Claiming Place

. . . .

On the Agency of Hmong Women

Chia Youyee Vang, Faith Nibbs,
and Ma Vang, Editors

University of Minnesota Press
Minneapolis
London

Published by the University of Minnesota Press
111 Third Avenue South, Suite 290
Minneapolis, MN 55401-2520
http://www.upress.umn.edu

Library of Congress Cataloging-in-Publication Data

Names: Vang, Chia Youyee, editor. | Nibbs, Faith, editor. | Vang, Ma, editor.
Title: Claiming place : on the agency of Hmong women / Chia Youyee Vang,
    Faith Nibbs, and Ma Vang, editors.
Description: Minneapolis : University of Minnesota Press, 2016. | Includes
    bibliographical references and index.
Identifiers: LCCN 2015022458| ISBN 9780816697762 (hc) |
    ISBN 9780816697786 (pb)
Subjects: LCSH: Women, Hmong—Social life and customs. | Women,
    Hmong—Social conditions.
Classification: LCC DS509.5.H66 C53 2016 | DDC 305.48/895972—dc23
LC record available at http://lccn.loc.gov/2015022458

Printed in the United States of America on acid-free paper

The University of Minnesota is an equal-opportunity educator and employer.

21 20 19 18 17 16   10 9 8 7 6 5 4 3 2 1

CLAIMING PLACE

Contents

Introduction: Hmong Women, Gender, and Power   vii
Chia Youyee Vang, Faith Nibbs, and Ma Vang

Part I. History and Knowledge Formation

1. Rewriting Hmong Women in Western Texts   3
   Leena N. Her

2. Rechronicling Histories: Toward a Hmong
   Feminist Perspective   28
   Ma Vang

3. Rethinking Hmong Women's Wartime Sacrifices   56
   Chia Youyee Vang

Part II. Social Organization, Kinship, and Politics

4. The Women of "Dragon Capital": Marriage Alliances
   and the Rise of Vang Pao   87
   Mai Na M. Lee

5. Hmong Women, Family Assets, and Community
   Cultural Wealth   117
   Julie Keown-Bomar and Ka Vang

6. Divorced Hmong Women in Thailand:
   Negotiating Cultural Space   144
   Prasit Leepreecha

Part III. Art and Media

7. Hmong Women on the Web: Transforming Power
   through Social Networking   169
   Faith Nibbs

8. Stitching Hmongness into Cloth: Pliable Identity
   and Cultural Agency   195
   Geraldine Craig

9. Reel Women: Diasporic Cinema and Female Collectivity
   in Abel Vang's *Nyab Siab Zoo*   220
   Aline Lo

Part IV. Gender and Sexuality

10. Thinking Diasporic Sex: Cultures, Erotics, and Media across
    Hmong Worlds   249
    Louisa Schein

11. Dangerous Questions: Queering Gender
    in the Hmong Diaspora   280
    Bruce Thao

12. Finding Queer Hmong America: Gender, Sexuality,
    Culture, and Happiness among Hmong LGBTQ   303
    Kong Pha

Afterword   327
Cathy J. Schlund-Vials

Acknowledgments   335

Contributors   337

Index   339

Introduction

Hmong Women, Gender, and Power

Chia Youyee Vang, Faith Nibbs, and Ma Vang

THIS COLLECTION EXPLORES the myriad roles Hmong women have played in society and the gendered ideologies embedded within the discourses that have surrounded them. In the literature on the Hmong, women have often been portrayed as victims of their patriarchal culture and of the wars that have dotted their history, as well as trapped between their cultural social standards and global industrialization. They are sometimes simply viewed as an emerging group beginning to "come into their own." In addition, early work that was dominated by anthropological and area studies often produced static depictions of Hmong culture and society as "primitive" and premodern, and in which gender relations—particularly portrayals of Hmong women—were central. These ideas became entrenched in academic and public discourse and have continued to heavily influence post-1980 research and literature on Hmong patrilineal society, portraying the exotic Hmong women as marginal yet crucial to the function of their society (see, for example, Symonds 2003; Rice 2000; Donnelly 1997; and Fadiman 1997). This book problematizes those portrayals and the academic paradigms that supported them, and re-examines the historical positions Hmong women have played in society. We locate our discussions in cultural agency as it relates to expressions of power throughout this volume and extend multiple critiques from myriad disciplines of existing scholarship about Hmong women. In doing so, we hope to de-essentialize the Hmong woman and reposition her as an agentic individual situated within a nexus of ever-shifting political, social, and cultural power structures capable of resisting and deconstructing forms of oppression.

Claiming Place is a collection of critical scholarship that counters the popular narrative about Hmong women by exploring how changing representations about this group challenge systems of patriarchy—both Hmong and Western forms—gender norms, race, war, and migration. Our objective is not merely to engage in a binary analysis about male versus female. Rather, we move beyond this dichotomy to illustrate how centering women in studies of history, family, society, media, art, and sexuality will expand the body of knowledge about a Hmong lived experience while contributing to broader conversations on gender, diaspora, and agency. While *Claiming Place* centers Hmong women's experiences, activisms, and popular representations, it also emphasizes the gender dynamics between women and men, sometimes highlighting men's stories to enhance the claim about Hmong women's actions in shaping their lives. Our project engages with the broader concern about the gendered status of the Hmong in historical and contemporary contexts within which Hmong men and notions about masculinity are also deeply embedded. It demonstrates how the prevailing scholarly emphasis on Hmong culture and men as the sole culprits of women's subjugation perpetuates the perception of a Hmong premodern status and makes unintelligible women's nuanced responses to patriarchal strategies of domination both in the United States and in Southeast Asia. Thus, this volume engages with and moves beyond a critique of Hmong patriarchy to expose imperial, state, and cultural regimes that structure subjectivity through the lenses of gender and cultural agency.

Collectively, this volume argues that Hmong women have been and continue to be active agents not only in challenging oppressive societal practices within multiple hierarchies of power but also in creating alternative forms of subjectivity and belonging within them. This position reflects broader paradigm shifts that depart from the descriptive scholarship and conceptualize Hmong women's subjectivities as revealing of broader social processes. The chapters take up particular issues in these popular representations to renegotiate and generate new meanings that show women's resistance and strategies as diasporic and racialized yet empowered subjects.

Because the study of Hmong women has ambiguously positioned them within different disciplines, we wanted our volume to be interdisciplinary as well. In doing so, we rethink the positions of research that posit the Hmong as refugee mental health subjects, Third World women, exotic "others," welfare subjects, and silent victims from within the disciplines that help define them. Our contributors come from a wide range of disciplines foregrounding alternative practices and readings on Hmong women through the various methods, theories, and critiques they employ. A majority of the chapters engage with the tools and concepts of anthropology to challenge the field's foundational research on Hmong, but the contributions also reflect that field's transformation to allow for critical scholarship on culture and society. Other contributors engage gender and diaspora studies, art, film, history, and ethnic studies. In addition to disciplinary differences, we have intentionally included works from scholars at different stages in their careers to illustrate the wide range of innovative Hmong studies scholarship produced by established and junior scholars. In this way, Claiming Place is not a survey of topics relating to the study of Hmong women. Instead, these scholarly contributions collectively work to bring Hmong studies into broader conversation with Southeast Asian and Asian American studies literature, feminist scholarship, gender studies, and migration discourse.

Critique of Culture and Cultural Agency

For contemporary Hmong women, a combination of subordinations imposed by those with different interests—such as Hmong experiences with French colonialism in Southeast Asia, Hmong struggles against the Lao state, U.S. military violence, refugee and diasporic experiences, and institutional inequities—produces their convoluted subjectivities. This complexity is often ignored in favor of centering analyses of power relations on their more easily targetable patriarchal social organization. Thus, we problematize this premise that the Hmong woman stands in for traditional culture. Historian Laurie J. Sears (1996), who examines Javanese shadow theater as allegory rather than as "tradition," explains that tradition and modernity came into focus at the same time, and scholars can only recognize tradition in the light of modernity (12). In this way, the idea of the "traditional" as fixed and unchanged is manufactured so that what is considered "traditional" culture becomes of more interest than the historical and social conditions of the people whose cultures are under exploration. Studies about Hmong women often reference "traditional Hmong culture" as a way to explain this group's experiences. Education studies scholar Eve Tuck (2009, 413) describes this approach to research from a deficit perspective as "damage-centered" in that it tends to look to historical exploitation for rationalizing a group's brokenness, thereby producing a "pathologizing approach in which the oppression singularly defines a community." Tuck proposes using a "desire-based research framework" that is more concerned with "understanding complexity, contradiction, and the self-determination of lived lives" (416). Our book contributes to this desire-based research by exploring the nuances of institutional and symbolic power as well as Hmong women's cultural agency, underscoring not only women's lived experiences but also how they are represented.

While Hmong women have and continue to sustain their culture in their roles as daughters, wives, and mothers, they also claim space through agentic and empowering acts that challenge the social practices that restrict their lives. *Claiming Place* does not suggest that Hmong women are one homogeneous group or that they experience disadvantages in the same way. Instead, we suggest a range of agendas and agentic processes that emerge from these various subjectivities. Agency and empowerment are generally recognized as a response to both institutionalized (Foucault 1978) and everyday (Scott 1985; Scott and Kerkvliet 1986) forms of power, and there has been much debate over what constitutes forms of agency and self-will. Sherry Ortner (1995, 175) emphasizes that agency must "attend to a variety of transformative processes, in which things do get changed, regardless of the intentions of the actors or the presence of very mixed intentions." While we acknowledge that those conversations exist, the interest of our book is less in deciding what constitutes self-will than in understanding how different forms of resistance are embedded in the sociopolitical complexity of Hmong women and their individual and collective realities. In this way, we find agency and empowerment useful categories to highlight the presence and play of power in relationships that exist within those realities.

Feminist literature suggests that a better understanding of the short- and medium-term strategies of women in different social locations can provide a corrective influence to these ethnocentric definitions of what constitutes a "feminist consciousness" (Kandiyoti 1988, 286). Deniz Kandiyoti points out that women strategize for power within a set of constraints that are particular to their culture. By looking within a particular societal structure, we can uncover the blueprint for how women negotiate power within the set of rules and scripts that regulate their gender relations—a process she calls "*patriarchal bargaining*." These "bargains," she suggests, are contested, redefined, and renegotiated in response to new environments and globalizing forces—influencing the specific forms of how

women choose to resist in the face of male domination—and are suscep-
tible to historical transformations that open up new areas of negotiation
between genders (289). In this way, *Claiming Place* contributes to scholarship on women and power in classic patriarchal societies that has moved
toward a systematic analysis of how these women devise strategies for
personal control and power over gender-based social disparities, and how
those choices are being shaped by levels of contemporary opportunities
and restraints (Wolf 1974; Ahern 1975; Martin-Liao 1988; Carsten 1995,
1997; Astuti 2000; Middleton 2000).

The chapters in this volume provide critical analyses of how changes in
landscapes, marriage, technology, education, and labor inevitably lead to
opportunities that question the fundamental, implicit assumptions behind arrangements of race, gender, and sexuality within the structures that
produce migration. They explore how women's access to power is created
through often complex and contradictory personal and political struggles,
demonstrating, as Kandiyoti (1988) suggests, that "patriarchal bargains do
not merely inform women's rational choices, but also shape the more unconscious aspects of their gendered subjectivity, since they permeate the
context of their early socialization as well as their adult cultural milieu"
(285). We suggest that a critical understanding of how Hmong women participate in their society is central to these broader discussions of women,
agency, and power.

As such, we employ culture as an important site from which to explore
Hmong women's practices of agency, resistance, and living. Queer and
gender studies scholars Roderick Ferguson and Grace Hong (2011) define
culture as exemplified by works of cultural production and inhering in the
"everyday practices of language and relationality, as the site where such
alternative comparative modes are imagined and brought into being" (3).
Following this expansive approach, we situate culture as the site for the
negotiations of power and agency. While we denounce cultural determinants as the sole cause of Hmong women's disempowerment or empowerment, and understand that there are always multiple narratives at play, we
also acknowledge that while distal, culture may indeed be a decisive factor
in analyzing Hmong women's agency. That is why we contend in this volume that culture may play a role in different situations when it comes to
disempowerment and agency, but acknowledge that cultural factors are
part of a wider gamut of social determinants that may also prove specious.
The contemporary paradigms of social determinism inadequately address

the seemingly more complex web of cultural causations of women and agency. We dedicate space to examine and intervene in this rather amorphous area of Hmong women and empowerment, acknowledging both the culturally specific and the broader social determinants that effect agency. By doing so, we hope to complicate the solely cultural scripts through which Hmong women have been analyzed and track the dynamics of history and individual biography to locate and compare Hmong women's agency across time and space (Chaturvedi et al. 2011).

Currently, Hmong studies scholarship has been in conversation with ethnic studies; American studies; Asian and Southeast Asian American studies; and migration, diaspora, and gender studies, which has shaped a new trajectory of the field to explore questions of race, gender, sexuality, war and U.S. imperialism, and transnationalism. For this reason, we sought authors who were recognized experts in various disciplines as well as emerging scholars who offer an interesting combination of theoretical, historical, and empirical approaches to the subject. They consider how Hmong women and cultural agency intersect with art history, anthropology, education, film studies, ethnic studies, and history. While a framework for a Hmong feminist critique has yet to be developed, we hope this work guides one that is sensitive to the unique sociohistorical perspectives of this group. Our authors draw attention to women as actors and address some of the key issues taken up from different disciplinary perspectives. Furthermore, we are opening up space to ask larger questions about sexuality and acknowledge the role that structures of power in Hmong culture play in its narrow definition. Several authors critique the ways in which sexualities are not merely reflections of biological imperatives but are instead controlled through socialization and formal mechanisms (Weinberg 2015, xvii). They interrogate "the everyday dimensions of lived experience and [describe] workings of heteronormativity, homonormativity, and their consequences" to illustrate the ways that people live their sexual identities with complexity and thus require questioning of the conditions of knowledge production when theorizing their lives (Rooke 2009, 151). Individuals navigate issues of belonging and the embodiment of desire as they create new identities and community as a result of today's leading edge of scholarship, which views "sex as fundamentally social" (Seidman 2011, 13). In the domain of Asian American studies, which has focused on more established national groups, such as Chinese Americans, Japanese Americans, and Korean Americans, the field has long been interested in representations beyond identity politics. Scholars in the smaller field of Southeast Asian American studies conceptualize diaspora, the refugee, and memory as important to rearticulating the histories of U.S. imperialism and war violence from the perspectives of those who must contend with historical trauma (Espiritu 2006; Nguyen 2012; Schlund-Vials 2012; Duong 2012).

The move in Asian American and Southeast Asian American studies to theorize a transnational mode of analysis that pays attention to the flows of people, ideas, and products across different geopolitical boundaries is especially informative for our book. Lisa Lowe and Elaine Kim (1997), in their *Positions: East Asia Cultures Critique* special issue, suggest a connection between the knowledge-producing fields of Asian and Asian American studies that would more adequately attend to the shifting demographics of the newest "racial formation" of Asian Americans since World War II (viii). Indeed, this call for new formations of knowledge has shifted the field toward a transnational approach that addresses how multiple forms of colonialism, racism, patriarchy, wars, and economic conditions compel Asian diasporic movements. In addition, Kandice Chuh (2003) proposes an Asian American studies critique to "imagine otherwise" in order to emphasize the links between body and discursively forged subjectivity (x). Therefore, we formulate a project that is grounded in Hmong women's experiences and transnational practices yet is linked to diasporic subjectivity in order to disrupt uneven historical and contemporary flows of power.

The transnational analytic has enabled engagement with cultural and political practices that are grounded in the narratives and memories of people who are critical of national narratives. It offers a perspective that politicizes people's transnational experiences and strategies of "homemaking" (Espiritu 2003), critiquing how colonialism, patriarchy, and nation have been constructed along the lines of race, gender, and sexuality. The field of Southeast Asian American studies, in particular, has taken up this transnational lens to examine the processes of refugee and diasporic migrations that are rooted in the U.S. wars in Southeast Asia as they are informed by patriarchy and state power. The recent edited journal volume on Southeast Asian American studies emphasizes the combined analysis of war and empire, refugee critique, diaspora, gender, and sexuality. According to the coeditors, as the emerging scholarship on Southeast Asian Americans has moved toward a "transnational analytic informed by recent critical theoretical and political interventions, Southeast Asian studies turns to address more complicated inquiries about assemblages of nations and states, refugees and residents, migrations and returns" (Ngo, Nguyen, and Lam 2012, 673). They call for new critical inquiries that move from the "historical to the historiographic, from the anthropological to the ethnographic, and from past frictions to lingering fictions" (672). We situate our book within the critical transnational inquiries in this field.

Hmong Women and Knowledge Formation

In their book *Exploring Women's Studies: Looking Forward, Looking Back,* Carol Berkin, Judith Pinch, and Carole Appel (2006) remind us just how difficult it is to remember how little scholarly attention women attracted just half a century ago (1). When Mary Beard published *Women as a Force in History: A Study in Traditions and Realities* in 1946, it caused hardly a stir in the academic world. Taken together, the chapters in this volume exhibit how contemporary methods, sources, and theoretical structures since that time can produce new perspectives on the role that Hmong women have played and are playing in society.

In the book, Berkin recalls how difficult it was as late as 1971 to find relevant literature for a course she taught on the social history of American women:

> To be sure there were a handful of biographies and biographical collections (but mostly relied heavily on myth and legend) and half a dozen serious history books published between 1914 and 1945. . . . In the United States, Eleanor Flexner's *Century of Struggle* had come out in 1958. Freud and others less notable had a good deal to say about the female psyche. A few anthropologists had paid attention to women in their field of research. Here and there a sociologist had included women in a community study. Some women's voluntary associations paid attention to their own history and, by extension, that of American women generally. But that was about the sum of what was available. (1)

Women were heavily excluded from universities when the PhD system emerged in the 1880s, and consequently, university departments that developed were overwhelmingly male. This led to a plethora of male-centric scholarship, in which everything from plants to people was analyzed through the social location of a man. The early (pre-1970) research on Hmong was written by men, informed through colonialist efforts in Indochina that depicted Hmong women first through a prism of Orientalist exoticism, and then through ideas of good science linked with concepts of the stereotypically masculine (Brunhes 1927; Dumont 1935; Gourou 1943; Condominas 1957; Spencer 1966; Hickey 1967). Through this historical prism, Hmong women's roles were understood in the agrarian context of slash and burn agriculture and the social organization of patrilineal descent particularly common in societies of southern China, from where Hmong migrated into Southeast Asia.[1] In this context, women's power and agency were understood as occupying the domestic sphere, as perpetuators of lineage and the Hmong life cycle, whereas men held traditional seats of power that came with operating in public spaces. The female shaman stood as an anomalous exception, because her opinions have historically been sought after for religious purposes.

Hmong women's sexuality was conceived in a heteronormative/ patriarchal perspective in which it is a virtue to be protected by men and managed by marriage to serve reproductive purposes. A woman was understood to remain a member of her father's clan for life; after marriage, however, she belonged exclusively to her husband's clan's spiritual world, where only members of his lineage could offer sacrifices to her soul after she died. Before marriage, girls and young women were expected to exist under the supervision of their parents or other adult kin to ensure that they behaved appropriately, thus increasing their marriageability. Divorce placed women outside the spiritual covering associated with a particular household, causing some women to enter into polygamous marriages as minor wives to ensure that protection. Being considered "other people's women" (Lee 1994–95), a daughter's subsistence and reproductive labor were also expected to benefit her husband's family. Thus, discussions about sex and sexuality often centralize Hmong women's reproduction, caregiving, and chastity.

Since those early depictions, changes in the life experiences of women, especially those who came of age as refugees or as the children of Hmong refugees in the West, opened up important articulations about the imperialist, racist, and gendered structures shaping their lives—from organizing powerful associations to generating art and literary movements to finally securing tenured positions alongside their established male peers. As female academics began producing scholarship, their own particular social location informed their approach and understanding of the subjects they studied. The result was scholarship that broadened the accepted knowledge produced.[2]

As a result of these influences in academia and a growing interest in new immigrant populations that came to the United States after the Vietnam War, a number of scholars of non-Hmong origin worked within their disciplines to reposition ideas of the "other" within communities of newcomers. Refugee resettlement in the United States meant changes and adaptations, which produced research studies that were overwhelmingly informed by the psychological health of Hmong refugee women. The perception of Hmong women as a voiceless group, unable to challenge patriarchy, has contributed to the proliferation of knowledge about them as submissive subjects in a male-dominated society. This is exemplified in the often documented high fertility rates of Hmong women and their practice of marrying at an early age—ill-coined by the American media during the 1980s and early 1990s as "bride theft." In the U.S. context, the health and sociological studies were discursively linked with media portrayals on the condition of Hmong women. Scholarship on Hmong women's changing lives remains focused on their continued adaptation to new environments and a globalized world.[3] Scholars who examine Hmong American women often portray them as "scarred yet undefeated" (Chan 2003).[4] This is best exemplified in Anne Fadiman's *The Spirit Catches You and You Fall Down: A Hmong Girl, Her American Doctors, and the Collision of Two Cultures* (1997), which investigates the news-making case of Lia Lee and the culture clash between her parents and doctors regarding her health care. This narrative is highly gendered in placing a young Hmong woman at the center of the cultural competency and compliance debate. As the Hmong began making their way up through the ranks of the Western education system into academia, it was the Hmong men who received their doctorates first, giving their accounts of what it was like to be Hmong. This insider perspective became the canonized versions of both male and female Hmongness.

Media and popular representations of Hmong women in the United States continued to focus on Hmong culture and traditions as detrimental to women's health and empowerment. Thus, even the purportedly positive depictions construct a fixed understanding of the position of Hmong women without getting at the larger structures of domination. The "positive" representations of Hmong women implicitly reproduce the idea of the liberated Hmong woman and the overall liberation of the Hmong through their resettlement in the United States. Linking discourses about culture with "assimilation" and "liberation" narratives structures an understanding of Hmong women as straddling and caught between tradition and modernity. Through a sociological framework, this body of literature indexed Hmong culture as a unique but damaging barrier to the exercising of women's agency, missing the opportunity to underscore acts of institutional and everyday forms of power exercised in their communities.

It was not until 2000—when Dia Cha became the first Hmong woman to earn a PhD—that Hmong women began to participate in their academic representation. As an anthropologist, Cha was a pioneer in beginning to rechronicle the story of Hmong women, starting with Lao and Hmong refugee women in Thailand and Laos. Since that time, a growing number of Hmong female academics have followed in her footsteps, engaging with the fields of history, art, social work, ethnic studies, psychology, and education; some of these women are represented in this volume. Hmong American women's perspectives have also been prominent in the literary movement, which was set in motion by the establishment of the literary arts journal *Paj Ntaub Voice* in 1994.[5] This women-led movement resulted in the publication of the anthology *Bamboo among the Oaks* almost a decade later (Moua 2002). The young writers wrote about their bicultural struggles with gender, family, history, and race, among other issues. Some of the contributors continue to expand and place their work in mainstream venues. Kao Kalia Yang's book, *The Latehomecomer: A Hmong Family Memoir* (2008), solidified Hmong American women's literary efforts by tracing the questions of war, refugee experiences, history, and belonging through the grandmother figure. Its positive reception has placed this work in classrooms across the country. Most recently, the Hmong American Writers' Circle contributed another anthology, *How Do I Begin? A Hmong American Literary Anthology* (2011), in which the writers explore the complexities of "Hmong identity" through concerns about history, refugee status, migration, home, race, and gender. A central issue driving these literary texts is the threat of a Hmong disappearance from history and culture because so much historical memory has been transmitted primarily through oral tradition. These literary texts have provided productive ways to establish Hmong women's perspectives.

Emerging research on Hmong women globally has begun to attend to their negotiations of power. In Vietnam, the topic of Hmong girls in Sa Pa has been a popular subject for exploring how women actively negotiate their identities and forms of belonging in a globalized economy. Duong Bich Hanh's (2008) study on the Hmong girls' negotiation with Vietnam's increasing tourism and its policies on inhabiting the mountain areas show how these young adults learn to adopt modernized practices that push social and political boundaries as they move to the city and interact with tourists and the local Vietnamese. The girls lead independent lives in the city, yet they are dependent on one another to survive and to acquire the skills they need to create new lives for themselves. This situation presents both dilemmas and possibilities for these girls as they navigate their new setting and newfound lifestyle. Duong argues that the Hmong girls have been able to occupy a position that is both socially and symbolically central, and to create an identity that cannot be subsumed by either the culture or the institutions of Vietnam (253). By paying attention to how systemic beliefs and institutional policies affect Hmong girls' lives, Duong explores both the possibilities of the girls' interactions and the instability associated with their daily lives. Our book engages with this recent trend in the scholarship to make visible the possibilities for Hmong women's claims to their belonging in multiple spaces and contexts that demonstrate the complicated formations of women's lives that can no longer be explained within the deficit model of Hmong culture and tradition.

Chapter Organization

For the purpose of this volume, our authors begin with two assumptions. The first, that Hmong women, as all women, have always been oppressed by societal structures—including academia. And second, that they have always been agentic in dealing with oppression. As a way of taking stock of those oppressions and Hmong women's power to resist them, each chapter's author was asked to situate his or her discussion within the sociopolitical complexities that configure Hmong women, as well as the pedagogical changes in the way those women have been represented by their disciplines. Taken together, their chapters make clear just how complicated understanding the power in relationships and the process of knowledge production can be. The book is organized into four thematic sections, focusing on history and knowledge formation, social organization and kinship, art and media, and gender and sexuality. These themes are key areas of contention and contribution by Hmong women in negotiating gendered ideologies and structures and in asserting agency. We have strategically ordered the chapters to reflect our book's reengagements with questions about history and social structure, followed by new inquiries about cultural expressions and sexuality in regard to gender and Hmong women's empowerment.

History and Knowledge Formation

This section looks at some of the historical roles Hmong women have played and how the way they were historicized has produced a particular knowledge about them. The chapters in this section centralize Hmong women's perspectives as an approach to critiquing discursive representations, privileging women's knowledge, and highlighting women's work during the war. Leena Her's chapter opens the book by critiquing those past representations from a discursive and literary perspective. By troubling the canon of literature on Hmong to interrogate the concepts and analytic frames used to depict Hmong women over time, she argues that women live within, resist, and negotiate systems of gendered ideologies. In addition, she examines works of literature by Hmong writers that offer alternative Hmong women subjectivities. This theme is echoed in Ma Vang's chapter, which is among a group of scholarship that critically examines Hmong perspectives on the historiography of the U.S. "secret war" in Laos. She demonstrates how the narrative about Hmong involvement in the war has been told through a masculinist and patriarchal perspective that valorizes Hmong men as heroes and the United States as a benevolent savior–rescuer. She notes that listening to Hmong women refugees' narratives about their wartime experiences centers Hmong knowledge and asserts women as knowing subjects. Vang argues that these oral histories articulate a nonlinear path of migration and an act of narrative refusal that rechronicle histories of war, violence, and displacement. Similarly, Chia Youyee Vang compounds this gendered formation of knowledge by examining the much overlooked record of women who worked during the war. Her depictions of how this precarious environment facilitated the social transformation of women into roles of nurses, entrepreneurs, and teachers draws our attention to Hmong women's multifaceted historical contributions, as well as their challenges to social expectations.

Social Organization, Kinship, and Politics

These chapters engage with the structures of family and society to show how Hmong women are the informal leaders and contributors of economic and political power to their families and communities. They also show how Hmong women rely on family as a source of strength for their leadership and educational goals. At the same time, Hmong women actively work to change gendered ideologies that are embedded in social practices such as weddings and divorce in order to establish gender equality in their society. Mai Na Lee's chapter offers new insights into the role marriage alliances played in General Vang Pao's rise to power.[6] She argues that Vang Pao's wives empowered Hmong male leaders and their families by contributing political and economic resources.[7] Shifting to more contemporary Hmong women, Julie Keown-Bomar and Ka Vang's chapter re-examines Hmong women's relationship to and reliance on family as cultural capital. They argue that a feminist inquiry can add new depth to the much examined subject of the supposed dysfunctional domestic space. Prasit Leepreecha's chapter explores the challenges that divorced women in Thailand face and their strategies for negotiating cultural belonging through everyday practices and through the Network of Hmong Women in Thailand. He examines the meanings and practices of Hmong marriage rituals that spiritually sever women from their natal lineage, and the precarious outsider status they take on when they divorce. He argues that women's participation in and strategies of negotiation through the network promote changes in power relationships.

Art and Media

The chapters in the next section explore the area of the arts and media by illustrating women's engagement with popular media and cultural productions such as art and film to transform their everyday lives and to create new meanings for cultural practices. Internet technology is one form of communication and strategy to create spaces of belonging, with a disproportionally higher use found among Hmong American women than in other parts of the diaspora. Interests have turned to the way women are using the Internet to sustain and create new modes of power. Faith Nibbs's chapter on Internet social networking examines the gratification young Hmong American women experience from participating in online forms of communication, how they negotiate the gendered forms of cultural politics in virtual spaces, and the way they perceive those experiences as empowering. She argues that social networking is helping Hmong women get around gendered norms of face-to-face engagement, opening up new spaces for power in the public sphere. Geraldine Craig demonstrates the impact of feminist theory on art history with a fresh look at the women who produce Hmong textiles, specifically Hmong story cloths. Craig's chapter traces story cloth producers and the shifting meanings of their craft through a thoughtful discussion of the empowering economic and communicative positions that Hmong women occupy. Aline Lo closes out the section using a similar feminist approach to analyze a little-discussed Hmong film. Through her examination of Abel Vang's *Nyab Siab Zoo/The Good-Hearted Daughter,* she finds Hmong women engaged in empowering structures of female networks. Lo situates a reading of the film within the field of diasporic cinema to highlight issues of displacement, longing, assimilation, and specifically the competing concerns of Hmong women in the diaspora.

Gender and Sexuality

Our final three chapters demonstrate the malleable nature of gender and gender roles in Hmong communities and the ways in which academics and subcultures have constructed them. They take up sexuality as a lens to examine normative diasporic relations. Together, the chapters highlight the contested boundaries between gender and sexuality (Manalansan 2006). Louisa Schein's chapter examines sexualities in the Hmong diaspora in relation to ideas about normativity, erotics, and sexual cultures, which advances our discussions of gender and cultural agency. She argues for the plurality of Hmong genders and sexualities by drawing our attention to how the preponderance of Western concepts can produce a false normativity that cannot account for the range of Hmong concerns around the globe. Bruce Thao's and Kong Pha's chapters follow by examining the feminist influence on queer studies and its power as a heuristic tool to produce new insights on how marginalized groups within the Hmong community are being empowered to create new social realities and ideals. Bruce Thao's chapter challenges the male–female gender binary and the heteronormative frame used to perpetuate patriarchy in Hmong families and customs. He situates queer Hmong within the diaspora and argues that they navigate and claim space and power within its diasporic possibilities. Kong Pha sheds new light on what it means to be queer and Hmong, exploring Hmong queer lives through a perspective of "happiness" rather than primarily through one of suffering and struggle. He notes the centrality of sexuality in shaping family, community, and happiness, suggesting that it can act as a form of empowerment for Hmong.

Notes

1. As in other agrarian societies, Hmong women were tied to fathers and husbands for economic security and well-being. The male head of household had the authority to make decisions affecting the household and the lineage. According to anthropologist Gary Yia Lee (1994–95), the foundation of the Hmong social system constituted one with "father-right as the norm." Nancy D. Donnelly (1997) claims that men determined how the overall welfare of the family and clan would look, although all "family members were expected to submit" to that well-being (29). It is for this reason that Patricia V. Symonds (2003, 8) concluded emphatically that "Hmongness is male." As such, women were considered "of no consequence insofar as clan membership is concerned; she counts for nothing in the handing down of the family name" (Yang 1993, 23).

2. Scholars began to address the huge gaps that existed in consideration of women's role in every aspect of human endeavor. Underlying the new scholarship were precepts that could be summed up in two words: gender matters. Examples of some of the other basic premises for women's studies were that until recently, the history of women throughout the world had largely been ignored; that works by women were omitted from the literary canon; that gender could be constructed differently across cultures; that gender, class, and race are interwoven; and that people who left no record still have a history (Berkin, Pinch, and Appel 2006, 5). These are some of the issues our contributors address.

3. See Symonds 2003; Liamputtong 2000; Donnelly 1997.

4. See also Lee 2005.

5. Throughout this book we are using the nonhyphenated "Hmong American" instead of the sometimes hyphenated term "Hmong-American" because the current practice in most academic fields is not to hyphenate. This stylistic choice does not negate the argument presented by Faith Nibbs in *Belonging* (2014) on the importance of some Hmong's self-identification with a hyphenated identity.

6. The late former general Vang Pao led U.S.-supported special guerrilla units in Laos during the Vietnam War.

7. In the Asian context, it is common to refer to individuals by their family name and then given name. When discussing historical figures, such as the late

general Vang Pao, we follow this format. All other Hmong names in the book are written with first name followed by last name, as is typically done in the United States.

Works Cited

Ahern, Emily. 1975. "The Power and Pollution of Chinese Women." In *Women in Chinese Society,* edited by Margery Wolf and Roxane Witke. Stanford: Stanford University Press.

Astuti, Rita. 2000. "Kindreds and Descent Groups: New Perspectives from Madagascar." In *Cultures of Relatedness: New Approaches to the Study of Kinship,* edited by Janet Carsten, 90–103. Cambridge: Cambridge University Press.

Beard, Mary. 1946. *Women as a Force in History: A Study in Traditions and Realities.* New York: Macmillan.

Beechey, V. 1979. "On Patriarchy." *Feminist Review* 3:66–82.

Berkin, Carol, Judith Pinch, and Carole Appel. 2006. *Exploring Women's Studies: Looking Forward, Looking Back.* Upper Saddle River, N.J.: Pearson Prentice Hall.

Brah, Avtar. 2003. "Diaspora, Border and Transnational Identities." In *Feminist Postcolonial Theory: A Reader,* edited by Reina Lewis and Sara Mills. New York: Routledge.

Brown, D. E. 1991. *Human Universals.* New York: McGraw-Hill.

Brownmiller, S. 1975. *Against Our Will: Men, Women, and Rape.* New York: Bantam.

Brunhes, J. 1927. "Geographie Humaine." In *Un Empire Colonial Francais—L'Indochine,* edited by Georges Maspero, 30–60. Paris: Van Oest.

Carsten, Janet. 1995. "The Substance of Kinship and the Heat of the Hearth: Feeding, Personhood, and Relatedness among Malays in Pulau Langkawi." *American Ethnologist* 22, no. 2 (May): 223–41.

———. 1997. *The Heat of the Hearth: The Process of Kinship in a Malay Fishing Community.* New York: Oxford University Press.

Cha, Dia. 2005. "Hmong and Lao Refugee Women: Reflections of a Hmong-American Woman Anthropologist." *Hmong Studies Journal* 6.

Chan, Sucheng. 2003. "Scarred, Yet Undefeated: Hmong and Cambodian Women and Girls in the United States." In *Asian/Pacific Islander American Women: A Historical Anthology,* edited by Shirley Hune and Gail M. Nomura. New York: New York University Press.

Chaturvedi, Sanjay, Narendra K. Arora, Rajib Dasgupta, and Ashok K. Patwari. 2011. "Are We Reluctant to Talk about Cultural Determinants?" *Indian Journal of Medical Research* 133, no. 4.

Chuh, Kandice. 2003. *Imagine Otherwise: On Asian American Critique.* Durham, N.C.: Duke University Press.

Condominas, G. 1957. *Nous Avons Mangé la Forêt de la Pierre-Genie Goo*. Paris: Mercure.

Delgado, Richard, and Jean Stefancic. 2001. *Critical Race Theory: An Introduction*. New York: New York University Press.

Donnelly, Nancy D. 1997. *The Changing Lives of Hmong Women*. Seattle: University of Washington Press.

Dumont, R. 1935. *La Culture du Riz dans le Delta du Tonkin: Etude et Propositions d'Amelioration des Techniques Traditionnelles de Riziculture Tropicale*. Paris: Editions Geograpiques, Maritimes et Coloneales.

Duong, Lan P. 2012. *Treacherous Subjects: Gender, Culture, and Trans-Vietnamese Feminism*. Philadelphia: Temple University Press.

Espiritu, Yen Le. 2003. *Home Bound: Filipino American Lives across Cultures, Communities, and Countries*. Berkeley: University of California Press.

———. 2006. "Toward a Critical Refugee Study: The Vietnamese Refugee Subject in US Scholarship." *Journal of Vietnamese Studies* 1, no. 2: 410–33.

Fadiman, Anne. 1997. *The Spirit Catches You and You Fall Down: A Hmong Girl, Her American Doctors, and the Collision of Two Cultures*. New York: Farrar, Straus, and Giroux.

Ferguson, Roderick, and Grace Hong, eds. 2011. *Strange Affinities: The Gender and Sexual Politics of Comparative Racialization*. Durham, N.C.: Duke University Press.

Foucault, Michel. 1978. *The History of Sexuality*. Translated by Robert Hurley. New York: Pantheon.

Freedman, Maurice. 1958. *Lineage Organization in Southeastern China*. London: Athlone Press.

Gopinath, Gayatri. 2005. *Impossible Desires: Queer Diaspora and South Asian Public Cultures*. Durham, N.C.: Duke University Press.

Gourou, P. 1943. *Land Utilization in French Indochina*. Washington, D.C.: Naval Division.

Greeley, M. 1983. "Patriarchy and Poverty: A Bangladesh Case Study." *South Asia Research* 3:35–55.

Hanh, Duong Bich. 2008. "Contesting Marginality: Consumption Networks and Everyday Practice among Hmong Girls in Sa Pa, Northwestern Vietnam." *Journal of Vietnamese Studies* 3, no. 3.

Haraway, Donna. 1988. "Situated Knowledges: The Science Question in Feminism and the Privilege of Partial Perspectives." *Feminist Studies* 14, no. 3: 575–99.

Harris, M. 1993. "The Evolution of Gender Hierarchies: A Trial Formulation." In *Sex and Gender Hierarchies*, edited by D. Miller. Cambridge: Cambridge University Press.

Hickey, G. 1967. *The Highland Peoples of South Vietnam: Social and Economic Development*. Santa Monica, Calif.: Advanced Research Projects Agency.

Hmong American Writers' Circle. 2011. *How Do I Begin? A Hmong American Literary Anthology.* Berkeley: Heyday.

Hune, Shirley. 2003. "Introduction: Through 'Our' Own Eyes: Asian/Pacific Islander American Women's History." In *Asian/Pacific Islander American Women: A Historical Anthology,* edited by Shirley Hune and Gail M. Nomura. New York: New York University Press.

Hutchison, Ray, and Miles McNall. 1994. "Early Marriage in a Hmong Cohort." *Journal of Marriage and Family* 56, no. 3: 579–90.

Johnson, K. A. 1983. *Women, the Family and Peasant Revolution in China.* Chicago: University of Chicago Press.

Kandiyoti, Deniz. 1988. "Bargaining with Patriarchy." *Gender and Society* 2, no. 3: 274–90.

Kaplan, Caren, and Inderpal Grewal. 2002. "Transnational Practices and Interdisciplinary Feminist Scholarship: Refiguring Women's and Gender Studies." In *Women's Studies on Its Own,* edited by Robyn Wiegman. Durham, N.C.: Duke University Press.

Keegan, J. 1993. *A History of Warfare.* New York: Knopf.

Lee, Gary Yia. 1994–95. "The Religious Presentation of Social Relationships: Hmong World View and Social Structure." *Lao Studies Review* 2:44–60.

Lee, Stacey J. 2005. *Up Against Whiteness: Race, School and Immigrant Youth.* New York: Teachers College Press.

Liamputtong, Pranee Rice. 2000. *Hmong Women and Reproduction.* Westport, Conn.: Bergin and Garvey.

———. 2004. "Being a Woman: The Social Construction of Menstruation among Hmong Women in Australia." In *The Hmong of Australia: Culture and Diaspora,* edited by Nicholas Tapp and Gary Yia Lee. Sydney: Pandanus Books.

Lowe, Lisa, and Elaine Kim, eds. 1997. *Positions: East Asia Cultures Critique* 5, no. 2 (December).

Mahler, Sarah J., and Patricia R. Pessar. 2006. "Gender Matters: Ethnographers Bring Gender from the Periphery toward the Core of Migration Studies." *International Migration Review* 40, no. 1: 27–63.

Manalansan, Martin F., IV. 2006. "Queer Intersections: Sexuality and Gender in Migration Studies." In "Gender and Migration Revisited." Special issue, *International Migration Review* 40, no. 1: 224–49.

Martin-Liao, Tienchi. 1988. "Dynasty." In *Zhongguo zhouogu shehui shi Inn* [A discussion of Chinese medieval social history]. Taipei: Lianjing chuban shiye gongsi.

McCann, Carole R., and Seung-Kyung Kim, eds. 2003. *Feminist Theory Reader: Local and Global Perspectives.* New York: Routledge.

McDonough, R., and R. Harrison. 1978. "Patriarchy and Relations of Production." In *Feminism and Materialism,* edited by A. Kuhn and A. M. Wolpe. London: Routledge.

Middleton, Karen. 2000. "How Karembola Men Become Mothers." In *Cultures of Relatedness: New Approaches to the Study of Kinship,* edited by Janet Carsten, 104–27. Cambridge: Cambridge University Press.

Millett, K. 1970. *Sexual Politics.* New York: Ballantine.

Mohanty, Chandra. 1995. "Feminist Encounters: Locating the Politics of Experience." In *Social Postmodernism: Beyond Identity Politics,* edited by Linda Nicholson and Steven Seidman. Cambridge: Cambridge University Press.

Morawska, Ewa. 2007. "Transnationalism." In *The New Americans: A Guide to Immigration since 1965,* edited by Mary Waters and Reed Ueda. Cambridge, Mass.: Harvard University Press.

Moua, Mai Neng, ed. 2002. *Bamboo among the Oaks.* Saint Paul: Minnesota Historical Society Press.

Ngo, Bic. 2002. "Contesting 'Culture': The Perspectives of Hmong American Female Students on Early Marriage." *Anthropology and Education Quarterly* 33, no. 2.

Ngo, Fiona, Mimi Thi Nguyen, and Mariam Beevi Lam. 2012. "Southeast Asian American Studies Special Issue: Guest Editors' Introduction." *Positions: Asia Critique* 20, no. 3: 671–84.

Nguyen, Mimi Thi. 2012. *The Gift of Freedom: War, Debt, and Other Refugee Passages.* Durham, N.C.: Duke University Press.

Nibbs, Faith G. 2014. *Belonging: The Social Dynamics of Fitting In as Experienced by Hmong Refugees in Germany and Texas.* Durham, N.C.: Carolina Academic Press.

Ortner, Sherry B. 1984. "Theory in Anthropology since the Sixties." *Comparative Studies in Society and History* 26, no. 1: 126–66.

———. 1995. "Resistance and the Problem of Ethnographic Refusal." *Comparative Studies in Society and History* 37, no. 1: 173–93.

———. 2001. "Specifying Agency: The Comaroffs and Their Critics." *Interventions* 3, no. 1: 76–84.

Rapp, Rayna. 1977. "Gender and Class: An Archeology of Knowledge concerning the Origin of the State." *Dialectical Anthropology* 2:309–16.

Reskin, B. F. 1988. "Bringing the Men Back In: Sex Differentiation and the Devaluation of Women's Work." *Gender and Society* 2:58–81.

Rooke, Alison. 2009. "Queer in the Field: On Emotions, Temporality, and Performativity in Ethnography." *Journal of Lesbian Studies* 13, no. 2: 149–60.

Rosaldo, M. Z. 1974. "Women, Culture, and Society: A Theoretical Overview." In *Women, Culture, and Society,* edited by M. Z. Rosaldo and L. Lamphere, 189–206. Stanford, Calif.: Stanford University Press.

Rice, Pranee Liamputtang. 2000. *Hmong Women and Reproduction.* Westport, Conn.: Bergin & Garvey.

Sacks, K. 1979. *Sisters and Wives: The Past and Future of Sexual Equality.* Westport, Conn.: Greenwood.

Schein, Louisa. 2000. *Minority Rules: The Miao and the Feminine in China's Cultural Politics.* Durham, N.C.: Duke University Press.

———. 2002. "Mapping Hmong Media in Diasporic Space." In *Media Worlds: Anthropology on New Terrain,* edited by Faye Ginsberg, Lila Abu-Lughod, and Brian Larkin, 229–44. Berkeley: University of California Press.

———. 2004. "Homeland Beauty: Transnational Longing and Hmong American Video." *Journal of Asian Studies* 63, no. 2: 433–64.

Schlund-Vials, Cathy. 2012. *War, Genocide, and Justice: Cambodian American Memory Work.* Minneapolis: University of Minnesota Press.

Scott, James C. 1985. *Weapons of the Weak: Everyday Forms of Peasant Resistance.* New Haven, Conn.: Yale University Press.

Scott, James C., and Benedict J. Tria Kerkvliet, eds. 1986. *Everyday Forms of Peasant Resistance in South-East Asia.* London and New York: Routledge.

Sears, Laurie J., ed. 1996. *Fantasizing the Feminine in Indonesia.* Durham, N.C.: Duke University Press.

Seidman, Steven. 2011. "Theoretical Perspectives." In *New Sexuality Studies,* 2nd ed., edited by Steven Seidman and Nancy Fischer, 3–12. New York: Routledge.

Spencer, J. 1966. *Shifting Cultivation in Southeast Asia.* Los Angeles: University of California Press.

Stafford, Charles. 2000. "Chinese Patriliny and the Cycles of Yang and Laiwang." In *Cultures of Relatedness: New Approaches to the Study of Kinship,* edited by Janet Carsten, 35–54. Cambridge: Cambridge University Press.

Symonds, Patricia V. 2003. *Calling in the Soul: Gender and the Cycle of Life in a Hmong Village.* Seattle: University of Washington Press.

Tapp, Nicholas. 2010. *The Impossibility of Self: An Essay on the Hmong Diaspora.* Berlin: LIT Verlag.

Tuck, Eve. 2009. "Suspending Damage: A Letter to Communities." *Harvard Education Review* 79, no. 3: 409–27.

van den Berghe, P. 1967. *Race and Racism: A Comparative Perspective.* New York: Wiley.

Vianello, M., and R. Siemienska. 1990. *Gender Inequality: A Comparative Study of Discrimination and Participation.* Newbury Park, Calif.: Sage.

Weinberg, Thomas S. 2015. Introduction to *Selves, Symbols, and Sexualities,* edited by Thomas S. Weinberg and Staci Newmahr, xiii–xxi. Los Angeles: Sage.

Wolf, Margery. 1974. *Chinese Women: Old Skills in a New Context.* Stanford, Calif.: Stanford University Press.

Wozniacka, Gosia. 2012. "Hmong Women in California Break with Traditional Roles." *Huffington Post*, June 10, www.huffingtonpost.com/2012/06/10/hmong -women-in-california_n_1585150.html.

Wyche, Karen Fraser, and Sherryl Browne Graves. 1992. "Minority Women in Academia: Access and Barriers to Professional Participation." *Psychology of Women Quarterly* 16, no. 4: 429–37.

Yang, Dao. 1993. *Hmong at the Turning Point*. Minneapolis: Worldbridge Associates, Ltd.

Yang, Kao Kalia. 2008. *The Latehomecomer: A Hmong Family Memoir*. Minneapolis: Coffee House Press.

Yoder, Janice, and Arnold Kahn. 1992. "Toward a Feminist Understanding of Women and Power." *Psychology of Women Quarterly* 16:381–88.

· I ·

History and Knowledge Formation

CHAPTER 1

Rewriting Hmong Women in Western Texts

Leena N. Her

> *The systems of thought which have patterned our social and political institutions, our universities, our archives, and our homes predispose us to a predictable beginning, middle, and end to untold stories. History books become copies of each other, mimicking style, organization, and content.*
>
> —Emma Perez, *The Decolonial Imaginary*

A PHOTOGRAPH OF MY MOTHER appears in a photographic compilation of Hmong living in Laos and the United States. In *Soul Calling: A Photographic Journey through the Hmong Diaspora*, photographer Joel Pickford (2012) presents pictures of the Hmong community he took in his journey through the Hmong diaspora. In this photograph, she is captured on a Friday morning picking vegetables at her farm. She is dressed in denim jeans and a long-sleeved, denim, button-up shirt, worn to protect her from the San Joaquin Valley sun. Her hair is unkempt and her placatory half smile reveals her disdain for being photographed on such a busy day. In one hand she is holding several bunches of long beans, and in the other hand, covered by latex gloves, she is holding a white towel she uses to wrap her head. My mother does not know that this photograph has been published in a book. I sense that she will be upset that an image showing her working at her farm is available for public consumption.

My mother's photograph is among other photographs of Hmong women in Pickford's collection that show them sitting with children, performing shaman rituals, farming, or wearing traditional Hmong clothing. Looking at these photographs, a number of questions arise: What story do these images tell about Hmong women? What ideas do they present about the experiences of Hmong women? What kinds of discourses do they continue to reify about Hmong women? Would others be able to read a photograph of my mother as a Hmong woman if it captured her away from the farm, in another context? Would images of Hmong women as artists, writers, scientists, and doctors signal Hmong women's identity?

Although the Hmong diaspora is diverse and Hmong women's experiences and everyday lives vary greatly, Pickford's pictures present Hmong women within a distinct Western construction of the woman as mother, nurturer, and bearer of tradition. She is obedient, hardworking, and a passive receptor of patriarchal practices, and as such, she is circumscribed and limited by Hmong society. While the understanding of what it means to be a Hmong woman is varied (and often contested) within the Hmong community, within Western academic texts this discourse is narrow, prescribing to limited perspectives. In these texts, Hmong women bear children; listen to their husbands; and conform to prevailing social and ideological gender norms dutifully, silently, and with little contestation (Donnelly 1994; Koltyk 1997; Rice 2000; Winland 1994).

As a Hmong woman, the singular possibilities of Hmong women's experiences as they have been written in Western texts belie the complex experiences not only of myself, someone whom others would say is a "modernized" and "acculturated" Hmong woman, but also of my mother and grandmother. The composite image of Hmong women in Western literature created by scholars, policy makers, journalists, photographers, and others is an act of discursive colonialism (Mohanty 1988). Mohanty describes this act as a process whereby the "material and historical heterogeneities of the lives of women are rendered invisible thereby making it possible to produce and re-present a composite, singular Woman" (62). In her critique, Mohanty draws a distinction between "women" who are "real, material subjects of their collective histories" and "Woman," which she represents with the capital letter W to designate the "cultural and ideological composite Other constructed through diverse representational discourse (scientific, literary, juridical, linguistic, cinematic, etc.)" (1988, 62).

This chapter challenges dominant academic constructions of the Hmong woman subject in Western texts by offering alternative subjectivities. My purpose is to interrogate the ideological concepts and analytic frames that dominate ways of seeing and speaking about the lives of Hmong women—and consequently about those of Hmong men—by revealing alternative constructions of Hmong women and their experiences. My exploration of works of literature by Hmong writers and scholarship from critical scholars of Hmong studies finds that although many Hmong women do live within systems of gendered ideologies, many resist, negotiate, and break out of them. To further complicate Western literary and scholarly constructions of the singular Hmong woman subject, I also draw from my fieldwork in Laos, where Hmong women are often perceived as antiquated vessels of cultural purity uninfluenced by Western feminist ideals.

Analytic Methodology: Ethnography as Discourse

Clifford and Marcus's (1986) seminal collection of edited essays in *Writing Culture* examines the construction of ethnographic texts. Through this work, Clifford and Marcus critically reflect on the systematic and institutionally determined composition of ethnographic texts and how they achieve their effect as knowledge of "others." They argue that the ideology that writing is a method of presenting the results of field experience has crumbled. Writing is no longer about keeping field notes or writing up transparent reports of one's experiences in the field. Instead, Clifford proposes that such writings are works of fiction, products made and fashioned not as falsehoods but as "something merely opposed to truth" (1986, 6). The constructed nature of the accounts represents partial cultural and historical truths. More importantly, these partialities are systematic and exclusive (Clifford 1986; Pratt 1986; Rabinow 1986).

My purpose is to explicate the making of the Hmong woman subject—that is, to reveal the methodology and fashioning of a cultural "other"—in ethnographic texts by using Foucault's (1972) archaeological analysis of discourse. Foucault outlines the method in this way: "We must grasp the statement in the exact specificity of its occurrence; determine its conditions of existence, fix at least its limits, establish its correlations with other statements that may be connected with it, and show what other forms of statement it excludes" (1972, 28). Inspired by the work of feminist historian Emma Perez, who uses Foucault's archaeological methodology of discursive analysis to challenge how Chicanas, Mexicanas, and female Indians have been "spoken about, spoken for, and ultimately encoded as whining, hysterical, irrational, or passive women who cannot know what is good for [them], who cannot know how to express or authorize [their] own narratives," this project is the first step toward "an archaeology of discursive fields of knowledge" that write Hmong women into academic archives (Perez 1999, xv).

I begin by examining the relationships among statements, images, and theoretical frames constituting discourses about Hmong women in ethnographic studies of Hmong women. As Foucault reminds us, "The frontiers of a book are never clear-cut; beyond the title, the first lines, and the last full stop, beyond its internal configuration and its autonomous form, it is caught up in a system of references to other books, other texts, other sentences; it is a node within a network" (1972, 23). The purpose, then, is to grasp the regularities and relationships that exist among statements and across texts so that one may be able to see how they coexist, mutually function, and reciprocally determine one another. It is to interpret the "'hearing' of an 'already said' that is at the same time a 'not-said'" (Foucault 1972, 25). It is an analysis of the work by the traditional chorus of speakers, who have consisted primarily of Western scholars. My purpose is not to critique or interpret the intentions of the authors. Echoing Foucault, this essay is not "a way of saying that everyone else is wrong. It is an attempt to define a particular site by the exteriority of its vicinity; rather than trying to reduce others to silence, by claiming what they say is worthless, I have tried to define this blank space from which I speak" (17), and others can speak about the lives of Hmong women. That is not to say that I am outside of the paradigms and discourse or closer to truth because I am Hmong. I recognize that there is no authentic story, no truth, "only stories—many stories" (Perez 1999, xv).

In what follows, I analyze the canon of Western academic literature on the Hmong and the different subjectivities that have been constructed. Then I focus my analysis on two ethnographic studies written specifically about Hmong women to reveal how the Hmong woman subject is a construct of intellectual and ideological notions of the cultural "other." In the second half of the chapter, I present alternative Hmong women subjectivities written from within and outside the Hmong community.

Unearthing the Ethnographic Archives

Ethnographic narratives of Hmong women generally categorize them into three figures: the authentic Hmong woman of the homeland, the refugee woman of Western relocation sites, and the acculturated and educated Hmong woman caught between two opposing cultural worlds. In the canon of academic narratives on the Hmong, the figure of the authentic Hmong woman of the homeland almost always originates in Laos and Thailand. The woman in these textual and visual inscriptions is frozen in traditional gender roles and constrained by traditional cultural values. She is depicted as faithful to tradition and a keeper of cultural heritage despite the infringement on her wants and desires. She is presented as the creator of Hmong clothing and the bearer of Hmong children. For example, in the opening of Pranee Liamputtong Rice's (2000) *Hmong Women and Reproduction,* the reader is greeted by the image of a shoeless Hmong woman in traditional clothing and a silver necklace squatting close to the ground. Her eyes are downcast, and her face is sullen. In the background, Hmong skirts and shirts hang on the walls of the woven bamboo hut. The caption reads, "Hmong woman in a traditional Hmong costume."

In the homeland, this woman occupied a lower social status as a marginal family member and obedient worker. Cooper (1984, 136) describes the relationship between a man and a woman in the homeland as one of "master-servant," premised on a psychological distinction in which a Hmong man can control a Hmong woman. The homeland serves as the site that authenticates Hmong identity and culture and perpetuates inequitable gender relationships. As Donnelly writes, a Hmong woman's "positional weakness was thus embedded in Hmong social structure as it was constituted in Laos" (1994, 30).

This gender hierarchy is premised on early anthropological accounts that describe Hmong society as patrilineal (Geddes 1976). While patrilineal descent does not necessarily reflect gender hierarchy and patriarchy, a patrilineal kinship system continues to be used to substantiate claims of oppressive gender hierarchy (Donnelly 1994; Koltyk 1997; Rice 2000; Thao 1999; Walker-Moffat 1995). In an ethnography of Hmong in the Midwest, Koltyk (1997) uses the metaphor of a tree to describe Hmong kinship structure and women's place within this structure. She writes, "The Hmong conceive of the links to their ancestors as their origins or roots; sons are considered the roots of the family, especially as families branch off into separate lineages within the patrilineal clan line. Daughters, on the other hand, do not carry the weight of the past. They will marry out and bear children for other patrilineal clans" (39). Within this patriarchal society, Hmong boys and girls are socialized differently. Although boys may be tolerated for challenging their parents, girls are often discouraged from having any voice at all (Lee and Tapp 2010, 158). Instead, young girls are taught to be good girls so that they may be able to attract husbands. Hmong parents want "obedient daughters-in-law and [urge] their sons to choose compliant girls" (Donnelly 1994, 139).

The second figure is that of the refugee Hmong woman who encounters Western ideas of gender equality while trying to make a new life for herself in Western relocation sites. The refugee Hmong woman figure was born in the refugee camps, where she began to acquire material wealth through the support of Western women who suggested that she sell her *paj ntaub* (needle work/embroidery) overseas. Later, when this woman resettled in Western nations, she began to work outside the home, which posed a threat to Hmong patriarchal society and to her husband, who experienced a loss of prestige, self-esteem, and authority (Bays 1994; Chan 1994; Donnelly 1994; Faderman 1998).

Leah Rempel's *Hey, Hmong Girl, Whassup? The Journal of Choua Vang* provides an example of the refugee Hmong woman figure. In this fictionalized journal of a young Hmong girl, Rempel blurs the line between ethnography and fiction. The book is described as a depiction of the "thoughts and feelings of a teenager" named Choua Vang, and it documents her experience growing up in Minnesota, "coping with her family's strict old-world traditions and her friends' and classmates' yearning to be grown-up and independent—and American" (Rempel 2004, book jacket). Rempel presents the text as an "authentic account" because she "workshopped" chapters of it with her Hmong students and because she interviewed members of the Hmong community to verify the "authenticity of the book."

In this fictionalized account, the gendered refugee figures of the Hmong man and woman continue to be construed within the narrow parameters of gendered Hmong subjectivities in Western discourses. The book begins with Choua explaining her family to the reader:

> Before you read, I think you should know a little bit about my family. My father is a very traditional Hmong man. He thinks we should still live the way we did in Laos: the men should be in charge and the women should take orders and never question.
>
> My mom started asking a lot of questions after they moved to America. She began asking, "Why do I have to keep having babies? We don't have a farm to take care of anymore so we don't need all the extra help." (My father says it's an honor to have children, and she's had four more kids since she asked that question.)

Last year she asked, "Why can't I take English lessons?" (Now
she takes classes twice a week, but my father doesn't like it.)
. . . My dad has problems with how my mom has changed. He
doesn't like it that she sews shirts at a factory all day and then
squeezes in English lessons at night. (Rempel 2004, 3)

Here Choua explains that her father is "traditional" and domineering and
uses his position to uphold Hmong tradition. Choua's mother, in contrast,
is eager to become American because it may liberate her from oppressive
patriarchal culture. She wants to learn English and finds a job working at a
factory. Yet she is unable to stand up to her husband and eventually submits to his demands.

The fictional depiction of Choua Vang and her mother and father do
not stray far from ethnographic and academic descriptions of refugee
Hmong women and men. Anthropologist Daphne Winland's (1994) study
of Hmong Mennonites in Ontario, Canada, explores how Hmong women
use the church not only as a resource to empower themselves in a new
culture but also to maintain their place in a patriarchal society. She argues
that "the Mennonite church (which preaches the importance of the family
and community) legitimated and reinforced certain Hmong patriarchal
values concerning the roles and responsibilities of women" (36), allowing
Hmong women to live in both worlds: the patriarchal Hmong world and
the new world they found themselves in. The Hmong women in Hobart,
Australia, encounter similar experiences as the Hmong women in Ontario
in Roberta Julian's (1998) study of constructions of Hmong femininity.
Julian is also interested in how Hmong women living in a Western context—where there is gender equality, autonomy, and independence from
male authority—reconceptualize Hmong gender norms. She concludes
that while there are multiple femininities emerging, Hmong women want
to be educated and independent but continue to be Hmong women. In this
way, they continue to prescribe to the traditional roles and gender rules
of Hmong culture. She concludes that even as Hmong women are active
agents participating in social change, they remain constrained by Hmong
patriarchal social order.

The third figure is that of the educated and acculturated Hmong woman
who refuses to abide by Hmong patriarchal social order. In the ethnographic archives, they are Hmong women who have adopted Western notions of
gender equality and modernity (Lee and Tapp 2010; Lee 1997; Ngo 2002).

Hmong women "who have assimilated mainstream values that promote equality between the sexes" include significant female figures in the Hmong community, such as former Minnesota state senator Mee Moua, Minnesota attorney Ilen Her, and community leader Mai Moua, who holds a PhD in leadership studies (Lee and Tapp 2010, 159). These women are considered "trailblazers" (Julian 1998) and role models, whose "initiatives will contribute to Hmong women becoming more confident and skilled in achieving better conditions for themselves" (Lee and Tapp 2010, 160).

In the next section, I delve closer into two ethnographic studies to reveal the fashioning of two of these figures in Western texts. First I examine the narrative of the good Hmong girl based on the authentic Hmong woman of the homeland in Rice's *Hmong Women and Reproduction*. Then I examine the rhetorical co-construction of the refugee Hmong man and woman in Donnelly's ethnography of Hmong women in Seattle.

Constructing an Authentic Hmong Woman of the Homeland across Ethnographic Narratives

Pranee Liamputtong Rice's (2000) *Hmong Women and Reproduction* is a study of the reproductive behaviors and customs of Hmong women in Australia. Rice, who is ethnically Thai, tells the reader that when she was young, she heard people speak disparagingly about the Hmong. For immigrants in Australia, ethnocentric views about the Hmong persist. Rice's book is written to "help to clarify many myths about the Hmong in general and Hmong women in particular" (xviii). In an early descriptive chapter, Rice gives an account of "A Good Hmong Girl." Her descriptive analysis of this "good Hmong girl" and her narrative method yield an insightful story of the limitations of the authentic Hmong woman figure as an analytic device.

Rice begins her account by posing the question, "What does it mean to be a 'good' girl in Hmong culture?" (2000, 27). Not surprisingly, Rice locates the answers within the domestic sphere related to *traditional* Hmong clothing and Hmong needlework. A particular item of clothing Rice focuses on is the *sev,* an apron worn by women and girls. Rice ignores the fact that Hmong women in Australia do not wear Hmong clothing on a regular basis. Instead, her analysis depends on an imagined premodern Hmong woman of the homeland who wears traditional clothing every day.

Rice states that women wear a sev when they are old enough to go to the farm and that "prior to puberty, a young Hmong girl is taught that sexuality is secret and she must keep her genital area covered by wearing sev.... They are taught that to leave home without a sev is to make oneself shameful, since people, particularly men, will see the outline of their genitals" (2000, 27). The sev is not only a modesty apron; upon reaching adolescence, the sev becomes a symbol of fertility. Like the plumes of a bird, Rice tells us, the sev "signifies the girl's readiness for courtship, marriage and motherhood" (28).

Rice's work is influenced by anthropologist Patricia Symonds's (2004) ethnography of birthing practices in a Hmong village in Thailand, *Calling in the Soul: Gender and the Cycle of Life in a Hmong Village.* Rice adopts Symonds's interpretation of the sev as a totemic article of clothing representing Hmong gender relationships. Symonds writes that "women wear [the sev] to cover their sexuality and to protect themselves" (2004, 27). According to Symonds, "sev signify femaleness, the age cycle, and sexuality.... The wearing of the sev for Hmong women constitutes the most visible act of modest deference. Women do not have to be coerced into wearing sev; through social conditioning they accept the necessity" (2004, 54).

Interestingly, this is Symonds's own interpretation and did not originate from within the Hmong community she studied. Symonds describes how, after talking to women and men about why the sev must be worn, she reached this interpretation: "My subsequent efforts at explication were met with puzzlement; it appeared to be knowledge they could not, or would not analyze further. Over time, I was able to relate their attitude toward sev to other aspects of Hmong life" (2004, 51).

Rice (2000) also finds a similar lack of interest or gendered interpretation of the sev among her informants in Australia. When she asks Hmong women in Australia why they wear a sev, they answer as follows:

With the Hmong, from generation to generation, we always wear the sev; that is *the way it is.* ... Ever since I was a girl I have been wearing it. ... For men you don't have to, but a woman she has to wear it for the rest of her life. (27, italics in original)

When she asks how a Hmong man would react to a Hmong woman who does not wear a sev, a Hmong woman said the following:

They will laugh at you and would not want to look at you. When you wear *sev,* you also wear the belt—sometimes just pieces of red and green cloths tied around your waist. Without these, people will not want to look at you, and will say that *you do not dress properly according to the Hmong way,* and they will laugh at you too. (8, italics in original)

The Hmong Australian's responses do not necessarily support the meanings that anthropologists have ascribed to the sev or to the reasons for wearing it. Their statement that "it is the Hmong way, it is the way it is," could be interpreted in many ways—not just with the gendered conclusions that Rice and Symonds have drawn.

Rice's analysis reveals how Hmong women are construed as subjects of analysis and yet are reproduced as objects of a patriarchal system who display "goodness, virtue and modesty." Furthermore, Rice discursively homogenizes the complexities and nuanced lives of Hmong women in Australia and presents a decontextualized and denationalized people—a people who are not situated in any particular context besides their own insular traditions, belief systems, socialization processes, and cultural practices. Furthermore, Rice's citation of Symonds's work draws on the ideology that Hmong from the homeland are untouched by modernity, and it is there that cultural practices and their meanings remain unchanged and authentic and always available for the analyst. Symonds's decision to go to Thailand, after all, arose from a desire to become more informed about the Hmong refugee population of Rhode Island.

Finally, Rice writes Hmong women as ignorant of their complicity in making and remaking gender hegemony. She presents them as women who wear the sev but do not know that doing so subjugates them to Hmong men and marks their sexuality in particular ways. Hmong women, the reader deducts, do not know that they are in fact reifying gender norms. It is the Hmong way, her informants tell her, and for Rice, the Hmong way is highly structured along asymmetrical gender relationships.

Constructions of the Refugee Hmong Woman Subject

Since its publication, Nancy Donnelly's (1994) *Changing Lives of Refugee Hmong Women* has been one of the most cited academic studies of gender dynamics in the Hmong community. Her influential study contributed to a transformational shift in studying gender dynamics in the Hmong diaspora by examining their lives in a Western resettlement context. Published from dissertation research in anthropology, *Changing Lives of Refugee Hmong Women* is an ethnography of the Hmong community of Seattle. Donnelly's study focuses on social change and cultural assimilation of Hmong refugees to the cultural norms of the United States, focusing on how resettlement into a new country affects gender norms.

Through her interactions with the Hmong community as a volunteer teacher in the Indochinese Women's Project, Donnelly's (1994) interest in studying gender dynamics within the Hmong community began with what she identifies as a "series of small observations" (8). These include an incident in which a Hmong man continuously shifted his pace to walk approximately five steps ahead of her despite her best ability to slow down or catch up with him so that they could walk side by side, observations of how Hmong women and men stood in a room during her visits to their homes, and observations of women "ducking their heads" and "avoiding eye contact" during various community meetings (9). Donnelly tells the reader that these observations led her to "think that the female is considered inferior in Hmong society" (9).

Hmong informants did not view the behaviors she associated with gender asymmetry as evidence of female inferiority. Donnelly explains: "A number of Hmong have maintained to me that although men and women do indeed occupy different spheres and pursue different activities, both male and female spheres are essential: Neither can do without the other, and therefore they are at bottom equivalent" (10). The disjuncture between Hmong interpretations and her own interpretation further provoked her interest in gender relations between Hmong women and men. Given the differences of perception between the Hmong view (in which there is no gender hierarchy) and her own view (in which there are great gender asymmetries), Donnelly formulated her research questions: "Would Hmong men and women feel misunderstood? Would they absorb American ideas about gender, and if so which ideas would they accept? Would they question their own behavior in light of these new hybrid ideas? Would Hmong women embrace American gender ideas and the men reject them—or vice versa?" (11).

Donnelly conducted her fieldwork with a segment of the community in gardening projects and in a sewing cooperative. She also collected life history interviews of seven women. Using her observations and these oral histories, Donnelly tells the reader that she wants to "construct a historical picture of the lives of a number of Hmong women from their own perspective" (14). Donnelly cites the importance of her identity as a woman as central toward achieving a new perspective on Hmong women's lives. Unlike the male anthropologists before her, who were unable to tap into the lives of Hmong women due to the women's reticence or to the men's inability to communicate with them, she tells the reader that her shared female identity allows her to "convey women's own perceptions of their experiences" (14). Yet it is not the women's perspectives that readers glean from *Changing Lives*. Donnelly's feminist and American identities become central analytic frames in her representation and interpretation of the Hmong women in her story.

The privileging of Donnelly's perspective and ethnographic agenda is revealed in the rhetorical construction of Hmong men in opposition to Hmong women. In her descriptions, Hmong men and women are constructed as opposing refugee and gendered figures. Their experiences are dichotomized into binaries: Hmong men want to hold on to culture and tradition, whereas Hmong women want to assimilate into U.S. society; Hmong men are depicted as weak, whereas Hmong women are depicted as strong; Hmong men are described as unable, whereas Hmong women are described as capable; Hmong men use their culturally sanctioned dominant position to assert themselves, whereas Hmong women maintain their obedience toward their husbands and families based on culture. Donnelly's constructions of Hmong women as strong and capable are only momentary. Just as easily as she constructs Hmong women as strong in contrast to Hmong men, Hmong women are rendered weak when she positions them as constrained by their culture and the men in their lives.

This is evident in a series of descriptions of a Hmong couple and the troubles they encountered as recent immigrants to the United States. Ker, the wife, is described as a capable woman whose English and knowledge of American society improved over time, while her husband, Chou Neng, is described as slow and unwilling to learn English and adapt to American culture. With Donnelly's help, Ker is able to communicate with her children's teachers and doctors and navigate other institutions. The reader is told that while Ker advanced at her job, Chou Neng had two car accidents and suffered from bouts of depression. The situation is summarized in this way: "In this family, the wife was becoming stronger and more capable, while the husband was trapped in a situation more and more out of his control" (81).

Donnelly argues that despite Ker's abilities and her husband's diminishing role within the U.S. context, the patriarchal conditions of Hmong culture continued to constrain her. Although Ker adopted the American concept of a nuclear family—a consequence of resettlement to the United States—this idea did not withstand the patriarchal belief system of her husband and his male family members. This indicates to Donnelly that Ker continued to be "an outsider in the family of Ly men" (81).

Donnelly surmises that Ker's position was even beneath that of her teenage brothers-in-law, who were more influential than her because "they, being male, were essential to the paternal line, while she, being female, was not" (82). Although Ker had the model of another Hmong woman who had divorced her husband and "did not yield to the patrilineal model," Ker "yielded to the men's conception of family" and did not protest her husband or her brothers-in-law's refusal to address their budget and spending issues. Donnelly argues that Ker "compromised her own ideas to retain her place in Hmong society" (82).

Just as Donnelly frames women and their actions within the narrow limits of her own conception of culture and gender hierarchy within the Hmong community, she interprets Hmong men and their actions within this frame as well. Donnelly presents Hmong men as authoritative and forceful in Hmong contexts, but insecure, hesitant, and timid when interacting with non-Hmong. Chou Neng, Ker's husband, is described as "timid," someone who did not have a "strong or decisive nature" but was empowered only through "tradition," where men's authority was sanctioned by patriarchal culture (82). This view and inscription of Hmong men is consistent throughout her book. In an early chapter, she describes Ly Chue, a man who served as a leader and translator for the Hmong community: "Ly Chue was bossy to the refugee women, but alert and slightly hesitant with Americans, and seemed to be trying hard to get his bearings" (5). Donnelly's feminist Western subjectivity is present again when she introduces Koua Kue, another man whom she meets early in her interactions with the Hmong community. "There was something odd—still and watchful—about this short, plump, self-contained man. He turned his head away and slid his eyes sideways to gaze at me in a calculating way from the corner of his eye" (5). Donnelly confides to the reader that she did not trust Koua Kue, and while his actions were "curious" to her, she "went along" with them for the good of the gardening project and the women. Donnelly concludes her study by arguing that gender and age are the "skeleton of Hmong social identity" (182). She argues that despite the changes that the cultural environment of the United States might pose for her informants, since gender and age define what it means to be Hmong, they remain persistent cultural forms. In the United States, "the definition of Hmong women as creators of beauty, skilled in devotion to their families, and embedded in a social order dominated by men, remained intact" (185). Despite the exclusion of Hmong women's voices from the text and the purposeful rhetorical framing of Hmong men and women as opposing gendered and refugee figures, Donnelly's ethnography continues to be seen as a significant study of Hmong gender hierarchy and cultural norms.

Donnelly writes about Hmong women from the presumption that she and they occupy divided and separate cultural spaces (Gupta and Ferguson 1992). Donnelly's informants are "nativized," and their experiences are placed within a separate cultural frame. Despite being written eight years after working and interacting with members of the Seattle Hmong community, from which she could have drawn from numerous experiences, Donnelly begins her book with a chapter titled "Discovering the Hmong." In this chapter, she relies on a common trope in ethnographic studies of constructing her arrival story and the meeting of the culturally different "other" (Marcus and Cushman 1982). Donnelly's "discovery" of the Hmong begins with her response to an ad to teach English to Southeast Asian women. She describes her initial meeting in the following way:

> The thirty-five Hmong and Mien women who were students in the Indochinese Women's Project were very good-natured and friendly to the six American volunteer teachers. But their behavior was unexpected: they blew their noses in the drinking fountain or wandered away during lessons. Some were intent on learning English, but others approached the classes like play, as if formal school were foreign to them. . . . I discovered that they did not understand money and could not add or subtract. (3)

Throughout her eight years working with the Hmong community, Donnelly interacted with Hmong women in a sewing circle and saw them operate a successful needlepoint business, yet she constructed and introduced a picture of Hmong women who did not know basic arithmetic, blew their noses into the water fountain, and wandered aimlessly like children while in class.

The spatial incarceration Donnelly uses to separate herself from the Hmong community allows her to analyze Hmong men and women as an exoticized "other" who do not share similar experiences with her

(Appadurai 1988). This exoticization is made apparent in her attempt to understand the communication breakdown she experiences with Hmong men. "They were not exactly sullen, but conservative, tradition-bound, earth-bound, stolid, and heavy, and seemed to be thinking: 'You are a city woman, and we are men, and farmers. You can tell us nothing.' I began to realize how different their values were from mine. Every move we made seemed to be governed by very different assumptions about society and reality itself" (Donnelly 1994, 7). To Donnelly, she was a woman and they were men; they were "conservative" and tradition-bound, while she identified as a feminist; they were "earth-bound," while she was from the city. Donnelly makes similar efforts to separate herself and her experiences from those of the Hmong women in the study. She exoticizes the women, rendering them as culturally backwards and ignorant, but a "good-natured" and "friendly" noble cultural "other."

Donnelly constructs this cultural "other" against the identity she inscribes for herself as a writer and researcher. She positions herself often within her analysis as a Westernized modern feminist subject. She reveals her subjectivity when she describes a conversation she had with a Hmong couple. Quoting herself speaking in broken English, she writes, "In America no husband is OK. Husband, too much time. Too much cooking, too much cleaning. I like no husband." As a divorced, childless woman, Donnelly claims that she held a "marginal" position within the Hmong community and that it was only after she "let them know it pained [her] to be childless or [after she and her Hmong subjects] could develop a joking relationship around her American feminism" that particular Hmong could "feel comfortable around [her]" (72).

Problematic Subjectivities: Authorship, Agency, Reification

There are several problems with the construction of the Hmong woman subject and the three figures she embodies in Western academic discourse. First, although gender asymmetries are found within Hmong culture, these asymmetries are contested and negotiated within the community. In the text analyzed, patriarchal Hmong culture is treated as a cultural fact that structures the lives of Hmong women. Furthermore, traditional patriarchal Hmong culture is not an idea that emerged wholly from within the Hmong community. It is also defined, generated, and reified by scholars in the studies previously cited. The composition of traditional patriarchal

Hmong culture, and consequently the depiction of Hmong women and men within this society, can be traced through the citation practices of the authors, who rely on the circulation and reification of this paradigm to affirm their work. The texts that Western academics produce are outcomes not only of "writing up" their research but also of the act of mapping onto and drawing from existing nodes of discourse. These texts are artifacts of the scholarly profession and of the different institutions to which they are bound. As a result, the references and the use of the paradigm of traditional patriarchal Hmong society to understand the experiences of Hmong communities in the diaspora predominate because they are visible and available for analysis.

The second problem is that of agency. This is of particular issue for the refugee and the educated/acculturated Hmong woman figures. In several ethnographic accounts (Donnelly 1994; Julian 1998; Lee 1997; Ngo 2002; Winland 1994), the authors give Hmong women agency. However, they interpret the actions and narratives of Hmong women as resistance against patriarchal oppression in Hmong society and structural oppression in the countries to which they have relocated. The problem is that the authors continue to analyze the actions of Hmong women within the framework of Hmong patriarchal culture and, as a result, perpetuate it as a central analytic paradigm. Even more problematic is that in these accounts, Hmong women's agency is derived solely from ideas they learned after being resettled in Western nations. Thus, Hmong women are only agents in a Western context, where circumstances such as war and resettlement have exposed them to ideas of gender equality, allowing them to change their culture.

Yet Hmong women have always been agents in resisting gender asymmetries. An account of one Hmong woman's agency is present in Donnelly's (1994) study but is silenced when she relies on an analysis of the experiences of Hmong women as *always* constrained by tradition, culture, and male patriarchy. In this narrative, presented as an excerpt from a life history interview, Mai, who is in her sixties, describes how she escaped a marriage proposal when she was fourteen.

As a young girl, while helping with preparations for a celebration, Mai was approached by two men and asked if she liked the younger of the two. Since she thought they were kidding, Mai responded by telling them that she did like the younger man. When asked if she would marry him, she responded with a yes. Later, when a letter arrived through a messenger asking Mai to confirm her response, she was told that the man whom she would be marrying would not be the younger man but the older one. Mai describes her response to the letter in the following way: "I had my uncle Chue write a letter back to them. I said if they wanted me to marry the younger one, I would, but if they wanted me to marry the older one, they could talk until their heads broke, and I wouldn't marry him. And I burned their letter" (134). The man persisted and asked the leader of the village to allow him to marry Mai, promising him a political promotion if he did so. Because she was an orphan, Mai assumed that she would be forced to marry the older man and was devastated, until one of her aunts tells her that she does not have to marry him: "If he comes to your house, just boil some water to burn him. If someone comes to your house, just kick them!" Then she tells Mai to go to town and find a boyfriend so that she can marry him. Still worried, Mai tells her aunt that she would not be able to do that. Another aunt admonishes her, saying, "Mai, you have to be smart. You don't want to die." Using herself as a model, she tells Mai, "Look at me. My mother's brother made all the arrangements for me to be his son's wife, they even had the party, but I didn't like that man. The party was almost over, and I went off with Chue." Emboldened by their stories, Mai marries another man.

Donnelly explains that the interpretation of the story depends on one's "gender concepts." In Donnelly's analysis, Mai is a victim of Hmong patriarchy. Mai is only successful because she exhibited "feminine actions"; that is, "without going outside her female role, she successfully manipulates the male who would control her. The model for female action set up by this story is clever and strong, but it is entirely contained within a male-ordered social universe" (137). An alternative reading of Mai's account is one of a young orphaned girl who, despite social and political pressure, is empowered to first tell the men they could "talk until their heads broke" and then burn the proposal letter and run off with the person she chooses to marry.

The third problem is the parallel figuring of Hmong men subjects in academic narratives. Hmong men of the homeland are portrayed as powerful in a context where a structural system of gender inequality imbues them with power. Once they leave this space and resettle as refugees in another country, their power is castrated from them. They are rendered weak, voiceless, and even more dependent on traditional Hmong patriarchy. As they disappear from the discursive landscape, the figure of a new generation of Hmong men emerges as hyperviolent gang members (Schein and Thoj 2009) or "effeminate, childlike geeks" who are meek in comparison to their Hmong sisters (Vang and Schein 2010; Schein, Thoj, and Jalao 2012).

Complicating Hmong Women Subjectivities

There are textual accounts that complicate and challenge traditional para-digms and prevailing constructions of Hmong women. While they echo the same concerns about the constraint of patriarchy, culture, and tradi-tion, they do not begin and end their interpretation and presentation of experiences bound by these ideologies. That is, these concepts are pre-sented as negotiable cultural facts created from within and outside the Hmong community. These accounts shed light on how ideologies of gender, tradition, and patriarchy are negotiated by men and women who sometimes reify the gender norms and sometimes challenge them. In the next section I examine the ways that scholars, artists, and writers are com-plicating the essentialist correlation of gender asymmetry with Hmong culture. To do so, I analyze literary and ethnographic texts produced by scholars and artists-writers as equivalents. As Perez (1999) asks, "Why is literature reduced to or expanded by the 'imaginary' while history can only be 'real'?" (xvii). Anthropologists who question the compartmental-ization of ethnographic writing from its literary qualities have asked the same question (Clifford 1994). Citing the works of Foucault (1973), de Certeau (1983), and Eagleton (1983), Clifford (1986) notes that "litera-ture" is a "transient category." Initially, Western science excluded particu-lar modes of expression, such as fiction and rhetoric, under the category of literature. By the nineteenth century, literature was tied to culture and art and viewed as a bourgeois institution (5). Clifford argues that the literary and rhetorical are "active at every level of science" (4). In this way, ethnog-raphy is artisanal, based on the definition of "art as the skillful fashioning of useful artifact" (6).

Troubling the Authentic Hmong Woman of the Homeland

Constructions of the Hmong woman subject depend on a nativized Hmong woman of an imagined homeland. Symonds's (2004) admonition that to understand Hmong women in Rhode Island she had to return to Thailand or Laos to study their birthing practices depends on this notion of Hmong in the homeland as culturally pure. She explains, "I hoped that the traditional Hmong way of life would be more or less intact in Thai-land" (xxx). Similarly, studies of Hmong women by Donnelly (1994) and Rice (2000) rely on the notion that the Hmong women whom they met

during the early resettlement period were more authentically Hmong because they had recently arrived from Laos and Thailand. In this way, they
hold Hmong gender norms intact because they have not been influenced
by Western ideals of gender equality.

Yet recent accounts produced by critical Hmong scholars offer competing portraits of Hmong women in Thailand and Laos that trouble
hegemonic images of Hmong women as uneducated, subservient, and
objects of cultural authenticity. Duffy's (2007) *Writing from These Roots*
provides insight into the literacy practices Hmong women engaged in first
in Laos and then later in the refugee camps of Thailand. Duffy describes
the experiences of Chia Vue, who attended elementary school in the village of Na Wae (81–82). In school Chia studied math, science, social studies, and art. She also learned to memorize and recite lessons, compose essays, and sing the Lao national anthem. Duffy also documents how Blia
Thao learned Lao not only to become a nurse and improve her economic
condition but also because she understood it as a marker of social status.
Thao was aware of linguistic hegemony and understood that learning Lao
was not only functional and pragmatic but also symbolic. She told Duffy
(in an interview): "It's like . . . if you don't speak Lao at all, then that means
that you are in a very low class. If you speak Lao and have an education
that means that you are in a high class" (88).

My own fieldwork in Laos finds that the story of the educational lives
of Hmong women is much more complicated than it is presented by either
bilateral organizations, such as the World Bank and the Asian Development Bank, or government institutions, such as the Ministry of Education, which draw on the discourse of Hmong culture as tradition bound
and patriarchal. In policy and development discourse, educational outcomes of students living in upland areas and villages composed heavily of
ethnic minorities are framed as a gender problem. This problem is articulated as the cultural preference of ethnic minorities—such as the Hmong—to
keep girls home to assist in household chores instead of sending them to
school, thus creating educational gaps between boys and girls. For example, a study examining ethnic minority girls' schooling explains the gender
gap in this way: "For most ethnic minority girls, the underlying problem is
the assumption that women and girls must carry the household responsibilities. . . . Based on *cultural predisposition,* it is principally daughters who
provide domestic and small home-based agricultural support in the family, and care for young siblings" (Government of Laos 2013, 11, italics mine).

The discourse of gendered cultural preferences silences policy recommendations to address problems regarding access to qualified teachers and instruction. My fieldwork in Laos finds that Hmong parents recognize the value of education for both their sons and their daughters. Despite encountering barriers such as access to quality education, economic constraints, and limited bilingual instruction, Hmong women in Laos work as medical doctors, lawyers, engineers, and teachers. They attend universities in Vientiane and Luang Prabang, and have earned scholarships to study abroad in China and Vietnam. My research finds that Hmong women in Laos face financial, political, and infrastructure barriers far more often than they face barriers imposed by Hmong gender ideologies.

Scholarship in this volume also troubles the limited and limiting constructions of Hmong women in Laos and Thailand. Ma Vang's analysis of the historiography of the U.S. "secret war" in Laos critiques the masculinist and patriarchal perspective of narratives of Hmong participation in the war. Vang finds that the stories Hmong women refugees tell of the war detract from the narratives of war violence and displacement. She argues that in these narratives, Hmong women assert themselves as knowing subjects. Chia Youyee Vang documents Hmong women's participation in the "secret war" by drawing attention to the role women played as nurses, teachers, and entrepreneurs.

These accounts of the experiences of Hmong women in Laos serve as an important contrast to the images of Hmong women in the academic archives, where they are depicted as ignorant of institutional norms and lacking literacy skills (Donnelly 1994; Faderman 1998; Rice 2000). Furthermore, the educational experiences of these women reveal how Hmong living in Laos or Thailand also inhabited spaces occupied by other cultural systems and nation-states. That is, they were subject to the socializing and assimilation processes of the states in which they were ethnic minorities.

Writing as an Act of Resistance against the Hmong Woman Subject

While research-based texts of and about Hmong women have been produced to help bridge the cultural divide between Hmong and the Western nations that have accepted them as refugee settlers (Donnelly 1994; Faderman 1998; Rice 2000; Symonds 2004), Hmong writers have produced texts as artistic expressions of their experiences that are relevant both to their identities as Hmong and to the many other identities they inhabit.

For these writers, the need to inscribe their thoughts visually and in print is an agentive effort to tell their own stories. As Mai Neng Moua, editor of *Bamboo among the Oaks,* one of the first anthologies of literature from the Hmong community, articulates in the introduction: "It is essential for the Hmong and other communities of color to express themselves—to write our stories in our own voices and to create our own images of ourselves. When we do not, others write our stories for us and we are in danger of accepting the images others have painted of us" (Moua 2002, 7).

The authors in *Bamboo among the Oaks* write against "simple, preliterate, illiterate, welfare-dependent, and, most recently, violent" images presented about the Hmong community by others (7). Moua reminds the reader that *Bamboo's* authors are not writing to essentialize the Hmong experience for others. The stories and poems should not be read as social histories to convey information about the Hmong, or as Moua aptly warns, "It is not an overview, 'Hmong life in America 101'" (14). Instead, the authors are trying to obtain power, a power that "consists in the ability to make others inhabit your story of their reality" (Gourevitch as cited in Moua 2002, 3).

The stories in *Bamboo* should be read as stories that others could inhabit, because they reflect universal realities. They address themes of identity, life in the United States, love, lost love, family, and place. Several of the writers also address gender ideologies. One particular piece, "We Women *of the Hmong culture*" by Mayli Vang, addresses male patriarchy. In this poem, Vang identifies a group of "she-witched women / 'possessed by this newfound knowledge / of excessive freedom' are weary / of participating in such patriarchal / rituals of the old motherland" (154). The ritual Vang describes is the practice of men eating first during ritual meals, followed by Hmong women. Vang's poem appears to echo the narrative that Donnelly constructs of the Hmong women in her study, yet Vang ends her poem with "we remember / we are women," ambiguously leaving the reader unsure if she is referring only to Hmong women or to the entire gendered category of women. Moua's introduction to the anthology helps frame the ambiguity of that last statement. Vang's poem is not just about the condition of Hmong women under Hmong patriarchy; it is about the condition of women under male patriarchy and its manifestations in rituals as well as in mundane everyday practices.

What would an account of the lives of Hmong women in Seattle look like if Donnelly's analysis were not premised on an essentialist reading of the experiences of the women? A close reading reveals that she and the

Hmong women shared similar geographic and cultural spaces. They participated in similar cultural activities conditioned by similar notions of gender and women's roles within the geographic and cultural terrain of the United States. Donnelly, like the Hmong women and men in her account, encounters gendered notions of acceptable behavior. She tells the reader that her divorce was due to her infertility, signaling heteronormative gender norms of women's role to bear children. Yet Donnelly does not position her experiences and those of the Hmong women within the universal experiences that all women share. Instead, she positions herself as a feminist who is able to escape gender-based oppression, whereas Hmong women, like Ker, are unable to because Hmong men do not let them.

Another literary text, *How Do I Begin?* (Hmong American Writers' Circle 2011), further disrupts the static portrait of Hmong women drawn by researchers in Western narratives. The stories in *How Do I Begin?* seek to redefine and represent the experiences of Hmong men and women who negotiate and contend with cultural, national, and gendered identities. Several of the authors focus on gender, gender disparities, and gender ideologies within the Hmong community. One story by Burlee Vang paints an intimate and moving account of a loving couple who decide to find a second wife after many years of not being able to conceive a child. While the ability of Hmong men to marry a second wife is often used as evidence of male dominance and severe gender inequality, Vang's account provides a complex portrait of the emotional toll that this culturally sanctioned (but not always acceptable) practice presents for the protagonist. Vang's protagonist wants children. Who will take care of her and her husband when they are old? While this decision can be analyzed through the lens of culture, it can also be studied through the affections and desires of the couple. Vang humanizes the characters, drawing us into their intimate world, where the desire to have children and fear of growing old and feeble are universal concerns. Vang shows readers intimate moments within the relationship to reveal that while women may be constrained by cultural traditions, they are also agents in making and remaking these traditions.

Conclusion

Gender hierarchies exist in all cultures. While men and women of all cultural groups and within all geographic locations make cultural assumptions about what men's and women's roles should be in society and how much power is afforded to each group, the decision to present a consistent Hmong woman subject as *always* conditioned and constrained by these ideologies is a Western fascination and phenomenon. While it may be true that the authors have authenticated their scientific, literary, or ethnographic accounts by drawing from narratives told by Hmong women and men, it is important to see that these accounts are invocations of gender ideologies that men and women have been taught as members of the Hmong community. That they are known and that they also generate discourse in the community does not mean that they determine what it is to be a Hmong man or a Hmong woman. Yet Western textual accounts continue to suggest that the experiences of Hmong men and women are determined by ideologies of culture, tradition, and patriarchy.

The metaphor of the photographs and the photographer serves as a useful tool to understand the crafting of the Hmong woman subject in Western text. Textual inscriptions of Hmong women are like the photographic images of Hmong women in Pickford's *Soul Calling*. Although they are photos of real Hmong women, the resulting collection has been mediated to capture particular kinds of images, and is presented as a series of decontextualized moments set apart from the rest of their lives. As a collection of images, they reflect previous depictions of Hmong women and reify the prevailing institutional discourse of the women. To continue to be meaningful to the intended audience, they must contain aspects of the old paradigm of these visual and textual discourses. What is promising is that new textual accounts are emerging from within and outside the community to disrupt the singular story of Hmong women that has been told in the academic archives. Researchers are collecting oral histories and interpreting them through less essentialist lenses. As artists and writers produce new accounts, they create their own images and stories.

Works Cited

Appadurai, Arjun. 1988. "Putting Hierarchy in Its place." *Cultural Anthropology* 3, no. 1: 36–49.

Bays, Sharon Arlene. 1994. *Cultural Politics and Identity Formation in a San Joaquin Valley Hmong Community*. Department of Anthropology, University of California, Los Angeles.

Chan, Sucheng. 1994. *Hmong Means Free: Life in Laos and America*. Philadelphia: Temple University Press.

Clifford, James. 1986. "Introduction: Partial Truths." In Clifford and Marcus, *Writing Culture*, 1–26.

———. 1994. "Diasporas." *Cultural Anthropology* 9, no. 3: 302–38.

Clifford, James, and George E. Marcus, eds. 1986. *Writing Culture: The Poetics and Politics of Ethnography*. Berkeley: University of California Press.

Cooper, Robert. 1984. *Resource Scarcity and the Hmong Response*. Singapore: National University of Singapore Press.

de Certeau, Michel. 1983. "History: Ethics, Science and Fiction." In *Social Science as Moral Inquiry*, edited by Norma Hahn, Robert Bellah, Paul Rabinow, and William Sullivan. New York: Columbia University Press.

Donnelly, Nancy. 1994. *Changing Lives of Refugee Hmong Women*. Seattle: University of Washington Press.

Duffy, John. 2007. *Writing from These Roots: Literacy in a Hmong American Community*. Honolulu: University of Hawai'i Press.

Eagleton, Terry. 1983. *Literary Theory*. Oxford: Oxford University Press.

Faderman, Lillian. 1998. *I Begin My Life All Over: The Hmong and the American Immigrant Experience*. Boston, Mass.: Beacon Press.

Foucault, Michel. 1972. *The Archaeology of Knowledge and the Discourse on Language*. New York: Vintage Books.

———. 1973. *Ceci n'est pas une pipe*. Montpellier: Editions fata morgana.

Geddes, William Robert. 1976. *Migrants of the Mountains: The Cultural Ecology of the Blue Miao of Thailand*. Oxford: Clarendon Press.

Government of Laos. 2013. *The Millennium Development Goals: Progress Report for the Lao PDR*. Vientiane: UNDP Laos.

Gupta, Akhil, and James Ferguson. 1992. "Beyond 'Culture': Space, Identity, and the Politics of Difference." *Cultural Anthropology* 7, no. 1: 6–23.

Hmong American Writers' Circle. 2011. *How Do I Begin? A Hmong American Literary Anthology*. Berkeley, Calif.: Heyday.

Julian, Roberta. 1998. "'I Love Driving!' Alternative Constructions of Hmong Feminity in the West." *Race, Gender and Class* 5, no. 2: 30–53.

Koltyk, Jo Ann. 1997. *New Pioneers in the Heartland: Hmong Life in Wisconsin*. Needham Heights, Mass.: Allyn & Bacon.

Lee, Gary Y., and Nicholas Tapp. 2010. *Culture and Customs of the Hmong*. Santa Barbara, Calif.: Greenwood Publishing Group.

Lee, Stacey J. 1997. "The Road to College: Hmong American Women's Pursuit of Higher Education." *Harvard Educational Review* 67, no. 4: 803–27.

Marcus, George E., and Dick Cushman. 1982. "Ethnographies as Texts." *Annual Review of Anthropology* 11:25–69.

Mohanty, Chandra Talpade. 1988. "Under Western Eyes: Feminist Scholarship and Colonial Discourse." *Feminist Review* 30:61–68.

Moua, Mai Neng, ed. 2002. *Bamboo among the Oaks: Contemporary Writing by Hmong Americans*. St. Paul: Minnesota Historical Society Press.

Ngo, Bic. 2002. "Contesting 'Culture': The Perspectives of Hmong American Female Students on Early Marriage." *Anthropology and Education Quarterly* 33, no. 2: 163–88.

Perez, Emma. 1999. *The Decolonial Imaginary: Writing Chicanas into History*. Bloomington: Indiana University Press.

Pickford, Joel. 2012. *Soul Calling: A Photographic Journey through the Hmong Diaspora*. Berkeley, Calif.: Heyday.

Pratt, Mary Louise. 1986. "Fieldwork in Common Places." In *Writing Culture: The Poetics and Politics of Ethnography*, edited by James Clifford and George E. Marcus, 27–50. Berkeley: University of California Press.

Rabinow, Paul. 1986. *Representations Are Social Facts: Modernity and Post-Modernity in Anthropology*. Berkeley: University of California Press.

Rempel, Leah. 2004. *Hey, Hmong Girl, Whassup? The Journal of Choua Vang*. Saint Paul, Minn.: Hamline University Press.

Rice, Pranee Liamputtong. 2000. *Hmong Women and Reproduction*. Westport, Conn.: Bergin & Garvey.

Schein, Louisa, and Va-Megn Thoj. 2009. "Gran Torino's Boys and Men with Guns: Hmong Perspectives." *Hmong Studies Journal* 10:1–51.

Schein, Louisa, Va-Megn Thoj, and Ly Chong Jalao. 2012. "Beyond Gran Torino's Guns: Hmong Cultural Warriors Performing Genders." *Positions* 20, no. 3: 763–92.

Symonds, Patricia. 1991. "Cosmology and the Cycle of Life: Hmong Views of Birth, Death and Gender in a Mountain Village in Northern Thailand." PhD diss., Brown University.

———. 2004. *Calling in the Soul: Gender and the Cycle of Life in a Hmong Village*. Seattle: University of Washington Press.

Thao, Paoze. 1999. *Mong Education at the Crossroads*. New York: University Press of America.

Vang, Bee, and Louisa Schein. 2010. "*Gran Torino's* Bee Vang on Film, Race and Masculinity: Conversations with Louisa Schein." *Hmong Studies Journal* 11: 1–11.

Walker-Moffat, Wendy. 1995. *The Other Side of the Asian American Success Story*. San Francisco: Jossey-Bass.

Winland, Daphne N. 1994. "Christianity and Community: Conversion and Adaptation among Hmong Refugee Women." *Canadian Journal of Sociology* 19, no. 1: 21–45.

CHAPTER 2

Rechronicling Histories

Toward a Hmong Feminist Perspective

Ma Vang

THE HISTORY OF THE U.S. "secret war" in Laos (1961–75) is a complicated story with multiple stakeholders and competing perspectives. The narratives of first and 1.5-generation Hmong refugees, in particular, have been an important source of knowledge contributing to the ongoing discussions about the Hmong involvement during this period of U.S. intervention in Laos against international mandates to leave the former Indochinese states of Vietnam, Cambodia, and Laos in peace, outlined in the Geneva Accords of 1954. Such narratives are especially crucial because the war was not publicly fought and there were few written records to document not only the diplomatic and military practices enforced upon and carried out by the Hmong "secret army" but also the human legacies of what was undeniably a project of U.S. empire. Yet these narratives have been framed either as testimonies of historical injustice, to garner U.S. government and public recognition, or as evidence of the degenerative psychological impact of war trauma that required culturally competent health-care practices. Although these narrative frames and their resulting material outcomes are important for addressing gaps in state accountability and health-care practices, they operate on methodological models that rely on a singular understanding of how Hmong refugees discuss their wartime and displacement experiences and for what purpose. They represent Hmong as what Randall Williams calls "appealing subjects" in the human rights framework—those seeking help and rights in a subjugated relationship to the state and international rights regimes. This gendered comprehension recuperates Hmong refugees and their stories when they are useful and rejects them when they contradict the state and its regimes. This latter move is evidenced in the *Radiolab* podcast titled "Yellow Rain," in which the show's hosts reject Eng Yang's claims of Hmong encounters with chemical warfare and repudiate his stories as distortions of Western scientific facts by a "Hmong refugee." This chapter intervenes in this broader gendered construction of knowledge that has informed Hmong subjectivity within restrictive historical genealogies.

To compound this gendered formation of knowledge, the narrative about Hmong involvement has been told through a masculinist and patriarchal perspective that valorizes Hmong men as heroes and the United States as a benevolent savior–rescuer. Hmong refugee women's narratives about their wartime experiences have been crucial yet marginal to a historical analysis of the conflict. With few written records, a past relationship of military alliance with the U.S. government has often been used to explain Hmong presence in this country. This has been a salient narrative about the Hmong because it aligns their sacrifices with the U.S. project to advance its militarism in Southeast Asia. The story of Hmong heroism and alliance supports the nation-state's liberal discourse of rescue and liberation in which the U.S. government purported to have saved the Hmong from the abject conditions of war by accepting them as refugees.[1] As such, Hmong Americans have had to recuperate this story in order to publicly communicate their history and to reclaim the thousands of Hmong lives that were lost in order to save American ones. This particular account on the part of Hmong men and women has been important in gaining some recognition for Hmong wartime sacrifices—especially the Hmong Veterans' Naturalization Act of 2000, which expedited Hmong veterans and their spouses' naturalization by waiving the English and history requirements of the test (Vang 2012a).

Although important in revealing the historiographic gaps about U.S. wars in Southeast Asia, the hero and ally narrative tends to portray a singular, masculinist depiction of Hmong agency through their wartime efforts. In this chapter, I am interested in the discourse about wartime experiences that do not fit within the masculinized retelling of history and cannot easily support the myth of U.S. rescue after the war. These are largely stories from Hmong women about their experiences of forced migration to stay ahead of the fighting and to escape Communist persecution in the immediate aftermath of the war. In addition, I examine the strategies of storytelling that reveal how warfare permeated Hmong women's everyday lives and how these stories reflect their subject formation.

By focusing on Hmong women's perspectives, this chapter does not presume that Hmong women have not been speaking or talking. Instead, it suggests that we have not been listening, and it also points to the gaps in the listening and reading practices that cannot account for the nuances in refugee women's speech acts. In fact, their stories are part of the everyday conversations and interactions that link what is in the past to the present to strengthen relationships between generations and family members. This chapter expands the scholarship on Hmong women's refugee experiences by highlighting their narrative strategies of recalling past experiences that refuse to adhere to linear forms of historical accounts. Therefore, I propose a methodological guide for listening that centers Hmong knowledge and asserts Hmong women as knowing subjects. I found that Hmong women's assertions about their wartime experiences of forced internal migration prior to the diaspora from Laos bring to the fore a central paradox about the so-called "secret war": the zones or spaces of military hostility overlap with and rub up against the places of Hmong civilian life.

I argue that Hmong women's narrative patterns in everyday practice, which emphasize a nonlinear path of migration and narrative refusal, rechronicle histories of war violence and displacement to disrupt the gendered project of militarism that institutes war violence as rescue. The narrative patterns as everyday practices challenge the production of knowledge about the Hmong involvement in war and Hmong women's place in that history. Historically speaking, the war permeated all aspects of Hmong life because the U.S. secret bombings and guerrilla warfare occurred in the northeastern region of Laos in Military Region II, where most Hmong lived. Hmong women experienced the difficulties of both sending their husbands and sons into war and having to flee their villages when the fighting got too close. Their narratives expose how the sacrifice of Hmong lives occurred not only on the front lines but also in the villages, where Hmong families became targets of bombings and Communist aggression, causing multiple displacements. I expand this argument about the indistinction between war violence and everyday life in the women's narratives to show how the accounts critically rechronicle Hmong wartime experiences as part of a historical process of U.S. militarism shaped by race and gender.

My analysis of the narrative strategies that Hmong women employed in the interviews takes a feminist approach that is informed by the scholarship on transnational and native feminist theories in which they interrogate colonialism, racism, U.S. liberal empire, and (hetero)patriarchy as ongoing structures of power through the lens of gender and sexuality. In addition, I borrow from the work of Native and feminist anthropologists who suggest "ethnographic refusal" and critical-listening practices, respectively, to articulate Hmong women's narrative strategies. In the following discussion, I begin first by teasing out a methodology of listening to Hmong women that is drawn from feminist anthropology and political trauma literature. Second, I show how accounts of Hmong forced migration, which produced their precarious diasporic condition, disrupt the U.S. Cold War imagination of Laos as an empty landscape for warfare. In their accounts, Hmong women recall war memories by naming the different places to which they moved and therefore assert their geographic knowledge. This discussion highlights some of the specific ways in which Hmong women and men rechronicle how warfare permeated Hmong daily life, which coerced their participation in the war effort through their everyday responsibilities and family obligations. Finally, I show how the pattern of Hmong women's life stories that are shaped by movement, by a refusal to fully communicate their stories, and by not remembering brings to the fore the crucial act of listening and interpreting stories as feminist practices that contend with the gaps in Cold War historiography's silence on U.S. military violence in Laos. These strategies open up possibilities to conceptualize a Hmong feminist perspective that centers gender and movement to expose the problems of Western knowledge formation and to theorize history.

Listening to Hmong Women

The scholarship on Hmong refugee displacement has primarily discussed their exodus from Laos across the Mekong River into Thailand's refugee camps and eventually to the United States or to another country of resettlement (Warner 1996; Hein 1995).[2] Those that focus on Hmong military activities often privilege the male perspective as the carrier of more accurate historical accounts (Morrison 2007). The scholarship that focuses specifically on Hmong women's lives has also missed the opportunity to situate their experiences within the historiography of U.S. militarism and a *critique* of U.S. liberalism. This research instead focuses on Hmong difficulties in adapting to U.S. society, especially through the oft-reported clash with Western medicine. Such portrayals reinforce Hmong cultural backwardness and their racialized status as a people who has been recently transported from the past into modernity (Fadiman 1997). Yet the literature that highlights Hmong refugee women's narratives overwhelmingly describes a pristine "pre-war" life in Laos to explain their daily lives and choices in the diaspora (Donnelly 1994; Rice 2000; and Mote 2004).

Hmong women have also served as objects of study in the research on the physical and mental health of Southeast Asian refugees who escaped from war, yet their perspectives are largely unwritten and unexplored in this scholarship. Oftentimes, mental health frameworks are used to understand Hmong and other Southeast Asian refugee women's wartime experiences to explain their depression and posttraumatic stress disorder among a host of other psychological concerns (Kroll et al. 1989; Rozée and Van Boemel 1990). Specifically, the study of refugee women and their recollections of wartime experiences and displacement have focused on their psychological trauma and their coping mechanisms (Cole, Espin, and Rothblum 1992). This range of scholarship emphasizes the needs of women and interprets their experiences within a deficit model that understands this group as requiring help to adjust to U.S. society. Often, their voices become muted as objects of study rather than as subjects who struggle with but also negotiate their traumatic wartime experiences. This chapter's concern with writing Hmong women's narratives is especially significant, since so much of the focus has been on Hmong men as soldiers who sacrificed for the United States. It also attempts to explore a style of ethnographic writing that would better capture the conditions of Hmong lives lived in war (Abu-Lughod 1993, 1–2). Writing Hmong women's narratives opens up the exploration of women and gender in history-making processes when that history has not been properly dealt with in official and public discourses.

The term "Hmong refugee women" is not used here as a descriptor for a monolithic group but as a category to expand on the analysis of the refugee figure in order to interrogate the gendered project of U.S. militarism. Examining Hmong refugee women's narratives, in particular, animates key questions about the U.S. project of "secret" intervention in Laos and the colonial relationship between the United States and the Hmong.[3] I have investigated elsewhere how the war as a historical period is also a project of knowledge production (Vang 2012b). I suggest that secrecy not only hides U.S. violence against "racialized peoples and terrains" but also produces racial knowledge to configure the Hmong as gendered racial subjects who belong in the past and exist outside historical time (Kim 2010, 16).[4]

Thus, systemic government secrets perpetuate the representational absence of Hmong Americans, which threatens to erase Hmong histories of war and displacement. Furthermore, secrecy enables a gendered military strategy of surrogacy, which involves the replacement of Hmong lives for those of Americans, when groups of Hmong soldiers would rescue American soldiers. My discussion here adds to the conceptualization of the refugee that expands the research on gender to the feminist critique of U.S. imperialism, war, and migration. I position the refugee as a transnational analytic to examine immigration histories that were produced by U.S. imperialism. Hmong diasporic women are a part of this refugee analytic, which expands the research on women and gender in transnational migrations. As such, their life stories represent an alternative site of knowledge from which to investigate the patriarchal structure of U.S. militarism.

In this way, transnational feminism is a helpful framework from which to situate a Hmong feminist perspective that links the processes of patriarchies, colonialisms, cosmopolitanisms, racisms, and feminisms (Kaplan and Grewal 2002, 73, 75). Caren Kaplan and Inderpal Grewal (1999, 350) propose transnational feminist cultural studies as a methodological guide and a practice of resistance and critique to transform traditional divisions that keep systems of power and epistemological innovation separated. Their concept offers a feminist analysis that "refuses to choose among economics, cultural, and political concerns" (358). Instead, transnational feminist cultural studies suggest using critical practices that link seemingly disparate processes, which for Hmong refugee women and men are war violence, displacement, and trauma. Alternatively, the work in native feminism provides an important guide to articulate Hmong feminist perspectives that challenges the structure of colonialism and Eurocentric knowledge formation. In addition to the work of Renya Ramirez (2007), Andrea Smith and J. Kehaulani Kauanui (2008), and others, which centers on gender and indigeneity in problematizing U.S. settler colonialism and U.S. empire, Maile Arvin, Eve Tuck, and Angela Morrill (2013) propose native feminist theories as an epistemological mode that makes claims to "an ongoing project of resistance that continues to contest patriarchy and its power relationships" (21). Native feminist theories make clear the interconnectedness across native and non-native feminisms, which places it with other feminist scholarship and within modernity (23, 26). Their important intervention in the field of feminist scholarship helps to imagine alternative forms of knowledge about gender and the figure of the Hmong women.

Therefore, I pursue a historical analysis by situating oral histories as "cultural products" that renew local, indigenous knowledge (Marshall 1994, 972). Over a two-year period, I conducted formal and informal interviews with twenty participants from Hmong communities on the U.S. West Coast. I interviewed fifteen men and five women, including former soldiers and community leaders and members. The interviews took place in the participants' homes or in their organizations' offices. My questions were structured around childhood memories and places of birth, war memories, camp experiences, and life in the United States. Because I was interested in Hmong experiences in Laos, during the war, and in resettlement, I initially approached former soldiers through veterans' organizations to learn about their stories. This contributed to the higher pool of Hmong men interviewed over women. I expanded my interview participants through acquaintances and the snowball method, seeking out women who would be willing to talk to me about their life experiences and family histories. Although some women were willing, others were more wary and reluctant about sharing personal histories, some simply saying that they did not have stories to tell.[5] This chapter's analysis is drawn from these five women's narratives, using the men's stories to supplement their accounts, because their unique perspectives incisively contribute to understanding Hmong wartime experiences through a nonmasculinist perspective of forced migration. Due to its small sample size, this case study does not presuppose its findings on Hmong women in general but does the work of illuminating the larger limitations of, and the need for, knowledge about this group.

Thus, I analyze Hmong women's narratives as life stories and as texts to be shared, listened to, and read. In doing so, I draw from feminist anthropologist Ruth Behar's (1990) use of the term "life story" rather than "life history" to name the ethnographic text, because it emphasizes "the fictions of self-representation, the ways in which a life is made in the telling" (224–25). Rethinking life history as a text denaturalizes the link between text and person. It also allows for a closer analysis of the narrative, using "critical forms of analysis and self-reflexive mediation on the relationship between the storyteller and the anthropologist" (227). Rather than approach the life history as a story full of information, Behar focuses on the "act of life story representation as reading," which transforms the listener into a storyteller (228).

By exploring the politics of Hmong women's wartime narratives, this chapter interprets and pays critical attention to the unspoken narrative strategies that empower these stories. The analysis employs a listening practice of these narratives that highlights how the experiences of forced migration serve as the context for women's memories about the war's violence.[6] The validation of these life stories as a listener, through representation and transformation into a storyteller, centralizes them as important for our understanding of the social world. Listening gives weight to a narrative: "It is up to anyone who listens to a woman's tale to hear the implicit message, interpret the powerful rage, and watch for ways in which the narrative form gives 'a weighted quality to incident,' extending the meaning of an incident beyond itself" (Dell Hymes [quoted in Behar 1990, 233–34]).

In listening to Hmong women, I also read their narratives as texts that do not reveal a truth about the past but rather work to expose history's gaps. The narratives constitute a decolonial practice of communicating how the past is always there as an interwoven network or repertoire of memories. Thus, I follow Behar's approach to "woman reading (and representing) woman," in which she uses the notion of "reading" to "ask anthropological questions about issues of representation" (228). As such, the process of storytelling contributes to an understanding of Hmong women's subjectivity because, as Behar suggests, it is an act that the storyteller engages in, and it reflects her processing and interpretation of experiences and events. Behar explains that women's orally related life histories in non-Western settings and "beyond to the ways in which women reflect on their experiences, emotions, and self-construction" (similar to women's written autobiographies) operate as a "vehicle for constituting the female subject" (233). Focusing on the five narratives, I show that they suggest possibilities for seeing Hmong women as multidimensional subjects. And because I also include two narratives from Hmong men, I suggest that the totality of narratives reveals a feminist dimension that shows how they critique power, patriarchy, and U.S. imperialism and war. If we understand that "women's stories about themselves have a concrete, context-specific texture" (233), then they are illuminating for our interrogations of the heteropatriarchal structures that produce violence, displacement/migration, and erasure of history and knowledge.

I find that these life stories convey a refusal on the women's part to fully tell or communicate a comprehensive narrative. Refusal has been a practice of doing ethnography that resists full depictions or thick descriptions of the lives of the group being studied for social scientific knowledge. Anthropologist Sherry B. Ortner (2006) critiques this practice of "ethnographic refusal" among postcolonial scholars. She claims that resistance is already in the writing of subjects in the text because they also push back so that "no text, however dominant, lacks the traces of this counter force" (61). Ortner concludes, then, that "resistance studies are thin because they are ethnographically thin: thin on the internal politics of dominated groups, thin on the cultural richness of those groups, thin on the subjective" (61–62). Native feminist scholar Audra Simpson (2007), on the other hand, takes up this very notion of "ethnographic refusal" and contends that this refusal is on the part of those groups whom we purport to study. The refusal of interviewees to tell, and the particular limits to the knowledge produced here, underscores "the sovereignty of the people we speak of, when speaking for themselves, [and] interrupt[s] anthropological portraits of timelessness" (68). Simpson argues that voice is "coupled with sovereignty that is evident at the level of interlocution, at the level of method and at the level of textualization." In doing so, she considers "what analysis will look like, or sound like, when the goals and aspirations of those we talk to inform the methods and the shape of our theorizing and analysis" (68). The stories I gathered "refuse" coherence and recuperation of a missing past for a "fuller" understanding of the subjects and their experiences. This refusal demonstrates narrative agency to convey events in a form that does not support and may differ from any popular notions about the past.

In the narratives, the refusal by Hmong women to fully discuss their wartime experiences brings into sharp relief the stories' incompleteness. Hence, I do not purport to offer a full portrayal of Hmong women's wartime experiences but to underscore the accounts about escaping the fighting and being coerced into the war efforts as the ways in which this group recalls how warfare permeates their daily lives. In her study of the internment experiences of Japanese Canadian Nisei women, including her mother, Pamela Sugiman (2006) explains that her mother continued to relay a story about one particular train ride as a way to talk about the internment. Sugiman states: "Through my childhood, whenever my mother was asked about the internment, she would highlight one story—the story of the long train trip that she endured from Roseberry, BC, to Toronto, Ontario, the site of her first job as a domestic worker" (71). This reflection shows how recollections of the past are always already incomplete, often culminating in a few well-remembered memories. Thus, what we learn from Hmong women about the historical moment of the war are episodic insights that invoke more questions than provide answers. Hmong women's fragmented narratives suggest that memories of the "secret war" are still ungraspable and shaped by the social and political contexts through which they surface. Lindsay DuBois (2000, 76) reminds us that personal memories are constructed and made sense of in social contexts so that social relations shape how the stories are told.

In addition, how much we know about the past is a result of both the lack of information and the inadequate language with which participants talk about that past because, as Jenny Edkins (2003) puts it, the unspeakable is a problem of language as a social and political process to comprehend traumatic events. The work on trauma theory in relation to historical analysis, then, approaches the historical power of trauma as rooted in its "inherent forgetting that it is first experienced at all" (Caruth 1996, 17). What gets passed on through trauma narratives, then, does not represent the violence of the event but "the impact of its very incomprehensibility," so that the thing that continues to haunt the victim includes the reality of the violent event and "the reality of the way that its violence has not yet been fully known" (6). The narratives I analyze dwell at this tension in grasping the trauma of the war as a violent event for the Hmong and its *secrecy* that has yet to be fully known. Trauma takes place when the site of protection and refuge becomes a source of danger, but traumatic events are a revelation of the contingency of the social order, compelling survivors to "bear witness to these discoveries" (Edkins 2003, 4–5). Edkins explains how this trauma introduces a politicized notion of time, a "trauma time" that intrudes and disrupts the linear progression of time maintained by the nation-state to forget its past violence (16). Hence, the state rewrites these traumas into a linear narrative of national heroism to conceal the trauma it has produced. Edkins maintains that resistance to the state's rescripting is resistance to sovereign power (xiv–xv).

Thus, Hmong women's narratives must be situated historically precisely because this group occupies an already hidden and unknowable place in this context of the "secret war." The significant gap in Hmong women's perspectives is explored in Doualy XayKaoThao's *National Public Radio* report "Family History: The General, His Sisters and Me." XayKaoThao, the granddaughter of one of General Vang Pao's sisters and a reporter for NPR, interviewed a couple of General Vang Pao's sisters shortly after his passing on January 6, 2011. She wanted to know what it was like to have a brother like the general, a prominent military and community leader, and revealed, "This is the first time the sisters of Gen. Vang Pao have been asked to speak publicly about their brother, and about their lives." By listening to their stories, she learns that "there are many more secrets and tales from the past," including one in which one of the sisters confided that, in her opinion, her brother did not marry his eight wives to unite the Hmong clans but rather for love. Through these interactions, XayKaoThao is charged with the task of "keeper of their stories," because these secrets from the past are often viewed as family histories to be passed down within the family, and they cannot be seen as important to our historical knowledge. Although this practice of keeping secrets is encouraged within the family to avoid shame or to contradict a public image, I suggest that the interactions between XayKaoThao and the general's sisters exemplify the social context in which Hmong women share their knowledge through their children and grandchildren. Yet Hmong men's narratives also bear witness to secrets that cannot easily be subsumed into the masculinist representations of warrior or hero, which must also be closely examined.

Life on the Run: Rechronicling History through Hmong Knowledge of Place

Hmong women's accounts of constant migration within Laos show how the multiple displacements of Hmong families, whose husbands and sons were off fighting, constitute escape strategies to stay ahead of the fighting. The women I interviewed describe this fleeing as *"khiav khiav laus li no"* (we have been running to this old age). This oft-repeated phrase reflects the structure of their lives around forced migration from their homes. Youa Yang, an elderly Hmong woman who was part of the more recent Hmong resettlement from Wat Than Krabok in 2004 and whose husband fought in the war, recounts, "I had three children by the time the war began, so we are at war until now, and we lost our country so we have been on the run until this old age." Her recollection of constant flight may be attributed to her more recent arrival in the United States, but it also suggests that resettling in the United States is a form of flight and escape even when it should constitute U.S. rescue. This ongoing impact of flight structures how she narrates her experiences when she explains that with three children at the beginning of the war they fled to " 'Naj Kias' to Long Cheng to 'Xam Xiam,' 'Khwv Lom Paub,' to the land of 'Taws Npoom' down to 'Muas Theeb' to 'Naj Vej' to 'Phuv Xev' until we followed General Vang Pao's flight to Nong Khai from where we went to Vinai and then Wat Than

Krabok." The process in which she summarizes and sums up all these places of her life—leaving and arriving—instantaneously draws together time
and place to illuminate how migration still persists in the present. This
method of narration shows how Hmong women recall historical memories through retracing the path of their forced migrations.

Hmong women's accounts about their life on the run during the war
allow for a rechronicling of history through Hmong geographic knowledge. In this way, their wartime experiences of forced migration actually
record the impact of war through their path of displacement. This path
follows places that are known only to Hmong because they reassign different names to the villages and geographic landscapes that have official
state and French colonial designations. These places that Youa refers to are
only known to the Hmong, because they were not yet mapped as knowable locations of the state. Thus, Hmong women's narratives about their
escape from place to place assert their geographic knowledge and capture
a Hmong sense of place that resists the colonial and war cartography. Glen
Coulthard (2010) suggests that "place is a way of knowing, experiencing,
and relating with the world—and these ways of knowing often guide
forms of resistance to power relations that threaten to erase or destroy our
senses of place" (79). While Coulthard's formulation of place is linked to
the indigenous connection to land as resource, identity, and relationship, I
find his analytic of place useful for understanding Hmong refugee narratives that are structured around the state's unmapped places (81). For my
informants, a place gathers history and embodies its events and people so
that it symbolizes a site from which to tell their stories. For instance, place
constitutes an epistemology to chronicle Hmong ways of knowing and experiencing the world in order to remember the violence and the erasure of
their flight. Hmong women's knowledge about these places of their escape
and arrival refuses to adhere to the U.S. colonial and war policy mapping
of Hmong as "natural" warriors onto the landscape of Laos.

This place-based knowledge unravels the totality of the colonial landscape sought by U.S. foreign policy to distinguish the Communist areas
that required military aggression from the neutral zones that warranted
protection. While there are few records about the war, the ones that do
exist overwhelmingly chart an empty Laotian landscape that was conducive to U.S. and Communist takeover, and map Hmong soldiers as "natural" warriors who could traverse the land (Vang 2012b). Alison Blunt and
Gillian Rose contend in *Writing Women and Space* (1994) that "maps were

graphic tools of colonization, themselves colonizing spaces perceived as empty and uninscribed" (9). As such, the routes built by the French colonial administration along with the U.S.-constructed Lima sites (aircraft landing strips) constituted the intertwining projects of colonial cartography and colonization and war. The development of roads and landing strips enabled France and the United States to represent Laos as a knowable landscape for the efficiency of colonial and military occupation. The process of unmapping and undoing this colonial cartography underscores how Hmong women's narratives complicate the historiography of U.S. war in Laos. Although scholars who study Hmong in Southeast Asia find that migration has been a Hmong historical practice for cultural, health, agricultural, and political reasons (especially their migration from China into peninsular Southeast Asia) (Michaud and Culas 2000), I insist that their displacement during the conflict in Laos exposes how U.S. political conflict produced forced migration.

While Hmong women used village or place names to mark their escape path, I found through my interviews that Hmong men recall place or village names that relate to well-known battle sites and as a way to chronicle their narratives as soldiers. This corroborates the masculinist war narrative, which tended to focus on heroic battle stories. Hmong veterans typically explained their wartime experiences in the context of their recruitment, training, and military duties. Their stories are detailed and formal as a result of more narrative practice. For example, my interview with Colonel Wangyee Vang, president of Lao Veterans, began in this way: "My name when I was younger and in school is Vaj Yis. I became involved in the war in 1961. An American took us to train on Route 6 in Laos" (Col. Wangyee Vang, 2009). This methodical introduction of his name, the year he became a soldier, and the location of his training frames this story in a familiar war narrative with identifiable characteristics. While useful for inserting Hmong involvement into the broader historical trajectory, this particular narrative strategy also serves the U.S. national image that the Hmong were its principal surrogate ally. The year 1961 was an important start to the beginning of Hmong armed conflict through U.S. aid. Furthermore, Route 6 represents a recognizable French colonial road that was crucial for carrying out U.S. military operations in Laos.

In undoing the colonial mapping of war strategies, the stories about escaping told by my female informants describe an instability of life on the run, in which they could not stay in one place for any significant period of time. They were constantly on the move because they "were at war and didn't have a stable or peaceful place to live" (Soua Lo, 2010). Soua Lo, whose husband fought in the war, recounts that she was born in Nong Het, but because there was war, they moved to Laj Huab. She explains that her family's "life is a refugee life" because her parents had been carrying her to escape from war since she was five years old. Her family moved from Laj Huab to Loob Kuas, then to Long Cheng until the war ended, and then they had to move again to "live in small places." This constant migration from place to place illustrates what it means to be "living in a country that is in turmoil," because they could not complete one season of farming before they had to move (Soua Lo and Youa Yang). Curiously, in a life marked by leaving, that leaving must necessarily be unmarked.

What interviewees remember are not events but the measures they had to take to erase their presence as they escaped from the bombings during the war and from Communist persecution afterwards. Yer Vang,[7] secretary for Lao Veterans, explained his family's escape after the U.S. retreat in this way: "We would just stay at a place for ten to twenty days, because if you stay at a place for too long the grass and plants that you step on will have your footprints" (Yer Vang, 2009). This description narrates place not as a specific location but as a process of leaving, so that what Yer conveys is how not to leave his footprints on the ground. Rememberings are marked by displacements and erasures, but such memories make poignant the spatial dimensions of leaving. These narratives represent decolonizing practices to relocate the fleeting Hmong presences in places where not even the grass was allowed to be permanently marked by footprints of movement, leaving, and escaping—lives lived in displacement. Indeed, the stories refuse the naming of such places as legible dots on the mapping of war, therefore exposing how the spaces of exception and violence are indistinguishable from the nation-state's territory.

Hmong women and families lived their lives on the edges of the escape paths in makeshift shelters constructed with banana leaves to shield the rain. The unrootedness of flight makes place and shelter precarious luxuries. Soua's niece, who was present during our conversation, asserts that they made lives on the side of the road and cooked in the rain under a banana leaf, like in the (Hmong) movies. Although they could not see the fighting, they heard gunfire (and saw fires burn) day and night. "We did not have any place of significance to set roots," said Soua, "I am sad whenever we talk about our life [tears up, long pause]." Soua shared a metaphor for her experiences during the war: "It was like we were being sifted, and whoever could hold on will live." She describes the experience of this makeshift life in the following way:

> You know that your parents and grandparents, we couldn't live in any secure place to raise any pigs or chickens to eat. With the bombing on vegetation, the animals were sick and we couldn't raise or eat them. Those who had businesses could get good meat but it was expensive. You can only buy one kilo of meat at a time to eat with vegetable and other foods. We struggled a lot when you talk about the refugee life. They dropped rice for us to eat but we didn't have anything to eat it with. We just ate so we wouldn't starve. . . . For us Hmong, you must bring a pot and a knife so that you can use it to find and cook food wherever you go. When the group leader decides that we'll stay there, then everyone will go cut down bamboos and trees to build shelter (*txiav xyoob txiav ntoo los ua tsev*). We'll live there for a while, but if Communists come then we have to move again. (Soua Lo, 2010)

This passage sums up the precarious life in Laos both during the war, when Hmong were displaced from their villages by the encroaching bombings and Communist takeover, and immediately afterwards, when they escaped from Communist persecution. Here she addresses me directly with a familiarity that says my parents and grandparents also lived through a similar experience. This reference of "you know" draws on the fact that I am a familiar listener and I should know from my elders what life must have been like. It asserts a shared experience of escape, fear, and starvation. Soua narrates the hardships in regard to livestock and the inadequacy of food because the bombings and "yellow rain" either destroyed or contaminated the vegetation and made the animals sick. The displacements and chemical warfare ruined their subsistence way of life, so they had to rely on United States Agency for International Development (USAID) rice drops for food. Without anything to eat except for rice, the Hmong "just ate so we wouldn't starve."

Long Cheng embodies the precarious quality of a Hmong life on the run. My informants recall Long Cheng—deemed the "most secret place on earth" because it was the site of General Vang Pao's military base—as a refugee settlement and an epicenter of Hmong cultural vibrancy during the war years. These stories about refugee escape and settlement paint a complex picture of Long Cheng, making it not only a "secret" military base or the site of Hmong cultural vibrancy but a place where Hmong refugees who had been on the run end up. Soua recounts:

> At that time, I was still very young and didn't know that much. But when they opened Long Cheng, everyone moved from the land of (*teb chaws*) "Pam Khaum" and Xieng to the place of Long Cheng. Then Americans began coming and General Vang Pao and them came to live in Long Cheng. They moved there, but there was always war, there was not a day with peace. (Soua Lo, 2010)

Long Cheng itself had not been a "place where people had always lived," as Soua Lo claims, but because General Vang Pao was displaced there to build his military stronghold, it became a place where the refugees also "came to live" (Soua Lo, 2010). Hmong refugees either were headed to Long Cheng or were pushed there to seek protection from the fighting. According to Soua, her family went to Long Cheng because they could not live in the other places anymore: "When we all came [to Long Cheng], the land of "Laj Huab" and Xieng were uninhabitable, the Communists already occupied them. We could live in Long Cheng because the soldiers protected it. War was always going on and we could not live in peace." Although she does not remember how long they lived there, Soua recalls living there from when she already had two children until they left Laos to go to Thailand and eventually to the United States.

Although Long Cheng provided some protection from the constant moving, it could not insulate the Hmong residents from other conditions of war, such as starvation and fear. Soua explains that Long Cheng was "not a well-built city": "it was a village in a ditch/valley (*kwj ha*). Mountains protect it on two sides. There was a small rise in the middle and they made the airstrip on its flat surface. It is not a good village." Long Cheng also represents the convergence of U.S. war strategies and a Hmong sense of place. First, the image of Long Cheng's airstrip is a well-remembered feature that was "not wide but very long" (Youa Yang, 2009). This landmark served as a reminder to residents that they lived in a time of war because they witnessed a constant flow of planes carrying out Hmong soldiers and bringing in body bags. Second, another poignant memory about Long Cheng is that of planes dropping rice for Hmong refugees. Soua explains,

"At that time, planes dropped rice for everyone to eat, so we ate like that. I don't remember when they started dropping us rice, but they had been dropping it since we lived there, otherwise we would starve." These rice drops were crucial for the survival of Hmong refugees in Long Cheng and those still on the move. They also demarcated certain Hmong places as knowable to U.S. militarism and humanitarian aid. Third, my informants also remember Long Cheng as a fun place to live. The Hmong transformed Long Cheng into a vibrant cultural center, creating radio stations to promote national propaganda and lift morale through Hmong folk songs and music, and many Hmong entrepreneurs built up thriving businesses. Because "everyone moved there" and started businesses and farmed (Soua Lo, 2010), Long Cheng constituted a vivacious place to live. Youa elaborates that because "there were a lot of Hmong and it was fun/lively (*lom zem*) with lots of activities," Long Cheng would have been a good place to live if the war had not ended (*lub teb chaws txhob tawg*). In this way, Long Cheng, as a dot on the map, represents the convergence and collision of U.S. war mapping and Hmong cultural knowledge of place.

Yet Long Cheng was not a permanent place for Hmong, as even General Vang Pao was forced to leave it, and thousands of Hmong who lived there had to escape the Pathet Lao and North Vietnamese armies in the aftermath of the Fall of Saigon. Even though Soua's family stayed longer, she still describes it as a refugee life: "We did have houses to live in but we couldn't live in peace." While some Hmong made Long Cheng a more permanent settlement after all their migrations, others did not stay long. Youa's family lived there for half a year because it "was primarily a place for soldiers and their families so there were many houses built closely together so we got to live there for a while." It could not become a haven for Hmong because "when the Vietnamese communists came [even] the General couldn't stay" (Youa Yang, 2009). This noted instability illuminates the Hmong diasporic condition that is compounded by war violence and the significance of a Hmong place-based knowledge.

Toward a Hmong Feminist Perspective

Hmong women's accounts about forced migration revealed how all Hmong were enmeshed in the fighting and violence. The narratives illustrate Hmong women and their families' roles as civilian "soldiers" who bore responsibility to the war efforts through their everyday practices, such as household activities. Witnessing the increasing numbers of dead Hmong soldiers that others did not see made Hmong women unwilling participants in the war. The women I interviewed talked about their lives as daughters, mothers, and wives, revealing their invisible efforts as those who stayed at home to help save the lives of their loved ones who were fighting in the battlefield. They explain the work of refraining from domestic responsibilities in order to protect their husbands' lives. Soua elucidates that she refrained from cooking and sewing while her husband was away on the front lines because "if you stab through cooking, then it makes it easier for others to kill or hurt him." She elaborates that "you must help from the home too so he is safe out there." For Soua, this practice is consistent with a Hmong tradition that dictates that the wife refrain from domestic responsibilities and the husband act morally (refrain from sexual misconduct) when he is away so that he will not be killed or taken as a prisoner. Once the husband is relieved from the field and comes home, his wife can resume her household activities. However, practice of this tradition occurred on an individual basis, and it was up to each person to observe it. Soua proclaims that it was partly due to her efforts of self-restraint that her husband was not hurt on the battlefield.

But the reality of the situation (in the time of war) for which some Hmong women like Soua practiced self-restraint was the increasing number of the Hmong dead brought in daily for those at home to sort through and mourn their loss. Young men who had left the day before were brought back in body bags via helicopter. Soua states:

> You know that they prepared body bags in the helicopters to retrieve the dead, right? They quickly put the bodies in these bags in the field with tags of the first and last names of these individuals and have the helicopters bring them back. At the airport, those at home will go sort through the bodies for their person to bring home. This made us very scared. So I thought about how your uncle [her husband] might one day have the same fate, and it made me not want to do anything. They gave us rice to eat so even if we didn't have anything else to eat, we just ate rice so we wouldn't starve to death. (Soua Lo, 2010)

This wartime reality of seeing and sorting the bodies of the dead constituted additional challenges that Hmong women endured. It also exposed the unequal numbers of Hmong deaths compared to American losses. When asked if the Americans helped with funeral and burial costs, Soua angrily responds that they did not because they had already paid General Vang Pao to hire the soldiers to fight on their behalf. She implores that "they probably only paid each person $20!" as a way to name the disproportionate value of American lives over those of Hmong soldiers and civilians.

These narratives reveal a gendered formation of the war that involved the commitment of everyone. Despite my informants' willingness to share the different places of escape in Laos, recounting the Mekong River crossing presented a challenge due to its particularly traumatic events of deaths and family separations. As such, the Hmong women I interviewed hesitated to fully reveal the details surrounding their escape into Thailand. While the other interviewees were too young to recall this historic moment, Soua briefly mentioned that they hired men with boats to help them cross. My interview with Youa in particular epitomizes this refusal to tell. I was excited to talk to Youa because her granddaughter and I attended school together, and she accompanied me to the interview due to her own interest in learning more about her family history. She had learned from an aunt a bit about the family's story of crossing the Mekong River and thought her grandmother might be able to elaborate more. But once we started talking, it was clear that Youa did not want to bring up traumatic memories.

When I asked about the family's Mekong River crossing, the story was brief, interjected with long pauses, as if she were trying to sort out what not to say. Youa states, "We crossed the Mekong River. We crossed the Mekong there so when we arrived at the bank of the Mekong . . . um . . . those who had already crossed to the other side sent boats to come get us, and that's how we crossed into Thailand." This monologue can only reveal as much as Youa wants me to know about that time in her life. Only with further prying from her granddaughter did she reveal that the family had been pursued by Communist soldiers and they split up right before they crossed the river, resulting in the death of one of the uncles. The family was reunited in Nong Khai after having crossed separately. In this strategy of selective telling, Youa herself enacts the silences into the story to leave open how that moment of crossing is such a well-known historical occurrence and yet it is filled with the unknowable pain and trauma its survivors endured. Youa explains at the end of the interview, "I only know how to tell the story the way I've told it" (Youa Yang, 2009). Her resistance to sharing this tragic moment in her family history results from both the necessity to withhold some secrets and the inability for stories to become knowable in trauma time (Edkins 2003). Youa's point that she only knows how to tell the story the way she has told it suggests that the story is incomplete but represents her perspective.

For elder Hmong women who experienced the war's violence and multiple displacements, what must be understood is how the war did not end with their leaving Laos. Two of the elder Hmong women explain that in the United States, their hearts and minds are constantly at war even when they no longer hear gunfire. They link the difficulties of navigating life in the United States with their struggles to survive during war. The difficulties they face include learning English, driving and taking advantage of opportunities, and relying on their children to take care of them. The symbolic forms of violence—the inability to share traumatic events and the continuing effects of war—constitute these women's ongoing struggles. Their accounts defy conventional war historiography, which demarcates clear-cut boundaries of when and where the war ended.

While some Hmong women had been running with their parents at a young age, others were born on the run, in the process of escaping, so their beginnings are shaped by not remembering. May Vue immigrated to the United States with her family at the age of thirteen. When asked to talk about where she was born and her childhood memories, she states, "I don't have much to say, I just tell you what I remember [laughs]. . . . I was born in Laos, I don't remember the name of the village. . . . No, I don't remember anything" (May Vue 2010). This repetition of not remembering the name of the village where she was born or anything else about her childhood exemplifies the erasure of having to forget. Kia Yang, a high school vice principal at the time of the interview, was born in Thailand and moved to French Guiana at a young age. She recounts her birth in this way: "I wasn't actually born in the camp because when we settled there, the Thais came to evict us. We ran through the jungle and then my mom gave birth to me in the jungle so that is my beginning" (Kia Yang, 2009). Kia's use of "my beginning" to describe her birth in the process of the family's escape in the jungle, even when they were already in Thailand, suggests a different tracing of Hmong beginnings interrupted and informed by flight. It is a precarious beginning that is constantly threatened as not existing. Oftentimes, such beginnings are not remembered but put together from the stories told to us.

Yet migration marks defining moments in one's life. Kia explains that her accounts are "just a story, I'm sure there are many more out there." She admits, after my urging, "Yeah, it's my story. . . . There are a few defining moments in your life where you look back and you wouldn't be where you are if those things [did]n't happen." Kia reflects that her mother's passing opened a path for her secondary migration to the United States. Because the family resettled in French Guiana, her father took four of the youngest children, including Kia, to live in the United States with their stepmother after he remarried. Kia reveals, "It's sad that she passed away when I was young but that one thing led me to what I am today to move from one totally different country to the next, to here" (Kia Yang 2009). Moving to the United States gave her the opportunity to continue her education and to pursue her career as an educator. Her family's migration history is unique, first moving to French Guiana and then resettling to the United States, because it makes visible the path of multiple overlapping French and U.S. colonialisms in Laos and their synchronized projects of refugee rescue. While her family's initial settlement in French Guiana was a part of the refugee rescue, the family's migration to the United States reflected their decision-making power and the social capital established through connections to the Hmong community in the United States through marriage.

Hmong women's narrative patterns that follow Hmong movement from place to place coupled with the refusal to fully communicate family histories suggest a reinterpretation of wartime stories that rechronicle the historical context of U.S. militarism. These strategies of storytelling make clear a need to theorize history through the ideas of movement and refusal in order to disrupt the existing gendered formation of knowledge about Hmong refugees who escaped from war—in particular, representations of Hmong women. Wendy Ho (1999) suggests that "in theorizing history from women's experiences and standpoints, one becomes more sensitive to their contributions not only to formations of individuals, families, and communities, but also to the theorizing of the political and public" (27). In this way, the narratives I analyze illuminate the possibility for a broader Hmong feminist perspective that problematizes militarism and U.S. empire as ongoing structures to expose them as problems of Western tools of knowledge and the nation-state. In addition, a Hmong feminist perspective would reveal the ongoing project and experiences of U.S. liberal empire's strategies of surrogate war beyond the Southeast Asian context.

This Hmong feminist perspective would bolster the refugee category to centralize gender and *movement* (in all its configurations relating to place, displacement, diaspora, and geopolitics) to theorize Hmong historical formation and subject making in a global context. Behar (1990) contends that a "life history narrative should allow one to see the subjective mapping of experience" (225). My discussion of Hmong women's narratives serves as a "mapping of experience" and a "mapping" of the migration path and pattern. Movement as an analytic more adequately describes and interprets women's experiences and subjectivities. It moves beyond the often binary representations between the diaspora and home country to assert that the ambiguous positioning within diasporas is an important place from which to theorize a feminist critique. Hmong women's narrations of their life stories are a process of becoming subjects. This perspective and analytic allows Hmong women to form their own subjectivities as actors who are engaged in the representation and creation of their own narratives and life stories. Centering gender and movement also marks an epistemological shift in the formation of knowledge about the U.S. empire's war technologies and the refugee's resistance and critique of those machinations.

For instance, a Hmong feminist perspective establishes how narrative refusal in life stories is a feminist practice that critiques the disciplinary logic of the patriarchal ally rhetoric about the Hmong–U.S. relationship. More urgently, this perspective comprehends acts of listening and interpreting as critical practices that rechronicle Hmong history making. These practices are necessary habits for members of the 1.5 and second generations—those who were born toward the end of the war or in the process of leaving, carried on their parents' backs in the journey from Laos to Thailand to the United States, and the ones who did not experience war except through their parents' and grandparents' stories. Kia Vang volunteered at Lao Veterans to assist the organization with its operations by providing transportation and translation services for its members. Because most of the veteran volunteers have limited English comprehension, her role is important to the daily functions and services of the organization. In this context, she asserts that Hmong elders relay the same story to one another, and as their children listen in on these conversations, they learn and anticipate "how the story will go." When asked if her father talks about his time in the war, Kia recounts:

> With these elders, if there's a new person especially when you see two elders who have fought in the war in Laos but they're not like in the same, the soldiers had many different groups, right? They

talk about how they went to fight in this village, that village, this mountain, sometimes you always remember how the story will go [laughter]. I don't know about others, but the way my dad talks about it seems as if he remembers it very well, right, about where everything is, he only changes a few words, but mostly his story is the same story. (Kia Vang, 2009)

Her response about how they always tell the same story, one that they remember well, and that she can always anticipate and remember how the story will go curiously points to how the narrative structure of telling the same story with few word variations establishes an impression for history making. When the stories about war are shared among the veterans or with their children, they have a different purpose that is about claiming a shared experience rather than inviting public sympathy. These are fleeting stories impressed upon the younger generations, yet they remind us how to remember—how exchanges are shared when elders meet—rather than what the recounting conveys. This emphasis on "how the story will go" rather than on what was told represents an important shift in under-standing how to recall the past. Kia's interpretation of her father's stories as well-remembered moments from his conversations with Hmong of his generation sheds light on Youa's refusal to fully convey her family's Mekong crossing experience. Rather than reading this narrative move as creating more gaps in the already hidden stories of Hmong refugees, listening to the silences reveals the fragmentary process of telling stories so that their pattern of absence represents the design of historical erasure.

Conclusion

At the risk of historical erasure in an already forgotten "secret war," these alternative histories offer another set of tools from which to excavate the past, not for what it truly was but for what they do not say. In this chapter, I focused not only on what Hmong women's narratives reveal about the past but also on how they are productive for the present and future in charting a Hmong active presence in global history. Deploying memory as a conceptual tool critically engages with the politics of historical knowl-edge. Specifically, it helps articulate the politics of our lack of knowledge about history and the production of such knowledge. Lisa Yoneyama (1999) contends that "memory is understood as deeply embedded in and hopelessly complicitous with history in fashioning an official and authoritative account of the past" (27). Employing this concept means that our investigations into the past must have an awareness that historical reality can only be made available to us through mediations in the present (27). Critical projects that engage in how acts of remembering can fill the void of knowledge must reckon with the question of "how can memories, once recuperated, remain self-critically unsettling?" (5). In other words, our communication of these narratives should make sure that they remain critical of how they emerge and for what purpose. While the information we attain through these narratives is important, capturing moments when the interviewees do not remember or choose not to convey certain things generates the most poignant lessons for our understanding of how historical knowledge emerges. Not remembering is a form of pushing back, and it reminds us of memory's complicity with history in comprehending the past.

In this chapter, I analyzed Hmong women's narratives to show the precarious diasporic positioning between places and their refusal to fully reveal these experiences. I contend that these practices help articulate some parameters around a Hmong feminist perspective that centers gender and movement as important analytics for doing historical analysis to critique patriarchy and U.S. liberal empire. It also sheds light on the politics of a Hmong public telling that is often fraught with questions about Hmong subjective, internal knowledge that purportedly distorts the "truth" to gain sympathy for their plight or is used to corroborate the U.S. government's policies, since the Hmong were its main ally in Laos. An analysis of Hmong histories, therefore, involves being faithful to the past by listening to the stories that emerge and reading them against the grain. Caruth (1996) states that "the possibility of knowing history is . . . a deeply ethical dilemma: the unremitting problem of *how not to betray the past*" (27; italics in original). This dilemma to not betray the past refers to how the very act of telling threatens to erase the very past it seeks to convey. Faithfulness means maintaining the event of violence against the larger narrative of personal/national redemption and refugee rescue (31). This practice shows how Hmong women's negotiations of the past reveal the traces of violence that are embedded in the process of displacement. In addition, it exposes the unequal grounds upon which history has been narrated to show that the struggle over historical memory is based on Western textual knowledge. My focus on Hmong women does not intend to feminize memory, in which the categories "woman" and "feminine" serve as a trope for the carrier of memory. Instead, I contend that listening to how Hmong women narrate their life stories offers a different language to access history.

Notes

1. See Espiritu 2006a and 2006b. For a broader analysis of the rescue and liberation discourse, see Yoneyama 2005.

2. This particular focus on Hmong exodus from Laos emphasizes the perspective of scholars and practitioners in the resettlement countries who attempt to understand how Hmong and Southeast Asian displacement and migration have impacted their "integration" into the new society.

3. Some of these key questions are as follows: How was the project of secrecy a U.S. military strategy of surrogacy to train and arm replacement soldiers? How did secrecy produce historical absence, and what does it mean to do research on a history that was not supposed to exist?

4. Kim's excavation of the Cold War as an "epistemology and production of knowledge" because it "exceeds and outlives its historical eventness" helps me pinpoint the "secret war" as a historical event and knowledge production project.

5. One particular challenge I faced in talking to some elder Hmong refugee women was their unwillingness to share their personal histories with me without their husbands' approval or presence. For example, I became acquainted with a couple, whom I call grandmother and grandfather, and was interested in pursuing formal interviews with them. However, the husband was either away from home or sick whenever I called, and I did not get to talk to him. Whenever I called, his wife always picked up the phone, and I would ask her if she would allow me to come by the house to talk to her. She conveyed that she wanted to wait until her husband came home before agreeing to an interview. This type of behavior made it difficult to reach out to some Hmong women who could have shared their stories with me.

6. Soua L. Lo reminds me that she wants the Hmong children of my generation, including her children and me, to achieve educational success so that we may live up to and atone for the experiences of the first-generation Hmong: "I am happy for you. You are a daughter who wants to learn about Hmong life and you are steadfast in your education. I think that, your parents think the same as me, we have sons and daughters and they do well (*tsim txiaj rau ntawm lawv*). Like I tell my kids, you should go represent/do your part for me for the Americans (*ua kuv tug rau Meskas thiab*). Do you know that I came to this country and worked for America as a servant, I want Americans to work for you as a servant like I've worked for them? I tell them that. I am satisfied that you are all steadfast in your education. Americans will work for you like we have worked for them." This multilayered statement captures the aspirations of Hmong narratives to speak to present and future goals for Hmong children. My intention in framing the interviews in

this way aims to show how the narratives can be productive for understanding the past in relation to the present. Most of the interviewees, male and female, impart this message as a necessary lesson for listening to their stories.

7. I met Yer Vang in September 2009 on a research trip to Fresno, California, to visit the Lao Hmong American Veterans Memorial and to interview members of the planning committee about its conceptualization and construction. At the time, he volunteered as the secretary for Lao Veterans of America, one of the major organizations involved in creating, in his words, the statue. I went to their office to interview Colonel Wangyee Vang, president of Lao Veterans and a memorial planning committee member. Yer happened to be in the office on the same day, and I asked to talk with him after my conversation with Colonel Vang. He graciously agreed to this impromptu request, and I interviewed him on the same day in their office.

Works Cited

Abu-Lughod, Lila. 1993. *Writing Women's Worlds: Bedouin Stories.* Berkeley: University of California Press.

Arvin, Maile, Eve Tuck, and Angela Morrill. 2013. "Decolonizing Feminism: Challenging Connections between Settler Colonialism and Hetero Patriarchy." *Feminist Formations* 25, no. 1: 8–34.

Behar, Ruth. 1990. "Rage and Redemption: Reading the Life Story of a Mexican Marketing Woman." *Feminist Studies* 16, no. 2: 223–58.

Blunt, Alison, and Gillian Rose, eds. 1994. *Writing Women and Space: Colonial and Postcolonial Geographies.* New York: Guilford Press.

Caruth, Cathy. 1996. *Unclaimed Experience: Trauma, Narratives, and History.* Baltimore: Johns Hopkins University Press.

Cole, Ellen, Oliva M. Espin, and Esther D. Rothblum, eds. 1992. *Refugee Women and Their Mental Health: Shattered Societies, Shattered Lives.* New York: Haworth Press.

Coulthard, Glen. 2010. "Place against Empire: Understanding Indigenous Anti-Colonialism." *Affinities: A Journal of Radical Theory, Culture, and Action* 4, no. 2: 79–83.

Donnelly, Nancy D. 1994. *Changing Lives of Refugee Hmong Women.* Seattle: University of Washington Press.

DuBois, Lindsay. 2000. "Memories out of Place: Dissonance and Silence in Historical Accounts of Working Class Argentines." *Oral History* 28, no. 1: 75–82.

Edkins, Jenny. 2003. *Trauma and the Memory of Politics.* Cambridge: Cambridge University Press.

Espiritu, Yen Le. 2006a. "The 'We-Win-Even-When-We-Lose' Syndrome: U.S. Press Coverage of the Twenty-Fifth Anniversary of the 'Fall of Saigon.'" *American Quarterly* 58, no. 2: 329–52.

————. 2006b. "Toward a Critical Refugee Study: The Vietnamese Refugee Subject in U.S. Scholarship." *Journal of Vietnamese Studies* 1, no. 1–2: 410–33.

Fadiman, Anne. 1997. *The Spirit Catches You and You Fall Down: A Hmong Child, Her American Doctors, and the Collision of Two Cultures.* New York: Farrar, Straus, and Giroux.

Hein, Jeremy. 1995. *From Vietnam, Laos, and Cambodia: A Refugee Experience in the United States.* Immigrant Heritage of America Series. New York: Twayne.

Ho, Wendy. 1999. *In Her Mother's House: The Politics of Asian American Mother-Daughter Writing.* Walnut Creek, Calif.: AltaMira Press.

Kaplan, Caren, and Inderpal Grewal. 1999. "Transnational Feminist Cultural Studies: Beyond the Marxism/Poststructuralism/Feminism Divides." *Between Women and Nation: Nationalisms, Transnational Feminisms, and the State,* edited by Caren Kaplan, Norma Alarcon, and Minoo Moallem, 347–63. Durham, N.C.: Duke University Press.

————. 2002. "Transnational Practices and Interdisciplinary Feminist Scholarship: Refiguring Women's and Gender Studies." In *Women's Studies on Its Own,* edited by Robyn Wiegman, 66–81. Durham, N.C.: Duke University Press.

Kim, Jody. 2010. *Ends of Empire: Asian American Critique and the Cold War.* Minneapolis: University of Minnesota Press.

Kroll, Jerome, Marjorie Habenicht, Thomas Mackenzie, Mee Yang, Sokha Chan, Tong Vang, Tam Nguyen, Mayjoua Ly, Banlang Phommasouvanh, Hung Nguyen, Yer Vang, Langsanh Souvannasoth, and Roberto Cabugao. 1989. "Depression and Posttraumatic Stress Disorder in Southeast Asian Refugees." *American Journal of Psychiatry* 146:1592–97.

Marshall, Mac. 1994. "Engaging History: Historical Ethnography and Ethnology." *American Anthropologist* 96, no. 4: 972–74.

Michaud, Jean, and Christian Culas. 2000. "The Hmong of the Southeast Asia Massif: Their Recent History of Migration." In *Where China Meets Southeast Asia: Social and Cultural Change in the Border Regions,* edited by Grant Evans, Christopher Hulton, and Khah Eng Kuah, 98–121. New York: St. Martin's Press.

Morrison, Gayle. 2007. *Sky Is Falling: An Oral History of the CIA's Evacuation of the Hmong from Laos.* Jefferson, N.C.: McFarland.

Mote, Sue Murphy. 2004. *Hmong and American: Stories of Transition to a Strange Land.* Jefferson, N.C.: McFarland.

Ortner, Sherry B. 2006. "Resistance and the Problem of Ethnographic Refusal." *Anthropology and Social Theory: Culture, Power, and the Acting Subject.* Durham, N.C.: Duke University Press, 2006.

Ramirez, Renya K. 2007. "Race, Tribal Nation, and Gender: A Native Feminist Approach to Belonging." *Meridians: Feminism, Race, Transnationalism* 7, no. 2: 22–40.

Rice, Pranee Liamputtong. 2000. *Hmong Women and Reproduction.* Westport, Conn.: Bergin and Garvey.

Rozée, Patricia D., and Gretchen Van Boemel. 1990. "The Psychological Effects of War Trauma and Abuse on Older Cambodian Refugee Women." *Women and Therapy* 8, no. 4: 23–50.

Simpson, Audra. 2007. "On Ethnographic Refusal: Indigeneity, 'Voice' and Colonial Citizenship." *Junctures* 9 (December): 67–80.

Smith, Andrea, and J. Kehaulani Kauanui. 2008. "Native Feminisms Engage American Studies." *American Quarterly* 60, no. 2: 241–49.

Sugiman, Pamela. 2006. " 'These Feelings That Fill My Heart': Japanese Canadian Women's Memories of Internment." *Oral History* 34, no. 2: 69–84.

Taylor, Diana. 2003. *The Archive and the Repertoire: Performing Cultural Memory in the Americas.* Durham, N.C.: Duke University Press.

Vang, Ma. 2012a. "The Refugee Soldier: Critique of Recognition and Citizenship in the Hmong Veterans' Naturalization Act of 1997." In "Southeast Asian/ American Studies." Special issue, *Positions: Asia Critique* 20, no. 3: 685–712.

———. 2012b. "Displaced Histories: Refugee Critique and the Politics of Hmong American Remembering." PhD diss., University of California, San Diego.

Warner, Roger. 1996. *Out of Laos: A Story of War and Exodus, Told in Photographs.* Rancho Cordova, Calif.: Southeast Asia Community Resource Center.

XayKaoThao, Doualy. 2011. "Family History: The General, His Sisters and Me." *National Public Radio,* May 27. www.npr.org/2011/05/27/133664172/family -history-the-general-his-sisters-and-me.

Yang, Kao Kalia. 2012. "The Science of Racism: Radiolab's Treatment of Hmong Experience." *Hyphen: Asian American Unabridged,* October 22. http://hyphen magazine.com/blog/archive/2012/10/science-racism-radiolabs-treatment -hmong-experience.

Yoneyama, Lisa. 1999. *Hiroshima Traces: Time, Space, and the Dialectics of Memory.* Berkeley: University of California Press.

———. 2005. "Liberation under Siege: U.S. Military Occupation and Japanese Women's Enfranchisement." *American Quarterly* 57, no. 3: 885–910.

CHAPTER 3

Rethinking Hmong Women's Wartime Sacrifices

Chia Youyee Vang

THE ONGOING DISCOURSES on war victimhood in Hmong American communities since they first settled in the United States in the mid-1970s and the continued privileging of men's military experiences by scholars, journalists, and policy makers are important contributions to the formation of a narrow narrative of Hmong wartime experiences. The dynamism of war provided some Hmong women transformative opportunities that were previously not available to them. In 1965, Choua Thao joined the United States Agency for International Development (USAID) Village Health Program to be trained as a nurse. She was twenty-two years old, and she could not have imagined then what would eventually transpire for herself and other Hmong men and women in northeastern Laos. Her counterpart, Diana (Dee) Quill,[1] a twenty-three-year-old American nurse, had signed up with the International Voluntary Service (IVS) in 1963 to expand her horizons. Two years after arriving in Laos, she was presented with the opportunity to work with Choua as part of the U.S. humanitarian effort supporting the "secret war" in Laos. Choua's and Dee's lives intersected in the remote northern Lao mountains just as the United States stepped up its military campaign in Vietnam, and the war demanded greater involvement of neighboring Laos and Cambodia.

This chapter explores Hmong women's responses to wartime opportunities and how the actions of employed Hmong women who lived in Laos during the Vietnam War contribute to the reshaping of discourses about the "secret war" era. Hmong women's accounts of their wartime experiences enable us to excavate the symbolic significance of this period. I argue that Hmong women strategically used U.S.-sponsored employment during wartime to liberate themselves from social and cultural constraints that disrupted gender roles and power structures. Although limited, employment and education facilitated the creation of a new social position for women in Hmong society and, for the first time, class differences due to women's earnings. Alternative heroic stories emerge from their narratives, shedding light on how Hmong women at the time constructed new identities and how their interpretation of wartime lives not only differs from but also contradicts that of others on the scene. Ethnic, racial, and gender tensions surfaced as they interacted with other local ethnic groups, Americans, Filipinos, and Hmong men in their new roles.

Methodology

My interest in the impact that the war had on Hmong women's lives expands on my extensive research on Hmong men's military service in Laos during the Vietnam War. In addition to stories I had heard about Hmong nurses and teachers during the war, the publication of Dr. Charles Weldon's memoir in 1999 confirmed that some women were engaged in nontraditional activities. From 1963 to 1974, Weldon served as chief of the Public Health Division with USAID in Laos, where he administered the agency's Village Health Program.[2] A chapter in the memoir describes the establishment of a nurse training program for local women in northeastern Laos. Their leader was a young Hmong woman named Choua Thao.[3] What the war meant for Hmong women and how they interpret the dominant, pro-American narratives that have been constructed became a part of my research undertakings as a doctoral student in the mid-2000s.[4]

Since no formal record is available, it is difficult to ascertain exactly how many people were involved. Choua Thao estimates that about one hundred young women and girls participated in the medical training provided by the Village Health Program at Sam Thong from 1965 to 1974, of which the majority were Hmong (Choua Thao 2005). Although nursing was the most common new profession available to women, some also became teachers or were employed in various U.S.-sponsored support positions. From 2005 to 2006, I interviewed ten Hmong women living in the United States who had been employed in Laos. I also conducted an interview with Diana Quill about her experiences working with some of the women. The reflections that interviewees shared with me constitute what sociologist and feminist scholar Ann Oakley (1981) suggested years ago: "Finding out about people through interviewing is best achieved when the relationship of interviewer and interviewee is non-hierarchical and when the interviewer is prepared to invest his or her own personal identity in the relationship" (41). When I set out to interview these women, most initially wondered why I would be interested in hearing about their pasts. They did not consider themselves important and their life experiences worthy of documentation. I often had to convince them that their lived experiences were important and that I was interested in recording Hmong women's own accounts of their lives so that their children, grandchildren, and others would hear their voices among the male-dominated military narratives. It was under this condition that they shared their memories with me.[5]

I contend that their stories serve as agents of historical change because their accounts demonstrate how they pursued ambitions amid much adversity. Given Choua Thao's prominent role during the war, this chapter revolves around her experiences. The viewpoints of six of the ten Hmong interviewees are incorporated into the larger narrative. The memories of Diana Quill and Dr. Weldon are also interwoven with Hmong women's recollections to further illustrate the underpinnings of a historical movement that disrupted Hmong social structure. I treat Dr. Weldon's reflections in his memoir as a primary source. The women's narratives reveal how they articulate their needs, resist oppression, and nurture power in their self-empowerment process. This approach enables the women to narrate their lives as they experienced them. As Lewis and Sandra Hinchman (1997) explain, the power of narratives is the "active, self-shaping quality of human thought . . . to create and refashion personal identity" (xiv). Writing about Vietnamese American women, Linda Trinh Vo (2003) found this process of women narrating their life experiences during and after the Vietnam War as empowering. Among Vietnamese refugee women in Australia, Nathalie Huynh Chau Nguyen (2009) also revealed that speaking about painful and difficult events in their lives allowed them to reinterpret their traditional role. Not only are they able to share their stories but they also feel that they have a story to tell and are prepared to bring it into the public domain (x).

Since the war was a catalyst that intensified the consequences of deeply rooted gender divisions and inequality in access to resources, I analyze the varied roles that women played and the thought processes that they underwent to pursue work and educational opportunities. I further explore how wartime presented opportunities to challenge existing attitudes about gender; to change women's consciousness; and to hasten broader processes of social, political, and economic transformation by engaging in what feminist scholar J. Ann Tickner (2001) called a "bottom-up approach [to analyze] the impact of war at the microlevel" (48–49). Their memories reveal their vulnerability, the ambiguities of their experiences, and struggles with socially acceptable behaviors. Thus, I further situate my analysis of their experiences within the literature on women's dangerous sexuality during wartime.

Understanding Gender and War

Whether it is in wars during ancient times or military adventures conducted by powerful nations in the modern era, women have always been involved. Jean Bethke Elshtain and Sheila Tobias (1990) observed, "When we think of war, we inescapably immerse ourselves in the horror and allure of collective violence, a violence from which women have been officially separated, at least in the era of modern nation-states, but to which they are, and have been, essential" (ix). We saw dramatic involvement of women during World War II. The comprehensive propaganda campaign created a progressive image of American women as competent workers in all fields (Honey 1984, 211). American women served behind the front lines as nurses in Korea and Vietnam. The role of women in war has, however, evolved as a result of the transformation of the U.S. military. Integration of women into combat and flight has become a means for both serving their country and achieving their own ambitions for advancement (Dombrowski 1999, 28). In *Women as Weapons of War*, for example, Kelly Oliver (2007) notes that for centuries women have been imagined as dangerous, especially in terms of their sexuality: "[Women] have been figured as either innocent virgins or dirty whores; and in fantasies one easily morphs into the other. . . . The virgin uses her innocence to trap and betray, the whore with heart of gold saves the jaded man from his humdrum life" (20). Oliver problematizes this dichotomous image with an analysis of how women's contentious participation in the combat zone has shifted to where seemingly innocent American girls gleefully tortured Iraqi male prisoners (20). While the female soldier's sexuality is still a threat, she is capable of performing violent acts often exhibited by male soldiers.

Hmong women's experiences during wartime Laos have never been described by scholars and other writers in any way other than that of poor, illiterate refugees in need of being saved. It should be noted that neither the level of prostitution seen in South Vietnam nor the nature of Korean women's sexual labor—which Grace Cho (2008) examined in *Haunting the Korean Diaspora*—occurred with Hmong women in Laos. The covert nature of U.S. involvement with only a few hundred advisers and CIA operatives in the country meant that few Americans had contact with the Hmong in northeastern Laos. The "dirty whore" characterization was primarily intraethnic.[6] Hmong women's experiences are best reflected in sociologist Philomena Goodman's (2002) articulation of British feminine identities and behavior during the Second World War: "There were fears that war would provide the conditions for women's sexual liberty and economic independence. Women would have the opportunity to colonise male space, to achieve their potential in the public domain, to achieve self-determination and perhaps, in some cases, challenge inequality" (103).

Existing scholarship on Hmong in the United States has primarily highlighted men's military sacrifices.[7] This tendency, as political theorist Jean Bethke Elshtain (1987) argues, is the result of historical dominant symbols of male fighters and female noncombatants (xii). In the early 1980s, scholars such as Karen Anderson (1980) and Sheila Tobias and Lisa Anderson (1982) documented how World War II freed American women from some role restrictions in mobilizing them for war work at home and some limited military and nursing service abroad. The nursing profession's link to the British military, as Anne Summers (1988) maintained, was thought to improve women's status because "services in war demonstrated their de facto equality with men" (295). In *Reconstructing Women's Wartime Lives*, Penny Summerfield (1998) described two main groups of women in Great Britain as those who embraced the war and those who endured the war. Hmong women suffered due to displacement during the war, so indeed most endured, but the women in this study and others like them embraced the war because they actively sought new opportunities to improve their socioeconomic status.

Clearly, the argument that modern war liberated women in industrial societies is not new (Rupp 1978; Anderson 1980; Elshtain 1987; Elshtain and Tobias 1990, 165; Dombrowski 1999; Oliver 2007). Wartime conditions in general freed some women from tradition and convention and transformed gender relationships in fundamental ways. As Leila Rupp (1978) explains, "[The] idea that wars 'liberate' women, that wars bring about social revolution, overlooks the fact that societies in time of war accept changes normally considered undesirable on a permanent basis" (176). D'Ann Campbell (1984) further illustrated that wartime emergencies lowered certain traditional barriers to facilitate gender changes. International relations scholar Joshua Goldstein (2001) argues that causality runs both ways between war and gender. Whereas gender roles adapt individuals for war roles, war roles provide the context within which individuals are socialized into gender roles. Gender relations are a part of the big picture of militarism and war (Cockburn 2007, 231). Unfortunately, when military conflicts come to an end, women's contributions tend to become marginalized.

One example in the Southeast Asian context is Vietnamese women's contributions to their country's military efforts against the United States. Historian Karen Gottschang Turner (1999) insists that any accounting of the American war in Vietnam that leaves out Vietnamese women tells only half the story (19). The American war produced a new crop of heroines, but following the war, few women were publicly recognized (35). Collective contributions are remembered, but not individual heroism. Turner quotes military historian and veteran Nguyen Quoc Dung:

> It was the simple, modest activities of Vietnamese women, armed only with small-bore 12.7 mm antiaircraft guns, that won out against the well-fed American pilots in their big heavy planes. Women used their small guns to shoot and their delicate hands to defuse bombs. We had to counter every U.S. plane and pilot with nine of our own people and most of the defense against the air strikes was carried out by women. Yes, their lives were hard. But many women learned to read in the jungles. Their teachers used raincoats as blackboards and forest plants for ink. Most women went home more confident and better educated, for the war liberated them from the bamboo gate of the village. (19–20)

Their participation was welcomed during wartime, but postwar conditions did not have a place for them outside of the domestic sphere. The erasure of Vietnamese women's wartime contributions is useful for examining Hmong women's contributions precisely because both have been overlooked.

Challenging Hmong Social Practices

When Dr. Weldon arrived in Laos in 1963, he was charged by the USAID with improving public health programs throughout the country, many of which were run by Filipinos through Operation Brotherhood (OB) since early 1957 (Bernad and Fuentecilla 2004).[8] Medical and socioeconomic teams from the Philippines operated a nursing school in Vientiane, the capital city. Upon touring the various regions, Weldon recalled:

> Very early in the planning phase, it became apparent that we needed two basic types of health care workers. One would be male, working at the village level in an outpatient dispensary. He would focus on first-aid, hygiene, environmental sanitation, plus symptomatic and curative treatment of simple ailments. The second could be female, and she would work in the hospital environment doing nursing tasks. (Weldon 1999, 120–21)

Weldon's assessment of health-care needs, and his conclusion that local men and women were needed, set the stage for Hmong women's involvement in nursing. It was at this particular juncture that the American humanitarian bureaucracy sought individuals like Choua Thao to build its capacity to serve the local population. Born in 1943 in Xiengkhouang Province, Choua was one of the few Hmong women who attended school. She recounted:

> My father was a district chief so his meetings with other leaders exposed him to little Lao girls like me going to school. This gave him an idea. That he had a daughter and he wanted her to go to school. So he obtained a birth certificate for me and enrolled me in school. I was so little and I did not speak any Lao. . . . This was back in about 1949/50. I still remember my first day of school. I had to learn Lao and French together. But within three months, I was fluent in Lao. (Choua Thao 2005)

Her inability to speak Lao illustrates the isolation of Hmong and other ethnic minorities from the major cities and towns in the lowland areas. Few Lao lived in the northern mountainous regions, so most Hmong did not interact with them directly. Despite her initial fear, Choua excelled in school. Going to school meant that she did not work in the fields like other Hmong girls and the women in her family. After school, she memorized her lessons, which she often could not wait to recite to her teacher the following day. This enthusiasm led her to attend the U.S.-supported nursing school in 1960, where she had the opportunity to learn English. Her ability to speak English would pave the way for her work in the Village Health Program.

Dr. Weldon identified the most significant problem faced by the Village Health Program to be the lack of candidates for training, since very few of the young people in the remote areas could read or write in any language. This challenge was exacerbated by the need to persuade local male leaders to accept the idea of a girl becoming a nurse or any sort of health worker. Weldon wrote:

> At Sam Thong . . . [Vang Pao] and the other clan chieftains were
> strongly opposed to the training of girls. Many reasons were
> claimed as to why such training was impossible: married women
> couldn't work in the hospital; the unmarried girls were too young;
> the male patients wouldn't accept nursing care from a woman—
> particularly not from a young, unmarried woman; women didn't
> have enough sense to be trained; women were too lazy to do such
> work; if the unmarried girls lived at the hospital, the boys would
> seduce them. (Weldon 1999, 122)

Hmong women and girls were thought to be incapable of taking on nursing tasks. Not only was their intelligence questioned, but Weldon also indicated that women and girls were believed to pose a danger to male desires. Weldon believed that Diana's arrival changed these perceptions. Originally from Harrisburg, Pennsylvania, she graduated with a bachelor of science in nursing in 1963. A few months before graduation, she met a cousin of one of the nurses with whom she worked. This young woman encouraged Diana to work abroad. She fondly recalled:

> I asked what she was doing and she said, 'Have you ever heard of
> an organization called International Volunteer Service?' I said no I
> haven't. She explained what it was and its mission. She said she was
> applying to go to Cambodia to teach English. This organization
> was working in teams in Southeast Asia. There were teams in

Vietnam, Laos and Cambodia. She said they take nurses. If you
don't know what you're going to do, it might be a good idea. I
could do some traveling, which appealed to me. So I called them
and they sent me an application. The next thing I knew was that I
was accepted and they had a position for me in Vientiane, Laos. I
didn't know the exact location, I had to go to the library and get an
atlas. (Diana Quill 2005)

Similar to many young Americans of her generation who answered the
call to engage in cultural diplomacy across the globe, Diana was intrigued
by the promise of adventure in a foreign land. Contrary to the nursing duties
that she expected to perform, once in Vientiane, she mainly provided
office support, since she spoke neither French nor Lao.

After fourteen months in the country, she was given an opportunity to
go to Sam Thong, where she would be the first and only American female
worker.[9] A house approximately thirty steps from the hospital was built for
her. According to Weldon's recollection:

Soon after Dee's arrival, we hired a Meo girl to work with her.
Chua was married to a Lao boy who worked for [the United States
Information Service] in Vientiane, and they had two children.
Although she was Meo from Xieng Khoung, Chua had lived in
Vientiane with relatives, and had gone through nurses training at the
OB. She was an intelligent, mature young woman, and—being fluent
in English, as well as Lao and Meo—was the ideal counterpart to
Dee, and an invaluable asset to the program. (Weldon 1999, 123)[10]

Unlike Diana, a house was not built near the hospital for Choua. She lived in
the nearby village with her family. A possible explanation is that she was
married and already had a house. Analyzing the situation more closely, however, one sees contradictory, paternalistic descriptions of Choua, which is a
common colonial mentality toward native populations. Her small stature,
which Westerners associate with children, may have influenced Weldon's
view of Choua. At the same time that he praised her as "intelligent" and
"mature," he referred to her as "a Meo girl" (and her husband as "a Lao boy!)
despite the fact that she was married with two children.[11]

Dr. Weldon, Choua, and Diana moved forward with plans to recruit
the first group of trainees, which Weldon claimed went against Hmong

military leader Vang Pao's wishes. He wrote, "Despite VP's resistance to training for girls, we went ahead and recruited two Meo, two Lao, two Lao Theung, and one Tai Dam" (126). Weldon referred to this group as "the Magnificent Seven," who were competent and motivated.[12] After a few months of basic nursing training, their skills would be put to the test by a progressing war. When Vang Pao saw them care for the wounded and distressed for the first time, no criticism came from him. In fact, Weldon described the contrary, "Later in the day, VP showed up—and was surprised to see them there. Nevertheless, he didn't say anything to Pop or me, and we didn't say anything to him. He exchanged a few pleasant words with Chua and the nurses, and everyone acted as if nothing out of the ordinary had occurred" (126).[13] As the military leader, Vang Pao held tremendous power. Had he wished to do so, he could have eliminated the effort altogether. Another major occasion for the women to prove themselves was caring for a group of eighty-five hundred people who had trekked through the jungle following major attacks by the enemy. Watching them work alongside male medics, Weldon praised their ability to "manage the dispirited mothers, the frightened children, and the debilitated and often disoriented old people," which he claimed set them apart from their male colleagues (129).

The effectiveness of this first cohort and the economic benefits resulted in a change in attitudes among some Hmong (see Figure 3.1).[14] Choua revealed that when she brought her 60,000 kip salary to her father, other parents began to envy him.[15] Furthermore, observing her descend from American helicopters from one village to the next to recruit young women, "[other] Hmong parents became crazy about sending their daughters to school" (Choua Thao 2005). Dr. Weldon agreed with Choua's assessment. He wrote:

> The fact that they were nurses who had trained at Sam Thong gave these girls new status—and greatly increased their marriage eligibility and their bride price. This, no doubt—especially the latter—influenced other parents to allow their daughters into training. . . . It was an honor to be one of the seven, and they were always pointed out at parties and ceremonies, and received special attention and courtesies. . . . Having broken some of the rigid bonds that tribal custom and tradition placed on women, they were indeed courageous pioneers. (Weldon 1999, 130)

Figure 3.1. Nurses in Laos, 1960s. [L–R]: Nurse Dee (shaking hands with King Sisavang Vanthana), Carol, Choua Thao, Onchanh (Lao), Ia Moua, Chanmala (Lao), and Unknown (Kmhmu). Author's collection.

As a representative of U.S. imperialism, Weldon credits himself for break-ing "tribal custom and tradition" that facilitated a change in Hmong wom-en's status. The seven were more valuable than other women via increased "bride price" and were paraded in front of the local population as evidence of imperial success. This is the kind of representation of war's impact on local populations that Yoneyama (2005) argues against, because it claims that war was good for Hmong women.

Expanding the Pool

The Magnificent Seven cared for villagers and wounded soldiers, but as the war dragged on, the need for additional nurses mounted. More people had to be recruited, and appropriate training materials needed to be developed. Weldon (1999) explained, "Dee inaugurated regular training courses for girls, and the program was even more successful than we'd anticipated" (130). Diana, on the contrary, stated, "Choua and I worked on a training program. We got a basic curriculum together. Nursing techniques for a three months training" (Diana Quill 2005). Again, race influenced Weldon's view of Choua. As a native female whom he regarded as *a girl,* Weldon erased Choua's contribution and credited the program's success only to Diana, a woman who shared his racial identity.

Choua and Diana agreed that training mostly illiterate young women required creativity. Diana recalled, "First thing we did was teach them the alphabet because all of the medication came from America and doctors wrote in English" (Diana Quill 2005). The young women received basic nursing skills training, including more difficult nursing techniques (intravenous), which Diana felt was difficult for many American nurses with college degrees to carry out. She authoritatively explained the reason for the effectiveness of the training: "Choua was the main force. I give her all the credit" (Diana Quill 2005). Diana also admitted that she did not know how Choua was able to convince parents to let their daughters take part in the training program.

Despite Weldon's problematic description of Choua, the female recruits were indeed teenagers, whose curiosity and aspirations to escape agrarian life motivated them to pursue careers outside of their villages. The training program increased the participants' knowledge and skills. Choua believed it expanded their worldviews and helped them rethink their roles in Hmong society. At the end of each session, they toured the hospital in Vientiane and clinics in other cities. For most of the young women, it was their first visit to the capital. Choua offered the following reflection on recruitment and training routines:

> Some finished, others left. There were Hmong, Lao and Yao girls. The majority of the nurses were Hmong, but there were Khammu, Lao, Pu Yi, and others. The Lao, I had to go pick up from Pakse, Savannaket, Luang Prabang. The parents wanted so much for their daughters to become nurses. Nurses were so popular in the 1960s through early 1970s because the pay was good. We had dorms for them. They didn't have to do anything, but we expect them to learn. . . . They didn't have to do anything except to take care of themselves. They kept themselves clean. They were beautiful.

People cooked for them. They just had to do their job. When they completed the training, they worked in Nasu and Sam Thong. Nursing duties. Administer medication. Look after patients. (Choua Thao 2005)

Both Diana and Choua pointed out that the work was demanding. While many took part in the training, not all completed it. Even when they completed the program, some could not work as nurses. Those who did complete the program and enjoyed the profession became a part of the more than thirty-five hundred village health workers throughout Laos.

Why Nursing?

The path that Chou Vang followed to become a nurse was complex. Her family was among one of the first Hmong families who converted to Christianity in the mid-1950s. Her mother insisted that she attend bible school. She recounted her mother's rationale: "[As] a businessman, my brother had visited places like Saigon where he met other Christians. He became a Christian so our whole family became Christians. We converted because we had bad experiences with evil spirits that took away the lives of two of my sisters. So my mother felt that I should go to bible school in Vientiane and become a missionary" (Chou Vang 2006). Upon completion of bible training, she changed her mind. She explained, "Since I did not want to go and live by myself as a missionary after I completed bible school, I decided to go to nursing school." This change of direction was due to her realization that as a young single Hmong woman, she faced barriers that Western missionaries did not.

Ly Vang, a former nursing student who has served as the executive director of a Hmong women's organization in Minnesota since its inception in the early 1980s, offered telling perspectives about how she became involved:

At that time [1968], I was 12 years old. I was recruited by the hospital in Sam Thong to enroll in the nursing program. They would go around from one province to another to recruit when a new class was starting. The clan and province leaders had a certain number they had to find. It's not like here where you go graduate then go train. The training was the same tasks that registered

nurses do here. The training was intensive. You had to be trained in all aspects from surgery to pharmacy to labor delivery room. You had to know all the skills because we had to be rotated. Most of my work was in emergency room and delivery room in Long Cheng.
(Ly Vang 2005)

From Ly's recollection, we see that the process for locating prospective female nurse trainees mirrors the strategy that military leaders implemented to recruit soldiers. Her age was similar to the thousands of Hmong boys who became soldiers. Because 1968 was a defining year in the larger Vietnam War, increased casualties and displacement of local populations as a result of the air war affected many areas throughout Laos. The cooperation of clan leaders was necessary to fulfill the slots. When asked why she had wanted to become a nurse, Ly explained:

I don't think I was thinking. At the time, I had a friend who was going. I was at the airport with her. When the airplane came, I was sort of forced to go. [The recruiters] needed two people and they only had one, so I was shoved into the airplane. My parents didn't even know that I had gone because at that time [my father] was doing some work in Long Cheng. Somehow, when I got to Sam Thong, my dad came from Long Cheng to visit. He didn't make me go back. He said that since I was already there, it was a good thing. He bought me some things and told me to keep going.
(Ly Vang 2005)

Given that Hmong parents held much power to choose a life path for their daughters, Ly's father could have forced her to return home when he found out. The urgent need for medical support likely influenced his decision to permit her to remain in the program, but it cannot be overlooked that like other parents, the financial reward and prestige of being recognized at community functions accorded to earlier recruits may have swayed his decision. Ly explained how people viewed nursing work: "[It was a] very important job for our community. . . . That's the only opportunity for women to be in the field. . . . People came from all over, so they had a dorm for the single girls. The people in charge were there to manage you and take care of you like your parents" (Ly Vang 2005). By the time Ly became involved, people generally viewed nurses positively. Although control of the trainees' lives by those in charge was evident, living away from parental control allowed the women to make decisions for themselves.

Lang Chanthalangsy was also inspired to become a nurse after she learned about Choua's success.[16] Lang initially joined because her father had died and her mother could not support her and three younger siblings. Only fourteen years old at the time, Lang said that she could not handle the intensity of nursing duties. "After nurse training I came back home. I worked for a hospital close to my house for about seven months, then I quit. I went back to Vientiane to take typing classes before I went to work for the military in 1971 until the country fell to communism," she explained (Lang Chanthalangsy 2005 and 2012). The violence of war was difficult for some of the young women. Choua elaborated on one of many incidents that would challenge young girls like Lang to reconsider nursing:

> One time a B-52 dropped the bomb on our soldiers. They loaded 270 casualties in the Nasu hospital. This was about 1970. The injured were everywhere. Before the doctors arrived, I had to check on the patients to see if they were awake, what their injury was, and what treatment they needed. I assessed them and provided emergency treatment to them. . . . You don't think about blood, smell, or other negative things. All you think about is saving someone's life. (Choua Thao 2005)

Choua remembered many days when she could not take meal breaks and had to eat in front of her patients. Chou Vang also immersed herself in the work. She described her responsibilities:

> I worked at Sam Thong hospital. I was in charge of emergency intake and discharge, especially the military ward. I took inventories and prepared patients for intake. When patients were ready to be discharged, I would process the paperwork. I was an administrator in 1967. I went on rounds with the doctor each day to check on patients. When the doctor finished assessing patients, I would file the records. (Chou Vang 2006)

Choua and Chou expressed much pride in this period of their lives. They may have witnessed much pain and suffering, but they also were fully committed to the work that they felt contributed to their community's

well-being. Their experiences represented a complex web of personal encounters with a variety of actors in support of the war effort. The roles
they played were direct responses to gender changes to meet wartime personnel needs, but the gendered structure in which men were fighters and
women were caregivers remained intact (Vuic 2010).

Women's Dangerous Sexuality

Stepping outside of the gender roles assigned to them came with high
costs. The women highlight ongoing, suspicious treatment from many directions. Choua, Ly, and Mao remembered the criticism they received
when they attended school:

> This is what other Hmong people said about me going to school.
> First, "What a dumb Hmong man to send a daughter to school.
> She'll probably just become a prostitute." Second, "Even if she
> becomes educated, she'll likely only become a nurse examining
> vaginas and do dirty work." I've never been a prostitute, but I did
> examine so many of their wives' vaginas and delivered babies for
> years before I left the country. (Choua Thao 2005)

> When we went to school, we were teased a lot by Hmong boys and
> were targets of criticism from the community. They would say to
> my father that if he let me go to school, I wouldn't know how to do
> household chores. They thought I would become lazy. My dad
> decided to let me go despite the criticisms. Guys tease you and
> they laugh and think that you would not make it. They sometimes
> make fun of you, called you bad names. They think it's funny for
> girls to be in school and not working in the farms under our
> parents' supervision. Sometimes our parents would have to
> accompany us to schools. They would say that if you're a woman
> and you go to school, then you're a prostitute. (Ly Vang 2005).

> Even though we were not able to farm, it was very unlikely for
> girls from poor families like mine to attend school. The mentality
> was that as a girl, your education would only benefit your husband's
> family. It would not be worthwhile for your parents to invest in
> your education. For a girl like me to go to school, it was almost a

miracle. My mother was responsible for my being able to go to school. My father did not want me to go at all. . . . My mother said to him, "Every day we just sit around here. There is no farming to do. Let her go to school." She told me, "Don't listen to your father. If I say go to school, then go to school. Here in the house, there is nothing much to do." (Mao Vang Lee 2005)

The connection that those who criticized Choua's father made between education and prostitution is problematic at first, but after listening to the women's accounts, another story unfolds to explain why the links were made. Choua revealed the contentious issue of sexual relationships among some nurses and high-ranking military leaders. She stated:

I worked with Vang Pao because he liked my nurses. He liked to flirt with them. . . . What I hated most about the General and Vang Fong was that they would take my nurses to sleep with. There were times when the women wouldn't return when their shifts began. Even when I was pregnant and ready to give birth, I would have to fill in for them until they returned because we had 400–500 patients. They were late four to five hours. (Choua Thao 2005)

This revelation of sexual activities between some nurses and military leaders justified parents' fear and community criticism of what might occur when daughters were unsupervised. Concern was expressed about the moral status of Hmong women. Since anxieties were articulated within families and in the larger community, nurses worked in perilous conditions. Some young and single women did behave contrary to what is considered proper, but it is not clear whether the women did so to express their newfound freedom or if they were pressured to engage in sexual activities precisely because they lacked parental oversight and were unable to repel unwanted attention.[17] Others may have intentionally made themselves available to military men with financial power.

Women's disappearance from their scheduled shifts, having been "borrowed" by Vang Pao and his military officers, illustrates the presence of informal sex work during wartime. The wealth that military officers accumulated gave them tremendous power. Rape or assault occurred, but such incidents could be shoved under the disguise of commonly accepted polygamous marriages. Rather than carrying the shame of being a victim, women in such conditions would become the minor wives of military officers. "After hours" sexual attention, as Summerfield (1998) found, resulted from the idea that women serving the military in various capacities were "fair game" because "[they] had stepped out of women's protected sphere in wartime, and their public appearance could be interpreted to mean that they had made themselves sexually available (137–38). Concrete experiences of women told a different story about Hmong women who had paid employment. Young women during the war had fun and experienced pleasure within self-imposed boundaries of respectability. Ly's early experiences suggest that it was not only elders who did not believe in the value of educating girls. Socialized to treat women as less capable through the gendered division of labor and cultural practices, male peers attempted to intimidate girls who desired to become literate. In addition to the fear of uncontrollable female sexuality that could affect their marriageability, an underlying assumption was that women who attended school would no longer be willing to perform household tasks, another important desired skill for marriage. Again, it was assumed that formal education would lead to sexual deviancy.

As Choua alluded to earlier regarding the conflicting situation with single Hmong nurses, Mao Vang Lee confirmed the underlying perception that people held at the time about women like her. She shared the following reflections:

> When I started at the radio job, my father did not like it. He did not
> want me to go. But again, my mother said that I could go as long as
> I was careful and not become involved in bad things. Even though
> I went to live with relatives in Long Cheng, my father always
> questioned whether I was doing proper work. At that time, there
> was a perception that unmarried girls who were not under their
> parents' supervision were engaged in prostitution. This made it
> very difficult for a lot of parents to let their daughters seek work.
> (Mao Vang Lee 2005)

Mao received her mother's unconditional support and trust, but it is important to note that she neither lived with other single women nor lived by herself. She resided with relatives who could watch over her in her parents' absence. Constant suspicion of single women's intentions seemed to be the norm. Though it appeared that single life was difficult, Mao suggested that employed women who married also encountered challenges. She said, "Life at this time was quite complicated for Hmong women, especially for those who had salaried jobs. If you get married, it is hard for many to keep their jobs." If certain tasks were considered unsuitable for single women, then they were certainly thought of as even more unfitting for married women to perform. Mao did emphasize that there were a few cases in which husbands stayed home to take care of the children while wives worked. Interestingly, Mao met her husband, Yia Lee, while both worked at the radio station. Unlike some women who became second wives of military leaders, both Mao and Yia were young and dated for about two years before getting married. As an administrator working with Choua at Sam Thong hospital, Chou also held decision-making power. Educated for her generation, she shared that it was difficult to find a suitable Hmong husband. She considered herself fortunate to have met her husband, a Hmong man who worked as a truck driver for USAID.

Although Mao's father may not have been supportive, Mao and many of the women were fortunate to come from two-parent households. As mentioned earlier, Lang's father had passed away, leaving her mother with four children. As the oldest, Lang decided to train as a nurse only to find out later that she did not enjoy the work. When she completed typing classes in Vientiane, she went to work for the military, providing clerical support. According to Lang, she was responsible for processing monthly salaries for soldiers. Through tears, she recounted the harsh four years she endured:

> In the military, many times I worked for 24 hours. Many times starving, no food, drink. Many times, scary, by nighttime. . . . Many times I've been sick. Nobody take care of me. Nobody give me medicine. Nobody come to say how are you. I was just there with my uncle. I missed my mother a lot. But I had no choice because I had no father to support my family. I had to work. I had three young siblings. Many times people might look down on me because I was the only woman walking with the soldiers. Sometimes they might think about maybe I was there to "feed the soldier." After two years they had three more girls come to help me. Sometimes there are many injured soldiers and some die. Sometimes we work for two weeks, 24 hours a day. We moved from place to place. It was dangerous. (Lang Chanthalangsy 2005)

Lang's work on the front line differed from all of the other employed women. She suggested that she had assumed the role that her father would have played had he been alive. Though not a combat soldier, she traveled with the company with whom she was assigned. She eventually earned the rank of lieutenant, a status that she indicated was used to pay her salary. The weight on her teenage shoulders to survive in this gruesome context along with the responsibility to support her family was unbearable. Like other single working young women, she received critical looks from bystanders as she walked among the soldiers. People's reactions indicated to her that they assumed she was among the soldiers only for sexual purposes.

Contested Progress

While the prospect of improved social standing lured some Hmong women and girls to nursing, social mobility for women also occurred in other ways. Among the professions, teachers were the most revered. Why was formal education in such high demand? To fully appreciate this phenomenon, it is important to briefly take into consideration the legacy of colonialism. As a French colony, the larger Lao society was introduced to French education as part of France's mission to civilize subjects throughout its colonies (*la mission civilisatrice*). Though limited, instruction in isolated Lao villages during the colonial era took place, exposing groups like the Hmong to the benefits of formal education, such as access to government posts. French colonial rule ended in 1954, but its education efforts were partially sustained by the United States during the late 1950s and subsequently increased in the 1960s through the early 1970s. Similar to nursing opportunities, the building of village schools with USAID funds enabled more Hmong girls than ever before to learn how to read and write in Lao. In 1960, there were about 1,500 Hmong students attending twenty village schools. By 1969, the number had increased to 10,000 students served by more than one hundred village schools, and seven elementary schools staffed by 450 teachers, who were primarily Hmong (Yang 1993, 98).[18] Most Hmong girls who received formal education attended village schools, and some subsequently attended high school in Vientiane. May A Yang made a name for herself as a teacher. As she recounted:

> In 1955, I went to school in Xiengkhuang province. But, my education was disrupted with the Kong Le coup in 1960. When we

relocated, there were no more schools available. My education
back then was quite minimal. In 1964, we lived in Long Cheng.
They asked for volunteers who were literate to help teach others. So,
as one of few women who were literate, I became a teacher. (May
A Yang 2006)

As a single young woman with a salaried job, May A was admired by many
people. Those who knew her at the time also commented that her beauty
surpassed that of many women of her generation. Wealth, knowledge, and
beauty resulted in her being able to choose which man she wanted to
marry: T-28 pilot Major Sue Vang. A household in which both spouses
had salaried jobs was unheard of prior to the American war in Vietnam.
The wealth they accumulated through their jobs enabled May A to have
options beyond the Hmong villages. She taught in Vientiane and had a
house there. She explained the choices she had following her husband's
death: "My husband died in the line of duty on October 18, 1972. After
that, I didn't teach anymore. After he died, I went back to Long Cheng. I
started to sew [Lao style] women's clothes and was essentially a business-
woman" (May A Yang 2006). Left with four small children when her husband died, May A was confronted with a cultural dilemma. Whereas it was
typical for a Hmong woman whose husband had died to marry one of his
brothers, May A chose not to follow this tradition. She had economic
power due to both her own savings and a death benefit from the military.
She explained that she was not interested in becoming a minor wife. Her
prominent status as a teacher influenced her elders to refrain from forcing
her to do something against her will. Her exposure to Lao culture and society as a result of living and teaching in Vientiane helped her to start a
tailoring business. While most Hmong women wore traditional Hmong
costumes, May A's clients were "upper class" Hmong women who had adopted Lao-style dress. Her entrepreneurial spirit and skills enabled her to
maintain her socioeconomic status. She remained unmarried until she
met her second husband, who was single and younger than she was, in a
Thai refugee camp in 1975.

Despite the tragic conditions, Hmong women did benefit from the
economic consequences of war. At school, Mao Vang Lee learned how to
read and write in the Lao language, but it was her ability to read and write
in the Hmong language that facilitated the dramatic change in her socioeconomic status. However, she did not gain Hmong literacy skills at

school. Instead, she learned alongside her friend, who was the daughter of a Hmong pastor from the Chang clan. Even though her family had not converted to Christianity, the pastor allowed her to learn with his daughter.[19] Mao described the unusual situation in 1970 that would change her life. Most of the teachers had fled due to increased fighting in the area. With no school to attend, one day she and her aunt decided to go shopping at Long Cheng. She recalled that fateful day:

> When we got to Long Cheng, my aunt decided to go try out to sing Hmong folksongs (*kwv txhiaj*) at the radio station. The people in charge were Moua Thong, Moua Tou and Koua Yang. They "interviewed" us. My aunt sang one song. I knew how to sing, but I didn't really like to sing. So, I talked to them about things I could do. Interestingly, before we left they told my aunt that she did not have to come back but that the next day, I was to return. They told me that they wanted me to help read the folksongs for the girls who sang, but could not read. (Mao Vang Lee 2005)

Mao exerted a new form of agency by presenting her skills and making her own decision without consulting her parents.

The power of the radio to transmit messages indeed reached the isolated mountains in Laos during the 1960s. The radio station, *Lao Houam Phao* (United Lao Races), was funded by Americans; thus, Mao was involved in the larger propaganda campaign against the Communists. In addition to making announcements regarding casualties, gains in battlegrounds, and other important issues for the community, the people in charge wrote songs with specific themes. Mao explained her role: "Because the singers were illiterate, I would read each song so that they could memorize the words. In a way, I was teaching them the songs, then they would sing it for all to enjoy through the radio" (Mao Vang Lee 2005). Using the Hmong folk song art form, Mao disclosed that pro-American Hmong men wrote lyrics for her to teach the singers. Houa Vue Moua shared a sample verse that she had memorized as a teenager in Laos with her ear glued to the radio:[20]

> Oh in this time and place to young men
> You red Vietnamese enemy do you not know
> It is a new world and we have gathered

Gathered our flourishing gardens
You have assembled your sons only to come and die in rows
Does this not cause you pain all the way to your gall bladder
    and liver [21]
You dedicated Vietnamese[22]

Such strategies have not been explored by any experts in the plethora of scholarship of the U.S. secret war in Laos, which has focused entirely on Hmong men's combat experiences and the actions of American military advisers. Perhaps more important is the fact that no non-Hmong experts of this period speak the Hmong language and did not consider Hmong language materials essential in their studies.

Clearly Mao's work had wide reach, but she served in the background. For Choua, wealth and power increased her status within the USAID bureaucracy, and she gained respect from other Hmong as a result of her leadership position. She was, however, not treated with the same reverence in the larger Lao society. Her status as a member of an ethnic minority group that was considered primitive affected the way people responded to her position as their superior when she was sent to work in Vientiane just before the country fell. She recalled:

Before I left Laos, I was actually sent to an OB clinic in Vientiane in January 1975 where there was a Filipino doctor. I was sent there because the Filipino doctor was apparently taking medications that the Americans provided and sending them to the Philippines. When I first arrived, the Lao staff hated me so much. They often referred to me as the "Dumb Hmong woman." They saw the Hmong as illiterate and so they despised the fact that a Hmong person was their boss. They hated that. But, I don't care. . . . The Lao staff at the OB clinic were so lazy. Only 40 patients with 5–6 nurses! They still complained that it was too much work. . . . The Filipinos did not like me either because they could no longer steal. (Choua Thao 2005)

Choua resented the non-Hmong treating her as inferior, but her statement reveals similar prejudice toward the ethnic Lao under her supervision, as well as the Filipinos. They did not seem to respect her, and she did not hold them in high regard either. Corruption and abuse of U.S.

funds by the Lao elite, Hmong military leaders, and American and other contractors—such as Filipinos—during the war are not new revelations. Development and humanitarian aid often did not reach the intended beneficiaries in full. Instead, significant portions ended up in the pockets of civilian and military leaders. Military leaders lived lavishly while front-line soldiers and their families faced starvation. Furthermore, some collected monthly pay from U.S. military personnel for soldiers that existed only on paper. They did so and got away with it because it seemed as though the financial aid would never end (Goldstein 1973; Warner 1995).

Conclusion

There is no doubt that economic, military, and political expansionism directed toward the creation and growth of an American empire resulted in a major U.S. position in Asia involving groups of people who viewed its arrival with conflicted curiosity. The narratives throughout this chapter show that displacement from their homes and villages created hardships for local women and their families, but at the same time, it laid the groundwork for changes that would occur within familial and community life. Wartime opened up new paths for some Hmong women and girls that liberated them from farm life. The self-generated empowerment process of the individual woman is vital to the collective empowerment that can help to challenge unequal social relations and bring about change. Although understanding women's relationship to combat and war is complicated and at times fraught with moral dilemmas, wartime opportunities certainly enabled these women to openly resist cultural expectations. The lived experiences of those who obtained formal education and worked in paid jobs reveal that their actions had contentious effects on Hmong gender relations and on the ways in which they saw their new identities and position within and outside of Hmong society. Within the traditions of a society that afforded women little decision-making power emerged a group whose actions disrupted Hmong patriarchal social structure.

Notes

1. Diana's maiden name is Dick. Earlier references to her use Diana Dick. Most Hmong who knew her referred to her as Nurse Dee.

2. The Charles L. Weldon Papers are available at the Eugene McDermott Special Collections at the University of Texas–Dallas. I conducted archival research at this collection in spring 2008.

3. Weldon claimed to have never heard of Hmong people calling themselves Hmong; thus, he referred to all Hmong individuals in the book as "Meo," which was the term that the Lao used to refer to them. Since "Meo" was the official term that the state used for Hmong, it is not a surprise that Weldon did not hear the term "Hmong." Like other Americans in Laos at the time, he did not speak the Hmong language, so even if it had been used in front of him, he would not have understood. Though the "Meo" term was used to refer to them, Hmong people have always called themselves Hmong. "Hmong" became used exclusively following their migration to Western countries after the Vietnam War.

4. As cochair of the 2005 National Conference on Hmong Women, "Building on Hmong Women's Assets: Past, Present and Future," I interviewed and helped a few women who had held prominent positions during the war write down their life stories so that they could share them at the conference.

5. When I contacted Diana Quill for an interview, her reaction was similar to the Hmong women's initial responses. She said that she was young and did not fully understand the larger political and military strategies that her government implemented. In our telephone conversation, she said that she felt terrible about what happened to the people she knew in Laos after the war ended and that she had tried to put that period of her life behind her. I gave her a similar rationale for my interest in her life experience as I did the Hmong women interviewees. When she agreed on a date for me to conduct the interview in her home in Antioch, Tennessee, I booked my flight from Minneapolis, Minnesota, and reserved a hotel room. Two days before, I called her to confirm our meeting and to let her know where I was staying. She was surprised that I was planning to stay at a hotel and told me that she had already prepared a room in her home for me. I canceled my hotel reservation. During the weekend, her adult children joined us for dinner one evening. Her daughter shared with me that Diana had occasionally spoken fondly of her time in Laos but that she often did not share details.

6. Interestingly, interethnic marriages occurred between some elite Hmong and Lao. Educated Hmong women like Choua Thao married outside of their ethnic group. Choua believed that some Hmong men and their parents were threatened by her status. In my research about the Hmong pilots who were trained in Thailand, I found that a significant number of them married Thai women.

7. Since the construction of the Vietnam Veterans Memorial in Washington, D.C., in 1982, Hmong veterans and Americans who served in Laos have collaborated to insert their stories into U.S. national memory of the war. Three memorials have been built since 1997 to recognize Lao, Hmong, and Americans who served

in Laos: a roadside plaque in the Arlington National Cemetery (1997), a six-foot bronze statue depicting two Hmong soldiers rescuing a wounded American pilot in front of the Fresno, California, courthouse (2005), and a twenty-four-panel circular memorial in Sheboygan, Wisconsin, overlooking Lake Michigan (2006).

8. This book documents the work of nearly one thousand Filipinos in Laos from 1957 to 1975, including doctors, nurses, social workers, nutritionists, agriculturists, dentists, engineers, accountants, and technicians of all sorts—from aircraft maintenance workers to artists, architects, teachers, and administrators.

9. In contrast to the CIA secret military base at Long Cheng (also known as Lima Site 20A), Sam Thong was the humanitarian location (also known as Lima Site 20).

10. Weldon spelled Choua's name "Chua." I use "Choua," which is the spelling she uses.

11. While Choua did not live next to the hospital, a dormitory was eventually built for the single nurse recruits.

12. Interestingly, the "seven" excluded Choua and Dee.

13. Edgar "Pop" Buell was the USAID refugee relief coordinator.

14. I would like to thank Diana Quill for giving me her photos because she felt they would be more useful to me than remaining in her closet. I thank Choua Thao for helping me identify the nurses in the photo.

15. Today, 60,000 kip is about $8.00.

16. Lang changed her last name from Yang to Chanthalangsy when she married her husband, who is ethnic Lao.

17. Interestingly, one of Vang Pao's wives was a nurse.

18. Xia Vang Yang keynote speech at the 2005 National Conference on Hmong Women, Minneapolis, Minn., September 16, 2005. Video of keynote address (author's personal collection). According to Xia Vang Yang, a few Hmong women were sent to the United States and France to pursue education, including Mao Yang, May Zoua Lyfoung, Mao Vang, and Bao Vang.

19. Written Hmong language using the Romanized Popular Alphabet (RPA) was developed by French and American missionaries in the early 1950s. Thus, it was common for the Hmong to gain literacy skills in their own language at churches.

20. Houa Vue Moua was in the audience during Mao Vang Lee's keynote speech at the 2005 National Conference on Hmong Women. Following Mao's speech, Houa stood up and praised Mao and others for the work they did during the war. Houa explained how much she loved to listen to the shows as a teenager and asked Mao to sing one sample song for the audience. As Mao had explained, she was not one of the singers. Instead, she helped read songs created by pro-American Hmong men for other women singers. She encouraged Houa to share if

Houa remembered any. Houa stepped onto the stage and sang. I was the moderator of this session. The speeches and songs are available in the conference proceeding videotapes (author's personal collection).

21. Note that "gall bladder" and "liver" are literal translations.

22. Original: Nib yaim ua ca tav no txiv lees tub em om / Nyiag yeejncuab nyablaj liab es / nej pua paub tias / Lub nyiag ntuj tshiab lawm los peb li pos / Pos tau peb hav vaj zaub hlas toog tej si li nciab / Es nej nyem sau tub sau kiv tuaj tuag tsheej kab es pws tsheej kev / Es pua mob tas neb cuaj tsib tuaj kaum rau mus nplooj siab / Ne cov nyiag nyablaj cob tsib om.

Works Cited

Anderson, Karen. 1980. *Wartime Women*. Westport, Conn.: Greenwood Press.

Bernad, Michael A., and J. "Pete" Fuentecilla. 2004. *Filipinos in Laos*. Queens Village, N.Y.: Mekong Circle International.

Campbell, D'Ann. 1984. *Women at War with America: Private Lives in a Patriotic Era*. Cambridge, Mass.: Harvard University Press.

Chanthalangsy, Lang. 2005. Interview with author on August 25.

———. 2012. Interview with author in Rockford, Ill., on May 19.

Cho, Grace. 2008. *Haunting the Korean Diaspora: Shame, Secrecy and the Forgotten War*. Minneapolis: University of Minnesota Press.

Cockburn, Cynthia. 2007. *From Where We Stand: War, Women's Activism and Feminist Analysis*. London: Zed Books.

Dombrowski, Nicole Ann, ed. 1999. *Women and War in the Twentieth Century: Enlisted with or without Consent*. New York: Garland.

Donnelly, Nancy. 1994. *Changing Lives of Refugee Hmong Women*. Seattle: University of Washington Press.

Elshtain, Jean Bethke. 1987. *Women and War*. New York: Basic Books.

Elshtain, Jean Bethke, and Sheila Tobias, eds. 1990. *Women, Militarism, and War: Essays in History, Politics, and Social Theory*. Savage, Md.: Rowman & Littlefeld.

Enloe, Cynthia. 2000. *Maneuvers: The International Politics of Militarization*. Berkeley: University of California Press.

Goldstein, Joshua. 2001. *War and Gender: How Gender Shapes the War System and Vice Versa*. New York: Cambridge University Press.

Goldstein, Martin E. 1973. *American Policy Toward Laos*. Cranbury, N.J.: Associated University Press.

Goodman, Philomena. 2002. *Women, Sexuality and War*. New York: Palgrave.

Hinchman, Lewis P., and Sandra K. Hinchman, eds. 1997. Introduction to *Memory, Identity, Community: The Idea of Narrative in Human Sciences*. Albany: State University of New York Press.

Honey, Maureen. 1984. *Creating Rosie the Riveter: Class, Gender, and Propaganda during World War II*. Amherst: University of Massachusetts Press.

Lee, Mao Vang. 2005. Interview with author in St. Paul, Minn., on August 8.

McCoy, Alfred. 2002. "America's Secret War in Laos, 1955–1975." In *A Companion to the Vietnam War*, edited by Marilyn B. Young and Robert Buzzanco. Malden, Mass.: Wiley-Blackwell.

Nguyen, Nathalie Huynh Chau. 2009. *Memory Is Another Country: Women of the Vietnamese Diaspora*. Santa Barbara, Calif.: ABC-CLIO.

Oakley, Ann. 1981. "Interviewing Women: A Contradiction in Terms." In *Doing Feminist Research*, edited by Helen Roberts. London, Boston, and Henley: Routledge & Kegan Paul.

Oliver, Kelly. 2007. *Women as Weapons of War: Iraq, Sex and the Media*. New York: Columbia University Press.

Quill, Diana. 2005. Interview with author in Antioch, Tenn., on October 14.

Quincy, Keith. 2000. *Harvesting Pa Chay's Wheat: The Hmong and America's Secret War in Laos*. Spokane: Eastern Washington University Press.

Robbins, Christopher. 1987. *The Ravens: The Men Who Flew in America's Secret War in Laos*. New York: Crown.

Rupp, Leila J. 1978. *Mobilizing Women for War: German and American Propaganda, 1939–1945*. Princeton, N.J.: Princeton University Press.

Summerfield, Penny. 1998. *Reconstructing Women's Wartime Lives: Discourse and Subjectivity in Oral Histories of the Second World War*. Manchester, U.K.: Manchester University Press.

Summers, Anne. 1988. *Angels and Citizens: British Women as Military Nurses, 1854–1914*. London and New York: Routledge & Kegan Paul.

Thao, Choua. 2005. Interview with author in Minneapolis, Minn., on August 10.

Tickner, J. Ann. 2001. *Gendering World Politics: Issues and Approaches in the Post-Cold War Era*. New York: Columbia University Press.

Tobias, Sheila, and Lisa Anderson. 1982. "What Really Happened to Rosie the Riveter? Demobilization and the Female Labor Force, 1944–47." In *Women's America: Recasting the Past*, edited by L. K. Kerber and J. D. H. Mathews, 354–73. New York: Oxford University Press.

Turner, Karen Gottschang. 1999. *Even the Women Must Fight: Memories of War from North Vietnam*. New York: Wiley.

Vang, Chou. 2006. Interview with author in Inver Grove Heights, Minn., on May 13.

Vang, Ly. 2005. Interview with author in Minneapolis, Minn., on August 18.

Vo, Linda Trinh. 2003. "Managing Survival: Economic Realities for Vietnamese American Women." In *Asian/Pacific Islander American Women: A Historical Anthology*, edited by Shirley Hune and Gail Nomura. New York: New York University Press.

Vuic, Kara Dixon. 2010. *Officer, Nurse, Woman: The Army Nurse Corps in the Vietnam War*. Baltimore: Johns Hopkins University Press.

Warner, Roger. 1995. *Backfire: The CIA's Secret War in Laos and Its Link to the Vietnam War*. New York: Simon and Schuster.

Weldon, Charles. 1999. *Tragedy in Paradise: A Country Doctor at War in Laos*. Bangkok: Asia Books.

Yang, Dao. 1993. *Hmong at the Turning Point*. Minneapolis: Worldbridge Associates Ltd.

Yoneyama, Lisa. 2005. "Liberation under Siege: U.S. Military Occupation and Japanese Women's Enfranchisement." *American Quarterly* 57, no. 3: 885–910.

· II ·

Social Organization, Kinship, and Politics

The Women of "Dragon Capital"

Marriage Alliances and the Rise of Vang Pao

Mai Na M. Lee

T HE PORTRAYAL OF HMONG WOMEN as passive victims needs revi-
sion to fit the paradigm shift already evident in postcolonial feminist
and family studies done on other groups. Chandra Mohanty (1991) first
drew attention to the discourse embedded in Western feminist scholarship that repositions Western women as subject/"norm" and Third World
women as the homogenized object/"other." Mohanty argues that by es-
sentializing Third World women as victims or passive dependents in need
of rescue within their own patriarchal societies, Western feminist discourse reproduces Third World women's subjectivity, depriving them of
agency within the contexts of their own societies. Saba Mahmood (2005)
also challenges the Western feminist construction of Muslim women's
false consciousness and the idea "that women Islamist supporters are
pawns in a grand patriarchal plan, who, if freed from their bondage,
would naturally express their instinctual abhorrence for the traditional
Islamic mores used to enchain them" (1–2). The works of Mohanty and
Mahmood emphasize how important it is that gender analysis of non-
Western, nonwhite women encompass the intersections of sex, race,
ethnic, class, religious, and historical (colonial) experiences. Mahmood
suggests we move to understand the workings of power and how women
resist within specific power systems. Defining "resistance as a diagnostic of
differential forms of power marks an important analytical step that allows
us to move beyond the simple binary of resistance/subordination," she concludes (9).

This chapter sheds light on Hmong women as informal leaders within
their families and community. It employs a postcolonial approach to examine Vang Pao's rise to power in order to explore Hmong women's influence

in the political sphere. I recognize the complex sociocultural interplay of patriarchal constrictions on Hmong women's lives but also challenge the idea that they were politically voiceless (Yang 1993, 24) or that they contributed little or nothing to the life of the clan (Lee 1994–95). I argue that while women may not have assumed bureaucratic titles in the realm of secular[1] political practice or presided as clan chiefs and ritual experts, they served as conduits of political legitimacy in highland Hmong society back in Laos by contributing economic resources and political influence to empower Hmong leaders and their families. Political authority, even titles, were transmitted through women from one generation to the next and from one clan to another. For this reason, ambitious males sought strategic matrimonial matches.

The importance of Hmong women's complex roles and the multiplicity of their contributions to society must be considered within the context that while men mostly serve the interest of their paternal clans, women promote their paternal clans as well as the clans of their husbands, thereby holding together Hmong people as a society. Hmong women's function in men's political legitimacy has eluded the scrutiny of historians, however. Thus, scholars who take a top-down approach attribute Vang Pao's rise during the "secret war" primarily to U.S. Central Intelligence Agency (CIA) support (McCoy, Read, and Adams 1991; Hamilton-Merritt 1993; Quincy 2000). Such an approach has worked to uphold the structures of U.S. imperialism and patriarchy. Instead, I employ a bottom-up analysis of Vang Pao's ascent that challenges imperialist power and privileges Hmong knowledge and perspective.[2] This chapter is not intended to document the narratives of Vang Pao's wives but to illuminate how Hmong view these women's important contributions to the political structure through their roles as daughters, wives, and mothers. Such a view elevates their roles and their marriages beyond the private sphere to underscore women's influence on public political leadership.[3] In relation, this bottom-up analysis imbues Vang Pao's rise to power within Hmong-specific negotiations of power rather than solely crediting the CIA and the United States for his political leadership.

My analysis draws from extensive research and insider knowledge (or reflexive ethnography) of the community, and it privileges Hmong knowledge. This is the first time anyone has centered women's roles in examinations of Vang Pao's leadership. I show how Vang's wives were important in his political objectives. He also benefited from prior ties forged by his family to the traditional elites. Consequently, the roles of female relatives and wives empowered Vang's authority as a Hmong leader. Vang's wives, in particular, each brought the manpower and financial backing of her clan, contributing to Vang's supremacy during the "secret war" period. The integral roles women played also made them vulnerable to the shifting political agenda, so that each wife rose or declined in favoritism depending on the political situation. In turn, Vang's wives also boosted the status of their male clan members by obtaining for them rewards in the form of titles, money, and prestige. Despite enduring gender inequality, these women affected the dynamics of male authority in Hmong society.

Hmong Marriage Alliances in Laos before Vang Pao

Marriage alliances were an important practice that contributed to the rise of Hmong leaders in Laos, as is often the case in lineage-based societies when chiefdoms are emerging, and also in feudal Asian societies of the lowland. The important role that women play in men's political ascent is emphasized in Hmong oral traditions that speak of how an orphan boy becomes a king by obtaining the hand of a dragon princess (Johnson and Yang 1992, 127–99; Tapp 2003, 439–43). Before arriving in Southeast Asia in the nineteenth century, the Hmong had long contacts with the Han Chinese, whose tactic of forming marriage alliances can be traced to the earliest dynasties. During the Han and Tang periods, betrothal alliances among Chinese elites became a threat to the ruling aristocracy, forcing the state to regulate marriages (Twitchett 1973; Johnson 1977; Ebrey 1978; Wong 1979). Robert Hymes's (1986a) study of marriages between seventy-three elite Chinese families in Fuchou, Kiangsi, in the Sung and Yuan periods also reveals that these marriages were motivated by the desire for strong political alliances. When the need to form ties with officials less-ened, these families married their children to local landowners and literati (11). Similarly, John W. Chaffee (1991) examines the royal marriages of the Sung dynasty, detailing how imperial clanswomen garnered political backing for their families through their marriages into elite groups. On the other hand, to prevent the seizure of power by the Han, the Qing forbade intermarriages between Manchu rulers and the Han bureaucratic elites (Rawski 1991). The informal political role of women through their mar-riages, therefore, forged critical alliances for political authority in the Asian context.

Marriage alliances in lowland Southeast Asia—in Laos, in particular—were also quite common. Like the Chinese, lowland Lao elites often engaged in strategic marriages, as evidenced by the meticulous family trees provided by Grant Evans (2009) in his study of the royal families of Luang Prabang, Vientiane, Champassak, and Xieng Khouang. Similar to the lowland aristocrats, Hmong tribal leaders like Vang Pao were quite strategic in their marriage choices in an effort to consolidate authority in the highlands. It is worth noting, however, that the Hmong do not distinguish between the Chinese categories of "wife," "secondary wife," and "concubines." Since the Tang period, Chinese men were allowed only one legal "wife"; thus, the titles "secondary wife" (a niece or sister who followed the "wife" into marriage) and "concubine" (a woman who is bought and does not come to the marriage with a dowry) were invented to circumvent state law (Watson and Ebrey 1991, 7). The Hmong, on the other hand, openly practice polygyny. Every woman married through matrimonial rituals to a man is considered a "wife" by custom law and is viewed as such by society. Polygyny made it especially easy for men like Vang Pao to employ matrimonial alliances to consolidate authority over segmented clans.

Hmong marriage alliance during the "secret war" period is an extension of matrimonial alliances between the traditional Hmong elites in the previous era. The women of former times also enhanced men's power by connecting families and clans. More significantly, women were the nexus of power for leadership inheritance in Hmong society. Political authority was transferred from one man to another through women. This historical reality challenges the claim of the eighteenth-century Han scholar Yan Riyu, who observed that the "Miao"[4] do not have a hereditary leadership system (Jenks 1994, 34). I argue that the Hmong do, indeed, have hereditary leadership, in which political rule was passed through women rather than men. The reason why scholars have missed this connection before is that they, like Yan Riyu, seek to understand Hmong political practices only through patrilineal successions. My discussion here traces for the first time the genealogy of Hmong political leaders to show how women negotiated political legitimacy for men within a patrilineal, patriarchal society.

In Laos, the Ly, Lo, and Moua clans have held power since the precolonial era. The Yang clan was also important, but it had not presided in the paramount position over the Hmong by the time of the post–World War

II revolutionary conflicts. However, Yang clan members belonging to the family of the Communist nationalist hero *Thao* [Mr.] Tou Yang are the most powerful Hmong figures in the Lao PDR (Yang 2004). Ly, Lo, and Yang clan marriage alliances dated to the mid-nineteenth century. Lo Pa Tsi, the father of Lo Blia Yao, was among the Hmong leaders from China who rose to prominence through calculated nuptials with the Lys [Lees] and Yangs. Pa Tsi had led revolts in southern China against the Qing authorities around the time of the Great "Miao" (1854–73) and Great Taiping (1851–64) Rebellions. Enduring defeat, he migrated south, accompanied by a bodyguard, Yang Zong Cher, who was also probably a kinsman through marriage (Mao Song Lyfoung 2002). Pa Tsi settled among the Hmong of the Fan Si Pan mountain range, west of the Red River in northern Vietnam. Another rebel leader, Ly Nhia Vu, who also traced his roots to southern China, had settled here a few years prior. Nhia Vu had led rebellions against the Qing in Sichuan Province. After years of struggle, Nhia Vu led his Ly kinsmen south. He had three brothers and a large clan, which allowed him to exert his influence over the population in the Vietnamese highlands (Na Jalao Ly 2002).

Alone, Pa Tsi sought an alliance with the Lys by marrying a female cousin of Nhia Vu as a second wife. That we do not know the name of this Ly woman even though she was the critical link between the Ly and Lo clans signifies the convoluted power and powerlessness Hmong women occupy in the historical past. She was important, however, as a conduit of power that solidified generations of alliances between the Ly and Lo clans, impacting Hmong politics in Laos. The Ly woman had been twice widowed. Her former husbands were from the Yang clan, another important ally of Pa Tsi. The Ly woman took her second son into the Lo clan and left her eldest by her first husband in the Yang clan. She had three additional children with Pa Tsi: Blia Yao, a daughter who married Sai Chou Yang (Mrs. Sai Chou), and Tsong Ger. Mrs. Sai Chou was the mother of the above-mentioned nationalist hero *Thao* Tou Yang. Reflecting an already strong bond between the Los, Lys, and the Yangs, Blia Yao, married two Yang women (his second and third wives) and one Ly woman (his fourth wife), a maternal cousin. He and his descendants remained close to the Yangs and the Lys because of these complex marriage exchanges among the three clans and because he had a half brother in the Yang clan. The alliances that Pa Tsi forged with the Lys and Yangs paved the way for him to become the preeminent Hmong leader in the late nineteenth century and for his son, Blia Yao, to become the paramount chief of the Hmong of Laos from 1910 to 1935 (Na Jalao Ly 2002; Mao Song Lyfoung 2002). Women were vital in the rise of the Lo clan to power.

After solidifying their relations with marriages, Pa Tsi and Nhia Vu relocated their clans and affinal Yang kinsmen from Vietnam to Muang Phuan (Xieng Khouang) in 1856. The Lo and Ly clans established the respective villages of Yeng Pha and Nong Khiaw, near the town of Nong Het on the Lao-Vietnamese border (Na Jalao Ly 2002). They were preceded by the Moua clan, which inhabited the Phou San mountain range farther west, at the edge of the Plain of Jars (McCoy, Read, and Adams 1991, 116). The Moua, Lo, Ly, and Yang clans quickly intermarried, monopolizing the leadership position over the Hmong of Muang Phuan. "The Moua, Ly, Lo and Yang clans intermarried only among themselves; not with any other clans," Dia Yang claims (2005). Empirical evidence reveals otherwise, but Dia's vehement statement can perhaps be interpreted to mean that when marriages occurred between these four clans, it took on political significance. Dia and her husband, Moua Long—a cousin of Touby Lyfoung and a former member of the King's Council in the 1960s—were direct descendants from Lo women related to Blia Yao. The three cousins—Dia, Moua Long, and Touby—were prime examples of the complex marriage exchanges among the Ly, Lo, Moua, and Yang clans.

From the mid nineteenth to the twentieth century, the Lo, Ly, and Moua clansmen, in-laws by marriage, took turns succeeding one another as the paramount Hmong chief in the region of Nong Het.[5] When they first arrived in Nong Het and before the existence of a Kingdom of Laos (1947), the Ly clan, led by Nhia Vu, was the first to obtain an honorary *kaitong* (sub-district) title by presenting a rhinoceros horn to the Lao Phuan scions who governed over Muang Phuan.[6] The Lo clan presented another horn later, thereby also obtaining a *kaitong* title for Pa Tsi, who soon distinguished himself as the wealthiest man in Nong Het (Na Jalao Ly 2002). A dispute regarding the theft of his buried silver led to his assassination by Yang Zong Cher in 1866, however, ending Lo clan power for the moment (Lee 2005, 149–56; Lor 2001, 8–10).

Following Pa Tsi's assassination, Ly Nhia Vu presided as the umbrella figure until he and his son, Tsong Na, led a rebellion against the French increase of taxes in 1896. The French had assumed authority over Muang Phuan and the Lao kingdoms straddling the Mekong River three years earlier. The Lo clan also participated in the rebellion, so they were equally compromised (Na Jalao Ly 2002). The clan leaders selected Moua *Kaitong* to negotiate with the French for a peace settlement. Touby Lyfoung writes, "They [the Hmong *kaitongs*] stipulated that if Moua *Kaitong* could reach a peaceful settlement he would henceforth be recognized as their paramount chief" (Lyfoung 1996, 10). Moua *Kaitong* appeared at Xieng Khouang and was designated as supreme Hmong chief and the political broker for the French (Yang 1993, 36; Lor 2001, 14; Mao Song Lyfoung 2002; Na Jalao Ly 2002).

By 1910, Blia Yao, who had matured into a man of distinction, reassumed his father's title. His maternal Ly clan supported his rise as the paramount Hmong *kaitong* in Nong Het as the aged Moua *kaitong* declined in influence. A brilliant strategist, Blia Yao garnered additional support by marrying a total of five women from the Vue, Yang (wives numbers two and three), Ly, and Hang clans. His daughters' and sisters' marriages into the Yang and Moua clans also assured the support of those groups. His sons, Fay Dang and Nhia Vu, also married women from the Moua, Yang, and Ly clans. When the French constructed Colonial Route 7 (CR7) along the traditional invasion route, which led from the strategic Plain of Jars, or Xieng Khouang, to the Vietnamese imperial city of Hue and the French administrative capital of Saigon, where the French governor-general exercised his authority over Indochina, they selected Blia Yao as the supervisor. Control of the road budget allowed Blia Yao to become rich and even more influential.

While the Ly clan supported Blia Yao, they competed for influence. In 1917, Ly Foung married Blia Yao's daughter, Mai, by employing the Hmong marriage practice of bride capture. Ly Foung aimed to establish political ties with Blia Yao, but the marriage was terribly strained as the two men competed for political prominence. Mai's suicide four years later broke up relations between the two men completely, but Mai did become the important linkage that legitimized Ly Foung's family. In 1939, Mai's son Touby claimed Blia Yao's title as the *Tasseng* of Keng Khoai. The Hmong accepted Touby because he was a descendant of Blia Yao, and the French agreed to his succession because literacy in Lao and French allowed him to perform the administrative work required by the colonial authorities (Lyfoung 1996, 146). In the case of Touby succeeding Blia Yao, we see direct evidence of political power transferring from maternal grandfather to grandson. Touby became supreme Hmong chief, while Blia Yao's son Fay Dang, disenchanted with the French, cast his lot with the Communists. It was during this murky period of nationalist struggles that Vang Pao, a relative of Touby by marriage, became a protégé of Touby.

Vang Pao's Marriage Alliances with Touby Lyfoung and Other Traditional Elites of Laos

The traditional elites of Muang Phuan—the Ly, Lo, and Moua clans—had jealously guarded their alliances, keeping the preeminent leadership position within their own circles and thus intermarrying primarily among themselves. These relationships, however, were far from harmonious and could be characterized as quite contentious. From the mid-nineteenth to the twentieth century, the three clans competed for the helm of power. It appears they reached a tense consensus by tacitly agreeing to alternate power, but it was not always clear which individual from which clan would succeed the previous leader. What is clear was that the clans not in power did not favor a hereditary system of primogeniture, in which the oldest son succeeds the father, or ultimogeniture, in which the youngest son succeeds the father. Such systems of father–son succession would promote the dominance of one single clan indefinitely while completely excluding other clans from power. The pattern was then for the position of paramount chief to pass to a close in-law from another clan, as in the circumstance that led to the rise of Touby. For this reason, women were important because the locus of power shifted along the female line through the women who married outside their paternal clans. Vang Pao's rise in the 1960s—his leadership inheritance from Touby—was similarly owed to women.

Born in December 1929 in the village of Pham Eng in the Phou Kong Khau District of Xieng Khouang, Vang was an outsider to the customary Hmong elites. Vang's father, Vang Neng Chue, was a *phutong*—a minor village chief or an assistant to the Hmong leader—who first staged the Vang clan's political climb. Neng Chue's first wife and Vang's mother from the Thao clan was also removed from the traditional elites. As such, "she was unfamiliar with the etiquettes of receiving guests of distinction," said Vang Chou, a nephew of Vang Pao. To remedy the situation, "Neng Chue married as a second wife, a widow of the Yang clan, who was a daughter of Lo Blia Yao" (Vang Chou 2013). This marriage bound Neng Chue with the Lo and Yang clans, and acquired for Vang Pao some Yang stepbrothers, who supported him and his family until today (see Figure 4.1).[7]

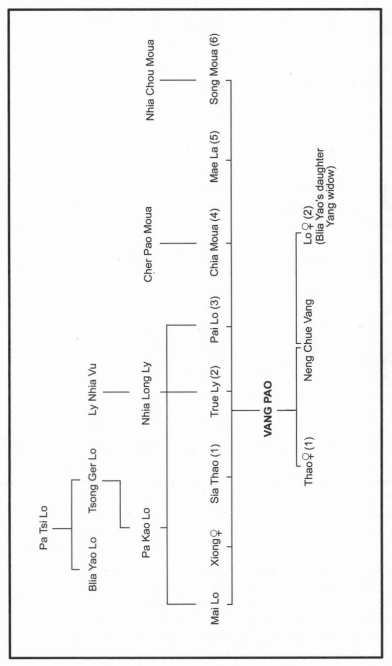

Figure 4.1. Vang Pao's marriage alliances with the Lo, Ly, and Moua clans. Author's tabulation. The numbers in parentheses represent the order of Vang's marriages to his wives. Sia Thao is recognized by the Hmong as "wife number one," hence I start the ordinal numbers with her, but note that she was preceded by two lesser-known wives.

Fortunately also for Vang Pao, in the early 1930s, Ly Foung had married as a fourth wife Vang Nao (Mao Song Lyfoung 2002; Lor 2001). Nao was, in accordance with the Hmong's classificatory system of relations, an "aunt" to Vang. When she became a stepmother to Hmong leader Touby, the two men became "brothers." Furthermore, in 1937, Touby's sister, Mao Song, married Vang Tong Ger, who shared clan affiliation with Vang. Mao Song was later widowed, but in accordance to Hmong levirate tradition, she remarried her husband's younger brother, Vang Ka Ge (Mao Song Lyfoung 2002). Meanwhile, Vang Pao's older brother, Nao Tou, also married Touby's half sister, Mao Nao Lyfoung (Charles Vannier 2012). These intermarriages set the foundation for Touby to become an important patron for Vang in the next three decades (see Figure 4.2). As a close affinal relative, Vang frequented Touby's home in the 1940s. When Touby fled to the jungle to evade arrest by the Japanese in March 1945, he asked Vang to remain in his home in Nam Kuang, which was occupied by Japanese soldiers. The teenage Vang ran errands for the Japanese while monitoring and reporting their activities to Touby and the French (Vang Pao 2004).[8]

After the Japanese occupation, Touby rewarded Vang with an administrative post, which he refused. Vang instead asked that Touby recommend him into the French *gendarmerie* (police corps), which was being created in anticipation of an independent Laos (Vang Pao 2004; Lartéguy and Yang 1979, 198). Touby's recommendation had political implications for Vang. The *gendarmerie* was reconstituted into a national army during the next few years. By 1962, Vang was the only Hmong general in the Royal Lao Army, and as such, he played a colossal role in the history of the Hmong and of Laos. Backed by the CIA, Vang quickly displaced Touby as Hmong leader.

Vang also was keen in creating his links to other elites (see Figure 4.1). During critical junctures of his career, he married women whose clans rendered him support. Toward the end of the 1940s he married Mai, the daughter of Lo Pa Kao. Pa Kao was the son of Blia Yao's younger brother, Tsong Ger. Had historical turn of events been different, Mai would have been significant to Vang's politics. The marriage did not help Vang establish a political alliance, however, as the split between Touby and Fay Dang widened by the 1950s. Fay Dang took his Lo and Yang relatives across the border to Vietnam. Vang, who had served Touby, was stranded in Xieng Khouang. Adding to this tragic turn of events, Mai died while Vang was in officer training school in southern Laos in 1951 (Vang Pao 2004). She left

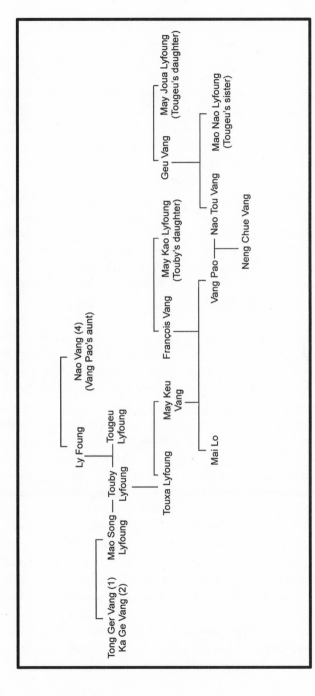

Figure 4.2. Vang Pao's marriage connections to Touby Lyfoung. Author's tabulation. Vang Pao's father, Neng Chue (at the bottom), should not be confused with Vang Pao's son by the same name. Vang's brother Nao Tou, his son Francois, his daughter May Keu, and his nephew Geu married individuals of the Lyfoung family.

three small children behind. Concerned for the children's well-being, Mai's father, Pa Kao, arranged for Vang to marry his younger daughter, Pai, so that she could care for them "like a real mother" (Mee Kue 2011). Unfortunately for Pai, the Lao revolution interrupted that plan, too. Her Lo clan, which was aligned with the Communists, ran off to Vietnam for a time. Pai would have been the top-ranking wife, but by the time her family returned to Xieng Khouang, Vang Pao had already married two other women. When she was betrothed to Vang in the early 1960s, Pai ranked third. The Hmong addressed her as "Niam Me" (Minor Wife).

As a minor wife with little standing or love from Vang, Pai's primary role was to be a mother to her sister's children. When the Lao coalition failed, most of the members of the Lo clan scrambled across the border again, leaving her behind. Pai's relatives, who were led by the revolutionary leader Fay Dang, became Vang Pao's primary opponents for the duration of the "secret war." Because she did not provide Vang with a strong alliance, he neglected her even though she bore him many sons. In protest, she "often declared that she just slept with him for money" (Warner 1995, 260). Pai and Vang Pao's relationship represented the shifting political climate among the Hmong leadership, which made her vulnerable to male political maneuverings. Although Pai appeared to have endured the most injury among the wives, she was not without spunk. One time in the mid-1960s, she was left home while the other wives attended a picnic with Vang. "When the general and the wives returned home from the picnic she grabbed an M-16 left lying around the house, aimed it at her husband, and pulled the trigger. The rifle was loaded but luckily for him she hadn't switched the safety off" (260). Pai's inferior position in Vang's household reflects how Hmong women's well-being was often tied to their clans. The other wives had authoritative relatives nearby, ready to render support to Vang. As such, he was cautiously considerate of them. Pai's relatives, however, were caught on the other side of the political divide. Pai's more vulnerable position within the Vang household adds a certain complexity to how we should analyze women's experiences and the operations of gender in traditional Hmong society. It also shows how women's position as a transmitter of power also exposed them to the contentious relationships between clans. Depending on who they were and from which clan they came, each of Vang's wives occupied various positions of power or powerlessness.

Exactly how many wives Vang had remains a bit of a mystery. "He has had quite a few women," said Vang Chou. Some were customarily sanctioned "wives," while others occupied positions closer to the definition of a concubine. One woman was a "mistress" of the Black Tai ethnic group, whom Vang supported financially. "Vang Pao built her an expensive house and he forced Madames Chia and Mae La to accompany him to pay her homage. There were other mistresses as well," said Vang Chou (2013). Among those categorized as "wives" were the one who died in 1951, the two whom Vang divorced, and the six who left Laos with him in 1975, making a total of nine (Warner 1995, 259–60). After his elder brother, Nao Tou, died, Vang was married briefly to Mao Nao Lyfoung in accordance to Hmong levirate tradition. "Irreconcilable differences" forced a quick divorce, however, and "they went back to being in-laws" (Vang Chou 2013). Another failed marriage was to a maiden from the Xiong clan, whom Vang divorced following a car accident and after having fallen in love with Sia Thao, who became his top-ranking wife.

Mee Kue, the wife of Colonel Nao Kao Lyfoung, who was close to the Vang family, related what she heard from Vang Pao about his marriage to Sia. Following Vang's military training in southern Laos in 1951 and after the death of his wife Mai, Vang was stationed on the Plain of Jars in Xieng Khouang. He had recently married his wife from the Xiong clan. During the New Year's Festival, there was a funeral in town. Sia and her sisters arrived in their finest clothes. According to Mee, "Vang Pao was driving a jeep along a road nearby. Entranced by Sia's beauty, he took his eyes off the road and his jeep plunged into a bomb crater beside the street. The funeral attendants had to help him push and pull the jeep from the crater using ropes" (Mee Kue 2011). Vang inquired about the striking beauty from the laughing crowd. He subsequently returned his Xiong wife and went to ask for the hand of Sia, who became "Niam Loj" (Main Wife) to the Hmong and "wife number one" to the Americans.

Vang's marriage to Sia may have been more politically strategic than the preceding story suggests. According to Vang Chou (2013), Touby Lyfoung had recommended that Vang Pao seek Sia's hand in marriage, saying that she was the daughter of his close cousin. By marrying Sia, Vang may have aimed to please Touby, an important patron. In any event, his marriage to Sia brought the support of her brothers, Thao Neng Chue and Pa Chay, who became close allies. During the "secret war," Vang promoted Neng Chue to the rank of colonel and appointed Pa Chay treasurer of his CIA-financed budget. According to Keith Quincy (2000), Pa Chay played a critical role in Vang's financial schemes by skimming CIA money for

Vang while also enriching himself: "By the early 1970s, Pa Chay owned two airplanes, several houses, and extensive property in Thailand" (241). Sia became the connecting link that made Vang and her male kinsmen powerful. Because of her significance, Vang cautiously guarded her public image. In 1968, he chose her over one of the younger, more svelte wives to accompany him on a visit to the United States (Warner 1995, 260).

As the main wife, Sia wielded domestic power in Vang Pao's household. She also monopolized Vang Pao's business interests, including his transport line from Long Cheng to Vientiane, which she charged the other wives to use. "She was a smart, good-hearted woman who delivered him a child every year, and who ran the food end of his household, a complex logistical operation including cargo flights to Vientiane, stalls in the Long Tieng [Cheng] market, and gardens tended by the bodyguards" (Warner 1995, 260). Sia aided Vang in other ways, according to Tsia Long Thao (2006). She was imbued with luck and possessed protective powers that helped Vang's political assent. After marrying her, Vang was invulnerable in the battlefield. Many Hmong elders believed events in 2007 confirmed this situation. Sia died that spring, on March 5, and her funeral had just been concluded in Fresno, California, when Vang was arrested in June. Some believed that without her protection, he endured the humiliation of imprisonment and house arrest until shortly before his death in January 2011. During a dinner party to raise funds for Vang's defense in 2007, a Hmong elder in Madison, Wisconsin, reiterated Tsia Long's words to me. Vang's arrest, he said, was due to his loss of protection after his first wife's passing.

A recent publication by Lyblong Lynhiavu (2015) makes an even more astounding claim about Sia's role in Vang Pao's rise and fall from power. As early as 1955, according to Lyblong, Madame Ly Mai Xao Kao and Ly Tso Lyfoung had predicted that Vang "will become a very important man. . . . But his fortune depends completely on the luck of his first wife, Xia [Sia] Thao. . . . When the time comes that Xia Thao is no longer with him, Lt. Vang Pao will only experience misfortune and calamities . . . [and] . . . the demise of Lt. Vang Pao will be a complete, public and spectacular circus" (94n10). Lyblong further tied an inexplicable event involving the transportation of Sia's body for burial in Los Angeles to a car accident endured by Vang's favorite minor wives.

> Not long after Xia Thao's death in 2006 [*sic*], misfortunes found General Vang Pao. Xia Thao died in Phoenix, Arizona . . . the

funeral took place in Fresno and she was eventually brought to Los Angeles, California for her last resting place. As Xia Thao's body was being transported, the driver felt that something was amiss and stopped the car. He then noticed that Xia Thao's pants had somehow caught fire. After Xia Thao's death General Vang Pao was arrested in 2007 in Sacramento, California . . . the fourth and the fifth wife of the general, Chia Moua and Xong [Song] Moua (Ntxhool Muas), respectively, went to visit Vang Pao. They traveled from Santa Anna to Sacramento. When they arrived at the very same spot where Xia Thao's pants had caught fire, their car suddenly experienced engine trouble, and they had to pull over. While they were stopped on the side of the road, a car hit both of them, causing serious injuries. (Lyblong 2015, 94n10)

Lyblong concludes that the breakup of Ly Tou Pao and others from Vang Pao in 2010, which forced two competing New Year's Festival celebrations in Fresno, causing Vang tremendous stress and leading to his final demise, was yet another consequence of having lost Sia's protection. Altogether, the testimonies of Tsia Long Thao and Hmong elders I encountered as well as that of Lyblong reflected a certain awareness of Sia's political significance. Sia's contribution to Vang's ascent was, however, attributed to the cultural rubric of possessing *hmoov* (luck), as opposed to the strategic maneuverings of perhaps Sia herself and, certainly, of the men connected to her.[9] During Vang's funeral in 2011, his family also paid homage to Sia by naming her eldest son, Neng Chue, the family spokesperson.[10]

Shortly after he married Sia, Vang also married True from the Ly clan. The Hmong called her "Niam Nrab" (Middle Wife) when Vang married Pai as a third wife. Sia was a love interest, but some believe Vang's marriage to True was political. Vang needed True's family's manpower and wealth. "The role of a Hmong chief is to lead, to demonstrate Hmong values, and to provide for and look after those who follow. This last required wealth," Jane Hamilton-Merritt (1993) writes. "Vang Pao was not a wealthy man; he had been a soldier all his life" (203). True was the daughter of Ly Nhia Long and granddaughter of *Kaitong* Ly Nhia Vu, one of the two original Hmong leaders in the nineteenth century (see Figure 4.1). For Vang, she was a bridge into the inner circle of the traditional Hmong elites. Moreover, before the CIA provided Vang with the largesse to build a clientele, True's family aided Vang financially, according to Dia Yang. "Nhia Long's family was so rich," said Dia (Yang 2005), "they did not farm rice for a living like other Hmong. They bought their rice with money they made from their businesses." Among their most lucrative business was the trade in opium. The family also invested in a huge herd of cattle that roamed the mountains and valleys around the Plain of Jars (Dia Yang 2005). Because of their businesses, they maintained a house in the district of Nong Het and one in Lat Houang, a city located near the provincial capital of Xieng Khouang, where Vang Pao sought shelter from Communist attacks in 1960. The Ly family's champion bulls competed and often won the annual New Year's Hmong-style bullfighting contest, in which bull went against bull. For this reason, in December 1970, when CIA operative Jerry "Hog" Daniels staged a Western-style bull-riding event in an attempt to raise Hmong morale after several heavy attacks on Long Cheng, he counted on Colonel Ly Tou Pao, the brother of True, to provide him with the bulls (Warner 1995, 252).

True's family used their wealth to fashion Vang into a rival leader, who eventually eclipsed Touby Lyfoung. "Nhia Long had used his money to help Vang Pao," Dia continued, "so Vang Pao loved 'Middle Wife' [True] the most among his many wives" (2005). True's Ly clan had aided Touby during the time of the French. Now, it also supplied the needed manpower for Vang. During the political chaos of the late 1960s, Vang fled east along CR7 from Khang Kay, accompanied by Ly clan members who urged him to seek American help. Then Ly and Thao members—relatives of True and Sia—helped Vang seize control of the Plain of Jars by arresting General Amkha Soukhavong, the area military commander (Vang Chou 2013). Vang handed Amkha over to the rightist factional leader, General Phoumi Nosavan, and was promoted as the first Hmong lieutenant colonel in the Royal Lao Army and given command of Xieng Khouang Province (Hamilton-Merritt 1993, 81). By 1962, the Ly and Thao clans had contributed to the founding of Long Cheng ("Dragon Capital"), Vang's military headquarters. As he did for Sia's brothers, Vang also rewarded True's brother, Ly Tou Pao, with the rank of colonel and made him chief of staff of his clandestine army. Much like Sia, True influenced the politics of the Hmong highlands. As the granddaughter of a former Hmong leader, she served as a link to economic resources and political authority for Vang. Moreover, she united Vang and her male relations toward a common political end.

When I interviewed Tou Pao in April 2004, he complained that Vang Pao cared little for his sister, who was infertile. "Nevertheless," he said, "I remain dedicated to his cause" (2004). (However, as noted earlier, Tou Pao broke with Vang publicly in 2010.) The contradictory statements by Dia, who associated closely with True back in Laos, and by Tou Pao in 2004 can be understood in the context of Vang's shifting relationship with the Ly clan. Vang may have favored True when her Ly clan served his political objectives, but her status declined as the Lys began to question his military tactics. Vang clashed with the Lys in early 1966, after he was shot at Na Khang, Vang's most forward resupply base in Military Region II, from where Jolly Green Giant helicopters rescued downed American pilots (Hamilton-Merritt 1993, 145; Warner 1995, 197). Until its seizure in 1968, this important site was guarded by multiple colonels from the Ly clan. In February 1966, when Na Khang came under heavy attack, Vang landed on the site against radio advice coming from the ground (Nao Kao Lyfoung 2002). As the general stepped off the helicopter, sniper bullets shot him down. He immediately saw a Ly clan conspiracy against him, according to Colonel Ly Pao (2002). After Vang was evacuated to Thailand for reconstructive surgery, his suspicions culminated into a scandal in Long Cheng. Vang publicly alleged that the Ly clan was staging a coup to prevent his return. The Ly colonels who headed Vang's army—including Ly Joua Va, who was a cousin of True—were each fingered as the culprit. Touby Lyfoung was accused of being the leader of this alleged "Ly Coup" (Hamilton-Merritt 1993, 145–46; Touxoua Lyfoung 2002).

Upon his return, Vang scrambled to promote his clan members to the rank of colonel so that they could replace the Ly battalion commanders, the older generation of officers who had risen during the time of the French under Touby's command. Vang also pushed the Lys out of his inner circle, handpicking Colonel Shoua Yang as his loyal field commander (Shoua Yang 2002).[11] Vang's connection to the Yangs can be traced to his father's second marriage to the Yang widow, as noted previously. Hence, although Tou Pao remained in Vang's confidence, it may have been, as he claimed, that his sister was no longer a favored wife.

Moreover, by the late 1960s, Vang no longer needed the financial support of True's clan even though he still relied on their manpower. According to Jane Hamilton-Merritt (1993), the CIA provided Vang with a "contingency fund to carry out his dual functions of military and tribal leader" (203). Colonel Bill Lair, the CIA operative who recruited Vang, said there was no such fund, but he applied creative means to obtain American dollars to bolster Vang's status. Vang had explained his need of money to build patronage, so Lair (2003) allowed him to inflate the number of infantry men in his battalions. Lair left Laos in 1968, but the methods he put in place were maintained until the end of the war. Vang's army was found to be below its payroll strength of 550 men per battalion in 1970 (McCoy, Read, and Adams 1991, 558n137).

After the alleged Ly coup, Touby and Vang renewed their alliances by marrying their children to one another, revealing yet another dimension that marriage and women played in Hmong politics. Women also became the gatekeepers of peace between the clans. In 1967, Vang's daughter May Keu married Touby's son, Touxa. Vang's son Francois also married Touby's daughter, May Kao. In 1970, Vang's nephew Vang Geu married May Joua, the daughter of Tougeu Lyfoung (see Figure 4.2). McCoy, Read, and Adams assert that "Vang Pao was threatened by military setbacks and mounting opposition from the Lynhiavu clan so felt compelled to arrange this last marriage to shore up his declining political fortunes" (1991, 560n157). The mounting strain between the Lynhiavus (True's family) and Vang may have stimulated him to embrace Touby again. Trust between Touby and Vang was never fully reestablished, however. "Our hens were in his coop and his ducks were in our pen, but the trust was never rekindled," Tougeu said (2002). Nevertheless, Ly women who married Vang and his sons legitimized Vang's authority as a supreme Hmong leader, allowing him to predominate well into the exile period.

As he did with the Ly clan, Vang married women from the Moua clan for political reasons. Once displaced from Nong Het into the Plain of Jars, he married as his fourth wife Chia, the stepdaughter of Moua Cher Pao (Hamilton-Merritt 1993, 139). "Vang Pao had his eyes on another Moua woman, but someone told him if he wanted political connections, he had better marry Chia," said Tong Pao Moua (2007). Vang heeded the suggestion. As it was uncommon for men to marry more than three wives, Hmong society had fashioned only the titles "first," "middle," and "minor wife." Chia and the wives after her were addressed by names, not by rank. Chia became "Niam Txiab" (Mother Chia) to the Hmong.

Chia was a member of the predominant Moua clan, which had pioneered the settlement in the Phou San mountain range during the previous century. Over the years, they had worked hard to become wealthy and influential. By contrast, Vang's humble origin was highlighted by the fact that one of his male cousins, Chong Toua, was sold into the Moua clan (Toulu Chongtoua Moua 2004; Mao Song Lyfoung 2002). Chong Toua worked hard to distinguish himself as a rich man, and his connections to the French earned him political distinction during the colonial era. By 1961, he had long passed away, but Edgar "Pop" Buell, who headed the refugee assistance program for the Hmong of Laos, was impressed by the legacy he left behind at the base of Phou San (Schanche 1970, 112). Chong Toua's achievements added to the prestige of the Moua clan, however—more reason for Vang to seek a Moua wife.

When Bill Lair united with Vang at Padong with a contingent of Thai operatives to train Hmong men in April 1961, Chia was the new favorite who accompanied Vang everywhere, even to areas under bombardment. Known as the "Field Wife" to Americans, she "cooked daily meals for the guests, who sat at long tables in a tent" (Warner 1995, 64). Also a stunning beauty, Chia's presence became an essential component of Vang's efforts to win the hearts and minds of the old leaders, who were still oriented toward Touby.

After the alleged Ly coup, Chia's clan was more essential to Vang's dominance. Her father, Cher Pao, who was rewarded with the rank of colonel, commanded the strategic site of Bouam Loung, a village located at five thousand feet on the Phou San mountain range, just twenty miles from the Vietnamese border. Cher Pao monitored CR6—coming from the Communist headquarters in Sam Neua—and CR7, coming from the Vietnamese border to the east. By early 1968, the northernmost site of Phou Pha Thi, which housed a radar control system that allowed the United States to bomb North Vietnam in all weather conditions, had been captured. Na Khang, "the Alamo," which had the only other electronic radar system, was threatened as well. As North Vietnam concentrated five battalions on Na Khang, American advisers scrambled to look for a backup site from which they could guide air strikes, monitor North Vietnamese activities, and launch black missions across the border. President Lyndon Johnson was also in the process of negotiating with the North Vietnamese and needed the capability to electronically monitor their military activities. This need brought renewed attention to Cher Pao's village, "from where, it was thought, sophisticated electronic equipment could monitor conversations and activities in North Vietnam. . . . American strategists asked question after question about Bouam Loung—just in case the Alamo fell" (Hamilton-Merritt 1993, 201).

Cher Pao's position was vulnerable, but as a loyal relative of Vang Pao, he vowed to defend it to the end. Hamilton-Merritt (1993) writes:

Moua Cher Pao . . . assured General Vang Pao and his SKY advisors that it [Bouam Loung] was different from Na Khang and Phou Pha Thi. It was not, he believed, compromised by enemy agents, and he intended to ask his followers to defend Bouam Loung to the death. He assembled his defenders, including a representative from each household, to participate in the powerful "drinking of the water" ceremony, in which one by one, the defenders drank water from a special vessel, binding them together in the defense of this position no matter what the odds. (201)

When Na Khang fell in March 1968, Jerry Daniels relocated to Bouam Loung with electronic surveillance equipment that was connected directly to the National Security Agency. A U.S. intelligence officer states, "The military information gathered at Bouam Loung about Hanoi's plans saved the lives of many American soldiers fighting in South Vietnam. This was another major Hmong contribution to us" (206). On May 20, 1971, twenty-five hundred North Vietnamese soldiers ascended to the site. Enemy soldiers outnumbered Cher Pao's men three to one. Bouam Loung survived, but the enemy left three Pathet Lao battalions to keep Cher Pao's soldiers from breaking out to destroy supply routes along CR6 and CR7 (261–62). Despite his pledge, Cher Pao abandoned Bouam Loung and evacuated by air to Thailand with Vang in May 1975 (371). He later returned to this base and continued to be Vang's commander on the ground in Laos until the early 1990s. Because of her father's importance to the homeland movement, Chia was one of the two wives who lived with Vang in exile (see Figure 4.3).

Meanwhile, Chia's son, Cha, enjoyed Vang's promotion. For a short time, Cha operated as Vang's public image, a role that gained Cha a position on the mayor's political staff in St. Paul, Minnesota. During the Chai Soua Vang shooting incident in northern Wisconsin in 2005, he also appeared on television as a local Hmong community representative. Cha's image was quickly tainted by a financial scandal involving his role in the Vang Pao Foundation, however.[12] He has since disappeared from public eye.

Vang Pao's marriage alliances extended among the Lao as well. In this regard, he may have been influenced by the Lyfoung brothers, Tougeu and Toulia, who had married wives from elite Lao families. In 1968, Vang confided in Pop Buell, "I must think of Laos. Most of the men under my com-

Figure 4.3. Vang Pao and his two favorite wives. [L–R]: Chia Moua, Vang Pao, and Song Moua in the backyard of their house in Westminster, California. Author's collection, 2004.

mand now are Lao, not [Hmong]. In order to keep face with them—to set an example of *samakhi* [unity]—it is time for me to take a Lao wife. That is what I plan to do next" (Schanche 1970, 287). Vang had added pressure from the Lao elites, according to Vang Chou (2013), who accused him of harboring prejudices against them, as evident in his unwillingness to marry one of their women. Vang had multiple incentives to marry "Mae La" (Mother La). It is unclear whether Mae La brought Vang more support from the Lao, but she did present an image of unity. She bore him sons, but she was the first wife that Vang divorced in exile, in 1978 (Vang Chou 2013).

By the early 1970s, Vang's political marriages were solid, but he fell in love with another woman from the Moua clan named Song. Vang's marriage to Song in 1973 stirred a scandal in Long Cheng that reverberated in the West. Song had been captured as a wife by Lo Ma, an educated young man, but she orchestrated a divorce in order to marry Vang. According to an informant:

Vang Pao first met Song when there was a nurse's strike in
Samthong. This was when the war was still going on and there were
a lot of soldiers being wounded due to heavy enemy attacks. Song
was a nurse working there. Concerned about the strike, Vang Pao
went to Samthong to ask what was up with the strike. Vang Pao, if
you would know, had a commanding voice and when he's angry, he
can really shout. He was shouting and asking why these nurses
were undermining his efforts just when he needed their support
the most. Everyone was afraid of him so each stood there with her
eyes cast down on the ground. No one dared to make eye contact
with him. When he finished shouting he sat down and asked the
nurses to come state their grievances. No one dared approach him.
Undeterred by Vang Pao's demeanor, Song went to sit right on
Vang Pao's lap like a child would do to her own father and said,
"Father, it is only because they're paying us so little that we don't
want to work. It's not because we do not support your efforts."
Vang Pao said, "Oh, if that is all then get back to work. I will
increase your salaries." (Anonymous 1)

Incredibly impressed by Song's courage and eloquence, Vang inquired
about her afterward. He learned she was the daughter of Moua Nhia
Chou. Following the incident, Vang often went to visit and court Song at
Samthong. The informant continues, "But our young lad, Lo Ma, did not
know about it. When he was on furlough and returned to Long Cheng,
he went to Samthong with his friends to court the nurses. He was attracted to Song as well. After a brief exchange of flirting, he had his friends
kidnap her to be his wife. He never knew Vang Pao had already had his
eyes on her or else he would never have dared kidnap her" (Anonymous
1). Song immediately protested her kidnapping and said she would never
relent to the marriage. Lo Ma refused to give her a divorce, since it would
be a loss of face for him. Another source, an elder who claims to be personally involved in the dispute case, said, "Madame Song said that she
had already made a vow to the general that she would only marry him.
She held his hand while they were dancing and she said this to him. She
had to keep her promise" (Anonymous 2). Once she revealed this, the
Hmong court urged Lo Ma to accept a divorce. Just then, there were heavy
attacks near Vientiane, and Song was summoned to tend to the wounded. "She just ran off to be with the Filipinos [doctors who tended the

Hmong,] so Lo Ma was forced to accept the court's ruling in the end" (Anonymous 1).

Song also told Hamilton-Merritt about her ordeal, but she claims that the source of her affection was a foreign man, not Vang (1993, 302–3). The following year, while still in Vientiane, Song happened to meet the general again. Hamilton Merritt (1993) writes:

> In early 1973, in Vientiane, at a gathering at the anniversary remembrance of T-28 pilot Vang Sue's death, General Vang Pao spoke with May Song and learned that she was no longer obligated to the arranged marriage and was now alone. Soon he asked her to consider marrying him. He promised to take care of her, saying that he would work it out with her family and his other wives. On February 18, 1973, in a *ba-sii* in Vientiane, May Song, age 17, married General Vang Pao. (303)

Song may have concealed her feelings for the general to Hamilton-Merritt due to a desire to downplay the scandal that had taken place decades earlier. Indeed, her family members confirmed her immediate attraction to Vang in her obituary: "She said it was love at first sight even though Vang Pao was nearly 20 years her senior and had other wives as was customary in those times" (*Asian American Press* 2013). Vang Pao was equally enamored of Song, as evidenced by the fact that he had to break a prior vow between himself and members of the Moua clan in order to marry her. Vang Chou explains:

> A few years earlier [but after he had already married Chia Moua] Vang Pao went to ask for the hand of Blia Ya Moua's daughter for his nephew, Vang Neng. Blia Ya was the elder son of Chong Toua Moua, Vang Pao's cousin who had been sold into the Moua clan. Blia Ya refused the marriage proposal saying that since his father was related by blood to Vang Pao, the two families—the Mouas and Vangs—should no longer intermarry. Vang Pao agreed. Now, he wanted to marry Mother Song and she was from Blia Ya's Moua clan, too. So, to get out of the situation, Vang Pao went to Colonel Toulu, the younger brother of Blia Ya, and said, "Toulu, I know we had a prior agreement, but you're not closely related to Nhia Chou [Song's father], right?" Of course, Toulu had to say, "Not really."

What else could he have said? After all, this was General Vang Pao
he was speaking to. (2013)

Song became Vang Pao's most minor wife and is addressed by the Hmong
as "Niam Ntxhoo" (Mother Song). Being Vang's newest favorite, she came
to the United States in 1975 as his legal wife and exerted her influence on
him from that stance.

Song, whose father also played a role in Vang's homeland politics, became the public wife in America. She was especially prominent after Chia's
death in 2009, following which Song was often pictured with Vang at city
and state events in California. Dynamic in personality, she was the out-
spoken wife who rallied Hmong supporters with passionate speeches during protests against Vang's arrest in 2007 for conspiring to overthrow the
Communist Laotian government.[13] Being chosen to make the announcement further revealed her influence within the Hmong community. Sure
enough, after Vang's passing, it was Song who appeared on his behalf at
national events, such as the Hmong New Year's Festival in Fresno, California, and the Fourth of July soccer tournament in St. Paul, Minnesota. In
July 2013, a month before she died, Song made the handshaking rounds at
Como Park next to Minnesota senator Al Franken and other political dig-
nitaries (Jurewitsch 2013). She also appeared at the inauguration of the
very first school named for the general, Vang Pao Elementary, in Fresno,
California (Asian American Press 2013). As she often accompanied the general everywhere during her lifetime, it appears that the Hmong accepted
her as his public spokesperson. Unfortunately, Song died on August 5,
2013, so we do not have the opportunity to see whether she would have
continued to prevail as Vang's public image or, more intriguingly, whether
she would have assumed a leadership role as Hmong American society
evolves. Reflecting her important status, Song was accorded a scaled-
down funeral ceremony that closely resembled Vang's in February 2011.
Hmong women in elaborate traditional garb and veterans in uniforms
lined the streets to pay homage as her casket was driven by. Former soldiers of Vang served as her pallbearers.[14]

Conclusion

Tracing Vang's connections to earlier leaders through marriage illustrates
women's important role in securing political power for men. On the sur-

face, Hmong politics seem disorganized and chaotic, as the most powerful clans competed for supremacy. Leaders from different clans seem to rise and decline in power without following any rational system of succession, as Yan Riyu observed in eighteenth-century China. When we examine kinship connections through women, however, a rational system of succession does appear. Over a century of history in Laos reveals how leadership transmission occurred through women from one generation of leaders to the next. Hence, Lo Blia Yao's rise to power can be traced to his five wives as well as to his mother, a cousin of the former leader Ly Nhia Vu. Similarly, Touby Lyfoung's succession in 1939 can be traced to Blia Yao through his mother, Mai. Finally, Vang Pao's rise in the 1960s can be traced to his female connections to Touby and to other traditional elites of the Lo, Ly, and Moua clans. Female links to predecessors made Vang a legitimate leader in the eyes of the Hmong during the "secret war" period. Leadership succession from the mid-nineteenth century reveals that Hmong women's marriages were used to ensure the political and financial success of husbands, fathers, brothers, and sons. Women were the nexus of power in Hmong society.

Notes

1. By the word "secular" here, I mean that women have not served in bureaucratic positions appointed by the state, but note that there have been documented instances in which women did assume positions of power as "queens" in Hmong messianic rebellions (see my chapter on Pa Chay Vue's rebellion, Lee 2005, 78–143).

2. I refer to the Hmong "perspective" here because non-Hmong sources about Hmong leaders' rise to power often emphasize external legitimation (by the CIA, the French, the Lao state), but when I interviewed Hmong informants, they highlighted kinship and marriage connections. Outside forces did not factor very much into the minds of my Hmong informants.

3. Because this chapter is not about active agency, the "voices" of Vang Pao's wives are not as integral, but more research about their perspectives is a definite plus. Only one wife survives the general today, however.

4. In China, the Hmong are subsumed under the category "Miao."

5. Although my informants construct the process of succession as a peaceful one that occurred with the consensus of the clan leaders, in reality, successions were often quite contentious, and there was much rivalry before a decision was made as to who would become the paramount leader. I argue in my dissertation

and my book that the individual who was able to obtain state legitimation became the supreme chief, as in the case between Touby Lyfoung and Lo Fay Dang (see Lee 2005 and 2015).

6. Believing that rhinoceros horns have supernatural and protective powers, the feudal lords of Asia coveted this precious object. The rhinoceros horn was a customary gift presented by the tributary states of Southeast Asia (such as Vietnam) to the Chinese emperor of the Middle Kingdom. Similarly, the Lao and Phuan tributary princes presented rhinoceros horns to their feudal lords (Thai) as gifts (Smuckarn and Breazeale 1988). Hmong leaders who sought the legitimation of the lowland authorities participated in this practice when they presented a horn to the Xieng Khouang royal family.

7. The simplified family tree shows Vang Pao's connections through marriages to the Ly, Lo, and Moua clans. From the bottom we see Vang Pao's father, Neng Chue Vang, married to a Lo woman, Blia Yao's daughter. Vang Pao, born to Neng Chue's wife of the Thao clan, also married wives who were directly descended from the powerful elites. The numbers in parentheses represent the order of marriages for Vang's wives. I start the ordinal numbers with Sia Thao because she was recognized by the Hmong as "First Wife," but note that she was preceded by two other wives, unknown to most Hmong. Vang's first wife, Mai, and his fifth wife, Pai, were sisters and the granddaughters of Tsong Ger, the younger brother of Hmong leader Blia Yao. Vang's wife, True, was a granddaughter of Hmong leader Ly Nhia Vu, and his two Moua wives were descendants of the powerful Moua clan. Vang never had to marry a Yang woman because he already garnered Yang support through his father's marriage to a Lo woman (the Yang widow).

8. This simplified family tree shows Vang Pao's marriage connections to Touby Lyfoung. Vang Pao's father, Neng Chue (at the bottom), should not be confused with Vang's son by the same name. Vang's brother Nao Tou, his son Francois, his daughter May Keu, and his nephew Geu married individuals of the Lyfoung family.

9. Although the Hmong emphasize Sia's protective power, or her "luck," we must be cautious in viewing her merely as a lucky charm for Vang Pao. For the Hmong, luck has its own kind of agency, which cannot be co-opted. Hence, Sia's good luck became a legitimating force for Vang Pao, which rendered him vulnerable after her death and led to his arrest and humiliation in jail. In this case, Sia's "luck" had legitimating elements tantamount to Benedict Anderson's (1972) explanation of how power operates in Javanese culture and how Javanese kings surround themselves with people believed to be imbued with certain essences and unique qualities.

10. Vang Pao's funeral was broadcast live throughout the seven days via the Internet by Hmong Satellite TV (see Widen 2011).

11. Yang Dao was the first Hmong to obtain a doctorate degree in economics from France. He returned in 1972 to become a close member of Vang Pao's inner circle, but he broke with Vang by the early 1980s and has since been perceived by Vang loyalists as a rival.

12. In 2005, the Minnesota state attorney filed a lawsuit against the Vang Pao Foundation, charging that it had violated state charity laws by not being able to account for $500,000 in spending. Cha Vang, the general's son, was the only signatory on the foundation's bank account. Cha spent money on trips, hotels, and jewelry. Cha and Lia Vang, the general's nephew, settled with the state and agreed never to be involved in charity work in Minnesota again. See Kennedy and McEnroe 2005; Jurewitsch 2005.

13. Since his permanent exile in 1975, Vang Pao has been working to overthrow the Communist Lao government. He was active on the ground in Thailand until 1992, when Thai political agendas began to shift in favor of rekindling relations with the Lao People's Democratic Republic (Lao PDR). Some claim that until September 11, 2001, Vang also had the tacit support of the United States, as evidenced by its continuing to deny normal trade relations with the Lao PDR, even though it had granted full diplomatic relations to Vietnam back in 1995. Vang's dream of retaking Laos was further inhibited by the U.S. effort to amass an antiterrorist coalition around the globe after 9/11. The United States courted the Lao PDR, a voting member of the United Nations, to its side by granting it full diplomatic relations in 2004. Then, in 2007, in a stunning about-face, agents of the U.S. government arrested its most loyal former ally and the archnemesis of the Lao PDR, Vang Pao, for violating the Patriot Act, which forbids American citizens from carrying out terroristic acts abroad. Vang, now an American citizen, was allegedly attempting to buy weapons, which he planned to use to retake Laos, from an ATF agent. The Hmong community saw the arrest as another betrayal and held massive protests across the United States, pressuring for Vang Pao to be released from jail. For Vang Pao's exile politics, see Keith Quincy (2000).

14. Song's funeral procession can be viewed at Suab Hmoob News, https://www.youtube.com/watch?v=Qsl4Ri85Fkg (accessed August 1, 2015).

Works Cited

Anderson, Benedict. 1972. "The Idea of Power in Javanese Culture." In *Culture and Politics in Indonesia,* edited by Claire Holt. Ithaca, N.Y.: Cornell University Press.

Asian American Press. 2013. "May Song Dies from Cancer." *Asian American Press,* August 11.

Baird, Ian. 2012. Email communication, March 21.

Chaffee, John W. 1991. "The Marriage of Sung Imperial Clanswomen." In *Marriage and Inequality in Chinese Society*, edited by Rubie S. Watson and Patricia Buckley Ebrey. Berkeley: University of California Press.

Ebrey, Patricia Buckley. 1978. *The Aristocratic Families of Early Imperial China: A Case Study of the Po-ling Ts'ui Family*. Cambridge: Cambridge University Press.

Evans, Grant. 2009. *The Last Century of Lao Royalty: A Documentary History*. Chiang Mai, Thailand: Silkworm Books.

Hamilton-Merritt, Jane. 1993. *Tragic Mountains: The Hmong, the Americans, and the Secret Wars for Laos, 1942–1992*. Bloomington: Indiana University Press.

Hymes, Robert P. 1986a. "Marriage, Descent Groups, and the Localist Strategy in Sung and Yuan Fu-chou." In *Kinship Organization in Late Imperial China, 1000–1940*, edited by Patricia Buckley Ebrey and James L. Watson, 95–136. Berkeley and Los Angeles: University of California Press.

———. 1986b. *Statesmen and Gentlemen: The Elite of Fu-Chou, Chiang-si in Northern and Southern Sung*. Cambridge: Cambridge University Press.

Jenks, Robert D. 1994. *Insurgency and Social Disorder in Guizhou: The "Miao" Rebellion, 1854–1873*. Honolulu: University of Hawaii Press.

Johnson, Charles, and Se Yang. 1992. *Myths, Legends, and Folk Tales from the Hmong of Laos*. 2nd ed. St. Paul, Minn.: Linguistics Dept., Macalaster College.

Johnson, David G. 1977. *The Medieval Chinese Oligarchy*. Boulder, Colo.: Westview Press.

Jurewitsch, Sao Sue. 2005. "Vang Pao Foundation Agrees to Close in Court Settlement." *Hmong Times*, October 16.

———. 2013. "33rd Hmong Freedom Celebration Brings Thousands to St. Paul's Como Park." *Hmong Pages*, August 1.

Kennedy, Tony, and Paul McEnroe. 2005. "The Covert Wars of Vang Pao." *Star Tribune*, July 2.

Kue, Mee. 2003. Interview with author in Vadnais Heights, Minn., on July 24.

———. 2011. Interview with author in St. Paul, Minn., on June 21.

Lair, J. William (Bill). 2003. Interview with author in Menomonee Falls, Wisc., on July 27.

Lartéguy, Jean, and Dao Yang. 1979. *La Fabuleuse Aventure du Peuple de L'opium*. Paris: Presses de la Cité.

Lee, Gary Yia. 1994–95. "The Religious Presentation of Social Relationships: Hmong World View and Social Structure." *Lao Studies Review* 2:44–60.

Lee, Mai Na M. 2005. "The Dream of the Hmong Kingdom: Resistance, Collaboration, and Legitimacy (1893–1954)." PhD diss., University of Wisconsin–Madison.

———. 2015. *Dreams of the Hmong Kingdom: The Quest for Legitimation in French Indochina*. Madison: University of Wisconsin Press.

Lo, Zong Blong. 2008. Interview with author in Vientiane Lao PDR on March 3.

Lor, Yia S. 2001. "Power Struggle between the Lor and Ly Clans, 1900–2000." Undergraduate thesis, California State University, Chico.

Ly, Na Jalao. 2002. Interview with author in Toulouse, France, on July 13.

Ly, Pao. Interview with author in Alençon, France, on July 27, 2002.

Ly, Tou Pao. 2004. Interview with author in Fountain Valley, Calif., on April 13.

Lyfoung, Mao Song. 2002. Interview with author in Maplewood, Minn., on October 18.

Lyfoung, Nao Kao. 2003. Interview with author in Vadnais Heights, Minn., on July 24.

Lyfoung, Tougeu. 2002. Interview with author in Herblay, France, on July 10.

Lyfoung, Touxa, trans. 1996. *Tub Npis Lisfoom Tej Lus Tseg Cia* [Words left by Touby Lyfoung]. Minneapolis: Burgess Publishing.

Lyfoung, Touxoua. 2002. Interview with author in Draveil, France, in July.

Lynhiavu, Lyblong. 2015. *The Liver and the Tongue: Memoir of Lyblong Lynhiavu.* Ontario, Canada: Lyblong Lynhiavu.

Mahmood, Saba. 2005. *The Politics of Piety: The Islamic Revival and the Feminist Subject.* Princeton, N.J.: Princeton University Press.

McCoy, Alfred W., Cathleen B. Read, and Leonard P. Adams. 1974. "The Politics of the Poppy in Indochina: A Comparative Study of Patron-Client Relations under French and American Administrations." In *Drugs, Politics, and Diplomacy,* edited by Luiz R. S. Simmons and Abdul A. Said. Beverly Hills, Calif.: Sage.

———. 1991. *The Politics of Heroin.* New York: Harper and Row.

Mohanty, Chandra Talpade. 1991. "Under Western Eyes: Feminist Scholarship and Colonial Discourses." In *Third World Women and the Politics of Feminism,* edited by Chandra Talpade Mohanty, Ann Russo, and Lourdes Torres. Indianapolis: Indiana University Press.

Moua, Tong Pao. 2007. Interview with author in Madison, Wisc., on August 1.

Moua, Toulu Chongtoua. 2004. Cassette recording sent to author from Denver, Colo., in March.

Quincy, Keith. 2000. *Harvesting Pa Chay's Wheat: The Hmong and America's Secret War in Laos.* Spokane, Wash.: Eastern Washington University Press.

Rawski, Evelyn S. 1991. "Ch'ing Imperial Marriage and Problems of Rulership." In *Marriage and Inequality in Chinese Society,* edited by Rubie S. Watson and Patricia Buckley Ebrey. Berkeley: University of California Press.

Schanche, Don A. 1970. *Mister Pop.* New York: McKay.

Smuckarn, Snit, and Kennon Breazeale. 1988. *A Culture in Search of Survival: The Phuan of Thailand and Laos.* New Haven: Yale University Southeast Asia Studies.

Suab Hmoob News. https://www.youtube.com/watch?v=Qsl4Ri85Fkg. Accessed August 1, 2015.

Tapp, Nicholas. 2003. *The Hmong of China: Context, Agency, and the Imaginary.* Boston and Leiden: Brill Academic Publishers.

Tsia Long Thao. 2006. Interview with author in Sun Prairie, Wisc., on August 6.

Twitchett, Denis. 1973. "The Composition of the T'ang Ruling Class: New Evidence from Tuanhung." In *Perspectives on the T'ang,* edited by Aurthur F. Wright and Denis Crispin Twitchett. New Haven: Yale University Press.

Vang Chou. 2013. Interview with author in St. Paul, Minn., on August 7.

Vang, Nao Chue. 2008. Interview with author in St. Paul, Minn., in September.

Vang Pao. 2004. Interview with author in St. Paul, Minn., on April 8.

Vannier, Charles [Vaj Neeb]. 2012. Email communication, October 17.

Warner, Roger. 1995. *Back Fire: The Cia's Secret War in Laos and Its Link to the War in Vietnam.* New York: Simon & Schuster.

Watson, Rubie S., and Patricia Buckley Ebrey. 1991. *Marriage and Inequality in Chinese Society.* Berkeley: University of California Press.

Widen, Steve. 2011. "Vang Pao Funeral to Be Broadcast Worldwide." *Sheboygan Press,* January 20.

Wong, Sun-ming. 1979. "Confucian Ideal and Reality: Transformation of the Institution of Marriage in T'ang China (AD 618–907)." PhD diss., University of Washington.

Yang, Dao. 1993. *Hmong at the Turning Point.* Minneapolis: WorldBridge Associates.

Yang, Dia. 2005. Personal communication with author on November 24.

Yang, Shoua. Interview with author in Nimes, France, on July 8, 2002.

Yang, Suddala [Sutdālā Yāthọtū]. 2004. Tū Yā Saichū : viraburut hæng dæn Lān Sāng. Vīangchan : Hōngphim Num Lāo.

CHAPTER 5

Hmong Women, Family Assets, and Community Cultural Wealth

Julie Keown-Bomar and Ka Vang

F AMILY IS OFTEN DEFINED as the cradle of patriarchy. By virtue of their sex, it should follow that Hmong women, as subordinate members of a patriarchal, patrilineal culture, are limited by their families in their exercise of agency. Yet the Hmong American women in this study often identified family connections and support as instrumental in helping them achieve their valued goals. In this chapter, we present a challenge to deficit-based frameworks that have characterized Hmong women as victims of oppressive patriarchal families and offer interpretations of women's agency that defy earlier portrayals of Hmong women as weak, passive, and marginalized. In our exploration of women's agency, we dismantle assimilative conceptions of Hmong women. The life trajectories shared illustrate personal abilities and women's struggles with the constraints of social structure. In particular, this chapter highlights sources of familial and community capital and the ways in which Hmong American women draw on relationships to influence their own functioning, life circumstances, and self-efficacy.

Alternative Modes of Agency and Empowerment

Human agency refers to a person's scope of power to achieve valued goals. While the power to act is an important component of human agency, exercising agency does not always grant power to the individual. Feminist writers such as Lila Abu-Lughod (1993), known for her research on the Bedouin, helped feminist ethnographers recognize gender- and cultural-based subjectivities and understand that women's subordinate position in a society or a family structure should not be considered a lack of agency.

Emphasizing the subtle and nuanced ways that agency is practiced in hierarchical cultures, Abu-Lughod's book contributes not only to Hmong studies but also to wider transcultural understandings of gender and power. We posit that agency manifests itself in many forms, and we seek to understand how women's individual or collective actions manage to affect, construct, and alter the world in which they live. We also seek to disentangle concepts of agency from individualist assumptions, for although agency is self-directed and self-determined, it is often enacted with and on behalf of a collective, whether a family or another group.

Markus and Kitayama (2003) help us understand why researchers may not recognize multiple forms of agency in cross-cultural research. In individualist societies, agency is seen as located within the independent self, while in collectivist societies, agency resides in relationships among individual selves. Markus and Kitayama (2003) provide evidence that agency is experienced differently by members of individualist and collectivist societies. Our work adds to this body of evidence by documenting the many ways that Hmong American women exercise their agency through relationships. Emphasis on acting alone as a measure of agency discounts the interdependence of family life and the many ways in which individuals help one another make decisions and act on those choices. We will share examples of situations in Hmong families and communities in which individual women may not have exercised direct, autonomous control but worked with others to make decisions, influence their situation, act on their behalf, or argue their case.

The theorizing and research on human agency have focused almost exclusively on the exercise of personal agency. Actions associated with agency are often constructed as personal autonomy or free will *versus* structure (family, religion, institutions), which distorts the extent to which a structure, like family, can expand the capacity of an individual to make his or her own choices, gain control, or, in many cases, empower themselves. In the world of Hmong studies, the structures that are most often associated with Hmong women's oppression are the patriarchal family and Hmong culture. Following the scholarly themes of this text, we deconstruct a dominating binary that privileges and elevates U.S. institutions (education, technology, labor) as the emancipators of Hmong women. We illuminate ways that female liberation is compatible with Hmong culture, family, and community. We want to honor Hmong women's agency across time and space and bring women to the very human project of transforming culture.

Gender and Family Discourses

A feminist epistemological shift in the social sciences includes women in inquiry, considers all women's life stories as meaningful, and renders women's agency and gendered power relations visible. Our contribution both to this book and to the field of family studies is to situate women's agency within a relative matrix of personal, interpersonal, and macrosystemic factors, and to view Hmong American women and their families using a resilience approach.

Women, as a group, are at a disadvantage in patriarchal cultures. This is true for all women in the United States, because they are living in a patriarchal society; men as a whole have privilege as well as more political and economic power. In Hmong communities, mechanisms of the kinship system also foster privilege and gender hierarchy. Gayle Rubin's (1996) landmark critique "The Traffic in Women: Notes on the Political Economy of Sex" identified the structural domination of women by men through mechanisms of the kinship system. Her focus on kinship structures as cultural productions challenged biological essentialism in social theory and signaled a major epistemological shift in the fields of kinship and gender studies. Feminist scholars and social constructionists have emphasized the social formation of these relationships. They have fostered a critique that uproots family and marriage from biology (Schneider 1984) and challenges the idea that kinship systems work to promote functionality, solidarity, and stability in societies (Vernon 1980; Yanagisako and Collier 1987). This epistemological transformation resulted in a preponderance of studies focused on individuals transforming, resisting, and navigating familial relationships. Scholars have also questioned whether subordination of women is universal and whether or not outsiders' views of women in a particular society are accurate. Local conceptions of family and the meaning it has for men, women, and community show substantial variation even within patriarchal cultures. We seek to document Hmong American women's conceptions of family and challenge the pervasive views that Hmong American women are victims of their culture and limited by their family relationships.

We are indebted to a long line of women of color feminists who challenged Euro-American stereotypes of ethnic and racial families as abnormal, broken, oppressive to women, and subordinate. *Race, Class and Gender* (Andersen and Collins 1992), in particular, influenced our understanding of the multiple overlapping systems of oppression that women of color face.

Within the field of Hmong studies, scholars have viewed Hmong families through a binary lens: functional–dysfunctional, assimilating–rejecting, modern–traditional. Their lens is undoubtedly influenced by a long-standing paradigm in the disciplines of family development and family psychology that accentuates difference as deficit. As other authors in this volume have argued, family stories that play on Hmong differences (Fadiman's *The Spirit Catches You and You Fall Down* [1997], the film *Gran Torino* [2008])—however well intentioned—have portrayed the Hmong family as in trouble, maladaptive, and a barrier to adjustment and success in the United States. Cultural practices that appear to imprison women are commonly documented in the literature with accounts of early marriage, polygyny, and bride theft (Donnelly 1994; Goldstein 1985; Walker-Moffat 1995). These practices do exist, but they are frequently overstated and presented as exotic, backward, or dysfunctional. As a result, Hmong culture is reified and easily fashioned as a deficit. The spotlight on Hmong patriarchy masks the agency of women to navigate the opportunities and limitations that exist in any society in which they reside. Moreover, it shrouds the cultural capital that is available to many Hmong American women despite their membership in multiple patriarchal societies.

Bic Ngo (2002, 2008) and Stacey Lee (1997) have broadened our understanding of Hmong immigration and adaptation by documenting the normative experiences of Hmong women and men as they encounter marriage, educational settings, and higher education. In contrast to earlier work that emphasized Hmong women's encounters with cultural clash and oppression (Goldstein 1985; Donnelly 1994; Walker-Moffat 1995), Ngo and Lee offer refreshing analyses of recurring cross-cultural themes, providing sophisticated and nuanced interpretations of agency, adaptation, and cultural negotiation. A renewed look at agency and gender within U.S. society moves the discourse beyond culture as difference and deficit and positions women as actors in their own life stories. Notwithstanding the difficulties that patriarchal ideology and structures impose, Hmong women use family and community relationships and, in some cases, gain considerable economic and political power in their communities.

We believe the case studies that follow illustrate that Hmong cultural practices are alive and adaptive and that Hmong women have been able to transform themselves without compromising their cultural identity. If one equates Hmong culture with traditional patriarchy, then it follows that a liberated Hmong woman must cast off her culture, ethnic identity, and pride. Moreover, if deficits are located primarily within the culture and family, problems and limitations experienced by Hmong American women are disassociated from macrosystems of oppression. Racism, inferior schools, lack of access to higher education, and low expectations oppress women of color. Sexism, classism, and racism create a "matrix of domination" that Hmong women experience on multiple levels, including the personal, familial, communal, and societal (Collins 1986).

Notions of what it means to be emancipated or liberated are historically and socially located. Hmong women's agency needs to be decoupled from a Euro-American understanding that equates women's agency with resistance to family norms, autonomous decision-making, or rejection of the "private sphere." Hmong women's motivations for action are often mediated by family and social relationships, and their capacity for action and resiliency is often enhanced by relationships with family, kin, and community.[1]

Perhaps because power and agency are often conflated, researchers and historians have portrayed Hmong women as powerless. It is true that historically, in Laos and Thailand, Hmong women were excluded from formal leadership roles and from participating in the public arena. Very few Hmong women held positions of formal power in Laos, even after Hmong became exposed to opportunities in education and the military (Vang 2008). Formal education in Laos required money that many Hmong families did not have. Only privileged families could afford to send their children to school, and when they did decide to educate a child, it was almost always a son.

Those who immigrated to the United States found educational opportunities for their children, regardless of gender. Evidence shows that more and more Hmong women are pursuing higher education and professional opportunities and are participating in community affairs. "A new kind of leadership—one in which women played some role—arose when Hmong refugees emerged as new leaders and served as cultural bridges between the Hmong and their American counterparts" (Vang 2008, 56).

Our research indicates that commitment and obligation to family as well as seeking help from family members figure prominently in the strategies devised by Hmong women to realize an "American dream" of their own. Family relationships can be a source of support to help expand individual opportunity and empowerment in the public sphere.[2] In conversations with Hmong American women from the Midwestern United States, we have documented determinants of agency that women use to their advantage to help them achieve goals, take risks, and achieve success on their own terms.

Methodology

To analyze the agency, determination, and support systems of Hmong American women, we drew on transdisciplinary training in anthropology, women's studies, social work, and education. The authors recognize that the experiential knowledge of Hmong American women is critical to understanding immigration, transnational identity, racial and gender subordination, and Hmong history. Our qualitative methods include interviews, field notes, and participant observation with Hmong American individuals from Wisconsin and Minnesota.

Our data sources include recent interviews as well as information collected in previous independent research projects. Keown-Bomar (2004) interviewed twenty-one Hmong American men and women in Wisconsin communities, and Vang interviewed eight participants for her forthcoming dissertation on Hmong American women in higher education. We augmented our research in 2012 by interviewing three women whose life stories are atypical in the sense that they defy cultural expectations: a single woman in her thirties, a woman who is married to a Euro-American, and a woman who is married to a younger Hmong man from Laos. We wanted to better understand how Hmong American women make difficult decisions, how they persevere in the face of obstacles, and how family and culture influence their decisions and actions.

In her research, Keown-Bomar (2004) documented multiple strategies women employ, including drawing on family ties, to attain their education. Keown-Bomar interviewed a variety of people of different ages with varied socioeconomic, educational, and immigration experiences. Vang's dissertation research highlights the strategies, motivations, and aspirations of Hmong American women who either are in the process of completing a doctorate or have attained one. We found many common themes in our research. Participants in Vang's research indicate that they had full support from their families. They credit their success as a community effort, acknowledging the support they received from family and encouraging mentors. Participants in both Keown-Bomar's and Vang's research indicated that their cultural identity and obligations to family and community were sources of motivation, strength, and constraint. Feminist sociologist Nazli Kibria's (1993) research on Vietnamese women similarly documents ethnic community as a source of solidarity and constraint for women.

As both learners and producers in this scholarly endeavor, we believe that our collaboration has transformed the nature of the research and interpretation. We bring different perceptions to this project because of our social locations and academic training. Vang came to the United States at the age of eight, and she has worked as a social worker, has lectured in social work, and is a diversity specialist in higher education. Currently, she is completing her EdD in educational leadership. As a researcher, Vang compares and contrasts her experience growing up in the United States with stories shared from other Hmong American women, reconciling these perspectives with scholarly assessments of Hmong cultural adaptation and capital.

Keown-Bomar is a Euro-American anthropologist with concentrations in kinship and gender studies. Her work as a community-based faculty member with University of Wisconsin–Extension focused on families and community development. Vang adds an insider's perspective to the research, having lived the questions that the authors asked participants. For the last seven years, we have collaborated on multiple Hmong American community and diversity projects in Eau Claire, Wisconsin. Given that we come from different social locations based on ethnicity, race, and national origin, our collaboration demonstrates a process for co-creating scholarship across lines of difference. We are keenly aware that we sit at the table of institutional power, where we may be given the opportunity to speak on behalf of others. Aware of the power imbalances that occur in this setting, we have been vigilant in representing our work as speaking with, not for, those who have been excluded from the table.

The following case studies offer a challenge to archetypal narratives that portray Hmong families as dysfunctional and Hmong culture as oppressive to women, as if they were not agents of change within it. As explained by many of the participants in this study, Hmong women were able to achieve their goals and gain opportunity with the support of their families and communities. Consistent with a number of previous studies (Supple, McCoy, and Wang 2010), our findings suggest that many Hmong American women are compelled to exercise their full potential, and they often credit their parents as influencing their drive. We wanted to take the analysis of family support a step further and ask if and how family relationships promote women's agency and empowerment. Whether through

outright statements of what was expected or through role modeling, participants said their parents clearly impressed on them that they expected their
daughters to do well and to be courageous and brave (*peev xwm*).

Expectations and Aspirations

Amanda came to the United States as a young girl, the oldest daughter in
a family of seven daughters and three sons. Amanda's father expects all of
his children to get an education and, to date, all seven daughters have an
undergraduate degree. The boys in the family are preparing for university.
Amanda, being the oldest, was expected to be a role model for her siblings
by achieving her degree. She recalled:

> There was pressure for me, being the oldest, to be the best. I had
> to lay the ground rules. I had to do a lot of the paving so that my
> siblings would understand they had no choice. That in America
> in order to succeed, there was no choice but for you to look at the
> education as the great equalizer; to allow you to do the things you
> need to do.

Amanda was an active agent in constructing her own identity without the
benefit of identifiable role models. As a daughter within a patriarchal family
system, an oldest child, a refugee in a new homeland, and an adolescent
trying to find her way, she is one of many Hmong American women who
forged their own subjectivities in relation to family, state, and international
forces.

Amanda's father fostered a strong belief in the family that education is
the key to obtaining a better life. Capitalizing on her ability to access education in the United States, she was able to create alternative forms of subjectivity and empower herself in ways that were impossible for Hmong
women in Laos and for many women her senior. To understand Amanda's
motivations and challenges, one must take into consideration what postcolonial, transnational feminist theorist Chandra Mohanty (1987) calls the
"temporality of struggle," which compels us to take into account the "historical, geographical, cultural, psychic and imaginative boundaries which
provide the ground for [her] political definition and self-definition" (31).
Amanda's boundaries included the educational goal set by her father that
all the children complete a bachelor's degree. Moreover, as the oldest, she

felt familial obligation to demonstrate that her father's expectations were achievable in the United States and that younger siblings could follow in her footsteps. As a woman who came of age as a refugee, Amanda also faced structural barriers in reaching her educational goals because of her marginalized status as a refugee and a Hmong woman, and because of her family's economic insecurity. Like many women of color living in poverty, Amanda faced numerous social and institutional barriers, and yet she succeeded with so many strikes against her.

Amanda describes education as "the great equalizer," and from her position as a refugee from a war-torn country and a woman from a cultural group that is often stereotyped as backward, stagnant, and traditional, this statement is particularly compelling. To become "equalized" through education is far more of a leap for Amanda than it would be for men, native English speakers, peers with role models who went to college, or any number of other privileged groups. Amanda's father underwent a paradigm shift of his own. Recognizing the shifting tides of opportunity that their new homeland offered, he encouraged all his children to pursue higher education. Amanda's position as the oldest and an abundance of girls in the family likely compelled the father to support and encourage his daughters' educational attainment as well as that of his sons; however, there were unique circumstances that allowed Amanda and her siblings to exercise their agency and empower themselves through higher education.

Superficially, this may seem to be a story of family pressure on the oldest child to do well and less a story about female agency, but Amanda sees it differently. She explained how these early experiences as the oldest child and role model helped her envision herself as a leader. Eventually she transformed these skills and her sense of self-efficacy into broader leadership within the local Hmong community. As a pivotal player in the family from a young age, Amanda developed her capacity to act and to position herself to make decisions, and she learned to act decisively. As we explain later, the experiences she and other Hmong women had growing up in immigrant families forged interpersonal skills and provided contexts for self-actualization that are key determinants of agency. Amanda stated that her experience as part of the 1.5 generation has influenced her throughout her adult life in terms of education and career choices and community leadership.[3]

For decades, ethnographers and feminist women of color have documented cultural assets and networks that help ethnic and minority groups adapt and persevere despite such obstacles as institutional racism, classism, unsafe working conditions, or concentrated poverty (Morawska 1985, 1990; Stack 1974; Yosso 2005). Our inquiry builds on this body of work by seeking to understand how familial ties, community networks, and linguistic ability influence Hmong women's agency. The tendency has been to look for signs of individual autonomy and to document the cultural implications of systems of gender (i.e., Hmong patriarchy) rather than focus on women's own description and analysis of their agency and empowerment. When women's agency is described as an individualist act, apart from interpersonal interactions or societal structures, we may miss complex and nuanced displays of self-determination, self-efficacy, and personal fulfillment.

Mee's story illustrates the influence of relational interdependence and family obligation on Hmong American women's personal goals and decisions about their future. A key factor that shaped many Hmong American women's sense of agency early in their lives was the role they played in helping their family navigate the outside world. Mee described how family members impressed on her the value of helping others and how they relied on her to interpret and serve as a youthful liaison between the family and mainstream institutions. This behavior was positively reinforced and affirmed, and she gained a sense that she could make a difference in people's lives. In Ka Vang's (2012) study, Mee was one of the youngest participants to complete her doctoral degree. In addition, she was the only one born in the United States and was still single during the interview. One can wonder if her single status, age, and identity as second generation have influenced her understanding of what is possible within Hmong and mainstream society. More important to this analysis, however, is the way that the people in her life helped shape her sense of the future and nurtured her ability to achieve goals.

As a young child, she was surrounded by family members in an urban Hmong American community. Her family wanted her to be successful, and she gained a sense of confidence and self-worth through their help. Yet her family did not possess all the skills necessary to help her move forward in a society in which they were marginalized. Lacking resources such as language skills, connections, higher education, and other enablers of social mobility, they nevertheless embraced high expectations for Mee. Although highly marginalized, they did what was within their power to maximize her educational opportunities within a matrix of political, social, and cultural power structures. For instance, they helped Mee attend a private high school, which afforded her a competitive advantage in terms of academic preparation, adult mentors, and a high-achieving peer group. Mee's parents wanted her to become a medical doctor (a coveted career goal expressed by many first-generation Hmong parents), but they had little knowledge of or access to these elite institutions.

Approaching college, Mee had the family support, the personal drive, and some of the necessary resources to pursue higher education, but she needed to build a realistic plan and negotiate the various institutional options. Up until this point, Mee's ability to successfully pursue higher education and graduate school was highly dependent on support from her family members and resources within her institutional networks. If she had been deprived of support from her family and had gone to a high school with a very low graduation rate, for example, the expression of her agency might have been quite different. Mee selectively assimilated prevalent social expectations and values and wove them into the realities of her life. Agency is this process of self-making within a context of interpersonal relationships, oppressive social barriers, and resources at hand. In Mee's case, the result was empowerment in that she gained power both educationally and professionally.

Mee chose a more realistic and achievable career path than medical school, but this choice had personal meaning. She explained that her doctorate degree may not be a medical degree, but she will be addressed as "Doctor" when she completes her PhD in leadership. Significant to Mee, this achievement gives her prestige and credibility within her community and the wider society:

> And what I've learned is that credibility in America is really about
> degrees, certification and education and I will say that my Ph.D.
> has helped because people look at the Ph.D. One second I'm
> Mee and you get a Ph.D. and all of a sudden you're Dr. Mee.

By establishing credibility within her family and the wider communities in which she operates, she has expanded her scope of power to achieve valued goals. Mee now has the credibility to do what she loves, which is to work with immigrant agencies and build leadership skills. Ka Vang has found in her research that women's early experiences serving in supportive family roles (problem solver, decision maker, interpreter, sounding board, negotiator, bicultural authority) set a strong foundation for exercising agency throughout their lives. Vang's findings build on the work of Yosso (2005) and others who argue that ethnic and racial communities have cultural wealth in the form of aspirational, social, linguistic, and familial capital. We take this a step further by arguing that family relationships and cultural assets also transform women's capacity to act and in some cases enable female empowerment. Yet Hmong women must still contend with social constraints at three distinct levels: the personal level, the group level, and the systemic level of social institutions, or what Patricia Hill Collins refers to as the "matrix of domination" (1986).

Nou's initial ambition was to be an actress, but her parents did not see any value in this profession. Sensing the normative boundaries of their generation, Nou's parents felt that acting would demean Nou as a Hmong woman and reduce her chances of making a good match later in life. Kissing on stage was seen by her parents as inappropriate, and they feared that people in the community would no longer think of her as pure and innocent. Nou's parents told her she could not pursue her love of acting. Nou recalled:

> I love participating in musicals . . . but I just remember a brief
> intervention that we had. . . . I was crushed . . . and then I went
> the complete opposite and decided to pursue [higher education].

Her parents could not see the value of performance arts, and they did not want their daughter to gain a reputation, but they still wanted her to pursue higher education. In fact, they expected no less than a bachelor's degree for all of their children, since they were being raised in America and were afforded the opportunity to better themselves through education. Nou surrendered her dream of being an actor and redeployed her energy toward a different career path.

Social theorists would tell us that personal experiences do not transcend normative cultural patterns; they are shaped, interpreted, and given meaning by that which is held in common. In this family's case, they were wrestling with changing cultural standards. Nou's behavior on stage pushed the boundaries of decency in her family's eyes, and so they intervened—as many immigrant families do to correct behavior when they feel their children are assimilating and losing touch with their values. Nou's case also suggests a gendered interpretation, because her parents would have likely reacted quite differently if Nou were a boy. We can read Nou's stage life as unruly performance and the subsequent parental response as disciplining her for her display of sexuality.

Nou's narrative illustrates women's agency and its persistence even under challenging circumstances. After some time exploring programs and degrees, Nou chose to pursue teaching, which, as all practitioners know, entails performance. She eventually obtained her doctoral degree in education, joining the ranks of a small but growing number of highly educated Hmong women who are challenging notions of what it means to hold prestige and power in the Hmong community. Researchers who focus on agency as autonomous decision-making and the pursuit of individual aspirations may scrutinize the role of family relationships in Nou's case. After all, her parents thwarted her dreams of a career in theater, and her agency was limited by conforming gender ideals. All of this is true. However, Nou's positive relationship with her parents, the support she had from them to go on to higher education, and her personal confidence were also factors that helped her pursue not only a bachelor's degree but also a doctorate. In this case, Nou was limited by her gender and the sociocultural norms constraining women's expression in the arts, a viewpoint that might be generational. At the same time, her parents wanted her to go far in her career by pursuing higher education, and with their encouragement, Nou was successful. Important in this analysis is women's perception of their agency and family relationships. While Nou may have felt "crushed" as a young woman, in retrospect, she does not feel that her parents restricted her from advancing her goals. Rather, they directed her energy to an achievable career that was gaining acceptance within the Hmong community.

Expectations about marriage and children were also a topic of conversation in our interviews. Participants said their parents did not pressure them to get married, but they felt it was a cultural expectation. Because of the heavy obligations that go along with being a daughter-in-law, mother, and wife, more Hmong American women are waiting until they graduate from high school and college to get married and start a family. Women are exercising their agency by making many of their own decisions, including prioritizing education over marriage and determining what constitutes a marriageable partner.

Amanda, who is in her thirties and dating, said she fears getting married now because she has had so much autonomy, feels that life is less complicated, is in complete control of her life, and doesn't have to share with or be accountable to anyone except her parents. She also said, "My love for education has really pushed marriage back." Her parents express concern about picking the right person to marry: "You get married only once. . . . This person's going to last your entire life. . . . Choose wisely because you are not blind." Her relatives do pressure her to get married by saying that if she waits too long, she won't be able to have children, and that her parents are the only ones in their generation who do not have any grandchildren. Amanda reported what her mom tells her about the old maid (*nkauj laug*) comments:

> Old maid doesn't mean anything bad. You should take that and turn it into a positive, you know, "you can label me as somebody who is an old girl, but hey, can you do what I've done?" She's like, if you just make your life extraordinary for you and live up to whatever expectations that you have set for yourself, nobody else can refute who you are.

Amanda's mother teaches a valuable lesson in this example. A pejorative term like *nkauj laug* has been owned and redefined, and Amanda seems to wear it with pride. The term implies the female subject is old, no longer desirable, and out of the marriage market. To transform this term as a positive attribute is a powerful act of agency in a patriarchal culture. It helps to reposition all sorts of status indicators, including gender, age, and relationship status. Family members have reinforced Amanda's resilience and helped her defy a lingering stereotype. Individual acts of agency such as this lead to collective acts of agency and are the first steps to dismantling gendered stereotypes.

Transforming Culture

Little is written about Hmong American women's resistance to sexual norms, and at least one Hmong scholar has labeled women who transgress as contributing to the instability and dysfunction of the family. In his book on Hmong people in Milwaukee, Fungchatou Lo (2001), using a deficit lens, describes adultery in the Hmong community, but he focuses on women who are unfaithful. He presents several case studies, and in two of the cases, the women were killed by their husbands. In a tone that blames the victim, Lo laments the transgressions of assimilated Hmong American women who are increasingly free to have extramarital affairs.

Decisions and behaviors that defy patriarchal practices and sexual norms are provocative and often come at a cost to one's reputation, relationships, and personal safety. Nevertheless, women are transforming cultural norms by waiting to get married, dating or marrying outside their ethnic group, and looking for Hmong partners thousands of miles away in Laos. Hmong plural marriage and infidelity are heated topics of debate. Globalization has increased opportunities for the flow of goods and people across borders for social and economic mobility. The relative degree of women's agency in these transnational exchanges needs to be better understood. Schein's (2005) study looks at Hmong men in the United States who travel back to China to initiate "multiform gendered relationships with the Asian-counterpart women, seeking them out for flirtation, entertainment, accompaniment, sexual tryst, mistresshood and marriage" (54). Little is known about Hmong women who journey to Laos to seek male companionship, but we do know that looking for potential partners—whether for sex, romance, or marriage—has gone global, and Hmong men and women are looking to Asia for new relationships.

A recent practice is developing in which Hmong American women travel to Laos to seek male companionship. Research is limited regarding this phenomenon, and we do not have quantitative data to understand how frequently it occurs. Antidotal evidence indicates that both Hmong men and women are practicing transnational dating, and marriages do result.[4] A major difference is that men are taking a second wife while Hmong women are taking a husband. While bigamy is considered a crime in the United States, polygyny (men marrying more than one wife) was traditionally allowed in Hmong communities in Laos. It still exists in Hmong American communities, albeit off the official record (Schein 2005). Second wives are married following Hmong customs in the United States. First wives may either leave their husband and divorce—a stigmatized choice—or live with the husband's decision to marry a second wife.

The developing practice of Hmong women marrying men from Laos is not well understood, but we sought to understand women's motivations, degree of agency, and factors that may influence their decision. Most research on transnational dating and marriage portrays women as commodities or victims in the trade. Kashia's story offers a different perspective.

Kashia married at fifteen and lived in what she described as a very unhappy marriage for thirty years. She stayed in this marriage for her children, to preserve her pride, and to avoid the stigma of divorce. Kashia tried many times to leave her husband, but cultural factors made it difficult to do so. Marriage has traditionally been seen and understood to mean "forever," and the wife is expected to accept all of her husband's faulty behaviors—even infidelity. Key to this concept is the idea that children have a father who is present, which allows them to be provided for in this life and exist as part of a family system and patrilineage forever. Because women and children are subordinates in this patriarchal system, they are dependent on a male figurehead for support, and he is their connection to a tightly structured family, kinship, and community system.

Kashia's husband did not allow her to go to college because he didn't want to be upstaged by his wife in any way. She describes him as a highly jealous and angry man. In terms of patriarchy and power, a "smart" college-educated wife may be perceived as a threat to the husband's dominant role in the family. Kashia worked outside the home throughout the marriage but did not pursue higher education. They had six children together, and Kashia recounted times when she would have to leave the house with small children to get away from her enraged husband. Relatives knew how unhappy she was because she would cry a lot. Kashia eventually went against cultural norms and divorced her husband. She dated a little after the divorce, but the men she met were disappointing. As she put it, "Sometimes you run from a snake and meet a tiger."

Kashia was encouraged by friends to call eligible Hmong men in Laos who were interested in dating. She started talking to a man who was eighteen years her junior. They corresponded for three months, then met in Laos and got to know each other. Kashia returned a year later to marry her fiancé. "The wedding was pretty much like the first time that you get married. You go to his parent's house. They came to the hotel and his family and other relatives came and we talked." She said she explained to his parents that she was eighteen years older than their son and that she could not have a baby. Kashia also made it clear when she took him as her husband that he could not have a second wife. "My husband and I already talked about these issues, but now we are talking to his parents."

Unlike Hmong men who may journey to Laos to find a second wife, Kashia was marrying for a second time, not taking a second husband. Kashia and other women who marry Hmong men from Laos are among a small but growing number of women who are taking bold steps in dating and marriage. Their behavior evokes a great deal of criticism from the Hmong American community. Kashia and her husband send money when they can to his family, but she said there was no dowry that went to his family. Hmong men in the United States that marry Hmong women from Laos pay about $5,000, following a long pattern of bride wealth, or payment to the wife's family for the loss of their daughter. Hmong American women who marry Hmong men from Laos typically pay no dowry, but they do sponsor their spouse. Once married, couples will often send money regularly to relatives in Laos. Although sending money to family in the old country is a practice based on economic and locational inequalities, the role of the woman in this story is anything but typical.

How one interprets Kashia's unconventional story depends on one's perspective. Kashia could be seen as a feminist heroine of sorts, inverting a transnational cultural model of male patriarchy. She could be seen as a rescuer, helping her new husband avoid a life in relative poverty. One might also see her as an independent woman—she took her life into her own hands and found love and happiness in a relationship with a younger spouse. Moreover, she found her voice and now stands up to people in the community who question her decision. Women who follow this transnational dating and marriage route, paved by men, are looked down on in the community. Like women around the globe who flip-flop gender norms, Kashia's boldness stands out.

Others may say Kashia is a victim of patriarchy. She stayed in a difficult marriage for thirty years. She sponsored her new husband and sacrificed her reputation in the community to find happiness. It is notable that Kashia has not been universally defiant of patriarchy. She has "bargained with patriarchy" (Kandiyoti 1988) in that she submits to male dominance but has rejected its most extreme form. She is subservient to her second husband but strategized to overcome an oppressive first marriage. As one example of the bargain, Kashia told us she had asked her husband's permission to give the interview. Is Kashia exploiting a global power imbalance? Most Hmong families in Laos are quite poor compared to Hmong families in the United States. Many Hmong families in Laos would be eager to negotiate a marriage that would benefit the family through wealth, education, and new opportunities. It just happens that the person exchanged in this transnational marriage arrangement is a man, not a woman. Theoretical positioning would be premature at this point because the topic has not been adequately studied. Plural marriage is so sensitive it rarely gets discussed openly in Hmong American communities. Few women have ever been heard on this issue, including those who emigrate as second wives. A phenomenological approach is appropriate at this stage of research. We advocate listening to the men, women, and families who are involved, and recording their perceptions and feelings before pigeonholing this transnational marriage phenomenon.

Kashia said that family members see that she is happier, and they have grown to accept her husband. Her children were opposed at first because they were worried about his age and limited English skills. Would he be able to support her? After some consideration, her daughter said, "You can marry whoever you want to. All I need is for you to have a happy life." Kashia was emotional when she talked about her mother's and children's reactions to her decision to marry a younger man from Laos. Kashia said that her mother knew that her life with her first husband had been miserable. Her mother gave her consent, glad that he had the same last name as her first husband, so that Kashia and her children could keep their last name. With tears welling up in her eyes, Kashia said, "She loves me so much, and she wants to see me happy, my life happy, before she dies. I was so happy to hear [that] from her." Kashia said, "Now I am happy. He is flexible and easy going, very different from my first husband."

A vibrant portrait of agency emerges from Kashia's life story. As an interpreter in the Hmong community, she knows there is a lot of gossip about her. People believe if you don't have children together, the marriage will not last. They gossip about the cost of marrying a "younger guy from Laos," and some predict her husband will run away. She was quiet in the face of this criticism for a while. With some encouragement from friends, this shy, rather unassuming woman is standing up for herself. "I can open my eyes, my mouth, and say something to them." She tells them her life is okay compared to the past and that they should not worry about her. Her responses might be: "Please take care of yourself" or "You have a daughter or son to care for—don't worry about me." The bad comments are less frequent as time passes. Some people, mostly women, do support her. She warns women interested in transnational dating that they will need to be patient, have a good job, and have a supportive family. Otherwise, when considering marrying a guy from Laos, Kashia says, "Don't waste your time." Kashia's agency is exercised in her self-expression of love and happiness, her growth as an individual who has found her voice, and her ability to build supportive relationships within her own family. Leaving her husband was difficult and took courage, and going to Laos to marry a younger man was even more daring and defiant. But in our conversations with Kashia, we also recognized that patriarchy is still operating.

Shoua, who stepped outside of her ethnic community to marry, has had to work with her family to gain acceptance of a partner who is Euro-

American. Shoua said her parents were always concerned about her dating, especially any non-Hmong boys because of their perceived tendency to leave girlfriends and wives. Shoua's parents believed that Americans were prone to self-interest and not able to stay as committed in marriage as the Hmong. When Shoua started dating Rick, she would not let him come to the house to pick her up, and she kept the relationship discreet because she did not know where it was going and she was afraid of her parents' reaction. Although she hid her relationship, she was still defying her parents' wishes, and this act of disobedience and concealment demonstrates several forms of agency. When she finally broke the news, her parents' reactions were explosive. Shoua said her mother "handed me a rope and told me to hang myself." Her father chased her around the house with a Hmong knife when he found out she was dating a white man, believing that her life would be over if she got involved. Her transgressions in the world of exogamous dating, or dating outside one's own group, compelled Shoua's parents to violently reprimand her. Despite this forceful display of control by her parents and the personal recognition that her parents loved her and wanted the best for her, Shoua didn't succumb to their demands to end her relationship. She stayed her course, waiting for the right time to maneuver Rick into her parents' lives.

Rick was handy around the house, and when the oven broke at Shoua's house, she seized the opportunity to invite him to the house to repair it. He gained respect by demonstrating his handyman skills in service to Shoua's family. Slowly her parents saw what he could contribute, and trust was built. Shoua said none of this was easy, and it was hard for Rick to understand that her family came first, and that when you "date a Hmong woman, you're not only dating her, you're dating the whole family." Despite a shaky start, the relationship between Rick, Shoua, and her parents has been positive. In order to make her relationship with Rick work, she had to integrate him within a cultural framework. Her agency is expressed by her ability to navigate family tensions and leverage the positive role her husband could play in her family.

Giving Back to the Community

Many Hmong Americans have enthusiastically exercised their civic duties and provided assistance to their communities (Vang 2008). For Hmong women in this study, many said their sense of civic responsibility came from their family. For Shoua, it was her father who inspired her and instilled within her a desire to serve her community; while for Amanda and Kashia, their service began out of family obligation and necessity. Shoua's father passed away several years ago, and she spoke lovingly about their relationship. Shoua is indebted to her father for many things, his commitment to the Hmong community standing foremost in her mind. In Shoua's case, we see evidence of familial cultural capital: high expectations, a strong cultural identity, service to others, and a willingness to work with family members rather than turn against them or sever ties. For over two decades, Shoua has been helping her family and members of the Hmong community as an interpreter and cultural liaison. Kashia found herself to be one of the only fluent English speakers among her relatives living in a small city in Wisconsin. She interpreted for her family from a young age. After her high school graduation, she became an interpreter for the community because she loved helping people and could read and write in Hmong and English. At that time, there were no formal credentials required for Hmong interpreters, so Kashia was able to find secure employment with healthcare providers in the area. Amanda reported interpreting and translating for her family from the time she was eight years old. Her love for leadership stems from these early experiences helping her family. Amanda said she was able to assist with bill payment, filling out forms, and communicating with a variety of adults; she became a little leader out of necessity.

Not only do these examples illustrate the importance of families and community in women's acts of agency, but they provide evidence of multiple forms of cultural capital (Yosso 2005). Linguistic capital includes the intellectual and social skills attained through communication experiences in more than one language or style. Translating for parents and relatives strengthens linguistic and communications skills for many children and develops a stronger command of the English language for children put in these situations. Marjorie Faulstich Orellana, Lisa Dorner, and Lucila Pulido (2003) examine bilingual children who are often called on to translate for their parents or other adults and find that these youth gain multiple social tools of "vocabulary, audience awareness, cross-cultural awareness, 'real-world' literacy skills, math skills, metalinguistic awareness, teaching and tutoring skills, civic and familial responsibility, [and] social maturity" (6). So rather than seeing bilingual children and individuals as different or English language learners as lacking in ability, as many dominant social institutions might label them, the participants in this study (as well as researchers like Orellana, Dorner, and Pulido) see that their juxtaposition between dominant and nondominant worlds afforded them skills. Showing love and concern (*kev sib hlub*), particularly as expressed in looking after the needs of another person, is a cornerstone of Hmong culture. Helping parents and relatives from a young age fostered *kev sib hlub,* but it also helped build community cultural wealth as these children became bilingual, bicultural adults. In many cases, these adults are the new leaders.

Community Leadership

Traditionally, Hmong leadership is determined by age, social and economic status, and gender (Vang 2008). Male elders have been deemed leaders in the Hmong community and in family life for centuries, but this changed to a great extent with emigration from Laos to the United States. Educated, bilingual, bicultural leaders were valued for what they could contribute to Hmong communities in a multicultural setting. Women have made many advances in all aspects of leadership because they have amassed skills and values that are deemed important for leaders to possess in the United States. In this chapter, we have touched on several, including communication, service to others, resiliency, and civic duty. Hmong women leaders are found in business, education, politics, and many other sectors. Despite many gains, when it comes to leading within the Hmong community, women have encountered challenges that are related to the patriarchal and patrilineal nature of Hmong culture.

Descent traced through the male line (patrilineality) influences connections, alliances, and leadership in the Hmong community. Hmong trace descent through the male line to a common person or tradition. Men, in particular, are taught how to trace affiliation by discussing how they are connected to others through clan, subclan, and ritual practices. Leading in the Hmong community depends to a great extent on gender and generational status and successfully working these networks. We have each interviewed a number of women in our research who are recognized leaders. Whether in higher education or in their jobs, many women stood out; but for the purposes of this chapter, we sought interviews with two women who stood out because of their leadership within the Hmong community. They described their strategies, challenges, and perspectives as women leaders in the Hmong community.

Amanda took on a major leadership role in an agency serving the Hmong community while her parents were out of town. When they returned, they could not believe what she had done. "This is what happens when your Dad and I are not in town. . . . You guys get yourselves in trouble," her mother said. Her parents contemplated Amanda's new role for a few days and then decided to help her as a family. Amanda recalled what her father told her:

> You have to be smart about this. You're a girl and they may not respect you, but you need to get the work done. That is the important thing. They may not like you. They may put up hurdles. They may make it difficult. They may throw everything at you to get your blood pressure up, but don't let it. Show them you can be better. Show them you can do the job better than they could.

At a family meeting, her parents told her that they had her back; she could depend on them for assistance. For example, she had a hard time getting enough help for the local Hmong New Year celebration, so her parents contributed by cooking and feeding the volunteers, and her siblings helped at the event. Amanda reported that her father sees that women can lead. He believes women are ready to be part of the solution; they are organized and articulate. Young people are passionate and transparent, which he believes are important leadership traits. Amanda credits her father with thinking outside the box and believing in women as leaders.

Both Amanda and Shoua have held leadership roles in the Hmong community. Both relied on their fathers to help them connect with male leaders of the Hmong community. Shoua, whose husband is not Hmong, invokes her father's name to make connections. Amanda said that sometimes she is completely ignored when trying to operate within a system that is clearly defined as male. In her interview, Amanda described how men make social connections through male-speak (language entrenched in gender and gender roles in the community) and the "good old boys club" of Hmong men. She said that because she does not socially interact with men the way other men do, and cannot because of her gender, she is sometimes met with indifference "within the Hmong structure," even if she is running a meeting. For women in community leadership roles, "It is like running up against a brick wall. . . . You get tired . . . and it is kind of painful." Amanda thinks this is why when you see Hmong American women in positions of power and authority they are often positions outside the Hmong community. Shoua, also a leader in the Hmong community, noted her encounters with racism in the dominant community. Not getting a job or consistently being invited to meetings as a representative of one's race or ethnic group is a lived experience shared by many women of color. The women we interviewed shared stories of discrimination and sexism that stem from their dual membership in U.S. society and the Hmong community.

We have found that these two women leaders in the Hmong community were effective because they relied on family for connections, support, and advice. To guide and infiltrate male-dominated power structures, they have had to depend on their fathers to a large extent. This is a patriarchal world that revolves around male relationships. These women must work with the relationships they have to the best ability their gender and situation in life allow. Shoua's husband is non-Hmong, and Amanda is single, but they both have familial cultural capital from their families of origin. We know that male relationships are important factors in Hmong women's leadership, but we need further study to help us understand how women with Hmong husbands or limited familial capital exercise their leadership within their ethnic community.

Conclusion: Community Cultural Wealth

Hmong women often draw on sources of dominant and nondominant forms of cultural capital to negotiate their positions in various environments. High expectations and family help are two forms of nondominant cultural capital that often go unrecognized and unacknowledged, as is the case with other communities of color (Yosso 2005). Mee, Nou, and Amanda, for example, were able to prepare for higher education through participation in such programs as Upward Bound and precollege programs. Nou participated in school plays and musicals, which gave her exposure to some mainstream "goods" of cultural capital—the kind of cultural capital identified with families of higher socioeconomic status. Our work builds on the notion that "all communities have cultural capital" (Nasir and Saxe 2003). Cultural capital is more than financial status, class, or connections, and it exists in more than one cultural realm. Yosso (2005) builds on the concept of "community cultural wealth" as a form of cultural capital possessed by communities of color. She identifies six forms of capital that communities of color cultivate to build cultural wealth: aspirational, navigational, social, linguistic, familial, and resistant. In this limited study, the authors have noted high aspirations, navigational tools, linguistic experience, and familial capital that Hmong women use to benefit themselves, their families, and their communities. While many Hmong parents and families could not provide some forms of cultural capital that are advantageous in the dominant culture (university experience, access to the best schools, help with forms), they could provide knowledge, preferences, norms, and supports that helped their daughters. As Vang has noted in her research, first-generation Hmong parents provided the high expectations for their children's education, while other organizations provided the exposure to higher education and tools that helped women gain access to social institutions where the deck is stacked against them.

Discourses that focus on difference as oppression in patriarchal and minority families cultivate an image of tradition and submissiveness. The findings presented here challenge the view of rigid Hmong patriarchy and Hmong women's submissiveness and point to multiple sources of cultural capital within their system of patriarchy. While Hmong American women must contend with challenges in general, many have grown in their capacity to be leaders, give back to their communities, find happiness, and practice self-determination by expressing agency, depending on family networks, and using the "goods" of their cultural wealth. Moreover, these stories of women's agency illustrate many ways of building empowerment within patriarchal cultural systems without sacrificing cultural values, family ties, and community connections.

Notes

1. Feminist scholarship in the social sciences has documented the importance of relationships in communities of color and in patriarchal communities, as well as the complexity of culture as related to the exercise of agency since the 1970s (Stack 1974; Abu-Lughod 1993).

2. Senator Mee Moua's successful campaign and election in Minnesota illustrate the benefit and role of extended family in elevating women in the public sphere. Moua was a member of the Minnesota Senate from the 67th district from February 4, 2002, to January 3, 2011. She was the first Hmong American woman elected to a state legislature.

3. Sociologist Rubén Rumbaut coined the term "1.5 generation" to describe the generation that arrives in the United States as young children. Individuals in this group identify with their homeland as well as their adopted country, are often bilingual, and often find it easier to adapt than those who emigrate as adults.

4. Information about plural marriage in Wisconsin and Minnesota was gleaned at a community meeting on transnational marriage held at the local mutual assistance association on November 19, 2012. It is estimated that about twenty men in the Eau Claire, Wisconsin, area have second wives from Laos or are dating Lao women. About ten women are using this avenue, and they tend to be middle aged and divorced from their first husbands.

Works Cited

Abu-Lughod, Lila. 1993. *Writing Women's Worlds: Bedouin Stories.* Berkeley and Los Angeles: University of California Press.

Andersen, Margaret L., and Patricia Hill Collins. 1992. *Race, Class and Gender.* Bellmont, Calif.: Wadsworth.

Collins, Patricia Hill. 1986. "Learning from the Outsider Within: The Sociological Significance of Black Feminist Thought." *Social Problems* 33, no. 6: 514–32.

Constable, N., ed. 2005. *Cross-Border Marriages: Gender and Mobility in Transnational Asia.* Philadelphia: University of Pennsylvania Press.

Donnelly, Nancy. 1994. *Changing Lives of Refugee Hmong Women.* Seattle: University of Washington Press.

Fadiman, Ann. 1997. *The Spirit Catches You and You Fall Down.* New York: Farrar, Straus and Giroux.

Goldstein, Beth L. 1985. "Schooling for Cultural Transitions: Hmong Girls and Boys in American High Schools." PhD diss., Department of Educational Policy Studies, University of Wisconsin–Madison.

Gran Torino. 2008. Directed by Clint Eastwood. Burbank, Calif.: Warner Brothers Pictures.

Hutchinson, Ray, and Miles McNall. 1994. "Early Marriage in a Hmong Cohort." *Journal of Marriage and the Family* 56:579–90.

Kandiyoti, Deniz. 1988. "Bargaining with Patriarchy." *Gender and Society* 2, no. 3: 274–90.

Keown-Bomar, Julie. 2004. *Kinship Networks among Hmong-American Refugees.* New York: LFB Scholarly Publishing.

Kibria, Nazli. 1993. *Family Tightrope: The Changing Lives of Vietnamese Americans.* Princeton, N.J.: Princeton University Press.

Lee, Stacey. 1997. "The Road to College: Hmong American Women's Pursuit of Higher Education." *Harvard Educational Review* 67:803–27.

Lo, Fungchatou T. 2001. *The Promised Land: Socioeconomic Reality of the Hmong People in Urban America (1976–2000).* Bristol, Ind.: Wyndham Hall Press.

Markus, H. R., and S. Kitayama. 2003. "Models of Agency: Sociocultural Diversity in the Construction of Action." In *Cross-Cultural Differences in Perspectives on the Self: Volume 49 of the Nebraska Symposium on Motivation*, edited by V. Murphy-Berman and J. J. Berman. Lincoln: University of Nebraska Press.

Mohanty, Chandra Talpade. 1987. "Feminist Encounters: Locating the Politics of Experience." *Copyright* 1:30–44.

Morawska, Ewa. 1985. *For Bread with Butter.* Cambridge: Cambridge University Press.

———. 1990. "Sociology and Historiography of Immigration." In *Immigration Reconsidered*, edited by Virginia Yans-McLaughlin. New York and Oxford: Oxford University Press, 1990.

Nasir, Na'ilah, and Geoffrey B. Saxe. 2003. "Ethnic and Academic Identities: A Cultural Practice Perspective on Emerging Tensions and Their Management in the Lives of Minority Students." *Educational Researcher* 5:14–18.

Ngo, Bic. 2002. "Contesting 'Culture': The Perspective of Hmong American Female Students on Early Marriage." *Anthropology and Education Quarterly* 33:163–88.

———. 2008. "Beyond "Culture Clash": Understanding of Immigrant Experiences." *Theory into Practice* 47:4–11.

Orellana, Marjorie Faulstich, Lisa Dorner, and Lucila Pulido. 2003. "Accessing Assets, Immigrant Youth as Family Interpreters." *Social Problems* 50:505–24.

Rossi, Alice. 1977. "Biosocial Aspects of Parenting." *Daedalus* 106:1–32.

———. 1985. *Gender and the Life Course.* New York: Aldine.

Rubin, Gayle. 1996. "The Traffic in Women: Notes on the Political Economy of Sex." In *Feminism and History*, edited by Joan Wallach Scott, 105–51. Oxford: Oxford University Press.

Rumbaut, Rubén G. 2004. "Ages, Life Stages, and Generational Cohorts: Decomposing the Immigrant First and Second Generations in the United States." *International Migration Review* 38, no. 3: 1160–1205.

Schein, Louisa. 2005. "Marrying Out of Place: Hmong/Miao Women across and beyond China. In *Cross-Border Marriages: Gender and Mobility in Transnational Asia*, edited by N. Constable. Philadelphia: University of Pennsylvania Press.

Schneider, David. 1984. *A Critique of the Study of Kinship.* Ann Arbor: University of Michigan Press.

Stack, Carol. 1974. *All Our Kin: Strategies for Survival in a Black Community.* New York: Harper and Row.

Supple, Andrew, Shuntay Z. McCoy, and Yudan Wang. 2010. "Parental Influences on Hmong University Students' Success." *Hmong Studies Journal* 11:1–37.

Vang, Chia Youyee. 2008. *Hmong in Minnesota.* St. Paul, Minn.: Minnesota Historical Society Press.

Vang, Ka. 2012. "Rewriting the Rite of Passage: Hmong Women's Experience in a Doctorate Program." Dissertation in progress, Minneapolis, Minn.: University of St. Thomas.

Vernon, Michel. 1980. "From the Social to the Symbolic Equation: The Progress of Idealism in Contemporary Anthropological Representations of Kinship, Marriage and the Family." *Canadian Review of Sociology and Anthropology* 17:315–29.

Walker-Moffat, Wendy. 1995. *The Other Side of the Asian American Success Story.* San Francisco: Jossey-Bass.

Yanagisako, Sylvia Junko, and Jane Fishburne Collier. 1987. "Towards a Unified Analysis of Gender and Kinship." In *Gender and Kinship: Essays Toward a Unified Analysis,* edited by Sylvia Junko Yanagisako and Jane Fishburne Collier, 14–50. Stanford: Stanford University Press.

Yosso, Tara J. 2005. "Whose Culture Has Capital? A Critical Race Theory Discussion of Community Cultural Wealth." *Race Ethnicity and Education* 8, no. 1: 69–91.

CHAPTER 6

Divorced Hmong Women in Thailand

Negotiating Cultural Space

Prasit Leepreecha

THIS CHAPTER CONTRIBUTES a new approach to gender studies and power relations in Hmong society by examining divorced women's active negotiation for spiritual belonging. For over a decade, the activist Network of Hmong Women in Thailand has pressed Hmong society to address divorced women's issues, specifically their postdivorce spiritual status.[1] I investigate the gender ideologies that structure Hmong marriage and divorce practices within the Thai space to illustrate the network's efforts to facilitate cultural belonging for divorced women within existing Hmong patrilineal practices. The network's accomplishments, I contend, were intimately tied to the solidarity among the young Hmong women involved and to their strategic alliances with key Hmong lineage leaders and outside scholars, who helped them raise awareness and garner support beyond their ethnic group.

Divorced Hmong Thai women's experiences of alienation and spiritual exclusion must be situated within an understanding of power. While structural-functional anthropologists such as Emile Durkheim (1995) have identified the many constraints that dominant structures place on people's lives, others such as James C. Scott take a political and anthropological approach to studying how the subalterns challenge such structures. Under the context of domination by rich farmers in a Malaysian village, the poor farmers exercised their own strategies of everyday resistance against the oppressing class structure. At the village level, Scott (1985) found that poor farmers used negotiation, gossip, petty theft, and reduced effort as forms of resistance. He also uncovered similar strategies taking place on a larger scale, such as poor farmers' resistance against the national government's policies that did not benefit them (1990, 2010). French cultural anthropologist and sociologist Pierre Bourdieu (1990) used the concept of contested "social fields" to explain the ways that marginalized groups competed for power or resources within a prescribed "field," or arena, of social activity. Here, political and cultural relationships maintained by the actions of agents within the field compete for resources or powers that are characteristic to that particular field. I employ Scott's and Bourdieu's approaches to analyze the processes, meanings, and consequences of Hmong power relations.

I also consider the network's activism within larger social conditions in the Southeast Asia region generally and Thailand specifically. Hayami et al. (2012) found that the region has undergone social and economic changes that resemble the family in crisis in the rest of the industrialized world. In Thailand, gender inequality and prevailing attitudes that negatively affect Thai women's well-being remain. Despite the inclusion of gender equality in its 1974 constitution, Thai family law continues to make it easier for husbands to use adultery as grounds for divorce than it is for wives (Songsamphan 2012, 101). Divorce in Thailand had increased from 19.4 percent in 1990 to 26.3 percent in 2000. Although statistical data are not available for smaller ethnic groups like the Hmong, community observations show that divorce among young couples in contemporary Hmong society in Thailand has become more prevalent, generating growing concern among ethnic community leaders. Community leaders tend to view the issue as a consequence of increased participation in globalization processes and the weakening of Hmong social structure. This chapter considers the latter concern about Hmong social structure by examining Hmong women's efforts to change cultural practices around wedding and divorce ceremonies.

Becoming a Hmong Bride

To understand the social pressures placed on divorced Hmong women requires an intimate exploration of wedding ceremonies.[2] As in other societies, the Hmong wedding ceremony serves as a transition of the bride and groom from single to married status. The various steps in the wedding process signify termination of the bride's membership in her natal clan and separation from its household spirits and the beginning of her inclusion in the groom's clan. Separation of ties at the conclusion of the wedding ceremony can be an agonizing moment for Hmong women because the transition between her parents' household spirits and the household spirits of her husband's parents has been structured as a complete break.

Unlike some Western wedding practices, in which the bride and groom express their commitment to each other with the symbol of rings in front of a religious leader, the Hmong wedding does not explicitly involve the bride and groom. Instead, a formal, multistep process for the bride to transition from her parents' household to the groom's family has been established and followed for generations. According to Vam Thai Txooj Txhim Yaj (1980), the complete Hmong wedding process contains four components that disconnect the bride from her natal lineage and link her formally to the groom's lineage.[3]

Lwm qaib (blessing ritual) is the first part, which takes place when the bride arrives at the groom's house. It symbolizes the bride's incorporation as a new spiritual member of the groom's family. Before the bride can enter, a rooster is turned around over the heads of the pair outside the door of the groom's parents' house. As Yaj (1980) explains, the *lwm qaib* is performed by an elder to drive away sickness, death, sadness, crime, burdens, and difficulties, all of which should be blown away by the wind. The ritual also functions as a time to bless the new daughter-in-law, so she may live a healthy and productive life (449).[4] In Thailand, a *lwm qaib* ritual performer from the groom's family closes this ritual by stating, "From now on she is our lineage member, she is alive as our people, if she dies she belongs to our spirit."[5] The groom and new daughter-in-law then enter the house through the front door (*qhovrooj tag*). Following this initial ritual, the woman no longer belongs to her natal household and clan spirits, and is under the protection of her husband's household spirits.

The second part is the performance of *pe* (bowing) to show gratitude and to inform the groom's ancestors and elders that there is a new household member. Carried out soon after the *lwm qaib* ritual, an elder guides the groom and his *phijlaj* (best man) to bow facing the house's *hauvplag* (central pole) and *xwmkab* (spirit alter). The elder refers to ancestors, parents, uncles and aunts, and brothers and sisters, and the men bow to them in a show of gratitude and deference. Then the elder guide has them bow to the groom's *pom dab pom qhua* (household spirits) to make them aware of the arrival of a new member.[6]

The third component is *laig dab* (offering whisky and cooked food to acknowledge ancestors and household spirits). It is performed twice during the wedding ceremony to acknowledge the household spirits of both sides. The first is carried out at the bride's parents' house. The groom's family brings cooked rice and boiled chicken, whisky, and a small glass for the bride's father to offer to ancestors and household spirits announcing the departure of a daughter. The second *laig dab* takes place back at the groom's parents' house to conclude the wedding festivities. Its purpose is to thank the wedding party members and to report the outcome of the wedding ceremony to the groom's parents and elders. Here, it is the groom's father who offers whisky and small portions of cooked food to ancestors and household spirits. He informs them about the official acceptance of the daughter-in-law and asks them to protect her.

The final part of a Hmong wedding is *qaib faib sia* (chicken for dividing life). Performed at the house of the bride's parents while the wedding party leaves, *qaib faib sia* occurs at the moment when the bride crosses over the entrance of her parents' house. As she straddles the threshold of the house, the ritual performer divides a cooked chicken into two parts. He then explains, "Divide mother's life to mother, divide daughter's life to daughter." Hmong ritual performers explain that this is to separate the daughter from her mother as she begins her new life, another act to spiritually disconnect a woman from her parents' household spirits.

Within these four main components of a Hmong wedding, there is tremendous sadness for the bride. Instead of being joyful, the last day of a Hmong wedding ceremony at the bride's parents' home is often a day of grief, particularly for the bride and her mother. While ritual performers and guests are busy celebrating at the main table full of food and whisky, the bride's mother chooses and packs the traditional Hmong clothes and other valuable belongings that she will give her daughter to signify their formal separation. The mother's face is filled with sorrow, and she often cries while talking with her daughter. Toward the end of the formal marriage ritual, the bride is invited to sit next to the groom and important guests at the special table set aside for them. Elder representatives of the groom insist that she and her elder guests eat and drink this last and most important meal of the wedding ceremony in front of the groom's side.

The *mejkoob* (go-betweens) from both sides sing a few wedding songs, and older brothers of the bride express their feelings and give the bride advice on how to be a good housewife for her husband and a polite daughter-in-law for other members of her husband's household and lineage. Her family also emphasizes the salient role of the bride and the groom in bridging lineage members on both sides. Most importantly, they tell the groom and his two *mejkoob*, "We give you the top of the rope [the bride], but we hold on to the bottom" (*Hauv hlua peb muab rau nej, qab hlua peb tseem tuav rawv*) (Symonds 2005, 68). This is the only formal occasion in which leaders of the bride's lineage not only coach her but also stress to the groom the important interclan ties that result from the union.

Subsequently, the groom and his *phijlaj* are told by his *mejkoob* to bow to show respect and honor the bride's parents and relatives. The bride's mother and other women from her clan comfort the bride. They express grief and concern, and also share their wisdom on how to be a good house-wife and daughter-in-law. Then a ritual umbrella symbolizing the new ties between the two clans is handed over to the groom's two *mejkoob*. The bride's belongings are carried out of the house. A *mejkoob* tells the groom to grab his wife's hands before leaving. The bride does not look back, as it is believed to cause bad luck. As they depart, the bride's parents have con-flicted emotions. On the one hand, it is a heartbreaking moment because they have lost their daughter, who will now be a member of the groom's family and clan for the rest of her life. On the other hand, it is a moment of deep pride that their daughter is starting a new life. It reflects their success as parents.

During interviews, Hmong lineage leaders were reluctant to clarify the details of the ritual processes performed during the wedding ceremony, stating simply that it is quite complicated to explain. Observations of many wedding ceremonies reveal that all of the steps signify the removal of a woman from her natal lineage. According to Hmong lineage leaders, ritual is a cultural inheritance created by Hmong ancestors and passed on from generation to generation (*poj ua cia yawm ua tseg*). They believe that the wedding ceremony rituals must not be changed, and need to be performed strictly in the same manner as stated by the ancestors. Performers should not omit or add any part to the rituals. Humans and spirits may impose fines if processes are altered.[7]

The processes were set up by Hmong ritual performers and leaders centuries ago, when Thai Hmong ancestors lived in southwestern China. The aim was to protect families from marital and social problems and ulti-mately to prevent divorce. Such practices are predominantly controlled by men, especially ritual performers, and they signify a gender imbalance in Hmong society, since men's lives remain intact regardless of their actions, whereas women enter a liminal state of being if marriages end in divorce. How are these processes relevant in contemporary Hmong life in Thailand?

In addition to social and cultural pressures, divorced Hmong women in Thailand continue to face spiritual exclusion, resulting in the need for collective action to challenge these centuries-old traditions.

Pressures on Divorced Women

As a rite of passage, the wedding ceremony lays out the terms and conditions for married status that the network seeks to address (Van Gennep 2004). Scholars who have conducted research among the Hmong in northern Thailand point out that Hmong society is patrilineal; thus, spirit and inheritance are received through the male lineage (Binney 1968; Geddes 1976; Cooper 1978, 1984; Lee 1988). Consequently, the Hmong practice patrilocal residence after marriage. In cases of marital disputes, lineage leaders of both sides play important roles in resolving issues. Divorce rarely existed in the subsistence economy context in highland villages due to a strong kinship network and the tolerance of polygynous relations. Women's marginal position likely prevented them from questioning such traditions.

Unlike Hmong from Laos living in the United States, whose lives were turned upside down during the Cold War in Southeast Asia, the majority of the Hmong population in Thailand were not involved in the same way. They have not been displaced and resettled in an entirely new and Western society like the Hmong from Laos; thus, the factors influencing family relations differ significantly. However, development programs brought by both Thai and international development agencies into remote Hmong communities since the early 1960s have subsequently influenced Hmong women's understanding of gender inequality in Hmong society (Leepreecha 2001; Manndorff 1967; Wanat 1989).[8] This is especially common among young Hmong, who leave the villages to attend school or work in cities. Elders from both sides have less influence on their children's marriage decisions than they had before.

Village leaders report that the divorce rate among Hmong couples in contemporary Thailand is increasing at a higher rate than in the past few decades,[9] and they often identify more relaxed gender relations and decreased kinship influence on social structure as contributing factors. Observations reveal that in addition to being excluded from participating in rituals at their parents' household, divorced Hmong women who return to live near their parents are often treated with disdain by some men outside of their natal clan because they are seen as sexually "loose."[10]

As mentioned earlier, a woman is cut off from her natal lineage by the rituals outlined in the wedding ceremony. The practices of marriage and divorce privilege the natal lineage. Therefore, a woman primarily returns to her parents' home following a divorce to seek temporary refuge while she waits to remarry. While a divorced Hmong woman can walk in and out of the house and eat meals with members of her natal lineage, she may not attend any rituals performed for members of her parents' household. She is banned from the following religious rituals: *ua neeb koos plig* (performing the shaman ritual to protect souls of family members), *hu plig* (soul calling in various occasions throughout the year), and *lwm tsiab* or *lwm sub* (ceremonies to drive out evil spirits during New Year events). If she becomes pregnant, a temporary shelter would be built where she would deliver the baby and be required to remain for a month after giving birth (*nyob nruab hlis*). In addition to the spiritual conflicts, daily tensions often occur between her and her sisters-in-law, especially if she has brought her own children into the household. Negative views of the divorced woman are subsequently transferred to her children. Consequently, her parents and brothers often build a small shelter near the main house for her and her children in order to avoid daily and spiritual conflicts. Such traditions and practices in Hmong society create a feeling of disappointment (*tu siab*) for divorced women. A divorced woman experiences alienation and exclusion from normative social practices in both life and death, and the spiritual alienation is complete when she dies. When a Hmong person dies, the body is usually kept in the home where the funeral rituals can take place. However, a divorced Hmong woman's body cannot be kept in her parents' house; instead, it is placed in a temporary tent outside.

Divorced Hmong women in Thailand today express much disappointment about these situations. Shoua Moua[11] shares how her experience has impacted her emotionally and socially. Shoua and Kong Thao were both from a mountain village in Chiang Mai province. Kong was studying at a university in Bangkok. When he returned to the village, he met Shoua. They had to marry in 2005 because Shoua became pregnant. The wedding ceremony was held according to traditional Hmong practices. Shoua stayed in the village with Kong's parents and siblings after the wedding while Kong returned to the city to pursue his degree. Shoua did not get along with Kong's mother. The mother-in-law accused Shoua of being lazy for not taking care of the house and not working with her in-laws in the fields. Shoua said that her mother-in-law often gossiped about her to neighbors. Kong received information from both sides but could not bring about peace between the women.

The conflict reached a critical point in 2009, and based on his parents' suggestion, Kong decided to divorce Shoua. A rumor also circulated that he had a new girlfriend in Bangkok. Kong and his parents finally brought Shoua back to her parents without asking for a return of any of the silver bars used to pay the bride price. Shoua and her daughter lived in her parents' house. According to Shoua:

> My daughter and I have lived with my parents and other younger brothers and sisters for two years. I was very disappointed about the way they treated us as though I was not a daughter or their sibling. They didn't allow us to attend any family rituals. Furthermore, my father had refused my request to give me a small plot of land to build a separate house for the two of us. Finally, I decided to leave the village and moved to town since I was not recognized to be a member of my parents' household. I saw no future for me living in the mountain village.

Shoua left her daughter with her mother because her daughter was only two. It would have been difficult for Shoua to take care of her while selling flowers in a lowland market. Despite the tensions in her parents' household, her mother was the only person she could rely on. Shoua's higher income benefited her and her daughter, and since her parents' income from farming was minimal, she was able to support them. Economically, it was a better option for her to work in town rather than live in the village and be dependent on her family. Interestingly, however, moving away allowed Shoua to escape some of the social and cultural oppression from members of her family and the villagers in general.

Migration to larger towns and cities is an important strategy for divorced women to avoid the discrimination in the villages. Being a *poj nrauj* (divorced woman) in Hmong society comes with low social status. The woman is usually the one who bears the blame for the failed marriage, regardless of the reasons, and she often faces contempt from others with whom she comes into contact. Moving from villages to cities not only removes the social pressures of the Hmong community but also is an opportunity for women to look for nonagricultural jobs, even if that work does not always result in higher social status or earnings. City life also provides anonymity due to the larger populations. These women are also more at ease with their social status living in Thai cities because Thai views on divorce are more tolerant. As Bussarawan Teerawithitchainan (2004) explains, "The relative ease of divorce in Thai society is partly owing to its religious tradition. *Theravada* Buddhism does not stigmatize divorce, even though social pressures might be there to maintain a marriage since family has an important economic function."

What impact does migration to cities and towns have on divorced Hmong women? Many have left the villages to live and work in cities or towns, while others travel back and forth. Some are able to maintain close connections with Hmong people due to the availability of modern technology, such as cell phones. Divorced women living outside of Hmong villages have more opportunities to choose new partners, and some couples live together without getting married, while others marry non-Hmong men. For women who are illiterate or unable to speak Thai, however, it is difficult to survive outside of the villages, because interacting with non-Hmong people and obtaining employment require at least some basic understanding of the Thai language.

What do the lived experiences of Hmong divorcées reveal about social practices, and how do they challenge the rigidity of Hmong cultural practices? Despite the complex relationships that divorced Hmong women have with respect to their natal lineage, it is their family that women rely on for survival, especially if they choose not to remarry. To Thai Hmong women, divorced status is a crucial period of time in their lives, since they enter into the "field" of power struggle (Bourdieu 1990). In Shoua's case, leaving her daughter in the care of her mother enabled her to work without having to find child care in the city. Children of divorced women are expected to help their mothers in the future. Even in instances in which sons remain with the woman's ex-husband, they would continue to help their mothers in daily life despite the fact that these women no longer belong to their ex-husband's lineage spirits. If a divorcée has only daughters, she would eventually depend on her daughters and their husbands for support, even though she is not allowed to be a member of her sons-in-law's lineages. A divorced Hmong woman without children whose parents have passed away could still count on her brothers and their children to care for her in her old age. They would provide food and shelter as well as help to oversee her funeral arrangements. Hmong cultural practices do ensure this minimum social security for divorced Hmong women.[12]

Although Hlee Kong was born and raised as a Christian and does not follow animist traditions, it is interesting that her life story differs little from Shoua's and that she encountered similar pressures. Hlee married Nong Khang, a non-Christian Hmong man, in 2003. As is customary in recent Hmong marriage practices, their wedding ceremony was held in a local church, and the ceremony followed Western traditions. They lived with Nong's parents after the wedding. Contrary to the expectation that she would follow her husband's ways, Hlee refused to embrace his animist religion, which led to tensions between them. The situation was exacerbated when it affected other members of the household. In 2007, Nong went to work in Taiwan and left Hlee and their two children with his parents and siblings. Alone and isolated, Hlee reconnected with her ex-boyfriend in the village. When this relationship was discovered, leaders from both sides met and discussed the situation. The marriage could not be saved, and Hlee and Kong divorced in 2010. Since both of her parents had passed away and her older brothers had their own families, Hlee did not move in with any of them. Instead, she rented a small room from a Hmong family and lived there with her two children. Hlee is not accepted as a member of any of her siblings' households.

Without child care, Hlee sent her children to a boarding school in another province. Not long thereafter, she became involved with a married Hmong man with whom she started a small business in Bangkok. After a few months, she returned to her rental apartment in the village. The man now lives with both Hlee and his family, but he does not plan to marry her as a second wife. She explains:

> As I'm a Christian, I don't want to be his second wife. Since we love each other and both of us are a new generation of Hmong, there is no need for us to marry according to Hmong tradition. Yet, if he divorces his wife and he becomes a Christian, I may agree to traditionally marry him.

Hlee's situation is not without problems. She is looked down upon by men outside the Kong clan—as well as by her own boyfriend—because she is considered a "public person." With the exception of men from her natal clan, a divorced woman is considered available and is expected to have sexual relations with any man who shows interest. Hence, she is vulnerable to the sexual advances of flirtatious men, even if they are married.

Although a divorced woman may reside with her parents and brothers, they are not able to protect her. Some men want her as a minor wife, while others are merely interested in playing around with her. Her position subjects her to their sexual advances, gossip, and condescending remarks. This precarious situation often leads many Hmong divorcées to accept propositions to become a minor wife, which enables them to escape such abusive treatment. More importantly, even as minor wives they become official members of their new husband's lineage.

Pang Yang, a thirty-eight-year-old mother of four, shared her heart-rending marital strife. Prior to the divorce, she and her husband sold souvenirs to tourists in Phuket in southern Thailand. They left their children in the care of his parents in a mountain village in Chiang Mai Province. Over the course of five years, her husband traveled back and forth to visit the children and his parents, and he brought products from Chiang Mai to sell in Phuket. He secretly had a girlfriend who worked in a restaurant in Chiang Mai city, and in 2009, he decided to marry the single woman as a second wife. Pang did not agree to this arrangement and decided to divorce him. During the clan elders' negotiation, the bride price was not returned to her husband, since his infidelity instigated the divorce. Their assets were divided equally. The two boys stayed with their father, while the two girls lived with Pang.[13]

Because of tensions between Pang and her sisters-in-law, she did not move in with any of them. A small house nearby was built for her and her daughters. Her young age and trading experience made her desirable to men outside her natal clan. A few men became her lovers, while others gossiped about fooling around with her occasionally. Most showed disdain toward her (*saib tsis taus*). Pang's "bad" reputation negatively impacted her natal lineage members. As Pang described:

> I had pressures from not just men of other clans who became
> involved in my life but also men of my lineage. Some of my elder
> brothers told me, via their wives, not to play around with many
> men unless there was the possibility of marriage. They said that
> doing so would make them lose face (*poob ntsejmuag*). (2012)

Among those who visited her, Meng Xiong, a forty-two-year-old man with a wife and three children, seemed the most sincere. To avoid the daily criticisms, Pang agreed to become Meng's second wife in early 2011. This second marriage failed by the end of the year due to conflicts within Meng's family. Following the second divorce, she placed her daughters in an urban Christian hostel where they are enrolled in school, while she temporarily resides with the family of her younger sister in the same town.

Becoming a second or third wife following a divorce is a path women use to overcome the social constraints of divorced status and gain male protection (*tobhau txivneej*), yet this form of "protection" is often a tenuous one. As illustrated in the preceding cases, divorced women are subjected to forms of male control embedded in Hmong social structure. As public women, they also become threats to married women, and they exist on the margins of their natal lineage.[14] This vicious cycle within the Hmong cultural landscape spurred Pang to join the Network of Hmong Women in Chiang Mai city, so that she could play an active role in fighting against the structural sociocultural oppression of divorced Hmong women in Thailand.

Agents of Change

From within the powerlessness that divorced women have experienced, a newfound sense of urgency to change their patriarchal culture has emerged. While suicide attempts are frequent among Hmong women in cases of forced marriage and when their husbands marry a second wife, few divorced Hmong women respond to this critical time in their life in the same drastic manner. In general, they are able to cope with their divorced status. As Pang exclaimed, "It's better to leave the smoking house, so I can freely breathe!" As they leave an unpleasant situation, some women have hopes of finding a more suitable husband than the one they divorced. Tainted by their divorced status, most do not find a better situation. Even more troubling is that if they do not remarry, their marginal position is transmitted to their children, who are also not permitted to their parents' household spirits. Given these multiple marginalities, individuals have responded in various ways to the lack of a cultural space in contemporary Hmong society available to them.

In the last decade, the Network of Hmong Women has allowed women to collectively address Hmong gender inequality in Thailand. Formed by young married and divorced Hmong women living in urban Chiang Mai in 2004, the network is an initiative of the Hmong Association of Thailand. Its primary goal is to engage with lineage leaders on women's rights issues and gender inequality that permeate Hmong social practices. Network participants were interested in developing strategies to negotiate with Hmong lineage leaders to change ritual practices in order to empower Hmong women. According to Mee Thao (2011), a key network leader, "Hmong women have a very low social status in comparison to men in our society. It is not just the ideology of inheritance, which predominantly favors men, but also gender inequality in daily practices. Those are the essential reasons behind the establishment of the Network of Hmong Women." She also pointed out that among the one thousand Hmong residing in urban Chiang Mai, the ten divorced women she knows live contentious lives.

They formed a network because as "social capital," the network is a form of power (Bourdieu 1990). It links individuals from a social group together either spontaneously or intentionally. Moreover, a network is constructed for a specific purpose to ignite a social movement (della Porta and Diani 1999; Diani 1992). Social movements arising from women's networks to empower themselves to negotiate with men are certainly common phenomena across the contemporary world (Mountjoy 2008; Scharff 2003). The Hmong network leaders actively organize around the idea of bringing women together. To make it feasible, they planned to organize a national seminar every two years. The first two gatherings took place in Chiang Mai (2004 and 2006), and subsequent seminars occurred in Phetchabun (2008) and Tak (2010). The number of participants increased from 50 in 2004 to 850 in 2010.

According to one female leader, the main reason for the significant increase in attendance is that Hmong women see such events as a brief escape from family and societal pressures. The three days allow them to be away from daily life activities, meet women from various villages, learn about other women's experiences, share their own views, and have fun together. At the end of each event, the safe space makes it comfortable for some women to cry not only with sadness because they are returning to their daily lives but also from the joy of having been empowered to take action that may bring about social change. While the socializing aspects of the meetings are important, participants cite the brainstorming sessions on strategies for negotiating with male leaders to be the most useful. Participants also leave with many new ideas and stories to share with their friends in their villages. Khou Chang, a housewife from Tak province, articulated at the end of the 2010 meeting:

This is my first time to get a chance to attend and meet many
Hmong women who face similar problems in our lives. The three
days we have been together here are both fruitful and they give
me a sense of relief and time away from family and community
responsibilities. I will certainly share my great experience here
with other friends who didn't get the opportunity to be here. If it
is possible, I would like our key leaders to organize the meeting
annually and rotate to different provinces so local Hmong women
can attend.

When asked if she felt confident using the new ideas she learned from the
meeting at home and in her village, she replied that what she learned would
be helpful in her interactions with others in the village. She further explained, "In terms of negotiating power with my husband and other Hmong
men in the larger village, it is still a long way to go. We need to educate our
people more, both men and women, to promote gender equality."

To Hmong women leaders, gender equality entails equal treatment and
respect in their families with regard to daily activities, support from parents for education, protection in ritual performance and traditions, and
equal access to inheritance of parents' assets (Mee 2011). Hmong women
who participate in the seminars realize that achieving gender equality in
Hmong society is a long-term process, and they understand that cultural
change does not happen overnight.

A fundamental part of the network's strategies is to educate Hmong
women about their basic rights. Committee members have organized
small workshops in different locations to provide information about the
international declaration on basic human rights for women and children.
The workshops also include an analysis of cultural and gender power in
Hmong society, and address dynamics at the local village level. Some of
these workshops are used to prepare local women to attend the national
conference. As Mee Thao explained,

Although it is impossible to reach all villages and Hmong women,
it is better than doing nothing. We have to nurture and empower
them for understanding their basic rights, so they would be stronger
in the future. They need to be empowered and well-prepared
before taking their individual and local issues to be shared with
women from other villages.

One sample workshop was held in urban Chiang Mai for twenty-three participants in 2011. Attendees included single and divorced women. Trainers consisted of both Hmong and non-Hmong experts on human rights. Contents included concepts and practices of human and women's rights at the international, national, and Hmong ethnic group levels. In small groups, participants discussed problems they faced and identified possible solutions. Action steps were developed by the end of the workshop to guide participants.

Collectively, leaders of the network created a list of demands and developed a petition to present to Hmong lineage leaders, which they distributed during a 2005 Hmong leaders meeting in Chiang Rai province (Network of Hmong Women 2005). The petition outlined the following seven points:[15]

1. The *lwm qaib* ritual's purpose is to welcome a woman as a new member of her husband's lineage at the door of his parents' house. In cases where she has to return to her parents due to divorce or the death of her husband, we ask for parents to perform the *lwm qaib* ritual to welcome her back to her natal lineage.

2. If a woman becomes pregnant out of wedlock, she must have the right to give birth inside her parents' house. The child's father must pay child support until the child reaches age 20, according to Thai law.

3. A divorced woman or widow who does not want to remarry or return to her natal lineage must be protected by members of her husband's lineage.

4. Parents should support daughters to pursue education at the same level as sons or further because a daughter leaves her parents to get married. Her future is at risk, so education ensures that she can survive when facing problems.

5. The bride price should be changed to "marriage money" for the new couple to start their life together. If it is defined as a bride price, it treats women as objects to be purchased. This sends her husband and his family the message that since they paid for her they are authorized to control instead of honor her. She should not be treated as "a wife under his feet."

6. Child rearing should not give priority to boys over girls. Both boys and girls should be raised as equal human beings.

7. Opportunity should be given for women to go out and learn from outsiders so they can come back with knowledge and experience to support a family.

In addition to these primary demands, the petition provides detailed explanations to support each point. They articulate Hmong cultural practices, such as guidelines for house structure and materials, the design and color of Hmong dress, language in daily life, placenta disposal, and daughters who are better caregivers of aging parents than sons.[16] The Hmong leaders who attended the 2005 conference acknowledged the petition. Some lineage leaders accepted the terms of the petition, while others were reluctant to take any action. Network leaders have had to continue to raise these issues to Hmong leaders at various meetings. To date, the first three points concerning divorced women and unwed mothers have not been practiced in any Hmong village. Some changes to the remaining issues are gradually taking place. Both girls and boys receive support to attend school, which has begun to equalize opportunities to work in the public and private sectors. In particular, Hmong women are involved in selling arts and crafts at tourist sites and local markets more frequently than are men. This has translated into increased power for women to express their viewpoints within families and negotiate their belonging in the public spaces. Interestingly, the most visible changes have been in the areas of education and economics within and beyond Hmong villages. These changes show how women's empowerment improves the status of their families. Issues related to divorced and unwed mothers have been more difficult to achieve because they require changes to preexisting social practices where male domination is intact. To alter them would require men to give up power, and at this time, it appears to be an uphill battle.

The lack of progress in some areas, however, has not discouraged the network leaders from continuing to build their own capacity. In late 2012, they began conducting participatory action research. Led by Mee Thao and Joom Xiong, a small group attended a workshop on women's health promotion in Bangkok. They developed a proposal on strategies to empower Hmong women and submitted it to the Thailand Research Fund, which approved it in early 2013. The project was implemented in Mae Sa Mai, a Hmong village close to Chiang Mai city, from February to July 2013. The research team included fifteen members representing local Hmong lineage leaders, elder widows, network participants, and university researchers. Local Hmong researchers conducted focus group discussions with male lineage leaders and divorced and senior women. They identified twenty-one problems that Hmong women in their community faced. One of the most urgent issues was the lack of spiritual belonging for divorced women, highlighted by the Hmong women's stories discussed earlier in the chapter. Hmong women's fight to be able to return to their parents' spiritual households is important because ancestral worship is patrilineal. As women, they are not allowed to establish their own spiritual households.

Following the conclusion of the research activities, the team organized three meetings with Hmong lineage leaders and official leaders in the village. The team reiterated the need for ritual performers to conduct a ritual to reunite a divorced woman with her natal family's household spirits. The leaders understood the problems faced by divorced Hmong women, but they were reluctant to take action due to the long-standing fear of negative consequences associated with divorced women. A breakthrough came in early October 2013, when seven key ritual performers in Mae Sa Mai village were invited to meet with the research team. The ritual performers explained that it was possible to perform a ritual to reunite a divorced daughter with her natal family. They pointed out that at the end of the divorce negotiation, the ritual performer already officially and symbolically handed the divorced daughter to her parents and thus affirmed (*phum*) her reunification with her parents' household spirits. The challenge, they argued, is that Hmong parents normally do not pay attention to such procedures and actively invite their divorced daughters to attend household rituals. It had always been culturally possible for a divorced woman to rejoin her family's household spirits, but long-lasting practices to segregate them from their natal family, compounded with the stigma of divorce, prevented parents from following through with a ritual to welcome back their divorced daughters. After listening to ritual performers' clarification at this meeting, male leaders of three families agreed to ask village ritual performers to perform the *phum* ritual the following week. The religious backgrounds of those three families include Hmong animist beliefs, Buddhism, and Christianity.

This ritual represented a fundamental shift in the way divorced women are perceived. In addition to family members, participants included four invited ritual performers, members of the research team, forty representatives of Hmong ritual performers, and network board members from other Thai provinces. Outside scholars and staff from funding agencies also attended. For the family who practiced Hmong animist beliefs, the ritual began with a soul-calling ceremony. After the required food items had been placed on the main ritual table, the four ritual performers stated that they were bringing the divorced daughter back to her parents. Tying strings around her wrists, they affirmed that "from now on she is allowed to attend any ritual ceremony performed by the family." They also blessed her and the family. The guests were also invited to tie strings and offer blessings. At this moment, the daughter and parents shed tears of happiness as they hugged one another, an unusual physical gesture in Hmong culture.

In the afternoon following the ritual, participants gathered in the village meeting hall to share their views. A few women from other Hmong villages spoke and cried. One stated, "Today is a historical day for the Hmong women in Thailand on reuniting divorced daughter with parents' family. We, the Hmong women's rights, had been ignored for generations. I expect to see the extension of these three families to Hmong in the whole country and also around the world" (Paiv Thao 2013). Two male ritual leaders, one from Nan Province and one from Tak Province, indicated that they planned to perform the *phum* ritual for their divorced daughters during the Hmong New Year at the end of December 2013. Following the successful event in Mae Sa Mai village of Chiang Mai Province, members of the research team were invited to present their research experiences and the ritual ceremony at a national Hmong leaders' annual meeting in Nan Province in early November. Other local Hmong networks also invited them to share their work. Most importantly, Hmong women's groups from Laos and the United States visited the village in January 2014 to learn from the research team. Mee summed up the experiences:

> We have already come to a right direction. Researchers who are mostly villagers and lineage ritual performers clearly understand what is the root cause of the problem and then cooperated to bring about change. The accomplishment of our participant action research is a great transition of Hmong belief and practice which will provide a cultural space and equal rights for Hmong women. It's not only the issue of divorced Hmong women but also other women's issues that we encounter so we have to continue to advocate more.

Mee acknowledges this important stride, but she is also quick to point out that much work remains to be done to achieve meaningful gender equality within Hmong society.

Conclusion

This chapter has examined Hmong patriarchal ideologies and practices, divorced Hmong women's coping strategies, and the Network of Hmong Women in Thailand's negotiation for cultural space within Hmong society in contemporary Thailand. Observations and ethnographic fieldwork reveal that divorced Hmong women have established their own strategies to cope with community pressures. Young Hmong women who have access to formal education have played a crucial role in leading a grassroots movement to put pressure on male leaders to change patrilineal practices that have been detrimental to divorcées regardless of the reason for ending a marriage.

The network's efforts have made a dent in patriarchal Hmong culture, but perhaps what is more important for researchers and community advocates is the need to carefully examine loopholes within patriarchal cultures to bring about change. For nearly a decade, divorced women and progressive young Hmong women and men called for change in ritual performances to welcome divorced women back to their natal family only to find out that the divorce negotiation process already included measures to support such ritual. Clearly, without their voices and the circulation of their petitions to Hmong male leaders and people and agencies outside Thai Hmong society, this success may not have occurred. The network has expanded its impact to reach more young Hmong women and men, in addition to Hmong women's networks in other countries, and networks of other ethnic minority women in Thailand. What was a small group of fifty women in 2004 has transformed to a movement that has caught the attention of international organizations and conventions concerning women's rights. The Convention on the Elimination of All Forms of Discrimination Against Women, which was adopted by the UN General Assembly in 1979, has been translated and publicized in Thai and ethnic languages, including Hmong. Leaders of the network often refer to the convention when dealing with Hmong women and men who are leaders in local communities. There is, thus, a greater awareness of women's rights and opportunities beyond Hmong villages that has begun to take shape around the way that divorced Hmong women see themselves and how others perceive their situations. While it will take time to gain greater power within Hmong social structure, the heavy burden on the shoulders of divorced Hmong women has been somewhat lifted. Hmong women in Thailand no longer struggle alone to negotiate cultural space.

Notes

1. I have observed the development of this network since its inception. Observations have taken place during various meetings and workshops since he was invited to participate as an adviser. From June to December 2012 and February to July 2013, he interviewed women participants and key informants. He has observed many wedding and funeral ceremonies as a result of growing up in a Hmong village and years of working with Hmong in other villages.

2. I acknowledge that Hmong wedding ceremonies in Asia and in the diaspora have incorporated practices from the different contexts, but our collective experiences suggest that expectations, restrictions, and the stigma attached to divorced Hmong women transcends all national borders. I thank Drs. Chia Youyee Vang and Ma Vang for helping to edit this chapter.

3. For more detailed Hmong wedding processes, see Yaj (1980).

4. Translation from Hmong to English by author.

5. Observation of Tua and Pang's wedding ceremony in the Highland village of Chiang Mai Province, January 2010.

6. It should be noted that *pe* is performed three times: when the bride first enters the groom's parents' house, at the bride's parents' house where the wedding ceremony takes place, and at the groom's parents' house after coming back from the wedding ceremony.

7. Interview with Bla Thao Xiong in Mae Sa Mai Hmong village of Chiang Mai Province, and Pa Cheng Lee in Paklang village of Nan Province.

8. Thai government and international agencies did not pay attention to Hmong and other highland ethnic minorities until the late 1950s. Modernizing initiatives included setting up resettlement sites and bringing socioeconomic development programs to mountain villages. Part of the efforts included "Thai-ization," an effort to assimilate them into Thai culture. Long-term consequences for the ethnic Hmong included a weakening of kinship structure and exposure to issues of gender equality.

9. Interview with Lou Xiong (pseudonym), a Hmong lineage leader in a mountain village of Chiang Mai Province, April 2012. According to Lou Xiong, during the last two decades, only around one out of ten couples divorced (10%); however, today that number has increased to about three or four out of every ten couples (30%–40%).

10. Marriage within one clan is a taboo in Hmong society. Even after a woman's husband dies or she is divorced, no man of her natal clan can marry her. She is still considered a sister or daughter of any man in her natal clan.

11. All names of the interviewees in this article are pseudonyms.

12. It should be noted that today the Thai government provides free health care and a small subsidy for anyone over the age of sixty.

13. This is a normal tradition in Hmong society. After they grow up and get married, sons have to take in wives and inherit their father's lineage, while daughters leave and become members of their husband's household and lineage.

14. If a divorcée becomes a minor wife, she may reside in the same house with her husband and his first wife, but she will always have a lower social status within the family. If the first wife moves out to join a married son and his new family, the second wife may live with the husband in the same house and may exercise more household power.

15. Translated from Thai by Prasit Leepreecha.

16. In Hmong tradition, when women still gave birth at home, the placenta of a baby boy was buried at the central pole (*ncej tas*) of the house, while a baby girl's placenta was buried under her parents' bedroom. The central pole symbolizes the household spirit, which the boy will inherit when he grows up, while the bedroom represents fruitful fertility, where the girl will give birth to many children when she grows up. Today, however, most Hmong women give birth in a hospital, where the placenta is disposed of as medical waste.

Works Cited

Binney, G. A. 1968. *Social Structure and Shifting Agriculture of the White Meo*. Final Technical Report to Wildlife Management Institute, Washington, D.C.

Bourdieu, Pierre. 1990. *The Logic of Practice*. Translated by Richard Nice. Stanford, Calif.: Stanford University Press.

Chang, Kong [pseud.]. 2010. Interview with Prasit Leepreecha in Tak Province in April.

Cooper, Robert G. 1978. "Unity and Division in Hmong Social Categories in Thailand." In *Studies in ASEAN Sociology: Urban Society and Social Change*, edited by Peter S. J. Chen and Hans-Dieter Evers, 297–320. Singapore: Chopmen Enterprises.

———. 1984. *Resource Scarcity and the Hmong Response: A Study of Settlement and Economy in Northern Thailand*. Singapore: Singapore University Press.

della Porta, Donatella, and Mario Diani. 1999. *Social Movements*. Oxford and Cambridge, Mass.: Blackwell.

Diani, Mario. 1992. "The Concept of Social Movement." *Sociological Review* 40:1–25.

Donnelly, Nancy D. 1994. *Changing Lives of Refugee Hmong Women.* Seattle and London: University of Washington Press.

Durkheim, Emile. 1995. *The Elementary Forms of Religious Life.* New York: Free Press.

Edgar, Andrew. 2002. "Bourdieu, Pierre." In *Cultural Theory: The Key Thinkers,* edited by Andrew Edgar and Peter Sedgwick, 30–32. London and New York: Routledge.

Geddes, W. R. 1976. *Migrants of the Mountains: The Cultural Ecology of the Blue Miao of Thailand.* Oxford: Clarendon Press.

Hayami, Yoko, Junko Koizumi, Chalidaporn Songsamphan, and Ratana Tosakul, eds. 2012. *The Family in Flux in Southeast Asia: Institution, Ideology, Practice.* Kyoto, Japan: Kyoto University Press.

Kong, Hlee [pseud.]. 2012. Interview with Prasit Leepreecha in Chiang Mai Province in June.

Lee, Gary Yia. 1986. "White Hmong Kinship Terminology and Structure." In *The Hmong World 1,* edited by Brenda Johns and David Strecker, 12–32. New Haven, Conn.: Yale Southeast Asia Studies.

———. 1988. "Household and Marriage in a Thai Highland Society." *Journal of the Siam Society* 76:162–73.

Lee, Pa Cheng. 2012. Interview with Prasit Leepreecha in Paklang village, Nan Province, in October.

Leepreecha, Prasit. 2001. "Kinship and Identity among Hmong in Thailand." PhD diss., University of Washington.

Manndorff, Hans. 1967. "The Hill Tribe Program of the Public Welfare Department, Ministry of Interior, Thailand: Research and Socio-Economic Development." In *Southeast Asian Tribes, Minorities, and Nations,* vol. 2, edited by Peter Kunstadter. Princeton, N.J.: Princeton University Press.

McCaskill, Don, and Ken Kampe, eds. 1997. *Development or Domestication? Indigenous Peoples of Southeast Asia.* Chiang Mai, Thailand: Silkworm Books.

Moua, Shoua [pseud.]. 2012. Interview with Prasit Leepreecha in Chiang Mai Province in July.

Mountjoy, Shane. 2008. *The Women's Rights Movement: Moving Toward Equality.* New York: Chelsea House Publishers.

Network of Hmong Women. 2005. Letter of petition to Hmong leaders (in Thai).

Scharff, Virginia. 2003. *Twenty Thousand Roads: Women, Movement, and the West.* Berkeley: University of California Press.

Scott, James C. 1985. *Weapons of the Weak: Everyday Forms of Peasant Resistance.* New Haven and London: Yale University Press.

———. 1990. *Domination and the Arts of Resistance: Hidden Scripts.* New Haven and London: Yale University Press.

———. 2010. *The Art of Not Being Governed: An Anarchist History of Upland Southeast Asia.* New Haven and London: Yale University Press.

Songsamphan, Chalidaporn. 2012. "Private Family, Public Contestation." In *The Family in Flux in Southeast Asia: Institution, Ideology, Practice,* edited by Yoko Hayami, Junko Koizumi, Chalidaporn Songsamphan, and Ratana Tosakul. Kyoto, Japan: Kyoto University Press.

Symonds, Patricia V. 2005. *Calling in the Soul: Gender and the Cycle of Life in a Hmong Village.* Seattle: University of Washington Press.

Teerawithitchainan, Bussarawan. 2004. "Modernization and Divorce in Thailand: 1940s to 1970s." *Journal of Population and Social Studies* 13, no. 1.

Thao, Mee. 2011. Interview with Prasit Leepreecha in October.

———. 2013. Interview with Prasit Leepreecha in July.

Thao, Paiv [pseud]. 2013. Interview with Prasit Leepreecha in Petchabun Province in October.

Van Gennep, Arnold. 2004. *The Rites of Passage.* London: Routledge. First published in 1960.

Wanat Bhruksasri. 1989. "Government Policy: Highland Ethnic Minorities." In *Hill Tribes Today,* edited by John McKinnon and Bernard Vienne. Bangkok: White Lotus-Orstom.

Xiong, Bla Thao. 2012. Interview with Prasit Leepreecha in Mae Sa Mai village, Chiang Mai Province, in September.

Yaj, Vam Thai Txooj Txhim. 1980. *KabTshoobKev Kos: Liaj Lwg Tus Cag Txuj, Rhwv Mus Tus Cag Peev.* Javouhey, Mana, Guyane Francaise: Association Patrimonie Culturel Hmong et Associaltion Communaute Hmong.

Yang, Pang [pseud.]. 2012. Interview with Prasit Leepreecha in Chiang Mai Province on June 2.

· III ·

Art and Media

CHAPTER 7

Hmong Women on the Web

Transforming Power through Social Networking

Faith Nibbs

A RECENT QUARTERLY REPORT from Facebook[1] estimated that 97 percent of all two-way telecommunication in the world is now coming through the Internet (Ferguson 2011), and as of September 2013, active Facebook users amounted to upwards of 1.49 billion people (Company Info/Facebook 2015). Bruce Overby (1996), in his study of social identity in online environments, describes cyberspace as "a vast territory" and a "space of representations." He adds that while people have operated in "representational spaces" for a long time, it is the "ease and flexibility" of travel in this environment that has enticed many individuals to its frontier. In fact, a recent Pew Research Center study found that 88 percent of all people living in America now say that the Internet plays a significant role in their everyday lives.[2] Scholars who work on issues of migration are, thus, taking an interest in the role of virtual space in sustaining and creating identity and, more recently, exploring its use and effects in refugee populations. More recent is the use of social networking in the United States, an activity that is only ten years old and thus research is just starting to emerge on how immigrant groups use this platform and what gratifications they get from it. This chapter examines some of the ways that young Hmong women in the 1.5 and second generation use Internet social networking to open up debates about their social position within society.

Internet use has been noted to play, among other things, a psychologically empowering role in people's lives. For example, scholars have lauded the democratizing and enabling forms of communication it offers users, arguing that its nonhierarchical structure allows a form of horizontal communication between people who might not otherwise communicate (Herring et al. 2004). Equally important are the views of the deterritorialized nature of online spaces, where scholars have noted the way that the Internet erodes the "ordinary ethological territories—body, clan, village, cult, [and] corporation"—that normally "fix" people to a precise point on the earth (Guattari 1992, 123; see also Ponzanesi and Leurs 2014). On the one hand, this form of deterritorialization has been demonstrated to empower marginalized users, making it easier to share information across group members (Kiesler and McGuire 1984). On the other hand, feminist scholars have critiqued the ubiquity of these claims, arguing that engendered forms of hierarchical communication and power do not necessarily disappear online, and suggesting that online interaction is fundamentally grounded in the realities of identities, relations, and cultural contexts experienced offline (see Lea and Spears 1992; Keyes 2006). Thus, one interest of migration scholars is in exploring how refugee women might use cyberspace to create better environments for themselves that foster more equitable relations and free them from complexly bound social inequalities in their offline lives (Balka 1986).

While there has been research on how immigrant groups in general are finding agency in the use of this technology,[3] very little exploration has been done on what gratifications female users from this group are getting out of participating in cyberspace, how they negotiate the gendered forms of cultural politics in virtual spaces, or what specific empowerment experiences they might be enjoying due to web access. The purpose of this chapter is to address these questions through a case study of Hmong women on the web, specifically in their use of horizontal communication—or, as it is more commonly called, social networking communication. How are Hmong women in America engaged in these processes through the use of social networking? To what extent does this kind of communication satisfy their needs for recognition, cognition, and socialization, or complicate the internal politics of culture, subjectivity, and gender roles? These are the questions that guided this study. This chapter highlights ways in which these practices are being used by Hmong women to generate a group context that has the potential to directly impact individual and collective empowerment and argues that it is vital to consider new technologies—and social networking in particular—when contemplating the strategies that young refugee women and their next generation use in order to open up debates about gender roles and engage in the cultural politics of gender representation.

In a study on how the global Hmong diaspora is using the Internet, male scholars found a "particularly active Hmong voice" online (Tapp 2010, 221).

This study suggested that one use of the Internet by some older Hmong leaders was as a space for turning their statelessness into a "virtual nation." This sentiment is echoed by Dr. Pao Saykao,[4] who has stated a personal goal of achieving "a caring Hmong culture that uses Internet communication to achieve its goals" (Allen, Matthew, and Boland 2004, 305). Such research and statements misleadingly suggest that Internet spaces for and by Hmong users are monolithic and male in nature and aim to achieve the same goals negating possible oppositional positions by marginalized persons within the group, such as women, the LGBT community, and youth. Such statements may be intended to counter perceptions of social networking as "frivolous or problematic" because of their association with youth and femininity (Harris 2013; see also Gregg 2006). This attempt to substantiate the use of this technology was personified in a recent study by Hmong men claiming that they found no representation of "explicit woman's voices" among the many Hmong vocalists on the web (Tapp 2010, 220). Yet as this book has argued, Hmong women have participated as active agents in their lives for centuries, and arguably today, in more agentic ways than possibly ever before. This would include having an active presence in many forms of public voice, including cyberspace. Indeed, a refined Google search using the keywords "Hmong Woman" conjures no less than nineteen thousand hits, ranging in topic from religion to dating and linking to blogs, YouTube postings, and old MySpace and new Facebook accounts. Particularly noteworthy among them are the number of horizontal communication sites occurring among Hmong women. A full 81 percent of those hits are currently dedicated to fostering free expression in Hmong women while formulating relations and virtual communities with other female Hmong users. It is within these spaces that we find new forms of the age-old prominent female Hmong voice.

The concept of "voice" features heavily in literary criticism and theory, and is frequently used in feminist anthropology. Foucault (1980) helps us recognize that voice entails the most "striking public revelations and private confirmations of our interior lives" (Giulianotti 2005). It stems from our subjective dispositions. It is the media through which forms of selfhood are both communicated and contested. Richard Giulianotti (2005, 341) theorized that voice is situated in the cultural political identities of gender, class, and national identity, and challenges anthropologists to explore the role of voice in constructing relations of power. Feminist anthropology, in particular, has drawn our attention to the diversity of women's experiences coming into voice and with issues of power and authority that accompany using it (Bernard and Spere 2012, 285; Keyes 2006; Herring et al. 2004). Caroline Brettell (2009) suggests that one way to understand voice and agency in immigrant women is to engage in the literature they write, suggesting that their books allow them to "speak for themselves, in their own voice, in a different voice, in a positioned voice" (69). Hmong women have historically claimed input from their unique understandings of culture and gender through poetry; embroidered story cloths called *paj ntaub;* and, in the United States, through new outlets in newspaper journalism, academic writing, and—most recently at the forefront of the Hmong literary arts—autoethnographic memoirs like Kao Kalia's award-winning *The Latehomecomer.* In her work about black female rap musicians, Cheryl Keyes (2006) posits that the movement they create as cultural producers and consumers becomes an "interpretive community utiliz[ing] representations of black women that they deem valuable in productive and politically useful ways" (22). By extension, a similar "interpretive community" is being created by Hmong women out of their art, poetry, journalism, and other writing for public consumption.

We have long understood the connection between autobiographical writing and empowerment (Benmayor 1991). Advances in technology urge us to consider that immigrant women and their children today have different, more accessible publishing outlets than their predecessors. With just one click of a mouse, the uncensored narratives of newcomers can be published over the World Wide Web. Ananda Mitra (2001) was the first to connect the process of expressing oneself in cyberspace through the metaphor of "voice," suggesting that it "is not unlike having a place at the table and utilizing that place to be heard and acknowledged" (31). Her examination of Internet dialogue reveals how technology aided marginalized immigrants in being heard by the dominant society. Scholars have since explored the gendered politics of migrant women's Internet use in ethnoracial identity construction (Parker and Song 2006; Ponzanesi and Blaagaard 2011; Nibbs 2015), in political activism (Van Zoonen, Vis, and Mihelj 2010), in user marginalization (Herring et al. 2004), and as a vehicle for border crossings (Diminescu 2008; Ponzanesi and Leurs 2014). In these studies, the Internet provides space for various testimonial speech acts that help foster a sense of a collective and validating framework for participants to tell their stories, thus linking Internet testimony to empowerment.

Early on in evaluating Hmong Internet spaces of testimony, it became clear that they were predominantly filled with voices from the 1.5- or second-generation children of Hmong immigrants. This finding follows national social networking trends, which suggest that the largest group of U.S. Facebook users by age are those between the ages of 25 and 34, followed by users in the 18–24 range. Moreover, 54 percent of users are female, and 46 percent are male (Pew Research Center 2013). This trend is reflected in more recent studies on how refugee women are expressing their voices on the Internet. Recent work on second-generation Moroccan Dutch girls (Brouwer 2006; Leurs, Midden, and Ponzanesi 2012), for example, demonstrates how they are turning to online discussion boards to express their voices in the Netherlands. This body of work has posited that "online minority voices—muted elsewhere—may foster a wider recognition of difference, which, subsequently, may invite majority members of Dutch society to begin unlearning dominant discourses" (Leurs, Midden, and Ponzanesi 2012, 172). This chapter on Hmong women will also focus on that "wired" second-generation refugee demographic, but it departs from Leurs and colleagues' work in its examination of how Hmong women feel that Internet social networking enables them to challenge the gender power relations *within* their refugee community while simultaneously complicating their myriad social positions in the host society.

Design and Method

For the purposes of this chapter, I use Boyd and Ellison's (2007) definition of social networking sites as "web-based services that allow individuals to (1) construct a public or semi-public profile within a bounded system, (2) articulate a list of other users with whom they share a connection, and (3) view and traverse their list of connections and those made by others within the system" (211). The data used in this analysis included observations conducted online over the course of six months; semistructured interviews in conjunction with a different study; and offline participant observation.

A sample of social networking web activity was drawn from a combination of existing female Hmong networks and by using a Google search for "Hmong Woman" in English and Hmong (*poj niam Hmoob*). From the list of sites netted from those searches, specific domains of Internet use were selected for evaluation that were Hmong women–centric *and* that satisfied the criteria of Boyd and Ellison's (2007) definition of social networking—namely Facebook, YouTube, WordPress blogs, Twitter, discussion forums, and websites that contained blogs geared toward communicating with a female readership. The sites analyzed as part of this study had to have activity within the previous twelve months and be constructed and maintained by Hmong American women who self-identified from the United States within the target age demographic. Seventy percent of the postings evaluated were written in English, and 20 percent were written in Hmong. Two second-generation Hmong American research assistants assisted in gathering and interpreting the material.[5]

As a result of this sampling criterion, my research assistants and I selected and monitored eleven Hmong women–centric association websites and interviewed eleven women who self-identified as engaging in those blogs. Additionally, we observed ten blog sites and forums that were not affiliated with a particular association but that identified as catering specifically to Hmong women. From those users, we interviewed five women. We also monitored twenty-five Hmong women's Facebook accounts and interviewed twenty women from this group. And finally, we examined two YouTube posts by Hmong women with a series of blog comments, and interviewed both originators of those posts. The total data for this study, therefore, are made up of monitoring 48 websites, 260 individual postings, and 38 structured interviews. We conducted interviews using a combination of mediums, including email, telephone, and face-to-face conversations. Participants were recruited by sending email requests for interviews on the basis of their web content, or by directly soliciting members of my, and my two Hmong research assistants', personal network, or by directly engaging women at a Hmong women's conference. There were an additional five men, whose comments on discussion threads with Hmong women merited further investigation.

One limitation in doing this emerging form of ethnography is that it is difficult to know (in the nonvirtual sense) whom you are talking to and thus to properly contextualize the various social interactions that become part of these people's online identities. To compensate for that, I simultaneously engaged in conventional face-to-face ethnographic fieldwork while conducting fieldwork online. This approach is informed by Wilson and Peterson's (2002) position that virtual ethnography cannot be done apart from traditional ethnographic methods, as the virtual is merely a "continuum of communities, identities, and networks that exist in the real" (457). There were also ethical concerns associated with this virtual research that were more difficult to maneuver than they typically are in the real—mainly that my presence and purpose were not fully open to every user of the site.

I made every attempt to let the owners of these websites know who we were and our intentions, and obtained written consent to use any material from their blogs. Despite those efforts, it was still impossible for me to know if all the users on those sites shared in the knowledge of my "observation" of their conversations. As I highlight themes and content from individual posts, I have tried to safeguard each participant's confidentiality by removing all names and pseudonyms. As technology advances faster than our methods, there is a caution to those doing this kind of research to find ways to make your online research as open and honest to as many secondary participants as possible.

Saving Face, Knowing Place

We know that Internet users, whether Hmong or not, draw on their own cultural understandings when engaging others over the web. Tim North (1994), in seeking to understand Net subcultures, points out that we need to consider the offline communication and behavior of a group when asking questions about how members of that group relate in cybersociety. From this perspective, we understand that not only will users bring their individual cultural understandings to the Net, but they will be dealing with myriad cultural representations brought by other users. Similarly, Mrinalini Sinha (1996) in her work on middle-class Indians, advocates for a more critical grasp of the ways women "come into voice" and the particular voices they assume. Such an approach, she maintains, should "take into account both the historical context which made possible the identity of the woman and the particular strategies by which they learned to speak in the voice" (479). To properly contextualize how Hmong women are using their digital voice, I first make clear that in talking about Hmong culture, I am not assuming some unitary Hmong American position in which young second-generation women share a homogeneous set of culturally constituted ideas of gender. What I refer to as *culture* is the complex "bricolage" Sherry Ortner (1995) suggests are "the pieces of reality, however much borrowed from or imposed by others . . . woven together through the logic of a group's own locally and historically evolved" position (176). I consider here some of those positions inhabited by Hmong American second-generation women, and how the different agendas born out of those positions are enabled through social networking, and to what effect.

For anyone, verbal activity is a vast and highly structured system of human engagement. Eckert and McConnell-Ginet (2013) call it a "project of meaning-making," and suggest that the "extent to which an individual or group or category of individuals actually contributes to meaning depends on their ability to get their contributions heard and attended to" (88). For a Hmong in America, the fate of a speaker's contribution is at issue even before it is uttered, as demonstrated in the popular Hmong saying, "Before you offer your opinion, you must first know your place."[6] Eckert and McConnell-Ginet offer that "the right to speak depends on the right to be in the situation and the right to engage in particular kinds of speech activities in that situation" (88). General understandings of the rules of social engagement in the Hmong American community have historically been explained through exotic practices of clan-centered patriarchy, but we now understand them as the accumulation of more complex forces imposed on all women. In cultures in which women do not speak in public places, for example, their ideas have trouble getting on the table. These gendered rules of engagement get institutionalized through a long process of limiting recourses and information gained in informal situations, and normalized through cultural practices. For the Hmong, this normalizing practice relies heavily on the adherence to the concept of "face."

Goffman (1955) defines face as the "positive social value a person effectively claims for himself by the line others assume he has taken during a particular contact" (213). In an examination of how face is understood in Asian cultures, Ho (1976) likened it to the Chinese concept of *lien*, which represents "the confidence of society in the integrity of ego's moral character, the loss of which makes it impossible for him to function properly within the community" (867). By extension, face is lost in the Hmong community when confidence in the expected moral character of a member is diminished. Because gender is a principal factor organizing social life, these cultural boundaries are enmeshed within Hmong ideologies surrounding gender roles and women's place in Hmong society and are exacerbated by new messages of gender roles and structures that undermine women through media and institutions in American society. Therefore, what is *approved* moral character is gendered, varies from community to community, may change over time, and can only be measured by "the extent to which a particular person's social functioning is adversely affected" (Ho 1976, 872).

The repercussions of losing face can be so demoralizing that face-protecting maneuvers are practiced in public at all times by Asian groups that uphold this worldview. Yen Espiritu (2001), for example, notes how this responsibility disproportionately falls on women, suggesting that Filipino American girls must carry the reputations of themselves and their families. Nancy Donnelly (1997) notes a similar pattern in Hmong American women whose behavior weighs heavily on the reputation of the extended clan. In an effort to protect these reputations, many young girls are encouraged by their families to pursue practices and ideals that have historically accorded them a subordinate status, and seek to cultivate virtues that maintain specific hierarchical rules of engagement. As one Hmong second-generation research participant put it:

> Knowing your place in the Hmong community requires insider knowledge of what issues are considered taboo, which side of a controversial argument to align with, where one stands in the social hierarchy, and when and where to speak.

One effect of these practices has been that Hmong women have not been seen as either leaders or experts of cultural knowledge, diminishing their voices in the public sphere. Women have, nonetheless, used various idioms to assert their presence in public, such as through poetry and song. However, cultural norms practiced in Laos usually limited these forms of expression to those who were competent in the arts and restricted them to New Years and a few other acceptable times of the year. These communicative rules of engagement disproportionately circumscribed women's voices over those of men. One informant expressed his observations of how these norms can play out in contemporary practice:

> In my own experience with women at public gatherings, whether social or formal, they have refrained from talking too much, in too much detail, or at all about any potentially controversial topics. Furthermore, they measure all their responses by the crowd; the more Hmong people present, the less opinionated they will be with their comments, and the older the crowd, the less likely they will engage in anything more than formal pleasantries.

This form of self-monitored behavior follows Weber's (1946) assertion that status, or quality of social honor, directly influences social class, and that maintaining social honor within a group requires the maintenance of a specific style of life and the rejection of others (405). Examples of the ways that Hmong women self-monitor their voice are numerous. A Hmong woman usually would not openly discuss internal family issues between herself and her spouse with other people, nor would she even suggest that there are such problems. In public, a Hmong woman is discouraged from stating that a Hmong man is wrong, especially about their culture. She is also reluctant to give public speeches—not because she can't but because words of inspiration are traditionally sought from Hmong men. She is reluctant to talk openly about Hmong cultural traditions, especially religion, because women have generally not been seen as experts in these domains. A Hmong woman is also unlikely to offer unsolicited advice to people she does not know, and typically doesn't discuss relationships with strangers. Practicing these face maneuvers has left many of the women I spoke with feeling limited in the way they can articulate a position for themselves in the public sphere, especially if they aren't skilled in more acceptable outlets of poetry, song, or *paj ntaub*.

This form of face maintenance is not unlike typical conversational practices of other cultures in which people enter into situations with power and status differences. James and Drakich (Berger et al. 1977) looked at U.S. interaction in terms of people's relative social status and found that it affected not only the more powerful peoples' tendency to talk but the less powerful people's tendency to let them. The gendering of conversation topics also affected who was thought to be more expert and, as Eskilson and Wiley (1976) found, greatly affected which gender dominated a given conversation. Even in U.S. conversations where there was a neutrality of expertise, new information offered up by male participants was far more likely to be taken into consideration than new information offered by female participants (Eckert and McConnell-Ginet 2013, 103). As face-to-face communicative conventions speak both to the gendering of topics and to cultured patterns of response, we might expect to find examples of Hmong women's empowerment in attempts to broaden either of these domains. I found both. The Internet and its ubiquitous nature among those under the age of thirty-five posed a new deterritorialized public space where domains of expertise and social regulations were not always clear. Assessing how young Hmong women are engaging the uncertainties of these spaces to articulate points of opposition to male authority provides insight into the universality of the desire to be free from relations of subordination in society.

Hmong Women and Social Networking

The women in this study used social networking sites to engage myriad audiences over a variety of topics. Those who communicated to a small group of known acquaintances used YouTube, and had discussions that ranged from trivial banter ("I just microwaved some popcorn") to more substantive discussion about travel, beauty and skin care, health, homework, schedule plans, family news, and venting about people who hurt them. Hmong women who wanted to engage a broader audience of both male and female loose acquaintances or anybody who would listen used more open formats, such as loosely restricted Facebook accounts with multi-hundred-strong "friend" lists, YouTube, Twitter, Hmoob.com, and Word-Press. On these sites, women were able to get their ideas into the Hmong discourse more readily by taking advantage of the unregulated social spaces to talk with a mixed audience of Hmong and non-Hmong, male and female, about a broad range of issues—from religion, dieting, and philosophy of life, to their struggles with prescribed gender roles, cultural knowledge, and depression—and to give unsolicited advice on life, relationships, skin care, and health, and then to generally vent about cultural frustrations and relationships gone bad. These sites had varied numbers of viewers and "users," ranging from a high of several thousand (YouTube and Facebook accounts) to a low of fourteen (Hmoob.com). There were also women who used Internet forums to specifically seek out and engage other Hmong women on female Hmong–centric issues, such as culturally prescribed gender roles, divorce, abuse, leadership, and education through websites sponsored by organizations that specifically cater to a Hmong female audience. The sites monitored from women's organizations were the Hmong Women's Heritage Association, the Professional Hmong Women's Network, the Association for the Advancement of Hmong Women, the Hmong American Women's Association, the Association for the Advancement of Hmong Women in Minnesota, the Hmong Women's Giving Circle, *Hnub Tshiab* (New Day), Portraits of Hmong Women, the Hmong Baptist Woman's Association, Hmong Woman Achieving Together, Hmong Women's Contemporary Issues, and the Hmong Women's Network. These sites had visitors and bloggers that ranged from a high of fourteen thousand to a low of twelve.

Like female Internet users elsewhere (Campbell and Jovchelovitch 2000; Herring et al. 2014; Leurs, Midden, and Ponzanesi 2012), the Hmong

women in this study are finding that the web offers different, and by extension safer, forms of self-representation. It is a public arena where they can
"come into voice." Within this arena, it was not unusual to find them exercising voice inside the bounds of their traditionally acceptable face-to-face
forms of expression. For instance, there were lots of poetry postings (in
English and Hmong) in which women talked about lovers, relationships,
pain, hurt, and even depression. What is different about posting poetry on
social networking sites is that every day is poetry day—there are no rules
of when it is or isn't acceptable to recite. This forum has expanded their
voice. This is typical of strategies taken up by Hmong women using social
networking to go beyond the face-to-face rules of social engagement and
hence challenge the multiple structures of power that have defined their
role in society.

Empowerment through Platform

One of the crucial components of social networking sites is the user's ability
to engage a large network of people who will view their musings, or "posts."
The label for these relationships differs depending on the site—popular
terms include "friends," "contacts," "fans," or "followers." Boyd and Ellison
(2007) suggest that the term "friend" in these contexts is misleading because "the connection does not necessarily mean friendship in the everyday vernacular sense" (213). The network lists on these sites contain links
to everyone's profile, enabling viewers to enlarge their voice by offering
invitations to and accepting invitations from a broad range of people. For
instance, one Facebook page dedicated specifically to Hmong women has
over seven thousand "friends," all of whom have access to the online lives
of the others. Equally as common were Facebook accounts of women with
large numbers of both men and women followers who regularly engaged
in their conversations.

According to a 2013 study by the Pew Charitable Trust, more than eight
million Americans have a personal blog or online diary, and roughly
275,000 blog entries are published in an average day. According to the
blog-tracking service Technorati, the number of active bloggers in the
United States alone has reached the audience size of prime-time networks.
Most blog publishing is personal in nature, with the majority of people
using these tools to talk about their lives. According to Steven Johnson

(2011), the blogging generation is operating under the reality that the computer screen "is not just something you manipulate, but something you project your identity onto, a place to work though the story of your life as it unfolds" (29). While this might be a logical evolution for American children who have been brought up to "be their own person" and express their staunch individualism, it is an awkward juxtaposition for Hmong coming of age in America against a cultural background that has operated for centuries under a collectivist and face-saving worldview. I asked Hmong women from this generation what role these applications have had in negotiating these two perspectives.

One informant said that she saw these networks as platforms where she was free to speak her mind, adding that her voice is heard every time she "throws" her opinions "out there," and that this would not be the case if she did the same thing offline. This ability to skirt offline rules of engagement was one of the reasons Hmong women said they spend so much time expressing themselves online. Take, for example, this second-generation Hmong woman living in Minnesota:

> If I had started a local off-line forum, most likely, no one would
> show because I'm a female, and Hmong women would be afraid
> to attend. Additionally, I would've been condemned as a trouble-
> maker and chastised. I needed a safe place to express myself,
> educate, and empower others. The World Wide Web was the
> perfect choice.

Another said that she liked to discuss, sometimes critically to a broad audience of both men and women, her family life on blogs and Facebook because "it's something that I can say, or more importantly, something I could not always say out loud."

One informant talked about how Hmong women desired a platform to express their thoughts beyond the traditionally acceptable means of female expression. Some were very passionate about wanting to engage with other Hmong women and provide information on certain issues that have been institutionalized in their community as taboo to talk about outside of the family. As such, the majority of web pages and blogs were dedicated to such issues as marital relationships; physical, mental, and emotional abuse; internal family struggles; questioning culturally prescribed gender roles; and sharing repressed emotions or anxieties. In telling their stories and giving informative advice on how to handle these situations, the authors of these posts said they hoped to make a difference in the lives of other Hmong women who read them. One participant, who ran an open-forum website dedicated to opening the lines of communication among Hmong women, put it this way:

> Reading something that someone shared or posted can lead an individual to learn new things, see things differently, or inspire someone to take action. To know that others care and support the same things you do helps individuals make a difference.

Other women said they used social networking to purposely post what would be considered controversial topics to get a dialogue going between Hmong men and women on things that would normally not be discussed in a large (fifty-plus) crowd of Hmong. For example, one young woman posted that she was "quite pissed off" at her husband for planning a trip without talking to her first. It worked. Within a couple of weeks she had drawn both men and women into a discussion that would not have taken place in a public domain outside the Internet, where everyone is supposed to keep their business to themselves. Reflecting on this discussion, she said:

> I use my Facebook to ignite conversations and provoke emotions. I choose this site because I have built up an audience. I post a lot about Hmong matters because most of my "friends" are Hmong. I basically give my opinion on a topic. . . . I write things that many of my Hmong friends would like to say in public but don't because they don't want to tarnish their reputation. Using the Internet allows me to speak-up more and give answers that would be deemed inappropriate if I express them in non-web-based modes.

Another way that I frequently found Hmong women gaining a platform on the Internet was by offering unsolicited advice over open discussion forums. Cultural Hmong American norms suggest that women refrain from offering unsolicited advice to people they do not know; however, they frequently take advantage of the opportunity to do so over the web. Take, for example, this one co-ed exchange prompted by a woman responding to a stranger's rants about his girlfriend's parents:

> WOMAN: IMO [In my opinion] you shouldn't talk about her in that way. I don't care if you are the man or woman, have some respect!!!
> MAN: You have some respect, whoever you are—what do you know anyway, you're just a *&^&() girl!
> WOMAN: I know respect, and you don't have it! Just my opinion.

This exchange exemplifies the idea that "the effect of one's verbal activity depends, among other things, on one's apparent legitimacy to engage in that activity" (Eckert and McConnell-Ginet 2013, 91). This woman's ideas and opinions, while openly expressed on the Internet, still struggle against the weight of current social and gender hierarchy. Nevertheless, the rules of engagement have changed online, where Hmong men and women *can* engage each other on topics they wouldn't discuss face-to-face. This is precisely the appeal of online social networking to some of the Hmong women I talked to. It makes certain kinds of connections easier. The desegregation of this informal space is empowering—it's a seat at the table where knowledge is gained in this next generation's equivalent of the locker room, the golf course, or the carpool, where women have been informally excluded for years. It is this seat at the table that changes the rules in ways that are favorable to women's voices being heard. As their legitimacy to occupy these spaces becomes more apparent, so will the positions they occupy within them.

Voice through Anonymity

The women in this study often cited the ability to remain somewhat anonymous through pseudonyms as one of the primary reasons why they felt free to express themselves in Internet forums. They also enjoyed the ability to control the public perception of how people respond to their posts. What they were referring to are some of the distinguishing technical features of social networking sites, which allow respondents' posts to be viewed at the owner's discretion. Someone with a social networking site, such as Facebook, can make her comments and discussions "public" or visible only to those she adds to her online network as "friends." These Internet sites also have features that allow viewers to leave "comments" or messages privately or make them visible to a select "friend" list, and that allow the owner to delete or "hide" undesirable comments. One informant commented on how she used these features as a form of agency:

> In my postings I can remain anonymous if I want. And if there are rude or abusive comments on my blog (I have experienced a few), I have the power to block or delete them.

Her postings included her dissatisfaction with her weight, calling herself "obese," and detailed descriptions of her weight loss regimen. Such intimate details may be shared with close friends in private, but airing them to a large group of strangers in a face-to-face setting is far outside the norm of a traditional Hmong lady. There were others who found the anonymity of the Internet empowering, one even calling her computer the "plastic crest of reality" that she could hide behind:

> I choose the Internet as a forum of expression because it gives me the ability to deceive and to control what I want others to see about myself. I have the privilege to "talk" behind a screen and that gives me the motivation to say something maybe that I, as a Hmong woman, would not or could not say in a group of people.

While some sites ask users to create a "profile" disclosing an array of information, such as their name, birthday, and town of residence, other forums, such as blogs and discussion boards, allow Hmong women to express themselves through a pseudonym that they can also hide behind. One Hmong woman commented on how this feature empowered her and others to assert opinions, noting, "We may be criticized, but since it's not in person, our pride isn't hurt as much."

One woman talked about how social networking sites allow Hmong women a space to share certain aspects of their identity that they might not otherwise share with people in their physical space. For instance, there are Hmong women blogging about being mentally unstable, lazy, or suicidal, or dieting to the point of anorexia—all things that would attract the stares of others and bring a sense of shame to an individual, or her family, if discussed face-to-face in a crowd of Hmong people. Take, for example, this woman who blogged regularly under a pseudonym about what she calls her "inner demons." When asked if she found this anonymity empowering, she responded:

Using the internet, I can hide who I am, my identity is hidden, thus I am free to be open enough to tell my struggles and ask questions without the fear of public judgment and humiliation.

The screen experiences of these users echo Mark Bauerlein's (2011) observations about offline behavior, in which he notes that it is often the disapproving looks of others that keep lesser intentions in check. "Not anymore," says Mark. "She can go anonymous in the virtual sphere and join the cyber-bullying, mobbing, and swearing, all the while appearing entirely decorous in the public sphere. . . . The sites she enjoys have no gatekeepers, but that's not all. With the screen disengaging her from the surroundings, others nearby have no gatekeeping power" (xiii). Social networking on the computer has allowed all of us to behave within cultural norms in the present while committing online acts that might fall outside of socially acceptable behavior. In this way, the Internet can provide means for yet another fragmentation of self—and a new cloak of privacy in which to hide it—or, as we saw in the last section, a stage on which to perform it. Hmong women have found empowering venues of social interaction that circumvent their social constraints.

Voice through Validation

Many of the individuals in this study discussed feeling a lack of support for their personal struggles from leaders in the Hmong community because, in the words of one informant, "talking about personal issues isn't something we do." Many wanted the opportunity to renegotiate their marginal identity within the community but hesitated to do so in most social settings out of fear that it would jeopardize their acceptance by other Hmong, even if they sensed their position was broadly shared. This was especially true if their position dissented from traditional female gender roles. While there are emerging outlets for these discussions, such as professional and gender-specific conferences, most women in the study did not have access to these forums. Internet access and social networking sites gave these women a way to gain public validation for their experiences from co-ethnics in a less threatening environment. One self-proclaimed "Facebook addict" in her late thirties put it this way:

> I always felt that I wasn't alone in my battles against Hmong traditional norms. I needed validation. I wanted to see if there were other women out there in the world who could identify with my life experiences and opinions.

Another young woman from California spoke about the pressure she felt to constantly withhold her opinions from other Hmong in public, "as if they didn't exist," because of the ramifications disclosing might have on her or her family:

> A part of me was hoping no one would notice my blog and I could just voice my opinions unnoticed in my little corner of the blogo-sphere. I was scared of what others would think of me. I knew that there would be people who would call me ignorant and blasphe-mous because I disagreed with certain Hmong traditional norms. But I had to get it out there.

While she did receive some criticism, such as one post in which a man criticized her for what he deemed her "incomplete" and "incorrect" knowl-edge, what she didn't anticipate was the acceptance, empathy, and validation that came from the online community of Hmong women who read it:

> The Hmong women really appreciated it. It has made me realize that words are powerful—creating these words and reading the words of others have empowered me. The validation of others continues to motivate me.

Many of the women who were interviewed noted a particular sense of empowerment that came from Hmong women sharing resources with or having access to other Hmong women as a resource. Such female co-ethnic voices were an important audience to whom they could present their views, which often remained unheard and unimportant within the main-stream discussions in their community. For instance, such forums generally offer sections devoted to biographies of inspiring Hmong women, resource pages with multiple links to other Hmong women–related websites, and profiles highlighting the successes and struggles of being both Hmong and female in America. All of these things indicate the need these women felt for support and validation of their gendered lives from their own ethnic community.

Other women in this study were frustrated by what they considered "an overall lack of community support" for trying to meet the expectations of being both Hmong and a woman in contemporary America. They spoke repeatedly of the myriad pressures on Hmong women to be silent about their internal family problems or cultural disagreements. As one woman put it, "Sometimes I feel like I am going to explode inside." The social message given to Hmong women was that protecting the face of the family came first, and internal struggles were best relegated to private arenas, invisible to the larger community. Feeling that the traditional means of communication were closed to women, one young female participant from North Carolina said she found the cyberworld a place to give voice to her thoughts to a willing audience of both men and women:

> Just the feeling of typing something from your head and visually
> seeing it on the computer is really therapeutic to me. It's almost
> like someone is reading my mind back to me.

Another example of women sharing their innermost thoughts came through on blogs and posts about dreams—descriptions of what they saw and what these dreams might mean. This is significant because Hmong women do not generally speak openly about their dreams in public or in private, as it is traditionally considered bad luck. Beyond dreams, many Hmong women were using their blogs and networks to share intimately personal experiences in hopes that someone reading them would be inspired. One woman put it this way:

> It's comforting to have someone respond to those personal posts
> because it means they either understand my situation or encourage
> me. It's human nature to want to feel like you are not alone.

For her, the Internet is fulfilling an expressed need to find validation, and through it she can "utter the call for acknowledgment" (Mitra 2001, 31). The power of this computer-aided form of voice was alluded to by Mitra (2001), who suggests that when these calls are acknowledged and validated in cyberspace, a new community emerges around this specific set of voices—one that has power to produce new narratives about their identity. "The dominant," she adds, "no longer need to be the primary and natural-ized narratives of groups" (45).

Examples of cybercommunity formation to gain validation can be found in the many online social networking communities that exist specifically for Hmong women. For these women, it is the far-reaching potential of voicing in cyberspace that they found empowering. As one woman put it, she became involved in creating such a blog because she thought "there must be more people out there who are struggling with these thoughts be-sides me." The discussion forum she created around exploring these issues gave her a sense of camaraderie with other Hmong women that she found difficult to achieve offline. One follower of this blog said that she became involved in posting on it to increase dialogue between Hmong women in a way that was discouraged offline. Thus, she used her cybervoice to over-come some of the challenges of developing and maintaining a positive female Hmong identity: "I feel that the more knowledge a Hmong woman can gain, the more she can take charge of her own life and the freer she is to be a Hmong woman."

Conclusion

Research has suggested that the Internet and social networking have be-come strategies of empowerment that are helping women of all locations and literacy levels to come into their own voice and thus exercise more agency over relations of subordination in their lives. As gender inequality works differently in various cultural systems, this chapter has extended that discussion to understanding how Hmong women use these sites to circumvent the particular conversational choreographies of their unique social location in America, particularly as it applies to the constraining in-teractional possibilities inherent in face maintenance. Complicating a broader understanding of women's voice, the social networking expres-sions of Hmong women should not be thought of as a freedom *from* cul-ture but rather as a historically situated movement and resistance *within* a culture to challenge ubiquitous structures of male domination.

Although the Hmong women who expressed their views and experi-ences online claimed numerous personal benefits, this was not generally their sole motivation. Most of the women in this study wanted things to change, something to happen, somebody to take note. Many hoped that their cybercommunities would grow large and vocal enough to change the marginalizing gendered structures of society. This has not yet been actualized. One explanation may be found in the words of Eckert and McConnell-Ginet (2013), who suggest that "the force of an utterance is not manifest in the utterance itself, but in its fate once it is launched into the discourse. . . . And that fate is not in the hand of the initial utterer, but depends on the meaning-making rights of . . . those who might take up the utterance and carry its content to other situations and communities" (89). Most Hmong elders with immediate cultural capital and power are not among the demographic most likely to be engaged with social networking and not present where these particular discussions unfold. Even within the generation of young Hmong men on the Internet, skepticism about the legitimacy of the causal Hmong female voice remains. Perhaps the strongest indicator that those who have always held power have yet to acknowledge Hmong women's voices as equally meaningful lies in the outcome of the only major study on this ethnic group's Internet use, which found no explicit representation of women (Tapp 2010). Thus, despite considerable advances in Hmong women's access to formal positions of influence (as professors, authors, politicians, and businesswomen), as women the world over know, men still primarily have the authority to perform speech acts that change people's civil status, leaving the calls of Hmong women somewhat unanswered—at least for now.

Despite these limitations, this chapter has demonstrated that within disempowering structures of society, explicit women's agency is not difficult to locate. Hmong female bloggers have retained a certain distinction by creating spaces from which to deliver powerful messages from their unique perspective. Web forums allow people to speak, and speaking empowers them. The Hmong women's open online engagement with men of the next generation of leaders also increases the political economy of their ideas and introduces once-marginalized private matters into public discourse. It is within these projects of meaning-making that the women in this study find their use of social networking agentic and empowering in the way that its forums help them realize the legitimacy of their own interests within their current cultural and historical location. This is important in that it simultaneously confirms the contemporary feminist critique that online interaction is fundamentally grounded in the realities of identities, relations, and cultural contexts experienced offline, while suggesting that efficacy and empowerment can be realized through online communication despite the gendered forms of hierarchical communication enmeshed within it.

Notes

1. "Facebook Reports First Quarter 2013 Results."
2. Pew Research Center 2013.
3. See, for example, Mitra 2001.
4. An older male leader of the first-generation refugees who fled Laos after the United States pulled out of the Vietnam War.
5. Kim Chang and Souvan Lee were the research assistants whose help on this project was immensely valuable and much appreciated.
6. Personal communication.

Works Cited

Allen, Margaret, Suzanne Matthew, and Mary Jo Boland. 2004. "Working with Immigrant and Refugee Populations: Issues and Hmong Case Study." *Library Trends* 53, no. 2: 301–28.

Balka, Ellen. 1986. "Women and Computer Networking in Six Countries." *Journal of International Communication* 3, no. 1: 66–84.

Bauerlein, Mark. 2011. *The Digital Divide.* New York: Penguin.

Benmayor, Rina. 1991. "Testimony, Action Research, and Empowerment: Puerto Rican Women and Popular Education." In *Women's Words: The Feminist Practice of Oral History,* edited by Sherna Berger Cluck and Daphne Patai, 159–74. New York: Routledge.

Berger, Joseph, M. Fizek, M. Hamit, Robert Norman, and Morris Zelditch Jr. 1977. *Status Characteristics and Social Interaction.* New York: Elsevier.

Bernard, Alan, and Jonathan Spere. 2012. "Feminist Anthropology." In *The Routledge Encyclopedia of Social and Cultural Anthropology,* edited by Alan Bernard and Jonathan Spere, 284–87. New York: Routledge.

Bourdieu, Pierre. 1984. *Distinction: A Social Critique of the Judgment of Taste.* Cambridge, Mass.: Harvard University Press.

Bourdieu, P., and J. C. Passeron. 2006. *Reproduction in Education, Society and Culture.* Beverly Hills, Calif.: Sage.

Boyd, Danah. 2006. "Friends, Friendsters, and MySpace Top 8: Writing Community into Being on Social Network Sites." *First Monday* 11, no. 12.

Boyd, Danah, and Nicole Ellison. 2007. "Social Network Sites: Definition, History, and Scholarship." *Journal of Computer-Mediated Communication* 13, no. 1: 210–30.

Brettell, Caroline. 2009. "Anthropology, Gender, and Narrative." In *Exploring Women's Studies: Looking Forward, Looking Back,* edited by Judith Pinch and Carole Appel, 68–86. Saddle River, N.J.: Pearson.

Broder, M. 1996. *The Therapist's Assistant.* Vol. 2. Philadelphia, Penn.: Media Psychology Associates.

Brouwer, L. 2006. "Giving Voice to Dutch Moroccan Girls on the Internet." *Global Media Journal* 5:9.

Campbell, C., and S. Jovchelovitch. 2000. "Health, Community and Development: Towards a Social Psychology of Participation." *Journal of Community and Applied Social Psychology* 10, no. 4: 255–70.

"Company Info/Facebook Newsroom." 2015. Facebook Newsroom. Accessed August 5.

Diminescu, D. 2008. "The Connected Migrant: An Epistemological Manifesto." *Social Science Information* 47, no. 4: 565–79.

Donnelly, Nancy. 1997. *Changing Lives of Refugee Hmong Women.* Seattle, Wash.: University of Washington Press.

Eckert, Penelope, and Sally McConnell-Ginet. 2013. *Language and Gender.* Cambridge: Cambridge University Press.

Ellis, A. 1993. "The Advantages and Disadvantages of Self Help Therapy Materials." *Professional Psychology: Research and Practice* 24, no. 3: 335–39.

Eskilson, Arlene, and Mary Glenn Wiley. 1976. "Sex Composition and Leadership in Small Groups." *Sociometry* 39:183–283.

Espiritu, Yen. 2001. "We Don't Sleep Around Like White Girls Do: Family, Culture, and Gender in Filipina American Lives." *Signs* 26, no. 2: 415–40.

Ferguson, Niall. 2011. "World on Wi-Fire." *Newsweek,* October 3.

Foucault, M. 1980. *Power/Knowledge.* New York: Pantheon Books.

Giulianotti, Richard. 2005. "Towards a Critical Anthropology of Voice: The Politics and Poets of Popular Culture, Scotland and Football." *Critique of Anthropology* 25, no. 4: 339–59.

Goffman, E. 1955. "On Facework." *Psychiatry* 189:213–31.

Grasmuck, S., and P. Pessar. 1991. *Between Two Islands: Dominican International Migration.* Berkeley: University of California Press.

Gregg, M. 2006. "Posting with Passion: Blogs and the Politics of Gender." In *Uses of Blogs,* edited by J. Jacobs and A. Bruns, 151–60. New York: Peter Lang.

Guattari, F. Chaosmois. 1992. *An Ethicoaesthetic Paradigm.* Bloomington: Indiana University Press.

Hadfield, Mark, and Kaye Haw. 2001. " 'Voice': Young People and Action Research." *Educational Action Research* 9, no. 3: 485–502.

Hall, Stuart. 1984. *Minimal Selves: Identity Documents.* Birmingham, U.K.: Birmingham Center for Cultural Studies.

Harris, Anita. 2013. "Young Women, Late Modern Politics, and the Participatory Possibilities of Online Cultures." In *Race, Gender, Sexuality, and Social Class,* edited by Susan Ferguson, 654–63. Los Angeles: Sage.

Herring, Susan, Inna Kouper, Louis Ann Scheidt, and Elijah Write. 2004. "Women and Children Last: The Discoursive Construction of Weblogs." In *Into the Blogosphere: Rhetoric, Community, and Culture of Weblogs,* edited by L. Gurak, S. Antonijevic, L. Johnson, C. Ratliff, and J. Reyman. Minneapolis: University of Minnesota Press.

Ho, David. 1976. "On the Concept of Face." *American Journal of Sociology* 81:867–84.

Holm, Ellis. 1996. *Better, Deeper, and More Enduring Brief Therapy.* New York: Brunner/Mazel.

Johnson, Steven. 2001. "The Internet." In *The Digital Divide,* edited by Mark Bauerlein, 26–33. New York: Penguin.

Kassing, Jeffery. 1998. "Development and Validation of the Organizational Dissent Scale." *Management Communication Quarterly* 12, no. 2: 183–229.

Kennedy, W. 1987. " 'Voice' and 'Address' in Literary Theory." *Oral Tradition* 2, no. 1: 214–30.

Keyes, Cheryl. 2006. "Empowering Self, Making Choices, Creating Spaces: Black Female Identity via Rap Music." In *Ethnomusicology: A Contemporary Reader,* edited by Jennifer Post, 97–108. New York: Routledge.

Kiesler, S., J. Siegel, and T. McGuire. 1984. "Social Psychological Aspects of Computer-Mediated Communication." *American Psychologist* 39, no. 10: 1123–34.

Kranaraem, C. 1988. *Technology and Women's Voices: Keeping in Touch.* New York: Routledge.

Lea, M., and R. Spears. 1992. "Paralanguage and Social Perception in Computer-Mediated Communication. *Journal of Organizational Computing* 2:321–41.

Leurs, Koen, Eva Midden, and Sandra Ponzanesi. 2012. "Digital Multiculturalism in the Netherlands: Religious, Ethnic and Gender Positioning by Moroccan-Dutch Youth." *Religion and Gender* 2, no. 1: 150–75.

Lopez, Nancy. 2003. *Networks of Marginality: Life in a Mexican Shantytown.* New York: New York Academic Press.

Mitra, Ananda. 2001. "Marginal Voices in Cyberspace." *New Media and Society* 3, no. 1: 29–38.

———. 2005. "Creating Immigrant Identities in Cyberspace: Examples from a Non-resident Indian Website." *Media, Culture and Society* 27:371–90.

Morgen, Sandra, and Ann Bookman. 1988. "Rethinking Women and Politics: An Introductory Essay." In *Women and the Politics of Empowerment,* edited by A. Bookman and S. Morgen. Philadelphia: Temple University Press.

Nanth, V. 2001. "Empowerment and Governance through Information and Communication Technologies: Women's Perspective." *International Information and Library Review* 22:317–90.

Napels, Nancy. 1997. *Community Activism and Feminist Politics: Organizing across Race, Class, and Gender.* New York: Routledge.

Nibbs, Faith. 2015. "'Too White and Didn't Belong': The Intra-Ethnic Consequences of Second-Generation Digital Diasporas." In *Identity and the Second Generation,* edited by Faith Nibbs and Caroline Brettell. Nashville: Vanderbilt University Press.

North, Tim. 1994. "The Internet and Usenet Global Computer Networks: An Investigation of Their Culture." Master's thesis, Curtin University of Technology, Perth, Australia.

Ortner, Sherry. 1984. "Resistance and the Problem of Ethnographic Refusal." *Comparative Studies in Society and History* 26, no. 1: 126–66.

———. 1995. "Resistance and the Problem of Ethnographic Refusal." *Comparative Studies in Society and History* 37:173–93.

———. 2011. "Specifying Agency: The Comaroffs and Their Critics." *Interventions* 3, no. 12: 76–84.

Overby, Bruce A. 1996. "Identification and Validation of a Societal Model of Usenet." Master's thesis, Paper 1251, San Jose State University.

Parker, D., and M. Song. 2006. "New Ethnicities Online: Reflexive Racialization and the Internet." *Sociological Review* 54, no. 3: 575–94.

Pew Research Center. 2013. *Coming and Going on Facebook.* February 5. www .pewinternet.org/2013/02/05/coming-and-going-on-facebook/.

Pinkett, E., and R. O'Bryant. 2003. "Building Community, Empowerment and Self-Sufficiency." *Information and Communication and Society* 6:187–210.

Ponzanesi, Sandra, and B. Blaagaard. 2011. "In the Name of Europe." *Social Identities: Journal for the Study of Race, Nation and Culture* 17, no. 1: 1–10.

Ponzanesi, Sandra, and Koen Leurs. 2014. "On Digital Crossings in Europe." *Journal of Migration and Culture* 5, no. 1.

Redding, W. 1992. "Response to Professor Berger's Essay: Its Meaning for Organizational Communication." *Communication Education* 59:87–93.

Siddiquee, Asiya, and Carolyn Kagan. 2006. "The Internet, Empowerment, and Identity: An Exploration of Participation by Refugee Women in a Community Internet Project in the United Kingdom." *Journal of Community and Applied Social Psychology* 16:189–206.

Sinha, Mrinalini. 1996. "Gender in the Critiques of Colonialism and Nationalism: Locating the 'Indian Woman.'" In *Feminism and History,* edited by Joan Wallach Scott, 477–504. New York: Oxford University Press.

Tapp, Nicholas. 2010. *The Impossibility of Self: An Essay on the Hmong Diaspora.* Berlin: LIT Verlag.

Tyler, S. 1983. "Post-Modern Ethnography: From Document of the Occult to Occult Document." In *Writing Culture: The Poetics and Politics of Ethnography,* edited by J. Clifford and G. E. Marcus, 122–40. Berkeley: University of California Press.

Valsiner, J. 2003. "Beyond Social Representations: A Theory of Enablement." *Papers on Social Representation* 12, no. 7: 1–7.

Van Zoonen, L., F. Vis, and S. Mihelj. 2010. "Performing Citizenship on YouTube: Activism, Satire and Online Debate around the Anti-Islam Video Fitna." *Critical Discourse Studies* 7, no. 4: 249–62.

Weber, Max. 1946. *From Max Weber.* New York: Oxford University Press.

Weidman, Amanda. 2008. "Gender and the Politics of Voice: Colonial Modernity and Classical Music in South India." *Cultural Anthropology* 18, no. 2: 194–232.

———. 2011. "Anthropology and the Voice." *Anthropology News* 52, no. 1: 1.

Wilson, Brian. 2006. "Ethnography, the Internet, and Youth Culture: Strategies for Examining Social Resistance and 'Online-Offline' Relationships." *Canadian Journal of Education* 29, no. 1: 307–28.

Wilson, Samuel, and Leighton Peterson. 2002. "The Anthropology of Online Communities." *Annual Review of Anthropology* 31, no. 1: 449–67.

Zentgraf, Kristine. 2002. "Immigration and Woman's Empowerment: Salvadorans in Los Angeles." *Gender and Society* 16:625–46.

CHAPTER 8

Stitching Hmongness into Cloth

Pliable Identity and Cultural Agency

Geraldine Craig

I N TRADITIONAL HMONG VILLAGES in Asia, women exerted cultural agency through their production of elaborate clothing. *Paj ntaub* (flower cloth) garments in Asia were a primary indicator of Hmong ethnic identity independent of geopolitical borders, challenging normative and homogenizing power structures of colony and nation. The *paj ntaub*—ascribed meaning by design and ritual use within an animist cosmology—can be seen as an alternative text and a visual manifestation of cultural maintenance in an ethnic group in which orality was a primary cultural script. However, the complex, layered aesthetic language of *paj ntaub* was not fixed—makers could reinterpret geometric patterns without losing group identification or lessening the role of the textile pattern in agentic resistance to national belonging and state-making projects. Hmong women strategically resisted assimilation into majority culture. Then as now, the evolution of *paj ntaub* traces the personal, economic, and political empowerment of Hmong women, despite living within other dominant structures.

The profound relevance of textiles as infrastructure in the Hmong social fabric is not strictly historical, as diasporic and Hmong women in Asia claim space for textile production's role in self-determinism in addition to collective cultural knowledge. Artist Maikue Vang and fashion designer Nonmala Xiong are among the American-born generation of Hmong women who find strength in Hmong textile traditions and serve as transformational agents in a complex aesthetic enterprise shaped simultaneously by history and twenty-first-century influences. The former narrative—cloth constructed for Hmong only, by women only, taught along with a complex set of values and rituals in which *paj ntaub* was essential—does not have the same relevance or possibility in the diaspora or in Laos today. However, the story of *paj ntaub* is one of tremendous cultural and aesthetic power, renewed with each generation, and now transformed by self-actualizing artists and designers who imagine alternative social and cultural purposes of their own. Their empowerment comes through a completely different socioeconomic filter than that of the mothers and grandmothers whom they saw sewing in early childhood, and *paj ntaub* suggests different incentives, identities, and social relationships for them than it does for most of the elders. However, the risky business of defining a unique identity while living within a powerful majority culture is still a shared, multigenerational, and complex experience vis-à-vis cloth.

Textile Histories of Representation

The new generation of Hmong women born in the diaspora are raised by parents and grandparents that for the most part did not attend college in Asia, or study textile making in a formal education environment. The concept of textiles as a fine art and design practice is an aspect of cultural assimilation typically introduced in universities, occupying specific fields of knowledge with their own histories of representation.

Maikue Vang is a graduate student in fiber art at the University of Wisconsin–Milwaukee who says that her interest in making art

> began as an attempt to figure out my Hmong and American
> identity. It was a way to explore the contemporary issues in Hmong
> culture and contemporary society. At the same time, it helped me
> to learn more about the traditional making of Hmong and Miao
> textiles. I would consider this a motivation, to want to learn about
> the origin in making these textiles as a way to self-teach myself
> about my own culture. It has been an issue with the first American-
> born Hmong generation, that we all sense a loss of culture with the
> post war trauma that has occurred to the Hmong people and our
> culture. I view art making as a problem solving and investigative
> process in the larger issues that directly relate to my experiences
> and identity. (Vang 2012)

Her work draws from traditional Hmong garments and designs, although she takes liberties with techniques and form, such as spirals that are silk-screened instead of rendered in reverse appliqué. She uses the garments as a signifier of gender identity, and wants her body of work to expand to represent aspects of her identity besides that of being a Hmong American. "I am also a person of color, working class, queer, and a woman. In general, my identities will always be an expression in my work as they are representations of my perspective" (Vang 2012). In her work, she seeks to bring attention to "the temporality of the role of Hmong woman in her native family, that the whole life of a daughter is raised to prepare her for life with her husband. In short, that when she is born, she is already expected to grow up into a woman who will marry into another family. My work critiques the issues of gender inequality not only in the Hmong but other cultures as well" (Vang 2012). Maikue looks to express meaning in an international fine art context, where her layered references in nonfunctional garments will be presented to a globalized audience accustomed to many binary forms of representation, but most will be unfamiliar with *paj ntaub* and its historic relationship to Hmong identity. Maikue's contemporary forms of Hmong representation exist within (and express) asymmetrical power relations today, just as traditional *paj ntaub* expressed an informal resistance to nationalistic subjugation through stitched cultural codes. Yet they simultaneously convey the deeply personal states of being/becoming and disintegration/loss embodied in her ethereal cheesecloth garments with the Hmong-patterned borders.

Hmong clothing in Asia was part of a rich cosmological and psychosensory world for centuries, where material constructs (textiles, architecture, jewelry) served their users in cultural, historical, and political ways. Direct social and aesthetic messages were said to be embedded in the visual and haptic language of cloth. Unlike Eurocentric art history traditions and their accompanying core principles—especially the concept of fine art produced primarily for visual contemplation—Hmong textile production was crafted for optical pleasure but equally for physical and cosmological functions.[1] Anthropologist Erik Cohen (2000) has noted, however, that Hmong visual traditions include neither drawing or painting, nor a history of naturalistic representation (129).[2] It is in cloth and thread that one sees a visual translation of culture, and thus a few points of reference to mainstream Western art history canons or visual traditions despite the extraordinary aesthetic level of Hmong material culture.[3]

Prior to the 1960s, textiles in Hmong villages were created according to local norms and for use among extended family with shared visual references. The Vietnam War would change their lives in unprecedented

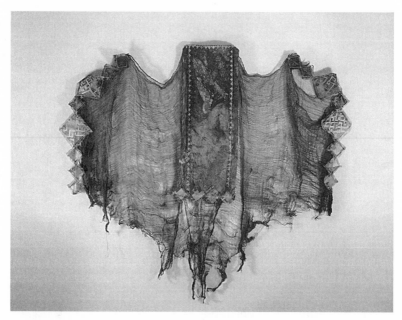

Figure 8.1. "Once Upon Our Homeland1" by Maikue Vang. Courtesy of Maikue Vang.

ways. Since the war, Hmong textiles have undergone dramatic transformations, including the introduction of pictorial representation in embroidered wall hangings, which first developed in Thai refugee camps; deeper changes to aesthetics; and techniques and forms influenced by immigration and diasporic tourism back to Laos, Thailand, Vietnam, and China. *Paj ntaub* clothing as cultural agent and artifact now has different symbolic relevance in both Asia and the diaspora (to Hmong and non-Hmong) but is still useful for maintaining group identity. Likewise, Hmong textile artists and designers become entangled in the larger conversation of what should be considered art (function vs. nonfunction, medium, etc.) and who are the power brokers (typically white males) that define value in the fields of art and design.

In the United States, Hmong immigrants were initially perceived as exotic when seen in traditional clothing. The elaborate *paj ntaub* garments were the most identifiable markers of "otherness," which mainstream Americans and politicians primarily saw at Hmong New Year festivals.[4]

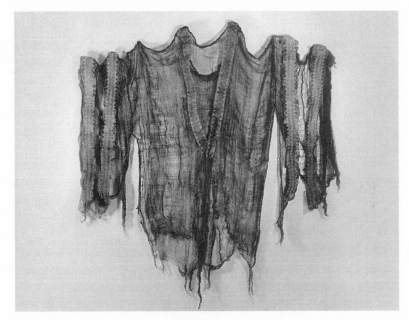

Figure 8.2. "Once Upon Our Homeland2" by Maikue Vang. Courtesy of Maikue Vang.

What is the role of Hmong textiles, then, in projecting both assimilation and nostalgic longing for a homeland? How are perceptions of culture written on the body, especially in gender politics as realized through performances of young female bodies? How are fashion shows, beauty pageants, and choices in clothing used to negotiate the process of assimilating into bourgeois American culture? Hmong American artist-designers such as Maikue and Nonmala draw inspiration from the visual and cultural uses of *paj ntaub*. To do so affirms their agency in crafting identity while it extends and problematizes the contemporary dialogue about art and fashion and how parameters or paradigms shift. Of significance to art and textile scholars, their work offers hope that Hmong textiles will continue beyond the refugee generation as an extraordinary art form, one that empowers women in advancing broad cultural transformation and rooted Hmong identity.

The difficult, fascinating, and paradoxical aspect of crafting identity and self-definition for young Hmong American textile artist-designers is that they are situated between two culturally prescribed art traditions: Hmong textile traditions that employ highly abstracted geometric codes in functional clothing, and a Eurocentric art history that privileges figurative representations and generally excludes textiles and crafts. The rich semiotic function of textiles is rarely on display in art museums. (Large urban museums with broad holdings are more likely to have textile collections, while museums such as the Metropolitan Museum of Art in New York include an encyclopedic collection of textiles and fashion.) In *Seeing Through Clothes,* Anne Hollander (1993) argues that fashion is a system of signs learned from art history representations of clothed bodies, perceived not directly but through a filter of artistic convention. Hollander writes, "Because they share in the perpetually idealizing vision of art, clothes must be seen and studied as paintings are seen and studied—not primarily as cultural by-products or personal expressions but as connected links in a creative tradition of image-making" (xvi). This subjective filter or convention continues to be the predominant lens used in art history texts. Two thousand years of Western art history are filled with figurative images and representations, with little disruption until the twentieth century. Figurative bodies, clothed (or not), were carved into clay amphoras or stone architecture or painted onto walls, using the artistic conventions of the day.

Fast-forward to the twenty-first century. Representations of clothed bodies exist not just in art collections and on architecture but on television, in printed books or magazines, or as global photographic images via the Internet and social media. These representations serve as culturally defining backdrops to identity. The difficulty in Hollander's (1993) attempt to elevate clothing through its link with traditions of art history, specifically figurative art, is that it diminishes other non-European costume traditions. Clothing as a subject within the canon of figurative art is what she states provides visual authenticity to *our* fashion or clothing,[5] its claim to importance, meaning, and appeal to the imagination. But this view ignores the historic value of clothing traditions outside the Western canon (ethnic textiles, among others). It also neglects to provide a framework for such developments as the rise of Asian chic. This supertrend in the New York fashion world reflects the idea of semiotics—as discussed by Roland Barthes (1983) in *The Fashion System*[6]—in the way that the trend exploited long-held stereotypes or representations of the exotic East, seen most widely in the media and not derived from fine art traditions.

Racialized representations of Asia as premodern—outside the march of progress and configured as an antidote to modernity—initially fueled the appeal of Asian chic. Discussed in detail by Thuy Linh N. Tu (2011) in her book *The Beautiful Generation*, she writes:

> As I will show, though Asian chic was ostensibly an expression of appreciation for Asian sartorial traditions, the production of Asianness in these sites actually worked to reinforce its inferior position within the dominant cultural hierarchy. This has been achieved in part through what Arjun Appadurai (2008) has called a "cultural economy of distance," in which exotic goods are posited as desirable and valuable because they exist at a cultural remove. Consumption of these goods, far from suggesting an intimacy with the cultures from which they purportedly emerged, demands a certain amount of distance: it is precisely because they are geographically and culturally distant that consumers have the cultural capital to see the value of these exotic objects and the economic capital to purchase them. (102)

She suggests that stereotypes of the exotic East, a glamorous form of Orientalism, were perpetuated in the New York fashion world from the mid-1990s to the mid-2000s by Asian designers as well as fashion editors. They used traditional signifiers, such as a dragon or lotus, to land a young designer's work in the pages of *Vogue* (137).

Since Hmong culture was not widely known outside of Asia before 1975, traditional clothing forms were not co-opted or complicit in the long-held representations of Orientalism (and an undifferentiated Asia) perpetuated by fashion editors. Hmong clothing designs were highly abstracted and not representational, and the popular press had not created stereotypes around them. However, representation in the fashion media—magazines, television, Internet—including written descriptions and photographic images, shaped a context for the clothing created by American-born Hmong designers such as Nonmala Xiong (2012). Her preview of international fashion systems and most important or conscious influence emerged from popular culture photographs and advertising of 1950s- and 1960s-era American fashion.

Maikue and Nonmala are the nexus in a fascinating visual tradition and part of the generation that contests and honors Hmong cultural heritage.

They watched their mothers or grandmothers hand-stitch *paj ntaub* as agents of personal- and collective-identity maintenance—immigrants who continued the tradition in spite of cultural assimilation pressures. For Mai-kue and Nonmala, self-determinism through textile production is a link to their elders. However, agency is equally shaped by large urban environments, advanced education, and globalized Internet commerce, with transnational and homogenized influences from multiple directions. History and identity deeply embedded in *paj ntaub* clothing was the precursor to economic, cultural, and material conditions that made international art and fashion viable choices for Hmong women in one generation. A meta-narrative in cloth—integral to complexly imagined rituals and traditions within the family and ethnic group—morphed into new roles for contemporary art and fashion in the nuances of social life. From any art history standard, the development of Hmong textile praxis in the last fifty years is quite extraordinary, with women at the center precipitating change. Tracing that path hopefully demonstrates the invisible power and overlooked accomplishments of the generations of Hmong women who helped shape and define Hmongness and female power within dominant public structures of patriarchy and powerful geopolitical bureaucracies.

Lost Writing Legends and Visual Narratives

The historic significance of *paj ntaub* textiles in Hmong cultural life is revealed in rituals, protections, and legends connected to traditional *paj ntaub*. Some Hmong believe that mothers and grandmothers must make *paj ntaub* baby carriers and hats that disguise children as flowers so that evil spirits will not take them away.[7] These tender performative acts, of making and protecting, are important rituals that linked generations, with the proper textile being the key ingredient. Young girls learn cultural values, history, and rituals through narratives they hear while sewing.

Another oft-repeated legend (shared with me in Providence first and repeated elsewhere) is that Hmong used to have a written language. As the story goes, when the Chinese made it illegal to speak or write Hmong, Hmong women hid the alphabet in embroidery and folds of the women's skirts. Complex layered geometric patterns were created by embroidery, appliqué, reverse appliqué, and batik in skirts made of twenty feet or more of hemp cloth compressed into tiny pleats. While traditional designs are not an alphabet in any strict linguistic definition, the patterns were a shared visual language or alternative text that fellow Hmong understood and that were important in the ritual functions of *paj ntaub*. Scholars Yang (2009), Hillmer (2010), Duffy (2007), and Scott (2009) have documented this legend of writing in the cloth along with other Hmong "lost writing" legends, many having to do with treachery or carelessness.[8] Designs were not a phonetic or alphabetic language, nor were they strict reductive symbols, as there was and is a high regard for design innovation among the makers and users. In the Thai refugee camps, new textile art forms developed that employed Western conventions of literacy or text, commonly reported to be influenced by relief workers and attempts to teach English with illustrated books.

In the Detroit-area Hmong community in the mid-1980s, anthropologists Dewhurst and MacDowell (1984) documented multiple nature references in the names of design motifs. Relational context was important to meaning and was not fixed. Collars worn on the back of the neck might signify a clan or village, but the same geometric forms used elsewhere could take on an altered meaning. Attempts to attach single names to intricate designs, such as "elephant foot" or "worm tracks," have been unsuccessful. In her study of highland Southeast Asian textiles, Monni Adams (1974) suggested that determining the framework for interpreting design names within traditional textiles could be based not only on the visual relationship but also on other qualities, such as smell or touch—for example, the prickly quality of leaves. All of these psychosensory effects played a role in design names. Adams writes that these broader qualities or effects became essential in determining not just design interpretations but how the designs related to the interests of maker-speaker, their identity, and the uses of ritual (61).

Unpacking the formal elements of a specific textile form helps one comprehend the strength of the narrative visual language. Hmong baby carriers (tied onto the back) and hats are typical items that would be made by mothers or grandmothers to disguise young children from evil that might lure the soul of a child. The complex designs of mazes and intricate lines were believed to confuse and disorient the evil forest spirits and send them in the wrong direction. The borders of the baby carrier also served an important ritual protective function, as they were believed to hold the soul of a sleeping child close to the mother's body. Cooper (2008) describes a Hmong cosmology in which everyone has many souls, but the playful "chicken soul" of children is the most likely to wander when the child is asleep, looking for other children's souls to play with (116). The triangle shapes on borders, most commonly identified as mountains and teeth, also add protection. Baby carriers are still stitched by hand today and remain the only part of traditional Hmong costume still in everyday use in Australia, according to Wronska-Friend (2010). Probably in most diasporic Hmong communities, the baby carrier is the traditional textile used most often.[9]

Because of the integration of ritual with visual symbolic design in traditional *paj ntaub*, I consider these traditional textiles to be spiritual and material narratives that defined Hmongness for performative-spiritual purposes. In addition, they gave tremendous visual pleasure. Hmong women understood the close and intimate stories that were propagated in stitched patterns and how that allowed for shape shifting on several levels—identity formation and historical independence being primary. Protection and the intimacy of home were believed to be tightly bound to *paj ntaub*, as Ia Yang (2009) says: "But all soldiers' wives would not sew or cut fabric when the men were at the front. They believed it could harm their husbands because they would feel the connection to home." In her memoir *The Latehomecomer*, Kao Kalia Yang (2008) describes a memory from before the war. She writes about her mother's wedding and the bride wealth in *paj ntaub* from her family: "My mother knew that the gifts her mother was handing her were pieces of the history. She also knew that a Hmong woman needed to have something of her mother's if she hoped to find her way back to her mother once life ended" (17). Textiles with specific "way-finding" patterns stitched by family members were elements in burial rituals to help "show the way" back to one's ancestors in the afterlife, as described by Cooper (2008); Mallinson, Donnelly, and Hang (1996); Lewis and Lewis (1984); and Symonds (2004). While these stitching practices contributed to cultural maintenance of the group, individual self-determinism of present-day Hmong women artists draws from the history of rituals with cloth and power negotiations (or bargains) with ancestors.

Postliterate Texts

I propose that textiles served as vehicles of personal aesthetic and cultural messaging control. They were also material agents of cultural way-finding and alternative texts in the context of an oral tradition Hmong society in Asia; and women, as the producers of *paj ntaub*, were empowered players in the story of Hmong literacy. In his book *The Art of Not Being Governed,* scholar James C. Scott (2009) writes that the many minority peoples in highland Southeast Asia who live with unique identities independent of geopolitical borders may have had texts and writing and chose to leave them behind—being neither preliterate, illiterate, nor nonliterate groups, but postliterate. Scott suggests that there was an active strategic dimension to the abandonment of texts to frustrate the state-making projects that require record keeping for taxes, conscription, property ownership, and so on, just as the swiddening agricultural practices and dispersion to the mountains impede appropriation (224). He writes that fixed written documents—of politics, genealogies, histories—can be a trap or an impediment, as they impede physical mobility and are an instrument of nation building; once texts were no longer useful in the social structure, they were left behind.

Scott (2009) also suggests that the social incentives driving the acquisition and transmission of conventional literacy would have diminished precipitously with migration to the mountains, and that the steep terrain and shifting agricultural practices provided a useful friction for not creating books or written records. Alternatively, I propose that the continuous narrative, or "text," of the textile patterns was maintained because there were social incentives for production, but unlike most literary projects, it was not connected to bureaucratic power or an elite. It was a text constructed for Hmong only, produced by women only, and taught along with a complex set of values bound to private and public rituals for which *paj ntaub* was elemental—birth, mating and courtship, death and proper burial, protection from evil spirits. There was little friction to impede design innovation, and the seminomadic lifestyle was conducive to record keeping in the cloth. Since fixed accounts of history could be dangerous depending on the political climate and power structure, innovation of textile patterns allowed for historic repositioning in ways that were less permanent than text. I think it relates directly to Scott's (2009) proposal that "to refuse or to abandon writing and literacy is one strategy among many for remaining out of reach of the state. It might seem far more prudent to rely instead upon 'knowledge that resists bureaucratic codification'" (229). I suggest that one needs to sufficiently reconsider and alter conventional ideas of text: pattern stitched in cloth could also keep information coded from the authorities. Hmong certainly were cognizant of the control that bureaucratic texts in the surrounding nation-states had on their independence, or even their hold on life. Jan Ovesen (2004) writes about the belief that all Hmong bring the "documents" they need when they enter this world, but if someone uses up his or her documents, the person becomes sick and the shaman must approach a divine spirit to extend the documents, or one's license on life (463).

Of course, Hmong *paj ntaub* has never been part of a fixed cultural tableau, as it was altered to fit changing political environments. Production of *paj ntaub* changed radically with the Vietnam War, which displaced the Hmong from villages to military settlements, and then to Thai refugee camps, followed by immigration to Western countries, with the largest populations of Hmong now living in the United States, France, and Australia.[10] The war's disruption of farming and cultural practices included dramatic shifts in Hmong textile making from a focus on clothing production to the creation of story cloths, and later to hybrid textile forms influenced by Hmong life in new countries. In spite of the trauma they experienced, Hmong women found new ways to maintain the relevance and efficacy of stitching Hmongness into cloth.

In the refugee camps in Thailand, relief workers encouraged Hmong textile producers to continue making traditional geometric designs in nontraditional forms—squares for coasters, wall hangings, pillows—and to use their skills to develop new commodities. (Cohen's [2000] research indicates that the sale of acculturated *paj ntaub* squares to tourists began in Laos as early as the 1950s, but that production and commerce were limited to less isolated villages.) A revolutionary new Hmong textile form began in the Thai refugee camps—the pictorial story cloth, a quasi-naturalistic embroidered narrative of images such as animals, clothed figures, and landscape. Cohen (2000) notes that the dramatic emergence from a geometric, highly stylized ornamental art to one of pictorial representation has rarely, if ever, been documented in detail in anthropological literature (138). It has rarely been documented in the literature of art history as well. While it is commonly reported that relief workers suggested the "illustrated" cloths as another salable commodity, it quickly became apparent that it was another way for Hmong to tell their own story.[11] Migration, bucolic village life, and tragedies of war were all vital subjects in the new form of cultural text, precipitated by the influences of war and resettlement. The prevalent Roman Popular Alphabet (RPA) for the Hmong language was incorporated into the new story cloths, along with English text, as titles and explanatory narrative to accompany the images.

Although the story cloth form was not a traditional cultural text, it became an important commodity that provided income to Hmong refugees. Sewing was one of the traditional skills that Hmong refugees brought to camps and later to Western countries. After the war, sewing empowered women as wage earners for their families, just as it altered the continuity of Hmong culture recorded in cloth. The overt commodification of *paj ntaub* in the camps even changed the producers. As Donnelly (1994) and Hillmer (2010) discuss, Hmong men who were bored began sewing or drawing images onto cloth as a way to help provide for their families. However, the separation or diffusion of traditional forms in the camps created a climate of innovation that allowed Hmong sewers born in the diaspora to adapt them further. Maikue's and Nonmala's art and fashion are an expression of assimilation and hybridized identities that give voice to evolving Hmongness within a new dominant culture that is completely familiar to them and yet exotic or separated from their elders' experience with cloth.

Textiles as Transnational Commodities

Textile production in village life before the war was local and specific to family or community needs, while in the camps it became historic documentation of political upheaval and presaged practices that made Hmong textiles global and transnational commodities within a few short years. Nontraditional forms like story cloths moved from the camps into remote villages and had an impact on production due to economic potential. Cash earned from sales may be the reason that the extraordinary textile skills survive, although it is much less pervasive throughout a community. Eventually, village-produced textiles were sent to relatives overseas to be sold for higher prices in a larger market. As alternatives to traditional forms, repurposed old *paj ntaub* are made into bed coverings or Western-style garments, and reverse appliqué designs are stitched onto tablecloths, napkins, aprons, slippers, purses and bags, and so on. Today these are sold in the night market tourist centers of Luang Prabang, Laos, Chiang Mai, and Thailand, or the Hmongtown Market in St. Paul, Minnesota, among many other places.

Wronska-Friend (2010) describes how after official refugee camps closed in Thailand, Hmong refugees living around Tham Krabok temple in Saraburi, Thailand, continued an impressive industry of handmade textile accessories and full suits destined for migrant Hmong diasporic communities (112). Today, hand-stitched story cloths and *paj ntaub* clothing sold in the diaspora are commonly handmade in Asia, where wages for labor-intensive work of this type are lower. As might be expected, many costume parts are machine-made now, especially in China. The skirts worn most frequently in Laos and diasporic New Year's celebrations are manufactured in China and imported.[12] The now polyester skirt still includes hundreds of tiny pleats, either left plain white or machine-printed to look like the indigo batik and embroidery patterns made by Green Hmong. The Hmongtown Market in St. Paul sells complete outfits in polyester from China, with only a few hemp skirts sold at much more expensive prices. The sellers report that these hemp skirts are made in Laos;[13] hardly anyone in the United States weaves hemp or makes batik anymore. Wronska-Friend (2010) notes that this is also the case in Australia (109).

However, in Asia and the diaspora, some of the more traditional elements of Hmong costume may still be made locally, especially those that require great skill. Most frequently, young women may continue to produce the counted cross-stitch apron piece for New Year's costumes, and then combine it with parts made elsewhere, either in a factory or by a family member. Basic components of a single costume may have been produced in several different states or countries based on where other families live.[14] The funeral jacket appears to be the garment least altered in the diaspora. As discussed by Cooper (2008), Hillmer (2010), and Symonds (2004), no synthetic materials are used, specific way-finding geometric designs cannot be altered, and special hemp or cotton "death" shoes with signifying patterns are required to traverse the rugged terrain on one's return to the ancestors. Wronska-Friend (2010) writes that her interviewees in Australia reveal that death shoes are mostly imported from Laos or Thailand.

One of the most striking features of the transnational traffic in costume pieces is that the codes, or categories, for each Hmong subgroup's identifying costume elements (e.g., blue skirt, white skirt, striped sleeves) have relaxed, resulting in a pronounced disregard for intragroup distinctions. Schein (2004) calls this a "decisive announcement of pan-ethnic identity" (282). The freedom from more fixed cultural conventions doesn't seem problematic and offers Hmong the opportunity to transcend national borders to consume and participate in culture with co-ethnics. The textile practices in rural Asia or the diaspora cannot have the same identifying specificity of the prewar era, and many young girls learn about Hmong culture through videos, not stitching. However, new social narratives are enacted through cloth, whether in Maikue's art, Nonmala's fashion, or variants of Hmong dress in beauty pageants that have become synonymous with many Hmong New Year celebrations.

Hmong Beauty Pageants

Rural life in Hmong villages did not include beauty pageants, and contemporary Hmong pageants did not begin in refugee camps or the diaspora. They developed in military settlements, where displaced Hmong moved in the 1960s. In an article in *Hmong Pages*, Malisamai Vue (2010) reported that the first pageant took place in 1968 in the military settlement of Long Cheng, Laos, where a young contestant by the name of Maiv Yeev Lauj was crowned the first Hmong *Ntxhais Nkauj Ntsuab*. In the beginning, Vue writes, the village leaders were asked to select "a female contestant who he felt most qualified and can represent their village with her true inner and outer beauty showing poise and adequate mannerism." Vang (2010) has suggested that only young women from wealthy families were able to participate in those early pageants, thereby rendering the event a marker of social class (111). In Long Cheng, other cultural influences were incorporated into Hmong life besides beauty pageants. Classical Lao dance and music performances were added to the New Year celebrations as Hmong became exposed to other forms of entertainment. As time passed and new additions became common practices, people began to appropriate them as Hmong traditions (Vang 2010, 104).[15]

While many urban Hmong New Year celebrations include beauty pageants, the textiles that young women wear reveal the beauty pageant organizers' conflicting cultural choices. In the large Hmong community in the Minneapolis–St. Paul area, two New Year celebrations are held each year, each with a different name, and the beauty pageant contestants wear different attire. Vang (2010) describes the role that clothing and culture play in reproducing and contesting social relations. The Minneapolis pageant is called Miss Hmong American, and the beauty queen wears a Western evening gown and is attended by Prince Charming; the St. Paul celebration is called Miss Hmong Minnesota, and the queen wears traditional Hmong costume (and stood next to General Vang Pao until his passing in 2011). The substantive difference between the pageants is that the Minneapolis event illustrates the flux of Hmong culture and the process of Americanization, as seen in the evening gown and Prince Charming, while the St. Paul event presents the immigrant generation's attempt to hold on to Hmong tradition, signified by *paj ntaub* garments (Vang 2010, 117).

Perceptions of culture become rewritten on the body, realized through performances of young female bodies, with textiles that project assimilation or nostalgic longing for a homeland. Other Asian immigrants from the Vietnam War have employed beauty pageants to imagine "the nation" in complex ways. Nhi T. Lieu (2011) writes in *The American Dream in Vietnamese* that the *ao dai* beauty pageants are one of the most visible examples of Vietnamese immigrants trying to negotiate the process of assimilating into bourgeois American culture while remaining ethnically Vietnamese. She suggests that the pageants are used to publicly assert feelings of cultural nationalism as well as anticommunism.[16] The traditional *ao dai* women's garment conjures romantic images of a fictional Vietnamese past that is pure, unified, untainted by war—a mythical homeland free of regional, religious, political, ethnic, and linguistic differences. For Hmong from Asia who identify more with their ethnic identity prior to immigration rather than any particular nation-state, *paj ntaub* garments in beauty pageants invoke tradition and modernity simultaneously, including pan-ethnic variants of costume styles. In 1994, a Miao young woman from China was chosen for the annual Miss Hmong Beauty pageant held in Fresno, California. Schein (2004) describes how "Hmong-Americans have regarded their co-ethnics' costumes from China, then, with a mixture of identification and exoticism. The styles simultaneously register as history, tradition, that which is alien and lost, and also as familiar and related to their own attire" (281).[17]

In the context of the beauty pageant, traditional costume is no longer a cultural text to be closely read by fellow Hmong, as regional and local distinctions are mixed freely or erased, and the most salient feature is the vision of being collectively Hmong. But the resiliency or cultural persistence of *paj ntaub* garments in the diaspora—for whatever cultural practice or meaning they serve—offers the best hope that some of the extraordinary Hmong textile skills will not be lost to history. Just as Hmong borrowed freely from lowland Lao music and dance in military settlements and then expanded those forms in the refugee camps and as immigrants, the emergence of new cultural expressions in clothing or fashion both confirms and alters what Hmongness means—in Asia and beyond. This condition of innovation—even when triggered by loss and uncertainty—creates fertile artistic ground for future adaptations of art forms in the diaspora amid dramatic cultural change.

Asian Chic

As mentioned at the start of this chapter, a tradition of pictorial representation was not part of the cultural legacy of pre–Vietnam War Hmong culture in Asia (in contrast to two thousand years of Western art history, which is filled with figurative images and representations). Naturalistic representation with clothed figures was introduced into Hmong story cloth production in the refugee camps; however, wide exposure to television or printed media was not common until Hmong immigration began in the late 1970s. For Hmong Americans born and raised in the United States, photographic representations of both traditional Hmong costume and Western clothing/fashion are part of daily life. The cultural subtext—that all images of clothing or fashion are seen through a lens of the history of images—is assumed today. The Hmong American experience includes watching *Project Runway,* going on school field trips to art museums, consuming *Vogue* magazine, and shopping for clothes online.

The first generation of Hmong born in America grew up at a time when Asian American fashion designers were gaining prominence in the New York and international fashion world. Young designers were setting up downtown boutiques and midtown showrooms as Asian students were filling fashion school classrooms. Tu (2011) writes: "This rare convergence—between the taste for Asian chic and the prevalence of Asian American designers—provides a unique opportunity to consider how this symbolic context shaped the material conditions of possibility for young Asian American designers" (100). She also asks readers to consider that some designers also contributed to racialized stereotypes. As she points out, "These designers spurred on the appetite for Asianness by offering the industry an Asia filled with romance and nostalgia, glamour and spectacle, and by embracing its strategies of representation and its logic of distance. There is ample evidence to suggest that Asian Americans can at times be as Orientalist as any other designer" (134). The pressure to *do something ethnic* often entailed "the incorporation of what fashion journalists and large design houses understood to be traditional signifiers of Asia—from dragons, lotus, and bamboo to slash necklines, and shantung silk—into some (though never all) of their clothing. The inclusion of just a few elements could yield big results for these small designers" (137). Ideas about Asianness had commercial value through a perceived embodiment of a lost ethos: the racialized conception of a premodern Asia.

While Hmong culture was not burdened with the same visual stereotypes of the East as other more widely recognized cultures, such as China and Japan have been, Hmong Americans soon inherited many Asian American stereotypes, as Hmong were undifferentiated from other Asian cultures. After immigration, Hmong were quickly burdened by conceptions of antimodernity and exoticism. While the textiles were the most visible condition of "otherness," Hmong design had no appeal as Asian chic because it wasn't reduced to a simple visual code. Fashion media representations offered a generalized Asian "look" shaped by majority cultures in China and Japan, as Asian chic and its media representations were created to drive the economic engine of the international fashion industry. New York fashion studios were not likely to invest in elaborate Hmong handwork or ideas of "ethnic" Asianness that did not have a preexisting cultural framework, so Hmong design wasn't commodified by the trend. Clothing influences for young Hmong American designers generally include the painstaking handwork of *paj ntaub* they observed at home but also advertising and representations in contemporary media—of Asian chic or any other fashion trend. The binaries of domestic handwork and machine-produced goods, with their equal media machine, create paradoxical influences that are unique. This may be the last generation in which the binaries of clothing production will be so explicitly lived in the Hmong diaspora, and in which designs have not all been influenced by media and its representations.

Hmong Chic

In the large Hmong community of Minneapolis–St. Paul, the nonprofit Center for Hmong Arts and Talent (CHAT) produces the Fresh Traditions Fashion Show each year, showcasing Hmong American designers. Publicity on its website states: "The Fresh Traditions Fashion Show is the only place where the union between the traditional fabrics of our culture and the contemporary designs of our community takes place."[18] The following descriptions of the collections of the six designers that were featured in 2010, the year I attended, appeared on CHAT's website:

CHONG MOUA: "HLUB HMOOB" (Hmong Love)—a graphic
    focused collection dedicated to our Hmong Youth. Traditional
    Hmong patterns and phrases layered with modern graphics
    make this collection youthful, fun, & culturally inspiring.
SEELIA VACHON: "Midnight Fantasy"—Eccentric, dark, wild, and
    dangerous.
KHAMPHIAN VANG: "Sparrow" Fashion for moving lives.
XEE VANG: "Refined" modern with vibrant colors, embellished
    designs, and distinctive structure.
NONMALA XIONG: "Lady in Red" With an emphasis on color,
    prints, and feminine silhouettes, each garment is ready-to-wear
    for the lady unafraid to make a statement.
LYLENA YANG: "Embroidered Elegance" Meshing Hmong *paj
    ntaub* with modern silhouettes to bring Hmong into the
    mainstream fashion world.

CHAT required designers to "incorporate the 5 traditional Hmong
fabrics" into one garment (or five colors or design elements) for their inspiration of Hmong traditions. The *paj ntaub* influences were indirect and
perhaps unrecognizable to most young Hmong Americans, which constituted a majority of the audience. The overall body profile or modesty of
traditional Hmong dress—which Symonds (2004) insists required an
apron for everyday use—was changed from traditional garments. A few
designs employed the wide pleated skirt. Most garments included more
exposure of the body, an increased amount of skin, or a tighter fit than
traditional garments. While body visibility in dress has frequently been
associated with increased sexual freedom, this construction of modesty is
framed more by gender politics than actual practice. Tu (2011) writes
about control of women and their bodies through visibility/coverage in
dress, framed by political power in almost every culture (200). Modesty as
a cultural trait is controlled mostly by representation, whether it is Hmong,
Muslim, or American sexuality that is under scrutiny. In this context, the
performances of young female bodies struck me as an assertion against
Hmong traditions of modesty, but they can also be viewed as assimilation
(which is also unrelated to actual sexual practice).

So how do young Hmong American fashion designers navigate the
tensions inherent in designing and making clothing from the perspective

of two distinct cultures? Fresh Traditions IV fashion designer Nonmala Xiong (2012) explained that she is most intrigued by 1950s- and 1960s-era designs and silhouettes, and that now she is more attentive to the local Twin Cities fashion scene than she is to national influences or media, such as *Project Runway*. She credits both of her parents for encouraging her to bring her artistic vision to life. Her mother also went to school for apparel design, and her father builds all kinds of things from scratch, which influenced her strong level of craft and love of creation and fashion. Her earliest memory of seeing someone sew was when she was about six years old and watched her mother sew doll bibs for Nonmala's stuffed animals. Her grandmother taught her to do cross-stitch embroidery as a little girl, and she shared this experience with her siblings growing up. Her mother taught her the basics of operating a sewing machine when she was young, but it wasn't until college that she learned to construct garments while she was studying apparel design.

Nonmala sews all her designs herself, and the majority are one-of-a-kind garments produced for fashion shows. They are not mass-produced yet, although that is one of her goals. This places her in the role of fine craftsperson, a link to *paj ntaub* garments that were entirely handmade, and sets her apart from designers in the fashion industry who are often less skilled at sewing and rely on sewers to tell them what is possible to stitch or put into production.[19] She said she thinks that "fashion is a form of expression. People all over the world use it to express who they are, personally and most importantly, culturally. I think that my fashion expresses what I like, not necessarily who I am. Since I am an emerging designer, I have not yet established a solid connection to my design aesthetic and who I am as a person. It is a journey and a goal I hope to be able to achieve one day" (Xiong 2012). Her "Lady in Red" dress featured in the CHAT publicity photos reflects her love of 1960s silhouettes, as it reifies the translation of *paj ntaub* (flower cloth) with hand-appliquéd red flowers and a green vine on a background of shifting black textures, demonstrating aesthetic influences from traditional garments.

While Nonmala has not attended the Hmong New Year celebrations since she was fifteen, she says that she would consider wearing traditional garments if she went again, but that her generation doesn't consider it important in courtship traditions of the Hmong New Year celebrations. "I think we enjoy being able to represent our culture through our garments during the Hmong New Year. Also, I think it is important for our parents and the older generation to see traditions being carried on and through the younger generation" (Xiong 2012). Her spirit of generosity and connectedness, combined with assimilated skills and influences, demonstrates enormous capacity for this generation of makers to continue as transformational agents in the complex aesthetic enterprise of Hmong textiles.

Conclusion

The work of Maikue Vang and Nonmala Xiong is informed by their formal education in art and fashion, and by cultural influences from their families that shape their sense of Hmongness. They are part of the second generation of Hmong immigrants whose lived experience will be very different from that of their mothers and grandmothers, and whose narratives reveal contradictory values, opportunities, and interests. Without the refugee or immigrant label, they are free to build a Hmong American identity through more urban avenues than was possible for previous generations of Hmong women. Their elders' example of cultural agency, seen through production of labor-intensive textiles that had spiritual and material value, had different social relationships and incentives, but the continuation of sewing as a practice with contemporary relevance is constantly redefined in American life. A career in fashion, fine art, or craft is financially precarious today, but the choice to create a unique identity in specialized, at-risk communities is a strong link between elders and young Hmong women.

The metanarrative of Hmong textiles continues to unfold, as it always has, in the empowered choices women make by using textiles as an expressive medium. Without an urtext for Hmong culture, the historic narrative stitched in cloth was always shaped by fleet-footed adjustment to political environments. The social and cultural border crossings that need to be intelligible for Hmong or Hmong Americans relative to powerful neighbors were and are negotiated daily, and globalization offers ever more complex ways for Hmongness to be honored and contested. For Hmong American women born in the United States, innovations of any "text" or textile forms still embody political, cultural, historical, and gendered messages and are historically positioned. However, there is a potentially deep and intimate reason for why many women, not just Hmong, continue to work with cloth: it links them to their mothers and grandmothers. They stitch new narratives of their own for alternative, shape-shifting identities, as they live in realities their grandmothers could not have foretold.

Notes

1. There is a long discussion—beyond the scope of this chapter—about whether only optical stimuli are sufficient for understanding art. My position is that all deep understanding of art/craft/fashion requires material and cultural sensitivity that should account for multiple sensory inputs. In this way, I am quite sympathetic to what I think I understand of Hmong cosmological and aesthetic traditions.

2. Cohen has researched a couple of early sources and found that there are no recognizable figurative representations in the traditional textile designs of the Hmong either in Thailand or in Laos except for an occasional, highly stylized flower or plant (2000, 129).

3. For a detailed history of Hmong textile meanings, see my paper, "Neeg Tawg Rog" (2012).

4. See Vang (2010).

5. Emphasis mine. Hollander's view allows for a narrow, Eurocentric slice of cultural production.

6. See Tu (2011, 106) for a concise description of Barthes's theory.

7. In 1982, I began volunteering at the Southeast Asia Co-op in Providence, Rhode Island, a nonprofit retail space established to help market *paj ntaub*. I learned many stories from the Hmong women friends I met there.

8. Scott has a succinct account of two legends of Hmong literacy, both of which involved the Hmong fleeing from the Han. In one account, the Hmong fell asleep and either their bones ate up their texts or the texts were mistakenly added to a stew and eaten. The other account claimed that the Han took their texts and burned them (2009, 223).

9. Wronska-Friend also writes of the exception: a small group of four families in North Queensland who moved inland, started using the name Amu, and wear some part of Hmong costume every day. This is seen as a negative practice by other Hmong, who consider it an extravagant and unnecessary effort to differentiate themselves from mainstream Australian society and not comply with the image projected by the dominant Hmong group.

10. According to the 2010 U.S. census, there are 260,076 Hmong living in the United States, with the highest Hmong populations in the following five states: California—91,224; Minnesota—66,181; Wisconsin—49,240; North Carolina—10,864; Michigan—5,924.

11. Many Hmong have told me this story over the years that I've worked with them.

12. During a trip to Laos in November–December 2009, I attended Hmong New Year celebrations in Phonsavan and smaller villages in Xieng Khuoang Province. I did not see young women wearing hemp skirts, only polyester imported

from China. The Phonsavan markets did have a few hemp skirts for sale, but they were substantially more expensive.

13. From my visits to the Hmongtown Market, St. Paul, in August 2011 and March 2012.

14. Wronska-Friend (2010, 114) describes Mai Yang's Green Hmong costume for the 2002 New Year celebration in Innisfail, Queensland, Australia. The indigo-dyed skirt was made by refugees in Thailand; it was sent to Mai's mother in France, who added additional embroidery to the skirt, made the hat, and embroidered panels for her jacket. Her pink sash was made from fabric that originated in Mexico and was sent to Mai's sister in California, then on to Australia. Mai did the cross-stitch for the sash in Innisfail, which was added to the sash along with silver coins and beads from Thailand.

15. Vang also points out that although beauty pageants were not completely new diasporic cultural inventions, progressive Hmong women criticized the objectification of women early on and opposed the beauty pageants.

16. Hmong may not feel compelled to assert feelings of anticommunism through beauty pageants in the United States because Hmong anticommunist rhetoric is well known. In the United States, the Hmong have been represented as freedom fighters and victims of communism.

17. Schein referred to Rebecca Mercer's "reconstitutive link" with the home-land to develop a wider theoretical framework that "asserted a pristine unity prior to the segmentation by the political borders of modern states" (2004, 282).

18. See www.aboutchat.org. I attended the 2010 Fresh Traditions IV event (November 7, 2010, Varsity Theater, Minneapolis, Minn.), which followed the format of contemporary Western fashion shows and included an elevated runway, a darkened room with strobe lights, and thumping electronic music.

19. Designing and sewing are interdependent forms of labor, and for designers like Nonmala, who have sewing skills and are doing it themselves, there is deeper understanding that design and sewing are contiguous practices. For a great analysis of the polarized labor structure of designers and sewers in the garment industry, see Tu (2011).

Works Cited

Adams, Monni. 1974. "Dress and Design in Highland Southeast Asia." *Textile Museum Journal* 4, no. 1: 51–67.

Barthes, Roland. 1983. *The Fashion System*. Translated by Matthew Ward and Richard Howard. Berkeley and Los Angeles: University of California Press. (Original work published in French, 1967).

Cohen, Erik. 2000. *The Commercialized Crafts of Thailand: Hill Tribes and Lowland Villages*. Honolulu: University of Hawai'i Press.

"Community Arts Project: Update #1." Center for Hmong Art and Talent. http://www.aboutchat.org.

Cooper, Robert. 2008. *The Hmong: A Guide to Traditional Life.* Lao People's Democratic Republic: Lao-Insight Books.

Craig, Geraldine. 2012. "*Neeg Tawg Rog* (War-torn People): Linguistic Consciousness in the Hmong Diaspora." Textile Society of America Symposium Proceedings. Paper 671. http://digitalcommons.unl.edu/tsaconf/671.

Dewhurst, C. Kurt, and Marsha MacDowell, eds. 1984. *Michigan: Hmong Arts.* East Lansing: Michigan State University.

Donnelly, Nancy D. 1994. *Changing Lives of Hmong Refugee Women.* Seattle and London: University of Washington Press.

Duffy, John. 2007. *Writing from These Roots: Literacy in a Hmong American Community.* Honolulu: University of Hawai'i Press.

"Fresh Traditions IV Fashion Show." Center for Hmong Art and Talent. http://www.aboutchat.org.

Hillmer, Paul. 2010. *A People's History of the Hmong.* Minnesota: Minnesota Historical Society Press.

Hollander, Anne. 1993. *Seeing Through Clothes.* Berkeley, Los Angeles, and London: University of California Press.

Lewis, Paul, and Elaine Lewis. 1984. *Peoples of the Golden Triangle.* London: Thames and Hudson.

Lieu, Nhi T. 2011. *The American Dream in Vietnamese.* Minneapolis and London: University of Minnesota Press.

Mallinson, Jane, Nancy Donnelly, and Ly Hang. 1996. *Hmong Batik: A Textile Technique from Laos.* Chiang Mai: Silkworm Books.

Ovesen, Jan. 2004. "The Hmong and Development in the Lao People's Democratic Republic." In *Hmong/Miao in Asia,* edited by Nicholas Tapp, Jean Michaud, Christian Culas, and Gary Yia Lee. Chiang Mai: Silkworm Books.

Schein, Louisa. 2004. "Hmong/Miao Transnationality: Identity beyond Culture." In Tapp, Michaud, Culas, and Lee, *Hmong/Miao in Asia.*

Scott, James C. 2009. *The Art of Not Being Governed: An Anarchist History of Upland Southeast Asia.* New Haven: Yale University Press.

"Southeast Asian Americans State Populations 2010 U.S. Census." *Hmong Studies Internet Resource Center.* http://www.hmongstudies.org.

Symonds, Patricia V. 2004. *Calling in the Soul: Gender and the Cycle of Life in a Hmong Village.* Seattle and London: University of Washington Press.

Tu, Thuy Linh N. 2011. *The Beautiful Generation: Asian Americans and the Cultural Economy of Fashion.* Durham, N.C., and London: Duke University Press.

Vang, Chia Youyee. 2010. *Hmong America: Reconstructing Community in Diaspora.* Urbana, Chicago, and Springfield: University of Illinois Press.

Vang, Maikue. 2012. Email interviews with the author, November–December 2012.

Vue, Malisamai. 2010. "Hmong Beauty Pageant: From the Past to the Present." *Hmong Pages,* August 1.

Wronska-Friend, Maria. 2010. "Globalised Threads: Costumes of the Hmong Community in North Queensland." In *The Hmong of Australia: Culture and Diaspora,* edited by Nicholas Tapp and Gary Yia Lee, 97–122. Canberra: The Australian National University E Press.

Xiong, Nonmala. 2012. Email interviews with the author, February–May 2012.

Yang, Dao. 2004. "Hmong Refugees from Laos: The Challenges of Social Change." In Tapp, Michaud, Culas, and Lee, *Hmong/Miao in Asia.*

———. 2009. "Hmong Culture Is Hmong Soul." In *The Impact of Globalization and Trans-Nationalism on the Hmong,* edited by Gary Yia Lee. St. Paul, Minn.: Center for Hmong Studies, Concordia University.

Yang, Ia Moua. 2009. Phone interviews with the author, August 2009.

Yang, Ia Moua, and Carolyn Shapiro. 2002. *The Pa Ndau of Ia Moua Yang: Keeping Alive the Treasure of the Hmong.* Detroit: Kenneth Yang and Ia Moua Yang.

Yang, Kao Kalia. 2008. *The Latehomecomer: A Hmong Family Memoir.* Minneapolis: Coffee House Press.

CHAPTER 9

Reel Women

Diasporic Cinema and Female Collectivity in Abel Vang's *Nyab Siab Zoo*

Aline Lo

R ELEASED IN 2009, Abel Vang's film *Nyab Siab Zoo* (*The Good-Hearted Daughter*) received little popular and critical attention and largely went unnoticed for many reasons. It played at various film festivals but garnered only a few reviews even within the Hmong community.[1] The film tells the story of a Hmong female displacement during a time before the "secret war" in Laos, and centers on the integration of two women into a new community. While it may not have prompted much initial interest, the film's focus on Hmong women and its complex portrayal of transnational longing is a strong example of the limitations and possibilities of diasporic cinema, particularly its concern with homeland nostalgia and changing gender roles.[2] More specific to this collection, *Nyab Siab Zoo* claims multiple places for Hmong women in its portrayal and exploration of empowered and subversive female characters. In addition, it represents various levels of patriarchal bargaining, creating a cinematic space for strong pre-diasporic female networks that resonates with contemporary issues of female empowerment and questions the gendered longing for the homeland. In this chapter, then, I argue that Vang's film negotiates the larger tropes of both diasporic cinema and Hmong media, simultaneously presenting a nostalgic portrait of Hmong village life while calling it into question by addressing issues of female agency and collectivity in pre- and post-diasporic communities. Indeed, one of the film's achievements lies in its ability to vacillate between a nostalgic fictionalization of a gender-structured past and a subversive cinematic space in which women are allowed to renegotiate their female roles and display their strength. As *Nyab Siab Zoo* represents female agency and obligation in a pre-diasporic setting, moving between male objectification to female empowerment, it also exemplifies the tension of diasporic nostalgia for the homeland and its seemingly stabilized gender roles.

In the film, Vang's female character, with the help of her mother-in-law, manages to begin a thriving new life, even though she is ultimately subject to male desire and masculine dominance and is conscripted into the male characters' idea of community. For the daughter-in-law, widowhood and lack of family briefly complicate her role as a Hmong woman before she eventually conforms to the established masculine norm. Yet even though the narrative eventually upholds the patrilineal community, it also showcases a secondary social structure that empowers women and establishes a legitimate form of agency for the daughter-in-law. The film is careful to highlight a system of female interdependence and cooperation, complementing its patriarchal ending with a women-centered communal network. Indeed, by emphasizing the marginal and unstable statuses of the two female principals, the film creates the ideal scenario in which gender roles are continuously blurred, thus drawing parallels to the experiences of Hmong American women. In this chapter, I begin with a larger reading of Vang's film as an example of diasporic cinema, as taking part in a tradition that highlights the issues of displacement, longing, and ambivalent assimilation. Rooting the conversation in diasporic cinema and feminist film criticism, I then make the case that *Nyab Siab Zoo*'s simultaneous portrayal of shifting gender roles and nurturing female spaces *and* its preoccupation with capturing the homeland reflect contemporary conversations concerning the role of women in an ever-changing Hmong American culture.

The Good-Hearted Daughter-in-Law

The plot of *Nyab Siab Zoo* focuses on the struggle of two widowed women, specifically a young woman and her mother-in-law, who leave their home in order to establish a new life in their husbands' old village. The movie moves slowly through the daily struggle of Nyab Seng (Ia Lee) as she and her mother-in-law (Mee Her) learn to live on the periphery of a culture structured by husbands and fathers.[3] Vang's film, written by Mee Yang Vang, portrays a time before the forced migration to America, reimagining lives relatively untouched by outside cultures and driven largely by agrarian subsistence. The film lingers on the small details of everyday activities and the labor-intensive work involved in merely getting by. There is no evidence of modern technology or factory-produced goods or materials, leading viewers to believe that the film is set in a time or place that has little, if any, contact with nonagrarian societies.[4] As such, the women must rely on their own strength and must abide by culturally normalized gender roles that limit unmarried women from fully participating in the community.

In many ways, the film conforms to the notion of the innocent, dutiful, and resilient Hmong daughter-in-law, as Nyab Seng's constant narration allows viewers to understand and know all her inner thoughts and motivations, establishing them as well intentioned and kind. Whether she is rising early to feed her small family of pigs, bathing her ailing mother-in-law, quietly working the fields of prosperous neighbors, or diligently performing the task of two people on her own, Nyab Seng never regrets her decision to return to her husband's land or blames others for her misfortune. Even when it is clear that her husband's kind and wealthy male relative Paochoua (Pha Thao) has taken an interest in her, she is unwilling to encourage him, since a second marriage would entail abandoning her current mother-in-law, who actually approves and encourages the match, for a new one. Nyab Seng is, after all, the good-hearted daughter (in-law), who follows her husband's impoverished and sickly mother back to a strange land, where she has no family and no landed security. Nyab Seng is a largely unwavering character, and her story ends happily, with the mother-in-law giving her and Paochoua her blessing to marry as she takes her last breath. With the death of the mother-in-law, viewers, who have watched Nyab Seng stoically endure loneliness and poverty, can celebrate her impending happiness and new life without worrying about the fate of the lovable mother. Simply glancing at the plot, Nyab Seng and her hard work and loyalty are finally rewarded in the end, securing her a loving husband and thus a prosperous place within a new community. However, this chapter will show how a female collective, which the film carefully constructs, makes this move from the periphery into the center possible. Moreover, I argue that this emphasis on female strength and collectivity reflects lingering tensions within the Hmong American diaspora concerning homeland nostalgia and destabilized gender roles.

Diasporic Cinema and the Female Subject

Although my focus is on the cinematic depiction of Hmong women, this chapter benefits from broader conversations on the critical work in diasporic studies and feminist film criticism. Because of *Nyab Siab Zoo*'s focus on female marginalization and collectivity, feminist film criticism provides useful strategies for understanding the interplay between the characters, the cinematography, and the eroticization of women's bodies within the diaspora. Although Sabrina Barton (2006) resists the "two major phases in the feminist film theory tradition" (332), her move away from these two methods marks their importance in analyzing cinematic representations of women. Barton identifies these two phases as "the 'images of women' approach" and "the 'Woman as image' approach" (332). For *Nyab Siab Zoo*, I approach the film through both phases, assessing how the female characters are "positive or negative reflections" of real Hmong women and thinking about how the film "produces and reproduces" the established representations that have served to define Hmong women (332). I also rely on critics like Laura Mulvey and Teresa de Lauretis, whose work on the male and female gaze helps me discuss the ways in which the position of the camera or the point of view shapes how viewers relate to the characters. In addition, scholars such as Lan Duong, Louisa Schein, and Jigna Desai, who work more specifically on the intersection between feminist film criticism and diasporic cinema, are essential to this chapter.

In *Treacherous Subjects*, Duong's (2012) analysis of the female figure, family politics, and transnational cinema highlights collaboration as a practice that can subvert and complicate traditional models of family and kinship. Most importantly, Duong is able to critique the relationship between family, nationalism, diaspora, and gender roles. Thus, her analytical mode of "trans-Vietnamese feminism" is inspired by "the works of writers and directors in Vietnam and the diaspora, who have used their art in order to challenge traditional notions of gender, family, and nation" (3). For Duong, "the work of trans-Vietnamese feminism needs to unseat the familial ideal as a trans-historical signifier for wholeness and completion" (187). "Yet," she adds, "ungrounding symbolic family ties does not have to connote loss" (187). That is to say, recognizing sites of transnational collaboration that work beyond the family does not have to imply a complete or negative break from the past. Instead, loss should be understood as a precursor to generative change and heretofore unseen multiplicities. Following Duong, my own analysis of *Nyab Siab Zoo* focuses on the film's interest in representing female collectivity as a counter model to patrilineal kinship. At the same time, I acknowledge that the film does not entirely dismiss the patriarchal social structure and, because of this dual interest, captures the differing attitudes about Hmong female gender roles in the diaspora.

Drawing on scholars in the fields of feminist film criticism and diasporic studies, I connect the more apt nuances in order to focus on the key tropes dealing with homeland nostalgia and the role women play in these pre-diasporic portrayals. At the most basic level, diaspora "are decentralised cultural formations that sustain real and imagined connections across spread populations and/or country of origin" (Georgiou 2007, 15). Looking beyond this idea of a dispersed collective, diaspora has taken on the characteristics of disconnection, a yearning for transnational ties, and a nostalgia or longing for the homeland. In his writings on the African diaspora, which has a specific history rooted in the transatlantic slave trade, Paul Gilroy (1987) notes that "modernity raised a different set of issues centering on the need to recover and validate black culture and reincarnate the sense of being and belonging which had been erased from it by slavery" (217). This "need to recover and validate" is very much tied to a desire to belong, to feel at ease with one's displacement. Edward Said (1984) echoes this sense of loss and homelessness in his work on exile and living within a diasporic community, but he also discusses the exalted memory of the homeland, the nostalgia for what has been lost. He writes, "Exile is predicated on the existence of, love for, and bond with one's native place" (55). These issues of loss, longing, recovery, and transnational collectivity help define diasporic cinema, which is an effort to depict such themes through film. As Olga Guedes Bailey, Myria Georgiou, and Ramaswami Harindranath (2007) argue in their introduction to an edited collection on diasporic media, "The assumption is similar [to general media studies] in that the daily, ordinary cultural and media practices of migrants and diasporic communities might help to forge feelings of 'belonging' and 'bridging,' creating mediated, symbolic spaces for political expression, senses of inclusion or/and exclusion, and hybrid identity articulations which transcend the binary of 'homeland' and 'new land'" (6).

Desai's *Beyond Bollywood* (2004) does not focus on Hmong American cinema, but her interrogation of cultural production and consumption in both the homeland and the diaspora provides an illuminating mode of critique and analysis. Desai—as well as other scholars, such as Duong—believes that diasporic films are not simply uncomplicated portrayals of the homeland or of displaced communities, but films that represent transnational issues or appeal. Separately, Koltyk and Schein, both of whom I discuss later, also understand diasporic filmmaking along the lines of expressing cross-national concerns, speaking more specifically to Hmong media practices. Because the two largely focus on the voyeuristic aspects of return films, I turn to Desai to consider competing understandings of diaspora and homeland and how cinema can help capture and complicate these imagined spaces. The films she discusses go beyond a singular, enclosed idea of nationhood or dominant cinema and are characterized by "disjunctures, heterogeneity, and hybridity" (2004, 36). She adds that "these heterogeneities and multiplicities indicate the different material and historical conditions of production that create specific and local cultural politics in relation to dominant forms" (36). That is to say, diasporic films are not easily located within one mode of production or within one national community or discourse. In the case of *Nyab Siab Zoo,* the filmmaker is Hmong American, the film is shot in Southeast Asia, the setting is an unmodern traditional village, and, as I will show, the gendered plot reflects contemporary issues. Furthermore, the film attempts to speak to a non-Hmong audience and, although the dialogue is entirely in Hmong, offers subtitles, opens with biblical lines, and lists all the film credits in English.[5] The film, as I will discuss later in this section, is also similar to older forms of Hmong American filmmaking that touch on diasporic themes of longing and loss. Thus, the film is very much a hybrid that is indicative of "different material and historical conditions of production." Beyond the film's scattered origins and interests, it also reflects some of Desai's, as well as Koltyk's and Schein's, nuanced discussion of the role of diasporic films.

While Desai is able to bring together many other concerns within diasporic studies, I have chosen to focus on issues of nostalgia and gender roles and the way in which Vang's film disallows an easy longing for the homeland by emphasizing Nyab Seng's limitations and her marginalization. In her text, Desai (2004) acknowledges the centrality of themes such as "nostalgia, longing, and loss" within "most discourses of diaspora" (102). Yet she is also critical of the relationship between homeland and diaspora, particularly "the idea of homeland as a given point of origin and as an original" (102). In this sense, the homeland cannot be understood as an unchanging ideal that serves as the measure of what has gone "wrong" within the diaspora. The notion of being nostalgic, of longing for a better past, must be questioned and complicated. Although a powerful force, nostalgia, especially in the form of film, is still fantasy. Here I want to reiterate Duong's (2012) idea of using art as a way to challenge traditional familial roles, to question "the imposition of the meanings of home and homeland on gendered subjects" (9). I will also draw on Koltyk (1993) and Schein (2004), particularly the former's discussion of "homeland videos" and the latter's characterization of eroticized longing and nostalgia. For *Nyab Siab Zoo,* I contend that the film resists a nostalgic portrayal of traditional Hmong life by emphasizing its difficulties and its restrictive gender roles. Even as the film takes on a longing gaze at times, it portrays the hardships of Nyab Seng's life and imposes a critical diasporic perspective on the traditionally peripheral role of Hmong women then and now.

The film's portrayal of the supportive mother–daughter relationship between the two female characters is in many ways dictated by their vulnerable circumstances, but its unambiguous codependence hints at deep-rooted anxieties of in-law relations and declining communal values recognizable to most Hmong viewers in the U.S. diaspora. These fears do not simply concern the changes in gender roles between men and women but also those between Hmong American women and their families and communities. This is not to say that such anxieties do not exist outside Hmong social practices—only that the film addresses very specific concerns that seem targeted at a Westernized Hmong audience. In many ways, the film goes beyond the basic narrative of the overbearing and terrorizing mother-in-law and the lazy, incapable, uncaring daughter-in-law, which are tropes prevalent in Hmong media. I return to these archetypes or concerns in my discussion of Hmong female writing, but they are also reflected in widely distributed films within the Hmong American community.

Two striking examples of the mother–daughter genre also represent different phases of Hmong filmmaking practices, pointing to a continuous fascination with this subject matter. The first is a 1992 Hmong dubbed version of a 1989 Hindi film originally titled *Chandni.* Under the distribution of ST Universal Video—a Hmong company that Schein describes at length in her article—the Hindi film, renamed *Kev Hlub Tsis Paub Kawg,* or Neverending Love (my translation), tells the story of a young woman who is bullied by her husband's family, who does not accept her. She sacrifices her happiness by leaving him once he becomes confined to a wheelchair. She then finds a new lover and a future mother-in-law who adores her, but she cannot go through with the marriage because of the undying love she still feels for her husband, who is now rehabilitated and asking her to return. Although not produced by Hmong, the film is characteristic of early efforts to create Hmong media, and I would argue that the popularity of this film rests on the translatability of the subject matter. The second film is a horror film called *Nkauj Nyab* (2009), which the producers translated as *The Awaiting Bride,* which retells the Hmong folk tale of a fiancée who haunts the village waiting for her would-be husband. This film explores an extreme version of the devoted daughter who angers the family by refusing to move on after her own death. It also represents a growing interest in the Hmong American community to explore different genres of film production. Yet what has not changed is a preoccupation with the daughter-in-law and her ability to be accepted or seen as good. Whether well intentioned or mean spirited, the daughter-in-law is always subject to the scrutiny of her family and the larger community, and she never seems to escape their gaze.

Portraying and Spying on the Good Daughter

Vang's *Nyab Siab Zoo* closely follows a simplified version of the Old Testament narrative of the Book of Ruth, gently observing one daughter-in-law's unflappable love of and loyalty to her husband's mother. Indeed, the film opens with these lines from the Book of Ruth: "Where you die I will die, / and there I will be buried. / May the Lord deal with me, / be it ever so severely, / if anything but death / separated you and me" (Vang 2009).[6] The original tale begins with the relocation of the mother-in-law, Naomi; her husband, Elimelech; and their two sons to Moab, whereupon the sons marry two Moabite women, Orpah and Ruth. After a decade, the men all die, and Naomi decides to move back to Bethlehem, instructing her daughters-in-law to return to their families. While Orpah reluctantly returns to her people, Ruth refuses to leave Naomi despite the challenges she will face in Bethlehem and vows to remain with her, as a true daughter would. This is the same beginning that Vang establishes in his film, opening first with the lines from the Book of Ruth, followed by a tearful scene between the two parting daughters-in-law. From here, the two stories remain fairly similar, with major differences emerging from the film's urge to address specific Hmong cultural traditions and anxieties. These divergences between the two stories, which both focus on assimilating through honorable acts of femininity and marital devotion, reveal how Vang's film is also interested in recapturing a now inaccessible Hmong way of life. *Nyab Siab Zoo* intentionally relies on Ruth's "shining example of virtuous devotion" to tell a story of the ideal traditional Hmong woman to a modern and mixed audience (Honig 2001, 41). By invoking Ruth, *Nyab Siab Zoo* estab-lishes a narrative in which the daughter-in-law can be accepted as a new member of the community and avoids any ambiguity concerning Nyab Seng's moral character or her ability to be integrated, imagining the per-fect scenarios to reward her model feminine behavior. This section of the chapter therefore focuses on the film's portrayal of Nyab Seng as the good daughter and how it often employs the male character's perspective to establish her as such.

Nyab Siab Zoo uses the male gaze to applaud Nyab Seng's devotion, emphasizing her temporary marginalization from the patriarchal system as well as her desirability to Hmong men. As Teresa de Lauretis (1984) defines in *Alice Doesn't,* the male gaze is a common cinematic device in which "the woman is framed by the look of the camera as icon, or object of the gaze: an image made to be looked at by the spectator, whose look is relayed by the look of the male character(s)" (139). Viewers literally see the woman through the male character's perspective and are thus likely to adopt the male's opinion of the female subject. Opening with lines from the Book of Ruth, the film establishes a patriarchal valuation of feminine behavior early on. By the time the audience actually sees Nyab Seng in the first scene, it already recognizes her as the loyal daughter-in-law, expecting her to fulfill her role as Ruth. As the film moves along, this initial male gaze is almost usurped by Nyab Seng's constant narration of her daily struggles. Indeed, the film continuously shifts between the male and fe-male perspective. While it sometimes establishes the female perspective over that of the male, it often changes to the male gaze, especially as a way to reinforce Nyab Seng's vulnerable and marginal status.

The placement of Nyab Seng's voice over the film's sequences frequently turns viewers away from the male gaze, replacing it with a female perspec-tive and interiority. From the narration, the audience comes to recognize Nyab Seng's isolation and the strength it requires to accomplish everyday tasks. Although she expresses little resentment about her situation, she makes it clear that much of her loneliness and difficulties stem from her widowhood and how it excludes her from fully participating in communal events. During the New Year's festivities, she tells the audience that she and her mother-in-law will not be able to celebrate in true fashion, since they have no men in their household to make the traditional sticky rice cakes. Her lack of place is not defined simply by their poverty but also by their detachment from any men. These sad moments, however, are not described in a bitter or an angry tone, for the film still wants to portray Nyab Seng as the good-hearted daughter-in-law. If anything, such details only reinforce her devotion, highlighting the sacrifices she makes in order to stay true to her marriage vows. These scenes also help establish the queer space in which women are able to live outside the patrilineal community. Nyab Seng and her mother-in-law exist on the edge of society, both in and out of the social realm, and the film explores this duality with competing moments of female interiority and male objectification. As such, scenes of inner and outward hardship are often disrupted by the physical presence of a male, reinstating the male gaze and Nyab Seng's fulfillment of the role of a good and dutiful daughter (in-law).

Because of her quiet suffering, Nyab Seng rarely expresses her pain, so it is significant that Paochoua comes upon her during the only scene in which she is outwardly grieving. Thinking that she is alone, Nyab Seng tells the audience about the sadness of losing a husband and the importance of Hmong sung poetry, and then begins to sing about her sorrow and the tragic circumstances of her life. A supposedly private moment, she is unknowingly watched by Paochoua, who happens to find himself there and stops to listen and observe her. This type of spying courtship, common in Hmong narratives, represents Nyab Seng's primary function as a desirable mate. She is not simply allowed to mourn for her own sake, but is put on display for the male's evaluation. The scene establishes Paochoua's perspective by opening with a shot of him before cutting to Nyab Seng as she shares her inner thoughts and then commences to sing. Watching from above, Paochoua's point of view takes precedence, and the camera lens angles down toward Nyab Seng. Later, viewers peek alongside Paochoua, seeing Nyab Seng through a frame of banana leaves. With Paochoua gazing on Nyab Seng, the scene of grieving changes into one of courtship, and his desires take priority over her sorrow. In this instance, Paochoua's gaze takes on what Laura Mulvey (2001) characterizes as the cinematic eye's ability "to build the pleasure of looking" (4). That is to say, from Paochoua's perspective, Nyab Seng becomes a desirable and eroticized subject. Her performance now plays into the ideal of the long-suffering widow who upholds the bond of marriage even after death. It also reveals her skill and talent at sung poetry, which is often seen as a desirable quality in a Hmong woman. Most importantly, the reinsertion of the male gaze during this private moment confirms Nyab Seng's inability to define herself independently of the male subject. However much she reveals about her inner thoughts and desires, she still exists in a world defined by the male's demands, and the film reminds viewers of this world through the explicit reintroduction of the male gaze. In the end, the conditions of her world determine that she continue to establish her place in the community by becoming yet another daughter-in-law. This constant shift of perspectives not only establishes Nyab Seng's ambiguous status in the village but also points to the film's complex diasporic representations of Hmong women and systems of kinship. While the film uses the male gaze to establish Nyab Seng's place as a daughter-in-law, it also constructs female-centered scenes and employs the female gaze to portray crucial moments of female solidarity and empowerment.

Looking Beyond the Male Gaze

Solely focusing on the patriarchal narrative of the female leads, it is easy to overlook the women who make up the larger social dimension of the film. While the betrothal ending seemingly champions male-defined worlds, *Nyab Siab Zoo* presents a complementary social structure that lends power and agency to its female characters. Indeed, the film's final shots are, tellingly, not of the marriage between the new couple but of tender moments that have passed between Nyab Seng and her mother-in-law, pushing audiences to reflect on the primary function of female relationships in Nyab Seng's success. But even beyond the mutually beneficial connection between Nyab Seng and the mother-in-law and her own ability to perform masculine tasks, there are other women whose friendship and special knowledge help reestablish the daughter-in-law's new place in the village. Many of these scenes of female collectivity are shot from Nyab Seng's perspective or are meaningfully free of men, producing cinematic spaces where women are knowledgeable, resourceful, and supportive of one another. In this manner, *Nyab Siab Zoo* imagines a unique space not only where women have the skills to support one another but also where men, because of Nyab Seng's unattached status as a widow, are largely incapable of helping in her daily life. Throughout the film, *Nyab Siab Zoo* inserts multiple moments of female collectivism and collaboration, showing how this alternative network provides support and knowledge even to women who are living on the fringes of society.

Although Anna Dempsey's (2009) article largely focuses on American frontier films, her discussion of female communities provides a narrative model for the construction of similar entities in *Nyab Siab Zoo*. Describing the "nurturing film genre," Dempsey explains that in such films, "the female protagonists subvert the masculine gaze through their creation of nurturing spaces and places" (116). These spaces are both located within the reality of the film, often created by women and "the help of those marginalized by the dominant culture," and constructed by the setting and cinematography (119). Thus, the character's actions as well as the camera's perspective play a role in defining and producing spaces in which female leads are not subject to male desire or reliant on a patriarchal social structure. In *Nyab Siab Zoo*, the moments of female independence and collectivism are often framed by Nyab Seng or are shot in a "cinematic landscape outside the patriarchal field of vision" (134). As widows and outsiders, both Nyab Seng and her mother-in-law, even with her deceased husband's relations in the village, do not have a stable place in a patriarchal system; however, the film aptly portrays the other levels of community that make it possible for the women to thrive. Of course much of their basic survival has to do with Nyab Seng's ability to perform male-specific tasks, which she often completes by herself and, significantly, without the presence of men.

Nyab Seng's patience and diligence are a sign not only of her daughterly devotion but of her actual strength and skills, as well as her ability to exist outside a male-centered society. Even as she constantly narrates how difficult it is for her to complete men's tasks, viewers witness her performing them nonetheless. In one scene, the filmic gaze focuses on how she patiently and carefully arranges a heavy and unwieldy load of water (roughly 7–10 gallons) in a large wooden bucket onto her back. The scene opens with the soft rush of the river and then pans to a single figure waiting patiently on the banks. This initial view of the river assigns no specific gaze to this scene and so the focus is solely on Nyab Seng's actions. Shot with no voice-over and with only the musical soundtrack and the sound of the babbling river, the film shows a solitary Nyab Seng filling and struggling to ease this cumbersome load onto her small frame. The visual representation of this laborious act juxtaposed with the soothing music illuminates her loneliness as well as her dedication. As the camera tracks her up the hill, shot so that viewers look down on her, she finally verbalizes her struggle, saying, "[Carrying water] is heavier than [carrying wood]" (Vang 2009). This delayed admission not only confirms what viewers have just witnessed but also recalls an earlier scene in which Nyab Seng speaks specifically about the difficulty of being on her own. However, what marks her strength in these scenes is not simply her ability to perform these tasks but the film's emphasis on her capacity to do them without the help of men.

Carrying the water home, the following scene reinforces Nyab Seng's lonely independence and why she cannot rely on male help. As she carefully approaches the house with her heavy load, Paochoua completely overlooks her, as he is too distracted by the mother-in-law's insinuation that he has fallen in love with Nyab Seng. Instead of seeing her and offering to help, Paochoua simply rushes away and turns in a different direction so that the shot is left once again with only Nyab Seng's figure. In this moment, where she could have been subject to Paochoua's yearnful gaze, she is left alone to finish her task independently. Thus, viewers see how Nyab Seng can nurture herself, witnessing how she can rely on her own strength even when men are in the scene. However, her physical abilities are improved by the help of three women who make up much of her social sphere. All three of these women are attached to female-centered scenes and to specifically gendered tasks and roles, establishing a space within Hmong society that is nurturing to women and that can subvert male authority.[7]

Falling into the cinematic tropes of the "nurture film," each of the three women within Nyab Seng's network appear in female-dominant scenes and shots. The first of these women is a friend (Chue Vang) that Nyab Seng makes as they both wash clothes in the river, a duty often assigned to women.[8] This friend provides life-changing advice and helps Nyab Seng take care of her sick mother-in-law at a crucial time. The scene in which they first meet opens with Nyab Seng's narration of her loneliness as the camera sweeps from a view of the cliffs to the two women working side by side. Just before the camera comes upon the women, Nyab Seng tells us, "Every time I come to the river I'm alone. Fortunately, today, there is a village woman here too" (Vang 2009). Once again, the viewer is reminded of her solitude, making this fortunate encounter a welcome change. Although Nyab Seng often keeps quiet, especially in larger groups and in front of men, she befriends this woman when the two are alone by the river. Noticing that the woman is with child, Nyab Seng offers to help with the laundry and makes a useful ally. Immediately after Nyab Seng insists on helping her, the new acquaintance tells her to work on another farm where the owners, Paochoua's parents, are known to pay more generously. After this beneficial exchange of information, the two women walk off together as Nyab Seng tells the audience that, from that moment on, they became friends. This friendship, while financially useful, is also emotionally important to Nyab Seng, who is alone and has recently parted from a close friend, her sister-in-law. As someone who is proximate in age and who is also a daughter-in-law, this new friend can act as confidante and helper, and she returns later in the film to help care for the mother-in-law and give Nyab Seng more advice. Significantly, this friendship scene in which Nyab Seng enters into a collaborative relationship is established through a female activity and is told from Nyab Seng's perspective. Her initial narration of the scene fixes the viewer within her gaze, grounding the scene with her thoughts, desires, and emotions.

When the film introduces the female herbalist, a figure with more social authority, it explicitly takes on Nyab Seng's point of view, highlighting her reliance on this knowledgeable figure. While not necessarily a friend, Aunt Za (Mee Vang) plays an important role in the film, providing Nyab Seng with medicine for her mother-in-law and also representing a mostly female role within traditional Hmong society. As Patricia V. Symonds (2008) explains in her discussion of Hmong women herbalists, "These women learn about herbal medicines from a mother or aunt and then pass on their knowledge to the next generation; their knowledge is closely guarded" (27–28). Herbal treatment is a form of healing that is usually only mastered by women and is passed on exclusively to other women. Thus, it represents a crucial duty that only women are capable of and responsible for maintaining. When the herbalist is first introduced in the film, she is presented as a clear authority figure, with the camera taking on Nyab Seng's actual gaze. From her line of vision, the camera lens/viewer looks down to Nyab Seng's hand as she reaches for the medicine and listens to the herbalist's detailed instructions. Only after looking up to the herbalist's face does the camera finally reveal Nyab Seng's face. The first shot of Nyab Seng's extended arm places viewers in the same position of grateful student, one who must defer to the special knowledge of the herbalist. Throughout this short scene, Nyab Seng asks multiple questions about dosage and medication, and each time the herbalist responds with extended and concrete instructions. From their exchange, the audience comes to understand that the herbalist performs an important task and that she holds knowledge that others, like Nyab Seng, do not. Later in the film, when the friend recommends the same herbalist, it is clear that not only must Nyab Seng rely on this woman's knowledge for medicinal help, but so must the other villagers who lack this skill.[9] The importance of this relationship, like the one with the pregnant friend, is also established through the cinematography, which represents another female network that is seemingly undisturbed by male authority. While the scenes with the friend and herbalist do not explicitly challenge the patrilineal system of Hmong kinship, those with the mother-in-law directly champion female collaboration and subvert the male-centered social structure.

The mother-in-law plays the most pivotal role in Nyab Seng's female network, and the film often portrays her as a sharp and powerful ally who is not afraid to denounce the system of patrilineal kinship. The mother-in-law provides companionship and a sense of home, and she possesses the foresight to secure a marriage for her beloved daughter-in-law. Indeed, it is the mother-in-law who encourages Nyab Seng to continue working for Paochoua's family and for him to visit their home. The film provides multiple shots of the mother-in-law approvingly catching moments and hints of Paochoua's interest in Nyab Seng. She is almost smug in her knowledge that she has a desirable daughter-in-law and that the two should be married. In the end, a scene to which I will later return, it is she who loudly protests the proposal of a forced marriage between Nyab Seng and a male relative, Xi (Ha Vang), who desires the new widow as his second wife. The mother-in-law's deathbed request secures the match between Paochoua and Nyab Seng, releasing Nyab Seng from her obligations and extracting a promise of love and marriage from the two. The mother-in-law's intuition and quick thinking finally ensure that her good-hearted daughter-in-law has an established place in the community, thus completing their movement from the periphery into the center. However, much of this movement has also been facilitated by Nyab Seng's own skills and kindness, and by the support and knowledge of her friend and the herbalist. The film's outcome is, as I have argued, largely achieved by depicting a collaborative network of nurturing women that allows Nyab Seng to slowly but successfully gain access back into a patrilineal society. Although Nyab Seng ultimately reenters the patriarchal system, the film focuses on the importance of female collectivity, especially when the patrilineal kinship system fails to support the women or recognize that a major social shift has occurred. In this sense, the film works to represent diasporic concerns, specifically those pertaining to the homeland, changing gender roles, and female empowerment.

Diasporic Longing and Subversive Women:
Dueling Representations of the Homeland

While it may be easy to explain the film's uncomplicated betrothal as an attempt to achieve a happy ending for Nyab Seng, I want to make the case that *Nyab Siab Zoo,* especially as a diasporic film, actually points to a contemporary and ambivalent interest in traditional Hmong gender roles.[10] Just as the film moves from portraying female interiority to male objectification, it vacillates between a nostalgic and dismissive representation of Hmong life as it might have been. At times, the film longingly captures a sense of the Hmong village, in its long shots of lush vegetation and its patient focus on daily tasks. Yet the basic plotline also shows how restrictive traditional Hmong life can be for women, especially those who do not easily fit into its social structure. Throughout the film, Nyab Seng's hard life is portrayed as both beautiful and oppressive, allowing for the mourning of a lost lifestyle and the celebration of modern possibilities. In this way, viewers, both Hmong and non-Hmong, can revel in the film's reconstructed portrayal of a bygone era, one that is far removed from their own in America. The idea of the Hmong village is, for a moment, visually recovered and no longer severed by the most recent displacement into the Western world or by the dissemination of advanced technology and growing economic and social change in Southeast Asia.[11] However, audiences can also feel confident that they are not subject to the same restrictions placed on Nyab Seng nor are they required to grind their own corn in order to eat. While trying to portray the daily routine of a vanishing Hmong agrarian lifestyle, the film also touches on surviving concerns about gender roles, providing both a nostalgic perspective and a model for contemporary Hmong femininity.

Although the film has the markings of a professionally produced project and clearly wishes to tell a fictional tale, its detailed representation of farming techniques and village life likens it to what Koltyk (1993) identifies as "homeland videos" (441). In her article on Hmong video production and consumption, Koltyk describes these homeland videos, which vary from amateur to semiprofessional, as videotaped testaments of Hmong culture as it is practiced in Asia, "put together in ethnographic fashion to make as complete a record of the Hmong lifestyle as possible" (441). She adds:

Filmmakers focus attention on the types of crops being grown and on the condition of fields, houses, villages, and clothing. Shots of farm tools and machinery are never shown in isolation; there is always a person using them. Work scenes reflect men and women's gender roles and children's duties, and provide viewers with a general feeling of what life is like in a Hmong village or community. (441)

In countless ways, Vang shoots his film as a "homeland video," with the film's gaze focused on Nyab Seng, slowly following her movements from one task to another and capturing her narration of these actions just in case her chores are not clear. In rare cases, the film even provides footage of tasks that she cannot perform, using her voice to describe the significance of these actions. When she laments that she and her mother-in-law will not be able to eat pounded rice cakes to celebrate the New Year because they "are made by men," the film depicts Paochoua and another male beating the sticky mass of rice with two oversize mallets (Vang 2009). This scene takes place within Paochoua's home and is inaccessible to Nyab Seng, but her voice helps give meaning to the task. In this moment, the film slips into a more documentary mode and provides a glimpse into what Nyab Seng and displaced Hmong are missing. Most often, though, viewers trail alongside her as she performs one large task through all its stages, from the shucking of the corn to the grinding of its kernel at the millstone and finally to the sifting of unwanted particles in the cornmeal. This close attention to her and the other villagers' work not only details a bygone homeland but also denotes a nostalgia for an older way of living that is often attached to diasporic films and, as discussed by Schein, the specific Hmong narrative of and longing for the ideal daughter/wife.

In her article "Homeland Beauty" (2004), Schein discusses the phenomenon of the male, Orientalist gaze—used in amateur videos and low-budget films—of post-diasporic returns to the homeland. She specifically focuses on how these films present "native" Hmong women as points of access to a nostalgic and eroticized notion of the homeland. Schein writes, "The lure of this girl is the lure of nostalgia mingled with male longing, longing *not only* for that feminized icon of home but also for an idealized and lost set of sexual mores" (444–45). A version of the homeland videos, these films capture the innocent beauty of Hmong women living in Asia as part of a larger desire to return home and to a simpler time. In her work on queer diasporic film, Gayatri Gopinath (1997) also touches on how

"Women's bodies, then, become crucial to nationalist discourse in that they serve not only as the site of biological reproduction of national collectivities, but as the very embodiment of this nostalgically evoked communal past and tradition" (468). Desai (2004) also addresses a similar issue when writing about diasporic films that depict transnational weddings, arguing that such films "pacify Western audiences anxious about the consequences of increased global migration while providing a nostalgic comfort in the possibility of life less transformed and ruptured by modernity" (229). Of course, the homeland can also participate in perpetuating this nostalgia. As Duong (2012) argues, "Both homeland and diaspora traffic in images of nostalgia about the past and the future, deploying familial rhetoric and gendered bodies to concretize the affective dimensions of what was and what could be" (186). In each argument, family and the role of women are vital to producing and maintaining a sense of nostalgia.

In some ways, *Nyab Siab Zoo* functions in this same manner as "homeland videos," using Nyab Seng as the example of the devoted and kind-hearted daughter-in-law as well as the perfect traditional Hmong woman. She is not only faithful to her husband's family but also skilled at farming, cooking, singing, and generally playing the part of the demure, soft-spoken, and obedient woman. Even if the film did not continuously shift to the male gaze, it presents Nyab Seng as the exemplary and desirable Hmong woman, especially as it also captures a sense of nostalgia for the "homeland." Yet at the same time, *Nyab Siab Zoo* challenges a simple admiration and longing for Nyab Seng's world by showing both the difficulties of her life and the restrictions placed on her. Although the film resembles nostalgic and often eroticized homeland videos, it also works against the genre by focusing on the female perspective and by emphasizing the limited roles women play in a traditional village structure.

Returning to the notion of marriage as a stabilizing force in nostalgic diasporic films, there is perhaps no better critique of the homeland video than the mother-in-law's challenging of male privilege during Xi's "proposal" to wed Nyab Seng. Although there are many scenes that depict the powerful bond between Nyab Seng and her mother-in-law, the moment in which the latter refuses Xi's marriage plans is most emblematic of the subversive nature of their relationship and the limitations placed on women. The scene curiously opens with a shot of an elderly Hmong man smoking opium from a long bamboo pipe before cutting to Xi's face, replacing the bubbling of the pipe with Xi's voice. As Xi reveals his intentions for the meeting—to speak about Nyab Seng—the camera briefly cuts to the mother-in-law, who is sitting farther away, seemingly feeble with her eyes downcast, her back hunched over, and her head resting on her hands, which grip a walking stick. Xi continues to recount the death of his cousin, Nyab Seng's husband, and the father-in-law, calling himself the "closest kin" (Vang 2009). As he speaks, the camera breaks away to focus on various men's faces, finally panning out to show five men sitting alongside Xi in a circle. Although there is a gap in the circle where the camera is positioned, it does not seem to represent the place where the mother-in-law is sitting. She is never shown within the circle, and the camera always jumps to another place in the room when showing her face. She is part of the conversation, and they have made room for her to look into the circle, but she is not actually invited to sit among the men. When Xi is finished sharing his intentions to marry Nyab Seng as his second wife, the camera quickly cuts to the mother-in-law, who silently expresses shock. When someone finally speaks, it is a man who points out, "We are all not as close as kin to them as you [Xi]. We don't know what to say simply because you already have a wife" (Vang 2009). Another man chimes in, suggesting that Xi first ask Nyab Seng if she would agree to such an arrangement. All the men seem to be in agreement that they cannot make any decisions because of their distance from the clan. Since Xi is the closest relative, his authority is greater, even among these older men. Although the second speaker suggests that Xi consult Nyab Seng first, they all imply that Xi, as the closest kin, has the power to marry her. However, the mother-in-law makes it clear that authority based on kinship will not apply to her or to Nyab Seng.

Contrary to her weak demeanor, the mother-in-law is able to wield influence with her accusatory words. When she verbally opposes a union between Xi and Nyab Seng, she does so by mocking the patrilineal kinship structure. After hearing her initial resistance, in which she recognizes that she has "no son as a husband for [Nyab Seng]," Xi is angered and responds by saying, "Aunt, you are old and unwise in these matters. You shouldn't speak like that" (Vang 2009). However, these attempts to silence her only compel the mother-in-law to dismiss the kinship system. She retorts, "Since our arrival here to follow the clan, none of you have been able to offer us a single meal. Except for the fact that my daughter-in-law must toil your fields in order to support us. Now that you've seen her, you clansmen talk of kinship and community!" (Vang 2009). She goes on to add that she has nothing else to say to the men and immediately leaves the home. The camera then turns to the group of men, who watch her leave in silence. Although this moment does not guarantee that Xi will not follow through with his plan, it illustrates the mother-in-law's dismissal of clan authority based on the extreme marginalization the two women have experienced. As the mother-in-law notes, the two women specifically moved back to rejoin the clan but have not received any aid from their close kin. Instead, their survival has depended on Nyab Seng, who could have gone to her birth family, as did the other sister-in-law, as well as the other women who bear no relation to them.[12] The two women have had to create their own nurturing space and so no longer feel obligated to the demands of the clan. If they are to reenter into the patrilineal society, then they will do so without the unearned impositions proposed by Xi, their closest male kin. In such moments when the film focuses on the women's subversive potential and actions, it challenges nostalgic homeland videos and reflects issues faced by contemporary experiences of diaspora—specifically the struggle that Hmong American women face, and the questions that arise concerning the changes in gender roles.

Conclusion: The Shift from Reel to Real

As a diasporic film, *Nyab Siab Zoo* vacillates between longingly portraying the homeland, which allows for some nostalgic yearning for an older way of life, and resolutely projecting concerns of the diaspora, which gives space for a critical reimagining of this older life. Because Nyab Seng and her mother-in-law both lack husbands and fathers, they live on the periphery and are always vulnerable to male desire, whether sexual or not. This temporary marginalization allows the film to showcase a female network of support and knowledge, and also serves as a reminder of how Hmong women, in a traditional setting, have few alternatives to being wives or daughters. Resisting the genre of purely eroticized homeland videos, the film portrays strong Hmong women who must question and readjust their proscribed gender roles. Instead of prioritizing homeland nostalgia, the film reflects the contested space and role of women in the Hmong American diaspora. To better understand these issues of Hmong American femininity, I turn to three Hmong women who have written about the difficulty of being Hmong women in the American diaspora.

Although most Hmong American women, in the best and worst possible way, have little chance of ever truly becoming the same type of Hmong woman as Nyab Seng, they are not completely removed from a society that seems to place more value on men and marriage.[13] In a recent essay on what constitutes a good Hmong girl, Ka Vang (2012) bemoans the servile role that women, especially daughters, must still play in the home: "Women have responsibilities in a traditional Hmong household that are valued by an agrarian community; however, none of those responsibilities transfer to equality and power for them" (105). Even as women become more involved in the public sphere as professionals, community organizers, or cultural liaisons, there is still a looming patriarchal order with which to contend. In the film, Nyab Seng may rely on herself and other women for a time, but in the end she must repel the unwanted suitor and become betrothed to the hero. Yet in much of the film, she is also able to renegotiate the rigid gender roles while still maintaining her desirability as a woman. Indeed the film, as I have argued, explores these successful spaces outside the patrilineal system. Within this peripheral and ambiguous position, Nyab Seng is similar to Hmong American women who have discovered that the blurring of gender roles has only made the question of who or what is a Hmong woman less clear.

Mai Neng Moua's (2011) short creative nonfiction piece "Being a Nyab" captures the modern dueling sets of obligations that pull Hmong women forward and backward, imagining, like in *Nyab Siab Zoo,* a space in which women are redefining their roles through daily actions and decisions. Similar to Nyab Seng, Moua's character struggles to be a good daughter-in-law while her husband's widowed aunt, Phauj Mee, comes to live with her and her spouse. A writer and considered "very independent," Moua's character wonders if she can fulfill the role of the good nyab (177). Around her husband's family, she already finds herself "revert[ing] to [her] mute five-year old self," not knowing "how to bridge the gap between [her] feminist self and the submissive Hmong girl [her mother] had taught [her] to be" (177). With Phauj Mee in her home, she deals with these two sides of herself daily and with even the smallest task, asking herself, "What should I do? . . . Get up and put in a movie for Phauj Mee like a good Hmong nyab?" (169). The character is not coldhearted and thinks warmly of Phauj Mee, but she is also unwilling to give up her independence and force herself into the role of the "good Hmong nyab." In the end, the aunt chooses to live elsewhere, but her brief stay in the house heightens all the tensions surrounding the role of women and the gap between "the feminist self" and "the submissive Hmong girl."[14]

Reflecting these same issues of conflicting obligations, Kou Vang's (2012) "Making the Invisible Visible" discusses the way Hmong women are treated and the way their roles are changing. She writes, "Although [Hmong women] may have successful careers in the larger community, they are not immune to such criticisms [gossip, belittling, and so on]. Because they do not fit neatly into the category of what is perceived as a good Hmong woman, they are ostracized" (220). Vang's remark on the marginalization of contemporary Hmong women is very much aligned with Nyab Seng's own inability to "fit neatly" into the Hmong village. Whether through widowhood, diasporic displacement, Western assimilation, or personal goals and opinions, these three women are pushed into the periphery and must challenge themselves to reexamine the roles laid out for them as Hmong women. Like Nyab Seng, Vang finds strength in other women, drawing personal and artistic inspiration from "the voices of Hmong women who have struggled to be heard, understood, respected, and loved for who they are" (213). She also takes note of successful Hmong women who have been able to find gender equality, at least within the home. In all three instances, the reconfiguration of gender roles must be corrected or normalized, either by conforming to social standards or by demanding that the standards change. What is significant about *Nyab Siab Zoo* is that the film is also willing to explore these seemingly modern issues but does so in a deceptively nostalgic setting. In this way, the film highlights both the beauty *and* limitations of the traditional Hmong village, as well as the struggle *and* possibilities of Western displacement, reflecting the hybrid and sometimes conflicting characteristics of diasporic film outlined by Desai (2004).

In broad terms, the film *Nyab Siab Zoo* brings together conversations about diasporic longing, Hmong filmmaking, and female narratives of collectivity. Yet as I have argued in this chapter, the manner in which these larger concepts intersect is fraught with unclear answers about how women must renegotiate their roles within a diaspora that still longs for the homeland. On the one hand, *Nyab Siab Zoo* depicts a restrictive fictional world into which two marginalized women must conform. In this vein, Nyab Seng seemingly represents the docile, nurturing, and hardworking daughter-in-law, silently fulfilling the role defined for her by the patriarchal community. For *Nyab Siab Zoo*'s characters, the traditional models of patrilineal kinship ultimately provide the only manner of integrating into a new society, which makes it difficult for Nyab Seng to be much more than another daughter-in-law. However, the film also presents audiences with a secondary community that enables its Hmong female characters to take some control of their lives and to call attention to the failings of the kinship structure. Nyab Seng's position as both insider and outsider allows her to befriend and make use of a nurturing female network even as she has no secure place in the village. Her use of and reliance on this female substructure ultimately allows her to become a full member of the larger society, revealing the importance of strong and knowledgeable women within the patriarchal system. Although the Hmong men may dictate her formal place in the community, Nyab Seng's survival and initial entrance into society depend on her own physical strength and the presence of a woman-centered network—a network that the film creates and highlights through the frequent use of the female gaze and the erasure of men.

While the film's depiction of this female collectivity is seemingly at odds with its more nostalgic rendering of the homeland, I have argued that its dueling representations reflect the hybrid and competing concerns of diasporic cinema. As such, the film transports modern Hmong American issues of femininity to a film that portrays a more traditional Hmong village life. *Nyab Siab Zoo* thus recovers the lost homeland while also questioning the traditional village structure and its treatment of women. Moreover, it is able to mirror issues of Hmong American femininity and, in this way, represents the Hmong American diaspora. The film vacillates between a nostalgic and critical framing of the homeland not only through its cinematography but also through its narrative focus on marginalized women. Portraying the limitations and resilience of Hmong women in the "homeland," the film simultaneously speaks to Hmong American women who also face a world full of blurred gender roles. In this way, *Nyab Siab Zoo* is not simply a nostalgic reimagination of a lost homeland or Hmong social structure but a film that highlights the possibilities in and advantages of redefining Hmong femininity within a hybridized, ever-growing, and continuously shifting diaspora.

Notes

1. Although the film's official English title is *The Good-Hearted Daughter*, the term "nyab" exclusively refers to a daughter-in-law or a sister-in-law through a male relative, thus clearly marking a woman's inclusion into a family via marriage.

2. It should be noted that Clint Eastwood's film *Gran Torino* (2008) was released just a year before Vang's. Eastwood's film, because of its wide release and the notoriety of the director/star, was met with glowing reviews from entertainment critics and unfavorable readings from academic scholars. For more critical work on *Gran Torino*, see Louisa Schein and Va-Megn Thoj's article "*Gran Torino*'s Boys and Men with Guns: Hmong Perspectives" (2009) and Tania Modleski's "Clint Eastwood and Male Weepies" (2009).

3. Despite being the lead character, the daughter-in-law's given name is unclear. Since she has moved back to her husband's land, she is only addressed as the wife of Seng or Nyab Seng. This title reflects Hmong culture and emphasizes her place as an outsider.

4. I use the term "modern" throughout this paper to denote a chronological division and not to make a judgment on what constitutes "primitive" and "advanced."

5. The film does not provide subtitles for all of the dialogue, but the omissions are rare and usually not crucial to the storyline.

6. While these lines are shown in English, the rest of the film is in Hmong. English subtitles/translations are provided and, when quoting directly from the film, I will use the English subtitles even if and when they vary from the actual Hmong words.

7. Of course not all the women in the village are happy about Nyab Seng's arrival. Nyab Seng poses an immediate threat to a male cousin's first wife who is rightfully afraid of the new rival. While it is clear that the male cousin wishes to marry Nyab Seng and attempts to do so, there is no sense that Nyab Seng welcomes this attention or is even aware of it.

8. This friend is not given a name and is only called "Pregnant Lady" in the credits.

9. Interestingly, a shaman is never consulted in the film. This typically male role is left out of the film and the female herbalist takes on the primary role of healer. In the context of the film, it would make sense that the women use an herbalist as they lack the funds for a shaman and because the herbalist is usually consulted first when an illness is not too serious. However, the absence of the shaman is also an interesting choice since this personae is so common in popular culture, appearing in almost every Western media portrayal that deals with the Hmong.

10. Although I do not have the space for it in this article, the use of a biblical story also reflects the presence of Christianity among the Hmong. While there is a history of missionary influence, there has been a sharp increase of Christian Hmong since Western displacement. The film's use of the Book of Ruth and its interest in representing a pre-diaspora world would make for a great discussion about the various ways of defining Hmong culture.

11. The issue of diaspora is especially complex for the Hmong, who have no modernly defined "homeland." Thus populations living in Southeast Asia, where

the film was shot, can easily be identified as part of the Hmong diaspora. With the advancement of technological communication and social media, the distinctions between those displaced into Asian countries and those resettled in American/ European countries may become even more blurred.

12. Although Nyab Seng calls the herbalist "Aunt Za," there is no other indication that they are blood relatives. It is most likely a formality since Aunt Za is an elder and a respected figure.

13. I cannot adequately address the issues of leading a non-heteronormative lifestyle in the Hmong American community, but it should be noted that those individuals are often increasingly marginalized.

14. Indeed it is not only the nyab, but also the aunt who has to continuously shift her ideas of feminine behavior and obligations. She has no real sons to live with and finds herself out of place in a world where older women have few avenues to become part of the larger American society. Moua is conscious of Phauj Mee's precarious position, but it is unclear whether the narrator considers the shifts that the older generation faces.

Works Cited

Bailey, Olga Guedes, Myria Georgiou, and Ramaswami Harindranath. 2007. "Introduction: Exploration of Diaspora in the Context of Media Culture." In *Transnational Lives and the Media: Re-Imagining Diaspora*, edited by Olga G. Bailey, Myria Georgiou, and Ramaswami Harindranath, 11–32. New York: Palgrave.

Barton, Sabrina. 2006. "Feminist Film Theory and the Problem of Liking Characters." In *Exploring Women's Studies: Looking Forward, Looking Back*, edited by Carol R. Berkin, Judith L. Pinch, and Carole S. Appel, 331–47. Upper Saddle River, N.J.: Pearson Education.

Chang, Kao, dir. 2009. *Nkauj Nyab*. New Age Home Entertainment.

Chopra, Yash, dir. 1989. *Chandni*. Yash Raj Films.

Dempsey, Anna. 2009. "Nurturing Nature and Cinematic Experience: The American Landscape and the Rural Female Community." *Journal of Cultural Geography* 23, no. 1: 115–37.

Desai, Jigna. 2004. *Beyond Bollywood: The Cultural Politics of South Asian Diasporic Film*. New York: Routledge.

Duong, Lan. 2012. *Treacherous Subjects: Gender, Culture, and Trans-Vietnamese Feminism*. Philadelphia: Temple University Press.

Eastwood, Clint, dir. 2008. *Gran Torino*. Warner Bros. Pictures.

Georgiou, Myria. 2007. "Transnational Crossroads for Media and Diaspora: Three Challenges for Research." In *Transnational Lives and the Media: Re-Imagining Diaspora*, edited by Olga G. Bailey, Myria Georgiou, and Ramaswami Harindranath, 11–32. New York: Palgrave.

Gilroy, Paul. 1987. *There Ain't No Black in the Union Jack*. London: Hutchinson Education.

Gopinath, Gayatri. 1997. "Nostalgia, Desire, Diaspora: South Asian Sexualities in Motion." *Positions* 5, no. 2: 467–89.

Honig, Bonnie. 2001. *Democracy and the Foreigner*. Princeton, N.J.: Princeton University Press.

Koltyk, Jo Ann. 1993. "Telling Narratives through Home Videos: Hmong Refugees and Self-Documentation of Life in the Old and New Country." *Journal of American Folklore* 106, no. 422: 435–49.

de Lauretis, Teresa. 1984. *Alice Doesn't: Feminism, Semiotics, Cinema*. Bloomington: Indiana University Press.

Modleski, Tania. 2009. "Clint Eastwood and Male Weepies." *American Literary History* 22, no. 1: 136–58.

Moua, Mai Neng. 2011. "Being a Nyab." In *How Do I Begin: A Hmong American Literary Anthology*, edited by Andre Yang, 169–79. Berkeley, Calif.: Heyday.

Mulvey, Laura. 2001. "Unmasking the Gaze: Some Thoughts on New Feminist Film Theory and History." *Lectora* 7:5–14.

Said, Edward. 1984. "The Mind of Winter: Reflections on Life in Exile." *Harper's* 269 (September): 49–55.

Schein, Louisa. 2004. "Homeland Beauty: Transnational Longing and Hmong American Video." *Journal of Asian Studies* 63, no. 2: 433–63.

Schein, Louisa, and Va-Megn Thoj. 2009. "*Gran Torino*'s Boys and Men with Guns: Hmong Perspectives." *Hmong Studies Journal* 10:1–52.

Symonds, Patricia V. 2008. *Calling in the Soul: Gender and the Cycle of Life in a Hmong Village*. Seattle: University of Washington Press.

Thao, Su, prod. and ed. 1992. *Kev Hlub Tsis Paub Kawg*. S.T. Universal Video.

Vang, Abel, dir. 2009. *Nyab Siab Zoo*. Red Sash Pictures.

Vang, Ka. 2012. "The Good Hmong Girl Eats Raw *Laab*." In *Hmong and American: From Refugees to Citizens*, edited by Vincent K. Her and Mary Louise Buley-Meissner, 101–12. St. Paul: Minnesota Historical Society Press.

Vang, Kou. 2012. "Making the Invisible Visible: Confronting the Complexities of Identity, Family, and Culture through Art." In *Hmong and American*, edited by Her and Buley-Meissner, 209–24.

· IV ·

Gender and Sexuality

Thinking Diasporic Sex

Cultures, Erotics, and Media across Hmong Worlds

Louisa Schein

THIS CHAPTER TAKES UP some of the key concepts and interventions in sexuality studies of the last half century in order to begin to think sex in the Hmong diaspora. I revisit some of the key insights of queer and sex-radical theorizing since the so-called sex wars in the early 1980s (Duggan and Hunter 2006). Specifically, I explore how a sexuality studies would look for Hmong diasporic networks if not subsumed under gender studies and if not infused with what Gayle Rubin (1993, 84) has called "sex negativity" (11). Without implying that gender could ever be irrelevant, and without being overly celebratory about sex positivity, I aim to position a collection of key conundrums in the sexualities of the Hmong diaspora in relation to such notions as normativity, erotics, moral panic, and sexual cultures. Interwoven throughout is consideration of how colonial and racial structures and ideologies shape sexualities.

Sexual Cultures?

Many of my reflections here grow out of a keynote I was asked to deliver at a conference on sexualities and history. Knowing that the scholars attending were mostly specialists from Europe and the United States, I faced a perennial challenge: How to talk generatively about sexuality and Hmong in a way that would avoid exoticizing or even fetishizing Hmong as culturally—and sexually—other? The weighty history of Westerners eroticizing the Orient, and the xenophobic reception that Hmong Americans have experienced in the United States in relation to gender/sexual practices all mitigated against writing Hmong sex. Yet to eschew writing about sex reproduces other pitfalls, such as naturalizing it as no more than an uncomplicated biological universal or, on the other hand, reproducing an alterity of Hmong sexuality that can only be egregiously complicit with externalizing Hmong Americans as somehow ill-fitted for the United States.[1]

I deploy an approach within sexuality studies that dovetails historical and cross-cultural analytics precisely to *denaturalize* many of the certainties about sex that have been generated in the contemporary West. What Euro-American precepts have held to be natural and unnatural turns out to be one particular social construction among many. To denaturalize would mean, in one sense, to de-biologize. A discourse premised on invoking the "natural" might maintain, say, that it would be a violation of biology for people of the same gender, or of the same sex, or of different generations, or of young ages, to engage in erotic activity with each other. Yet what much of sexuality studies has emphasized is that—if historical and non-Western mores are taken into account—it becomes amply evident that there has been and continues to be a great deal of variation in both sexuality discourses and erotic practices across history and around the globe.

Universalizing discourses don't always rest on biology to authorize their tenets. They also rely on taken-for-granted *norms* of what is considered socially acceptable and proper. These norms may draw their authority from, say, religion rather than from ideas of the natural. My approach here also seeks to *denormalize* sexuality: in other words, to suggest that what some may take as basic certainties—that sex work is wrong, or that children should not be exposed to sexual knowledges—turn out to be contingent and variable positions that have emerged as dominant in particular sociohistorical moments. These positions are underpinned by such moral force that it becomes imperative for a sexualities analytic to start from the stance of suspending morals—at least as a basic methodological approach.

I proceed with and beyond a notion of "sexual cultures" as a strategy for making these denaturalizing and denormalizing moves. A sexual cultures framework—a decidedly plural framework—would assert that multiple sets of norms can be found across societies. These norms cohere around their own internal standards, only sometimes reiterating universalisms like biology or absolute morality. But asserting this is a very fraught strategy. Why? Putting forward alternative sexual cultures, bringing them under the scrutiny of the mainstream Western gaze, can also have the effect not of pluralizing conceptions of sexual norms but of providing a basis upon which some can be condemned as uncivilized, deviant, or exotic.

It has been a long-standing technique of "othering" practice, or what Edward Said (1979) called "Orientalism," to describe the "other" as sexually excessive or perverse (Nagel 2003).[2] Indeed, as with many racist and discriminating ideologies, the notion of culture tends to be subjected to a double standard in which groups who are less powerful and more marginal are represented as having more *culture,* while dominant societies are portrayed as having more *civilization,* more uprightness, more morality. It is a central principle of my work that the ostensible multiculturalist inclusiveness upheld in so many Western countries is inexorably haunted by this hierarchical tendency. Having "culture" can come to be a marker of inferiority and unassimilability and, in this instance, a shorthand for sexual impropriety; just as non-Western "others" are framed as having too much culture, so their sexual practices spill over beyond definitions of American normalcy. As Kong Pha (this volume) points out, this ostensibly neutral discourse of culturally different sexual practice can take the form, for Hmong, of the mainstream vilification of what he calls "hyperheterosexuality."

As a non-Hmong, white Westerner, what I say is irrevocably implicated in this intercultural dynamic—a dynamic that in some ways might be described as colonial discourse production. If there is a mode by which my speaking about Hmong and sexuality could be appropriate, it would have to abandon or resignify the notion of sexual culture in order to somehow take others' norms on their own terms rather than demonize them. But given global power asymmetries, as well as those between Euro-American "experts" and their "others"—this may be an unattainable goal. It is for this reason that I take space here to clear the ground before talking about specifics.

Normativities in Motion

In this chapter, then, I will work through a notion of shifting *normativities* before getting to specific women's situations in, say, polygynous or arranged marriages. Through the concept of normativity I hope to do several kinds of work. I hope to show the dynamic process by which groups come to concur on certain expectations and assumptions, sometimes on certain moral precepts, and in the process designate some members of that group or of other groups as outside, nonnormative, and implicitly perverse. Early queer theorist Michael Warner (1999) registered the consequences of these judgments by counterpointing this sexual control with sexual "autonomy":

Most people cannot quite rid themselves of the sense that controlling the sex of others, far from being unethical, is where morality
begins. Shouldn't it be possible to allow everyone sexual autonomy,
in a way consistent with everyone else's sexual autonomy? . . . The
culture has thousands of ways for people to govern the sex of
others — and not just harmful or coercive sex, like rape, but the
most personal dimensions of pleasure, identity, and practice. We
do this directly, through prohibition and regulation, and indirectly,
by embracing one identity or one set of tastes as though they were
universally shared, or should be. Not only do we do this; we
congratulate ourselves for doing it. (1)

What I strive for in this chapter is to suggest how normativities operate on
multiple scales, from within small local communities to between, say,
American minorities and the implicitly white, Christian mainstream, and
also between sites distributed around the globe. As well, I hope to explore
normativities as contested, as targets of social praxis, which are taken up
consciously and agentively by actors who would like to see norms change.
And I will ask questions about how normativities are produced and reproduced inadvertently in many approaches to sexuality.

Attempts across time to regulate Hmong practices of polygyny are a
vexed case in point. I use "polygyny," not polygamy, for it is only the
former — one man marrying more than one woman — that has been at
issue in relation to Hmong sexual norms. "Polygamy" — which also includes
the arrangement of one woman marrying more than one man — is not on
the table, not debated, and probably has never been for Hmong or Miao in
various parts of the world.[3] Note, of course, that marriage is a social structural form, not a sex act, but the moral freight enforcing the standard of
monogamy is co-implicated with regulating sex. Polygyny is contested.
It is unproductive to ask questions about timeless sexual culture, such as:
Is Hmong culture polygynous? Is polygyny permissible in Hmong mores?
Under what conditions is polygyny allowable? These kinds of questions
use a verb tense that is sometimes called the "ethnographic present." They
describe values, norms, codes, beliefs, and practices as the cultural characteristics of a people outside history. My position here is that there is
no place outside history and that we can see polygyny as a site of struggle
over many moments in the Hmong/Miao *longue durée*.

In China, for instance, scholars of Miao history widely concur that polygynous marriage was generally frowned on and only practiced by certain

elite Miao with economic and political privilege. Some portray this practice almost as an *abuse* of privilege. Here we can grasp a distinction between moral norms and de facto practices and how contestation might be lived out in sociohistorical process. Even under widespread moral disapproval of the practice of taking multiple wives, it has taken place nonetheless. Even when tolerated, it may have been reluctantly so. We can say that a *practical norm* was in effect when, during the upheavals of war in Laos, many more Hmong men were killed than women, and polygyny became more tolerable so that widows would be able to remarry rather than remain alone.[4] Meanwhile, immigration to Western countries enforced the norm of monogamy, again shifting the family form. We might analyze the Western aversion to polygyny, firmly encoded in immigration law, as akin to what Rubin (1993), Herdt (2009), Lancaster (2011), and others have referred to as "moral" or "sexual" panic imposed by outsiders, in which a de facto social arrangement comes to be "burdened with an excess of significance" (Rubin 1993, 11). These controlling norms, though, have also been vehemently championed by Hmong in many quarters. My intention here is not to take a stand on the tolerance of polygyny but to underscore how fluid, divisive, and debated its status has been across time and space.

Media and Moral Crisis

In the 1990s, I stumbled into a heated cultural dispute over the status of polygyny that was also about arranged marriage, about media, about masculinity, and about transnationalism. I had been working on a book about Hmong media (Schein n.d.; see also Schein 2004). Hmong Americans had been making hundreds of entertainment videos to market within the Hmong diasporic community. I focused on films shot in Asia, with Hmong American directors and minimally trained Hmong local actors. Especially popular among Hmong consumers were melodramas that depicted the homeland and that trafficked in nostalgia for remembered cultural mores. Among these memories were young men's courtship of nubile young women and the romantic tremors of first love.

Up until the blockbuster series *Dr. Tom,* nostalgia films had always staged romances that took place between Hmong in Asia, either tucked away in the exotic highlands in "timeless" farming villages or during the war years. *Dr. Tom 1* broke new ground in the 1990s, for it portrayed a transnational relationship. The basic plotline is as follows: Tom, a predatory Hmong American, who is nothing but a janitor in Fresno, jets in and flashes his cash in a refugee camp, claiming to be a highly paid doctor. Although already married in the United States, his aim is to pursue a lovely young woman, Ngao Ia, whom he's spotted at market, and to pry her away from the local refugee man she's in love with. In a Hmong cultural context that favors feeling-based courtship, Tom connivingly activates a rival Hmong courtship mode. He approaches the family and proffers a better material and geographic future for all if they marry off their daughter to him. Strong-arming through economic and national power—the lure of promised remittances and migration to the United States—carries the day. The family agrees to Tom's marriage proposal and twists heartbroken Ngao Ia's arm, pressuring her with obligation to act on her family's rather than her own behalf.

This filmic text takes its place among a panoply of condemnations of arranged marriages, some of which are polygynous. It is commonplace in Western treatments of arranged marriage to champion the "companionate" form—free choice, voluntary courtship, romance, and mutual attraction—as the far preferable counterpoint to a coercive "traffic in women" (Rubin 1975) that reduces women to mere objects of exchange. However, as newfangled social forms such as digital mate searching emerge in the West—undermining the time-honored value of spontaneous romantic courtship—the putatively coercive gendered exploitation element of marriage arrangement needs to receive more rigorous scrutiny. We might ask, for instance, about elements of women's own marriage strategizing, even within systems where arrangement and polygyny are practiced, and whether narratives like *Dr. Tom*—in which women are taken to be passive victims—serve to reinforce that image of lack of agency. There are several presumptions bundled with the evaluations of arranged marriage and polygyny that deserve unpacking: patriarchal privilege, effacement of women's subjecthood, disempowerment of women, and erasure of women's desire. I will return to most of these later in the chapter, but let us first consider masculinities.

Masculinities and Eroticisms in Excess of Patriarchy

As suggested by the *Dr. Tom* series and a veritable genre of didactic video retellings of the stories of privileged Hmong Americans exploiting Hmong women in Asia, a kind of hypertrophied patriarchal privilege is portrayed as operating, intensified by the location and citizenship of the men. This transnational relationship, especially when entailing substantial disparities of age, is a source of a great deal of grief and reprobation on the part of Hmong both in Asia and in the diaspora.

What I highlight here, however, are the aspects of gender and erotics that are underexamined in these condemnations. Is it tenable, for instance, to straightforwardly aver that it is because Hmong American men have been emasculated upon immigration to the United States that they return to Asia to reclaim their patriarchal authority, particularly through young women? Quite possibly, but keeping a sexuality framing in play, other more complex diasporic subjectivities might come in for consideration. In other work (Schein 1999), I have undertaken a close reading of the videos produced by Hmong American men to draw closer to the affects that eroticize the image of the homeland Hmong woman. Rather than argue that men's seeking of young women is but an artifact of a reified "Hmong sexual culture" that privileges youth, I suggest that the videos may represent *constructs* of Hmong sexual culture that play to émigré nostalgia. In other words, it would be not a cult of young women per se that accounts for the age imbalance in actual relationships, but rather that Hmong returnees may pleasurably and desiringly recall their time in the mountains and refugee camps of Laos and Thailand as their coming of age, their coming into erotic awareness, their early courtship and nascent romantic feelings. Could it be, then, that it is the pursuit of these nostalgic imaginaries that have generated the contemporary exploitative gendered relations of age disparity and of procuring sexual partners through the social form of marriage arrangement?

One evening I was watching one of the *Dr. Tom* series with a group of Hmong American friends. As with all the installments, the story traced the exploits of the philandering Tom as he traveled Asia in search of gullible young women who would sleep with him and have their arms twisted into "marriages." In most cases, these putative marriages translated into temporary erotic dalliances followed by long periods of solitude, waiting in Asia as second wives to a U.S. life that Tom could not escape. But Tom kept coming back, and what the stories dwell on is the obsessive quality of these transnational erotics—the way that Hmong American men will go to such great lengths to pursue a transnational tryst. As we watched that night, a forty-something mother of four blurted out: "Hmong men are crazy. They will fall in love with a young woman and think about nothing else for the rest of their lives!"

Which "Hmong men"? Before any unitary characterization of Hmong American men, and their gender and erotics, becomes too stable, another reason to unpack this issue is that certain Hmong American men occupy feminist and social-justice activist positions and have also been among the most vocal against homeland exploitative practices. Filmmaker Va-Megn Thoj, for instance, had been trained in production by the minority activist organization Third World Newsreel in New York City, and came to his craft with the intention of impacting both Hmong and the wider communities in which they are situated. His vision of working for the Hmong community was forged in part out of concerns for social justice, which he sharpened during his time away in New York.[5]

Thoj's *Death in Thailand* (2002)—a thirty-minute film that was aired by the local Minneapolis–St. Paul PBS affiliate KTCI as part of a six-part series on Hmong social issues—is a searing indictment of Hmong gender relations between Asia and the United States. The quasi-documentary came into being in an incidental way. An associate of Thoj's, Cy Thao, traveled to the Hmong camp at Tham Krabok in Thailand to visit relatives. While he was there, a young woman took her own life out of agony over a Hmong American man who had hired her to act in movies, slept with her, promised marriage, then spurned her a year later. Thao recorded the reactions of the people of Tham Krabok with his camcorder as the event unfolded. In anger and dismay, relatives and onlookers—including senior Hmong men—spoke into the camera in direct address to Hmong Americans about the scandal of this kind of relationship and its consequences.

Thao brought the video material back to the United States, and Thoj set about to edit it into a kind of documentary, dedicated to the deceased young woman, Nplias Yaj. He intercut scenes of Tham Krabok camp and the lifeless young woman surrounded by crowds of curious children and mourning women with interviews of men and women. He then ingeniously inserted clips of the videos that Nplias Yaj had acted in as ironic illustration of the phenomenon that interviewees were describing. Building on the strong statements made by interviewees, Thoj composed and added narration read in a woman's voice. In this text, he uses the pronoun "we" to address Hmong Americans, thereby assuming responsibility or at least complicity—as part of a Hmong American collectivity—for these acts of exploitation. The opening narration, in Hmong with English subtitles, is as follows:

How many of us have gone back to Thailand? How many of us have asked ourselves why we go? . . . If we go with honor and honesty perhaps this young woman would not have died. Her lifeless form lies here like an animal, a spectacle for little children.

After some clips from her movies, which portray her as an object of male desire, the narration continues:

Who is responsible for her death? Who is to be punished? Who is to blame? Are we responsible because we watch these movies encouraging Hmong men to exploit these young women?

Death in Thailand highlights more than any other film I discuss the fractures that provoke so much consternation among Hmong at home and abroad. Not addressed to relations with any dominant society, it is strictly about the kind of exploitation that dispersal to disparate nation-spaces facilitates. The pronouns used throughout underscore this point through their production of "us" and "them." Not only does the narrator use "we" to talk about Hmong Americans in contrast to those in Thailand, but the interviewees in Tham Krabok camp speak into the camera, using "you" to emphasize the status of Hmong Americans as other than, but acting upon, "us."

Here, then, is another reason to be wary of any reified construct of "sexual culture," and it is the same reason that we should be wary of *any* notion of culture:[6] it smuggles in premises of internal homogeneity and cultural determinism—the idea that everyone who is, by identity, part of a cultural group will effortlessly and unquestioningly live by that group's presumably unitary culture, often without so much as reflecting on it. These notions have been under fire in fields such as anthropology for decades, but they still have a strong hold in the mainstream, where "multiculturalism" prevails as a dominant discourse. Their implication would be that if Hmong are somehow sexually "other" in their mores— in, for example, tolerating polygyny or in reviling homosexuality—then all Hmong are presumed to be this way. Clearly this effaces the deep divisions and disparities that characterize Hmong diasporic sexualities.

Not only are such generalizations belied by social realities, which reveal a huge range of variation—individual, subcultural, or regional—but they have also been in flux over huge sea changes in Hmong history.[7] These include the impacts of such external elements as the Immigration and Naturalization Service and U.S. legal requirements that persons be legally married to only one spouse. They also include elements that are no longer so external, such as the moral tenets of many Christian denominations to which Hmong ascribe—tenets that might hold premarital sex, homoeroticism, or masturbation to be impermissible. At the same time, they include progressive social-justice stances of feminism and homotolerance. If a notion of sexual culture is to be deployed, then it must be extremely supple; it must allow for sexuality to be sexualities, to be plural, fluid, and polymorphous, if it is to take account of these multiplicities. Likewise, any East–West dichotomy needs to be destabilized by the phenomenon of Hmong multilocality: Hmong in the West avow a panoply of positions on sexuality, a range so great that it is not reducible to the unidirectionality of assimilation qua Westernization. The mere coexistence of a lesbian and gay movement alongside fundamentalist Christian repudiation of homosexuality in Hmong American society is but one example of a very plural and dissonant field. The ongoing process of certain Hmong American individuals revising their personal stances on homosexualities makes this point even more strongly. Other instances will be examined later in the chapter.

Pluralizing Manhoods

The moments of internal division discussed here illustrate how unthinkable is a notion of Hmong manhood separate from global location. And yet disparate global location still does not do justice to the variations among Hmong men, whether in "patriarchal," "feminist," or other standpoints. To expand this insight, we detour into the outcomes of putative emasculation within the U.S. racial order.

Hmong *American* masculinities cannot be thought about independent of the relentless slotting of Asian men as the most effeminate, asexual, or homosexual in an American racio-sexual dominant discourse. David Eng (2001) famously called this "racial castration." In his ethnography of hip-hop, import racing, race, and masculinity, however, Pao Lee Vue (2012) argues that Hmong should not be regarded as generic Asians: "Hmong youth occupy a unique position within the racial order," specifying that "as generally poor non-Whites, the Hmong are racialized like Asian Americans, but also stratified like poor African Americans" (13). In the complex positionality of the Hmong youth Vue studies, "race is understood only *through* their understanding of gender, heterosexual masculinity, and social class" (20, emphasis mine). Vue's powerful contribution here is to insist that the masculinities that Hmong men proactively fashion are their own productions of identity in response to dominant society's racialization of them; moreover, this holds even when they appear to be mimicking blackness.

Meanwhile, Bee Vang (2013) has argued vociferously that Hmong and other Southeast Asian men, as newcomer refugees, are regularly typed as unruly "exceptions" to the model minority standard of accomplishment and respectability, and are thereby subject to an alternative image, which Vang calls "butch." This image derives from perennial journalistic reporting on Southeast Asian street gangs and, to a lesser extent, shooters and perpetrators of domestic and sexual violences (Schein and Thoj 2008). This portrayal of new post–Vietnam War immigrants as less assimilated and more lawless, as perpetual aliens that represent a particularly violent kind of yellow peril, we have elsewhere thumbnailed as "perpetual warriors" (Schein and Thoj 2009; Schein et al. 2012). A recent version of this blanket characterization was reiterated in the white-authored line placed in the mouth of Hmong sister Sue in Clint Eastwood's *Gran Torino* (2008): "The girls go to school and the boys go to jail."[8] Menacing gangster criminality is often hypereroticized, as seen later in *Gran Torino*'s scripting of an extremely transgressive Hmong gangbanger rape of their own cousin. Lisa Marie Cacho (2012) put it pointedly: "Young Hmong men who form gangs are represented as *perversely* unassimilated" (89, emphasis mine).

What Vang points out is that dominant discourse bifurcates Asian Americans into the static categories of quiescent, hyposexual/gay Asians versus threatening newcomers who are hypersexual and deviant. This not only puts under erasure those Southeast Asian men, especially Hmong, who are high achieving, feminist, or conforming to dominant American mores; it also makes inconceivable a gay space for Asians that is at the same time masculine or butch. Asian American critics have done much to critique those strictures that rank Asian men as perpetual bottoms in gay hierarchy (cf. Fung 1991). Opposition to this slotting has for the most part been along the lines of remasculinization achieved through compulsorily heterosexual identity (Nguyen 2002, 87–106). Others suggest pathways to reconciling with this feminization by embracing an alternative, perhaps gay, masculinity (Shimizu 2012) or by refusing the social subordination associated with sexual bottomhood (Hoang 2012, 2014). But this begs the question of how, in the prevailing racial order, could Hmong and other Asian men occupy a social-symbolic location that could be at once masculine and homoerotic?

Indeed, one might hypothesize that the straight-affirming self-fashioning of the cultural subjects studied by Vue actually plays a role in muting homoerotic expression among Hmong male youth. As Gonzalez (2007), following Connell (1995), has explicated, we can think of two counterpoints to what is called the "hegemonic" masculinity monopolized by whites: "marginalized masculinity," which is raced nonwhite and heterosexual, and "subordinated masculinity," which is considered inferior and often homosexual (Gonzalez 2007, 30–31). Young Hmong American men hover between these possible identities, often subject to extreme (and homophobic) pressures to locate themselves within the former.

One of the points I am making here is that while a notion of sexual cultures may be useful, it can only be deployed within a theoretical model that accounts for representations, for cultural imaginaries, for "othering" and "Orientalizing," and for ongoing identity production in relation to these processes. The gender struggles experienced by Hmong immigrant men cannot be separated from their fraught situatedness within American regimes of racio-sexual typing that are shifting and contested but also constraining and disciplining. It may be that the much-noted Hmong immigrant emasculation is less an artifact of shifts in gender roles per se than about the symbolic violence of a racial order that frames them in lockstep ways. Reinscribing a dissonance between Hmong generations irrespective of racialization in which elder heteropatriarchy is counterposed to gay youth identities would be far too simplistic (Boulden 2009; Mayo 2013).

We can move here to the politics of the closet that are highly fraught in and beyond the United States, especially for men of color. As documented in other chapters in this volume (Pha, Thao), there has been steadily increasing lesbian and gay identification and highly vocal lesbian and gay movement in the recent decade, and yet, as Bic Ngo (2012) affirms for Asian Americans, avowing homosexuality may be taken as an affront to values of family (2–5). Coming out, as Bruce Thao (chapter 11) emphasizes, forces "dangerous questions" not only about what gets included as "authentic" Hmong culture but also about whether that purported—and sometimes fiercely defended—cultural essence can change over time. Hmong sexual subjectivities are proliferating in this historical moment, as some—especially Hmong who are publicly out—call others to avow their homoerotics as a declared identity, at the same time that homophobia is rife in some quarters, not only among elders but also among certain Christian Hmong. Multiple scenarios are conceivable. Movement can create backlash, but silence can be intolerable. Many occupy a third space, one of undeclared but tacitly known homoerotics (Decena 2011). In some cases, this is a space of homoerotic practice that may, for some subjects, coexist with heterosex; in some cases, it is a space of identity that is known to the individual but actively or passively kept from those around her or him. In still other cases, bisexuality may be avowed as an identity.

This plurality cannot be shut down, it cannot be re-binarized into strict homo/hetero categories, but it *can* be silenced by normativities. Not only the necessity of the closet, but also the necessity of coming out can be questioned as norms that risk coerciveness. The first NFL basketball player to come out, Wade Davis, speaks to the contingency of such acts:

> Disclosing our sexual identities can be a political act. For example, I often disclose that I am gay if I am in a space where heterosexuality is assumed to be the norm. But, I don't feel the need to "out" myself. People seem to think that anyone who isn't "straight" has a responsibility to make that known. And, for what? The privilege of being straight, like whiteness, is such that it is imagined as the norm. Because of that, heterosexuals don't have to deal with the demand to "come out" of anything, because in the eyes of the society, they don't exist in a closet that renders them abnormal. (Moore and Davis 2012)

As men of color weigh their racialization against their sexual identification, these choices become especially difficult, since they will be called upon to be exemplars of some kind of respectability for their people that will be relentlessly coded as straight. Concomitantly, as one gay Hmong described his parents' perceptions of homosexuality: "It's a White disease, a White issue" (Boulden 2009, 143).

Fleshing Out Sexual Variation

Questions of homo/heterosexuality and of coming out or not are questions of identities, perhaps even identity politics. They work within a certain codified set of categories and norms that tend to obscure some of the lived messiness of erotic life. By contrast, I appropriate here a notion of "polymorphousness" for the pluralizing work it stands to do. Polymorphousness, or polymorphous perversity, was, for Freud, a characteristic of babies who started out with undifferentiated erotic feelings but were to mature through oral, anal, and genital stages or suffer mental illness as a consequence of their veering off the track. The implication was that there was a single path to sexual maturity and normalcy; it is just this singularity that stands to be challenged by the phenomenon of plurality in erotics and sexual practice. What Freud condemned as undesirably perverse and unhealthy was found by others, most notably Alfred Kinsey in the United States (1948, 1953), to be within the range of variation of erotics practiced by mature adults.

I think we can mobilize polymorphous perversity to greater end if we make room for its persistence throughout the life course, and not always as the opposite of adult mental health. Polymorphousness can be thought of as another way to talk about erotic variation, and here we are required to think in several scales—from the variation *between* sexual cultures, to the competing norms *within* them, to the highly individual variation in erotic proclivities, to the fluidity over time that characterizes so much of erotics. How, then, to genuinely implement what Rubin (1993) called a "benign" approach to sexual variation (15)?

In the much-cited chapter "Axiomatic" in her monograph *Epistemology of the Closet* (1990), foundational queer theorist Eve Sedgwick advances several axioms for complexifying so-called sexuality. The first axiom is, "People are different from each other." She proceeds to offer a sample list of some of the erotic differences that typically go unaccounted for in investigations of sexuality.[9] These investigations, she suggests, tend to foreground such sexual distinctions as homo/hetero, creating a kind of straitjacketing of thought and obscuring other very consequential forms of variation, which, she contends, have the "potential to disrupt many forms of the available thinking about sexuality" (25).

I focus on two axioms that are about meaning and about fantasy and thereby challenge any overly biologized framing of sex. The first, "Even identical genital acts mean very different things to different people" (Sedgwick 1990, 25), asserts that there is no neutral, biological genital act. What there might be, instead, is a range of subjective experiences, in which, for some, there is raw, corporeal sex, a quasi-biological act, where for others, that act is laden with idiosyncratic significance. These are contingent eventualities and may differ from moment to moment in the same individual. Genital acts are never identical, then, because of meaning. And diaspora is one of the processes that produces meaning.

The second axiom doesn't even entail physical acts: "Many people have their richest mental/emotional involvement with sexual acts that they don't do, or don't even want to do" (25). This take on fantasy is apposite to the role of media consumption in sexualities. Much in the rich world of fantasy is never acted on—that goes without saying. But where does it take us to look closely at the idea that much of sexual fantasy is about acts people don't even *want* to do? It takes us to a place of images and scenes dancing in peoples' heads and gripping their bodies, images that matter not because they are acted out but because fantasizing itself is corporeal, even if it is not about practice or about physical entanglements between bodies.[10]

I find Sedgwick's axioms provocative in large part because they are about what I am calling erotics, a kind of sexual feeling that is never reducible to genitals and acts, indeed does not necessarily entail genitals *or* acts, but does include, by necessity, affect—a kind of social affect that can be intersubjective and embody specific cultural and historical valences. Certain scenarios, things, people, places, smells, whatever, are rendered erotic by an accumulation of personal and social histories. Some of these eroticisms might be the outcome of individual sets of experiences; some are the outcome of interpersonal synergies; and some are collectively held products of shared histories, economies, and politics.[11]

Fantasy, the Visual, and Homeland Erotics

It is in the polyvalent and inchoate workings of the *visual* that much of fantasy/erotics is generated. In the *Dr. Tom* videos previously discussed, the storyline, while condemning Tom's abuse of privilege, also offers lush frames saturated with feminine beauty and both vérité and aestheticized Asian scenes. Hence, the gendered structure of Hmong transnational relations may not only be a matter of Hmong migrant men recuperating their threatened masculine privilege by returning to their homelands with First World cash and using it to procure women. A scenario such as this would naturalize their sexual desires, making those desires a given rather than something to be interrogated. If such men wanted to purchase cheap sex while in Southeast Asia, there are any number of red-light and entertainment districts they could visit. But instead, some seek out youthful Hmong women who may evoke memories of their coming-of-age years, of romantic courtship, of passionate love before they left Asia. The aural looms large as well, for Hmong language, song, and musical instruments all figure in evoking nostalgic yearning.

I have suggested that nostalgia intertwines powerfully with erotics in this scenario. Migrant men, often dislocated and disenfranchised in the United States, not only remember the land and lifestyle of their homelands with tenderness but also reminisce about a sexual culture that has been affectionately canonized in the Hmong movies they consume in the West. In such movies, the allure of the ethnically costumed woman is a stock item, a must for marketability within Hmong American consumer circles. This woman evokes culture lost but also constitutes an erotic object, highly visual, marked by both beauty and ethnic specificity. This category of woman appears as abundant, available, and very young. She can be an object of courtship for men who want to journey through the erotic memories of their pasts. In their youth, this woman was, perhaps, an unconsummated love; now, due to First World economic power and citizenship, she can be a source of erotic fulfillment.

In filmmaker Su Thao's *China Part 3,* the director travels to a large Miao festival in China. His camera zooms in to range over the faces of homeland feminine prospects. At times, he is even seen flirting with them or narrating their availability to the camera. Erotic desire, I suggest, can be generated not only in the *practices* of homeland returns but also in the imaginaries promulgated by Hmong and other media. As Sedgwick (1990) reminds us, both forms constitute erotics, and neither should be privileged. Again, the domain of fantasy far exceeds that of social practice and envelops many in affects that won't be acted on through genital sex. One of the things I am doing in this chapter is thinking about media in terms of this kind of spilling over: media as incorporeal, but media consumption as bodied. Is the drama that takes place in the psyche during media consumption fantasy or act? What about when the context is collective viewing?

Whither Women's Desire?

In the previous discussions, the plural paths and identities of Hmong American men are seen to mitigate against a singular portrayal of them, or even of Hmong men in Asia, as simply and uniformly patriarchal. Any "culture" of Hmong gender must be complicated by these variations and take patriarchal values as one factor among many. Meanwhile, a much noted risk of focusing on men and masculinities is that not only do women's subjectivities and agencies get sidelined but—in tandem with sex negativity—women's desires and eroticisms can be wholly submerged. It is arguable that Hmong women's location in the American racial order is less marked than that of men, or at least less marked as *nonnormative* in terms of gender and sexuality. While they stand to be classed among exotic-erotic Asian women, what Susan Koshy (2004, 17) designates as the highly marriageable "sexual model minority" who have come in for so much overrepresentation (Nagel 2003; Tu 2003), this is crosscut by the persistence of their extreme victimhood in representation. As we have pointed out elsewhere (Schein et al. 2012, 779–80), the young woman, Sue, in *Gran Torino* begins as a strong, highly vocal character, arguably stronger than her emasculated brother, Thao. Yet the arc of the story returns her to a passive position as harassed and later raped; well-nigh speechless; preyed on by transgressive men of color whose sexuality is again out of bounds. It is noteworthy that her victimization is along a sexual axis, and that she is only avenged or rescuable by an older white man. The age dynamic further infantilizes her as helpless, but it also serves the function of making her violation more egregious, since—as childlike—she is *rendered asexual*.

These are recurrent dominant tropes, most of which apply to all Asian women—sexually desirable but victimized, abused, sexless, childlike, and so on. What would it take to narrate and visibilize Hmong women in terms of *their own* sexuality, a felt rather than imposed erotics, and a self-awareness of playing a role in their own sexual engagements? And how to do this without playing into their sexualized objectification in dominant culture? In earlier sections, I have taken care to put specific erotics into considerations of polygyny, arranged marriage, and transnational and age-differentiated liaisons, but it is time to think harder about women's situations. In what follows, I will also raise some issues around methods, and the unspoken and unresearchable—about ways of achieving insight into unarticulated domains. This requires a nonlogocentric, attentive stance "to strain for, listen to, and, ultimately, respect the stutterings, hesitancies, indirections, and silences surrounding erotics" (Mankekar and Schein 2012). Yet as I continue to refer to media texts—which would imply a high degree of accessible visibility—questions of reading, discussing, and interpreting come to the fore, returning us to language.

There is a sequence in the first *Dr. Tom* film that showcases the bride's erotics in a way that interrupts the passive, trafficked victim role within which homeland women are regularly framed. Ngao Ia has just been betrothed by her family to the predatory Tom. Tearfully she goes to her boyfriend, pleading with him to elope, starting to undress, and recklessly offering her virginity to him as one last gift before they are wrenched apart. "I love only you," she utters. "No matter where I am, under what sky. My heart will always be with you." Her distaste for Tom is palpable. The boyfriend, however, icon of honorable masculinity, turns her down for sex. Ngao Ia goes to her marital bed as a reluctant virgin.

A couple scenes later, she is married and going out for noodles and coke—luxuries in the refugee camp—with the chimerically affluent Tom. He skulks off to make a phone call, during which he finds out that his U.S. wife, furious, refuses to wire him more money. He is broke and has no choice but to leave his new bride in the camp and go back to work in California. In a parting scene, they sit close on a bench and Ngao Ia proclaims: "I apologize for not loving you in the past. Today I'm realizing the love between you and me. How am I supposed to wait until you come back?" Only a few days have passed since she professed undying love for her boyfriend—how can this young woman be saying such things to her abhorred spouse? Or is he still abhorred?

This professed transformation in subjectivity has become a research question for me. The scenario appears in a Hmong male-authored script but has been taken by many viewers as a variously plausible situation. I have showed the clip over and over again to Hmong audiences and asked them how this can be. What does Ngao Ia mean when she says these things? Some heated debates have ensued, underscoring just how much sexual culture can be struggled over. Many viewers, especially women, insist that she is using her words strategically to serve her own purposes. She is afraid that Tom will never come back for her, and she is attempting to secure his commitment through proclaiming love. But many viewers, men and women alike, interpret the scene otherwise. After a new wife sleeps with her husband for the first time, they explain, she will come to love him in a way she had not anticipated. They are talking about the wedding night, the conjugal bed, and the loss of virginity. They do not reiterate the much-rehearsed story of the unwilling arranged bride who knows little of sex and experiences pain, shock, shame, and something like rape on her wedding night. To the contrary, sex is the answer, they are saying. Having experienced sex for the first time is the reason for her emotional turn-around. My respondents are narrating a sex-positive version of sexual culture that goes against the grain of many mainstream Western assumptions about how sex, marriage, and emotion articulate. By what conventions would such a narrative be a surprise? I'd suggest a couple, all of which rely on premises of categorical purities. And I'd suggest that these conventions might be informing our scholarship in unexamined ways.

The first is that of the bifurcation of companionate and arranged marriage forms. Companionate marriage, as I've said, has been typified as romantic and hence as the site of sexual attraction and erotic fulfillment. Arranged marriage, by contrast, is emotionally dry but may offer other fulfillments, such as a suitable partner, social approval, and—for women more often than men—access to wealth or citizenship. So is arranged marriage an erotic desert? Has erotics been conflated with "romance" such that, by extension, it must be considered absent when romance is lacking? Is this an outcome of the privileging of the companionate form as the historically progressive form in our recent era? And is this privileging reflective of a normative stance that has so tightly twinned eroticism and romantic feeling that a moral glance of disapproval would also be cast upon such practices as casual sex, sex work and its patronage, "hooking up," "friends with benefits," and so on, as lesser eroticisms?

What if erotics rather than emotion were to take the lead temporally and conceptually? In this scenario, erotic pleasure would be the baseline for romance, rather than vice versa. In the Tom instance, as we've seen, the act of sex is portrayed as making a difference, altering erotic and emotional subjectivity. It would not be a contradiction, then, that Ngao Ia would desperately want her boyfriend one week and come around to wanting, even loving, Tom the next. It is about a transformative act of sex—an act that, due to its transformative power, suggests that not only genital sex acts but also erotic subjectivities can happen after unwanted marriages between resistant partners. I am arguing here that we have work to do in allowing for sex acts and erotics to be more socially consequential.

This line of inquiry sits precisely at the juncture of structure and affect. When we ask questions like: "How can there be erotics to a relationship where the parties didn't know each other, or actively disliked each other, or where some kind of pressure or force was involved?" we are privileging structure to the exclusion of affect. We are assuming that an alliance created by kin, a trafficking in women, a selling off of a bride, is, by virtue of its being structural, necessarily devoid of feeling (except for those negative feelings of resistance that distinguish the individual from the collective). When feeling kindles in the social process of these alliances, our categories are breached.

Which brings me to another categorical distinction—that between coercion and consent. I am wondering if we might nuance the coercion reading of arranged marriage so that it doesn't always already and by definition preclude the kindling of erotics. In many instances like this one, dutiful sons and daughters acquiesce to having their arms twisted into accepting matches they wouldn't have chosen. What is this "consent"? A subjugation of the individual to collective will or, conversely, a different form of agency? Does having acquiesced to the union have anything to do with erotic subjectivities within it? Might there be a form of desire in the motivation to make it work? This is not to suggest that arranged marriage is easy or straightforward, or to question the reality that many arranged marriages are miserable, lonely, isolating, and even abhorrently violent. Rather, it is to question our sexuality analytics, to scrutinize whether the weight of arranged marital misery in experience has become a conceptual normativity, rendering erotics in unwanted unions nearly illegible and therefore unthinkable.

Methods and the Unresearchable

But how can a line from a cheesy Hmong movie tell us something about erotics and sexual agency? What kind of scholarly method is in play here? I want to get beyond media as a text for the *scripting* of subjectivity and of erotic feeling. Media consumption in its less logocentric characteristics— its sensory multidimensionality that often privileges the visual, the aural, and even the haptic[12]—should not be reduced to a mechanistic process of the structuring of emotions. As Brian Massumi (2002) suggests, this latter process bestows priority onto an already encoded "ideological master structure" that inscribes, indeed codes, the body in predictable, and legible, fashion. In much media consumption, however, not only does the body become involved, but these moments of what we might call "affect" blur distinctions between the psychic, the cognitive, and the corporeal. Pornography is, of course, the most apparent example of this, but as Linda Williams has pointed out (1991), other genres, such as the tearjerker and the horror story, necessarily implicate the visceral as thickly entangled with meaning or ideology. Here, then, is a prime instance in which the synergy between media and embodied practice should be factored into a nuanced analytics.[13]

Part of my agenda in telling and thinking through the *Dr. Tom* story in this way is to push questions about how we proceed in what I characterize as the domain of the "unresearchable." For so many reasons, it is not plausible to imagine that research participants would or could articulate their erotic subjectivities in interviews or other formal dialogues, whether in person or in writing, in ways that would directly address the questions I am asking here. For one thing, what occurs around sexuality *in consciousness* may be quite distant from what goes on in that inchoate and corporeal living out of erotics. For another thing, there are many who feel moral constraints, shame, secrecy, or prohibition about such telling. For a third, erotic subjectivities are always in motion, and any discrete moment of narrating them would be tantamount to a freeze-frame excerpted out of a story-in-progress.

Fourth, especially given that I am a non-Hmong researcher, there are many ways in which probing these questions directly with research subjects could be unethical or invasive. Indeed, I have never set about to conduct research expressly on sexualities. And yet after years of researching media and transnationality, it turns out I have garnered quite a bit of incidental insight. There are many moments when erotics and norms are not the explicit subject of research but they arise nonetheless, and should not be discounted as irrelevant to the issues at hand.

There are certain instances where *cultural products* are particularly useful—especially melodramas such as *Dr. Tom* for the way they delve into hypertrophied feeling, and the romance genre for the way it traffics in desire, compelling the reader or audience through affective involvement in longing. Moreover, they constitute and in turn elicit Hmong commentaries on social and erotic phenomena. Many viewers of Hmong movies love these oft-maligned genres. These seductive narratives make for minglings of pleasure and desire, for multiple meanings. Gleaning what Hmong audiences get from the media they consume may seem a circuitous approach to thinking erotics. What I've done here is attend to the polyphony in how people *talk* about media meanings. Nonetheless, when it comes to erotics, a domain so much involved with body and affect, the media—visual media, especially—become salient for the ways they pull at affect, independent of lines and plots. In addition to focusing on one clip and posing questions, it is crucial to be mindful of peoples' spontaneous reactions when watching videos. These reactions include bursts of visceral affect in the form of laughter and tears, not just commentary. All of these elements constitute what I refer to as an ethnotextual approach to the study of media, situated within a complex and far-from-unitary community of production and reception (Schein 2004; see also Mankekar and Schein 2012, 25–27).

Desires of Homeland Women—Redux

But I want to suggest one other possible scenario that pushes us out beyond bodies and once again toward socially constituted and contingent erotics. This scenario compels us to ask what it is that the homeland women in transnational relationships get out of them. There are, of course, the predictable economic and geopolitical answers—that is, they get material rewards and the possibility of migrating to the West. These answers are based on two assumptions: (1) that homeland women's relations with Hmong Americans are instrumental, tantamount to sex-economic exchange, and therefore not erotic for the women; and (2) that, consequently, the sexual attractiveness of the men is irrelevant to the encounters. A deeper gendered assumption might be bundled here as well: the pervasive construction of women's desires as anything but sexual—that is, the negation of women as desiring sexual subjects. I want to suggest that there is potentially another normativity at play here, one that might smuggle in a considerable moralism: the assumption that sexual-economic exchange must be by definition unerotic for the person with less economic power—in other words, that sex is, and must be, unpleasurably delivered in exchange for other returns.

What would happen if we tried to think outside the box, to put erotics back into the equation on the women's side? If a rational calculus of sexual-economic exchange falls short as an answer, then we might suggest that a multiplex form of erotics is being hinted at, one that does allow for Hmong American men's attractiveness despite forms of physical repugnance, hypertrophied, for instance, in Hmong movies where these men are predictably old, sometimes disabled, always unfit, and almost always pudgy or flabby. But what if erotic attractiveness is not thought of in terms of the predictable diacritics of masculine good looks but rather in the deliciousness of relative wealth?

Perhaps returnee men incite a diffused eroticism for homeland women, less centered on the corporeal presence of the actual heterosexual partner and more situated at the scale of global relationality. In its contemporary incarnation, this body would be desirable precisely for its cosmopolitan reach, its globality, its mobility. The accompanying erotics would incorporate the array of the physical pleasures a woman could access through a liaison with a suitor from the West—luxurious foods; accoutrements such as jewelry and clothing for beautifying the body; liberation from rural labor; and a reveling in plush comforts, such as carpeted hotel rooms or residences with running water.

What I am suggesting is that we think of such corporeal pleasures as *within* the scope of erotics, not as other pleasures acquired by trading in one's sexual body. Is it possible that, at least in the sensibility of Hmong/Miao women, the otherwise unattractive corporeality of the transnational suitor could become one object of sexual desire by virtue of his positioning within a universe of delectations enabled by his cash and citizenship? If all, or even some, of these latter types of meaning are present in such encounters, then it becomes possible to think of the transnational Hmong male body as always already situated within a larger material body beyond the skin. And we could then think of the deficiencies in this body as not obviating sexual desirability or reducing the liaisons to mere sex work but as recasting the construction of desire—narrating the erotics of a material pleasure in excess of more bounded sexualities involving conventionally desirable bodies.

The mobile, meandering yearnings of homeland women beyond the bodies of Hmong American men to their alluring wealth and its corporeal comforts, to commodities that make the experience of one's own body more enjoyable, to the dreamlike prospect of migration overseas to another life—these might be taken together as an assemblage of desiring processes, occasionally—but not necessarily—congealed in moments of bodily contact. Such yearnings would reflect the rhizomic patterning that Deleuze and Guattari (1988) are so noted for developing in contradistinction to what they called the "arborial" form, in which everything proceeds from a central trunk. The rhizome does not have a unifying base but is characterized by perpetual outcroppings in unpredictable directions: "Once a rhizome has been obstructed, arborified, it's all over, no desire stirs; for it is always by rhizome that desire moves and produces. Whenever desire climbs a tree, internal repercussions trip it up and it falls to its death; the rhizome, on the other hand, acts on desire by external, productive outgrowths" (Deleuze and Guattari 1988, 14). We might think of the motivations of homeland women in transnational trysts as arborified if they are reduced to asexual material instrumentality and as rhizomic if erotics spill over in many directions above and beyond the specific man who is the suitor. Displacing the more reductive adjudication of agency or not, constrained or unfettered, this framing would rather put forward a notion of women as polymorphously desiring subjects.

Conclusion: For Erotics

This chapter has synergized three tasks, which might be disaggregated as (1) exploring insights of sexuality studies, (2) pluralizing Hmong genders and sexualities, and (3) deploying approaches to media analysis as method. Sexuality studies and queer theorizing, as developed in the Western academy, encourage us to shift the lens through which a plethora of gendered practices are viewed. In this chapter, I have touched on many flashpoint issues, including monogamy versus multiple partners, arranged versus companionate courtship or marriage, intergenerational relationships, sexual-economic exchanges, the eroticizing of homeland "others" and of the very young woman, the incommensurability of fantasy and bodied sex acts, questions of homosexual identification versus tacitness or bisexuality, questions of homophobia and coming out of the closet, and more. How do Hmong sexual politics fare in these highly contested discussions?

Assuming that there are very specific Hmong and diasporic modalities by which these issues play out, how might we mobilize a notion of changing and plural sexual cultures to counter unitary Western paradigms of sexuality? Using Hmong sexuality studies to talk back to Eurocentric approaches—what is made visible? Desire in arranged marriage, the cult of the very young homeland woman, polygynous actualities, and the erotics of transnational privilege could all be considered forms of polymorphousness, with its myriad promiscuous imaginings, that breaches categories held constant in so much of gender and sexuality studies. There is a narrow path to be charted here—navigating between the dual ills of painting Hmong sexualities into an otherness that is judged as less "civilized" versus imposing existing Euro-American categories and rendering invisible the specificities of Hmong ethnic, racial, and transnational socialities (and in both these potential excesses, my non-Hmong positionality is again highly implicated).

I have suggested that the concept of "sexual cultures" is fraught, for while it dislocates some Eurocentric certainties, it can overly homogenize and obscure the vital variations that are actually lived out in social and erotic process. The many versions of masculinity—some highly racialized—that come into view when concepts of patriarchy, or the homo–hetero binary, or the agent–victim dichotomy, are disturbed affirm that "sexual culture" for Hmong Americans is not to be frozen or generalized. Nor is men's sexual "drive" to be naturalized and assumed. Much highly negotiated social process risks being overlooked if biology, or even male privilege, comes to explain men's sex acts. Hmong masculinities, even as they are held constant as the roots of Hmong women's oppression, are also buffeted by considerable unfixities: how to fashion one's manhood in a racial context that alternately ascribes effeminacy and perpetual warriorhood?;[14] how to decide whether to come out as gay in a larger social field where such identification may be coded white and assimilationist?

The purpose of this work is not limited to doing a close reading of how Hmong (and Miao) homeland women are represented in diasporic imaginings, or to assessing whether their depicted engagements with Hmong American men are exploitative or not. It is also to take a step back from these judgments to make methodological points (1) about how sensitive community topics—especially those involving sexuality—can be explored ethically, and (2) about the validity of looking at mediated forms of cultural production for social analysis. What, if anything, can media studies tell us about Hmong gender and sexuality? I have intertwined media with social methods to interrogate erotics, asking what we might get from the intricate subjectivities incited and reflected by media.

The account here raises further queries: What is the relationship between Hmong-made images and larger global and gender imaginaries? What are the social effects of such images being in circulation, and how would we get at this? How can analyzing images get us beyond them to looking at women and men as social actors? And how would we go about producing such knowledge responsibly and with insight? A more dispassionate attention that perceives sexual variation, eschews sex negativity and moral panic, and makes room for erotics and fantasy will allow fuller development of rich and insightful Hmong diasporic sexuality studies.

Notes

1. The most extreme example of this is the coverage of Hmong gang rapes in the popular press, coverage that implies that a cultural reflex drives this phenomenon. Among many such stories, see, for example, "Shamed into Silence," *Minneapolis Star-Tribune*, March 23, 2012, www.startribune.com/shamed-into -silence/11608836/.

2. My extension of this is the axiom that "where there is othering, it will always be gendered, whether the Other is portrayed as masculine or feminine"; and "this Other will always be sexually nonnormative, whether hypersexual, hyposexual or somehow perverse."

3. Here and elsewhere I use "Miao" to denote Hmong co-ethnics in China. For more on the use of the "Miao" term in China, see Schein (2000, 36–41).

4. Note that some Westerners have argued for the legal protection of those in "de facto polygamous" marriages as reducing the vulnerability of women who might otherwise be on their own with no claim to spousal support (cf. Alexandre 2007).

5. Even though he has rejoined his community, Thoj describes his work in the 1990s as "not oriented to the Hmong market." What this meant was that he and his Hmong associates were willing to speak out in their films about sensitive issues that would otherwise be unmentionable and that didn't have a place in conventional Hmong entertainment media. His funding base, as a consequence, could not be sales of videos to Hmong consumers; but, on the other hand, to the extent that he took up larger social issues, his work stood to interest nonprofit funding organizations concerned either with social issues or with the arts.

6. One of the most elegant arguments against using culture to explain social process and personal experience was Lila Abu-Lughod's classic "Writing Against Culture" (1991). Her cautions against the implications of imputing a determining force of culture over social action and values remain acutely apposite when we think of the excesses of Fadiman's *The Spirit Catches You and You Fall Down* (1997) and the retrogressive cultural portrait that has stuck to Hmong Americans who continue to be treated as new arrivals and awkward misfits by readers influenced by the book and the construct of static Hmong culture.

7. For an exploration of this, see our write-up of a co-facilitated sexualities workshop at the 2015 Hmong National Development conference (Pha, Schein, and Vue n.d.).

8. A chilling example reveals how readily these attributions can be propagated. After the release of *Gran Torino*, the L.A.-based Media Action Network for Asian Americans (MANAA) posted on its website a review that lauded as pedagogical what a majority of Hmong Americans considered among the most objectionable lines in the script: "Girls go to school and boys go to jail." When a scholarly alliance, the Critical Hmong Studies Collective, challenged this position in a cosigned letter, MANAA professed willingness to be "educated" but ultimately, in an acute instance of de facto exclusion, downplayed the Hmong cautions that lawlessness and gangbangerhood were egregious reductions that can ratify police profiling. Insisting on their own take, finding the gangster attribution to be "sociological," they exercised their de facto privilege to speak in a pan-Asian voice over the protestations of Hmong audiences. See http://manaa.org/?p=31 (accessed August 12, 2015).

9. "Some people like to have a lot of sex, others little or none"; or, she suggests, "Sexuality makes up a large share of the self-perceived identity of some people, a small share of others" (Sedgwick 1990, 25). Such differences affect social process but almost invisibly, for we have not deigned to take them seriously in our analyses.

10. Am I talking here about the celebrated "bodies and their pleasures" that Foucault championed in *The History of Sexuality*, vol. 1 (1980), as that pristine space outside discourse? Perhaps, except that for Foucault, and so many readings of him, the bodies-and-pleasures space was somehow a resistive one, maybe even an oppositional one. What he celebrated in that well-nigh utopian vision of "pleasure," Deleuze (1997) refused in favor of "desire." The problem with pleasure, Deleuze suggested, was that it implied a reterritorialization, a zoning of erotics into those binarized spaces of the encoded (sexuality) and the resistant (pleasures). A conventional demarcation of arranged marriage and erotic love, for instance, into separate categories can be seen as a form of what Deleuze might have called coding or reterritorialization. "Desire," by contrast, offered deterritorialization; what he called "assemblages" of desire could be much more shifting, contingent. Assemblages always retain heterogeneity, can enfold power, can desire power's exercise, whereas pleasure, at least if I understand Deleuze's perspective, could only either evade or be complicit with power. What this Deleuzian angle adds is that what might seem to congeal as a static sexual culture with fixed sets of erotically charged meanings could also be shifting, realigning, and in constant motion—reassembling.

11. Think, for example, of Anne McClintock's (1995) powerful historicization of what we now identify as the sexual subculture of fetishism. What she so deftly showed in her magisterial study was its specific emergence from changing labor relations and global geopolitics in the nineteenth century. Far from being a transhistorical, psychically generated "perversion," it was a specific assemblage of

factors that came together to make leather, whips, and strict discipline so highly charged in that era.

12. In a useful discussion of haptic visuality, Laura Marks (2000) describes how "the eyes themselves function like organs of touch. . . . While optical perception privileges the representational power of the image, haptic perception privileges the material presence of the image. . . . Haptic visuality involves the body more than is the case with optical visuality" (162–63).

13. For an expanded discussion of this, see Mankekar and Schein (2012, 20–22).

14. For a reflection on this fashioning at the level of oppositional grassroots media production, see Schein and Vang on the YouTube video "Thao Does Walt," https://www.youtube.com/watch?v=dMaIOFMg64M.

Works Cited

Abu-Lughod, Lila. 1991. "Writing Against Culture." In *Recapturing Anthropology: Working in the Present,* edited by Richard G. Fox, 137–62. Santa Fe, N.M.: School of American Research Press.

Alexandre, Michele. 2007. "Lessons from Islamic Polygamy: A Case for Expanding the American Concept of Surviving Spouse So As to Include De Facto Polygamous Spouses." *Washington and Lee Law Review* 64:1461–81.

Boulden, Walter T. 2009. "Gay Hmong: A Multifaceted Clash of Cultures." *Journal of Gay and Lesbian Social Services* 21, no. 2: 134–50.

Cacho, Lisa Marie. 2012. *Social Death: Racialized Rightlessness and the Criminalization of the Unprotected.* New York: New York University Press.

Connell, Robert. 1995. *Masculinities.* Berkeley: University of California Press.

Decena, Carlos Ulises. 2011. *Tacit Subjects: Belonging and Same-Sex Desire among Dominican Immigrant Men.* Durham, N.C.: Duke University Press.

Deleuze, Gilles. 1997. "Desire and Pleasure." In *Foucault and His Interlocutors,* edited by Arnold Davison, 183–92. Minneapolis: University of Minnesota Press.

Deleuze, Gilles, and Félix Guattari. 1988. *A Thousand Plateaus: Capitalism and Schizophrenia.* Translation and foreword by Brian Massumi. London: Athlone Press.

Duggan, Lisa, and Nan D. Hunter, eds. 2006. *Sex Wars: Sexual Dissent and Political Culture.* 10th anniversary ed. New York: Routledge.

Eng, David. 2001. *Racial Castration: Managing Masculinity in Asian America.* Durham, N.C.: Duke University Press.

Eng, David, and Alice Hom, eds. 1998. *Q & A: Queer in Asian America.* Philadelphia: Temple University Press.

Fadiman, Anne. 1997. *The Spirit Catches You and You Fall Down: A Hmong Child, Her American Doctors, and the Collision of Two Cultures.* New York: Noonday Press.

Foucault, Michel. 1980. *The History of Sexuality*. Vol. 1, *An Introduction*. New York: Vintage.

Fung, Richard. 1991. "Looking for My Penis: The Eroticized Asian in Gay Video Porn." In *How Do I Look? Queer Film and Video*, edited by Bad Object Choices, 145–68. Seattle: Bay Press.

Gonzalez, M. Alfredo. 2007. "Latinos on DA Down Low: The Limitations of Sexual Identity in Public Health." *Latino Studies* 5:25–52.

Herdt, Gilbert, ed. 2009. *Moral Panics, Sex Panics: Fear and the Fight over Sexual Rights*. New York: New York University Press.

Hoang Nguyen Tan. 2012. "I Got This Way from Eating Rice: Gay Asian Documentary and the Reeducation of Desire." In *Resolutions 3: Global Networks of Video*, edited by Ming-Yuen S. Ma and Erika Suderburg, 241–57. Minneapolis: University of Minnesota Press.

———. 2014. *A View from the Bottom: Asian American Masculinity and Sexual Representation*. Durham, N.C.: Duke University Press.

Kinsey, Alfred C., Wardell B. Pomeroy, and Clyde E. Martin. 1948. *Sexual Behavior in the Human Male*. Philadelphia: W. B. Saunders.

———. 1953. *Sexual Behavior in the Human Female*. Philadelphia: W. B. Saunders.

Koshy, Susan. 2004. *Sexual Naturalization: Asian Americans and Miscegenation*. Stanford, Calif.: Stanford University Press.

Lancaster, Roger N. 2011. *Sex Panic and the Punitive State*. Berkeley: University of California Press.

Mankekar, Purnima, and Louisa Schein. 2012. "Mediations and Transmediations: Erotics, Sociality, and 'Asia.'" With Purnima Mankekar. In *Media, Globalization and Asian Erotics*, edited by Purnima Mankekar and Louisa Schein, 1–31. Durham, N.C.: Duke University Press.

Marks, Laura U. 2000. *The Skin of the Film: Intercultural Cinema, Embodiment, and the Senses*. Durham, N.C.: Duke University Press.

Massumi, Brian. 2002. *Parables for the Virtual: Movement, Affect, Sensation*. Durham, N.C.: Duke University Press.

Mayo, J. B. 2013. "Hmong History and LGBTQ Lives: Immigrant Youth Perspectives on Being Queer and Hmong." *Journal of International Social Studies* 3, no. 1: 79–91.

McClintock, Anne. 1995. *Imperial Leather: Race, Gender and Sexuality in the Colonial Contest*. New York: Routledge.

Moore, Darnell L., and Wade Davis. 2012. "Tongues Untied: On 'Coming Out,' Anderson Cooper and Frank Ocean." *Huffington Post*, July 6. http://www .huffingtonpost.com/darnell-l-moore/anderson-cooper-frank-ocean -gay_b_1653017.html.

Nagel, Joane. 2003. *Race, Ethnicity, and Sexuality: Intimate Intersections, Forbidden Frontiers*. New York: Oxford University Press.

Ngo, Bic. 2012. "The Importance of Family for a Gay Hmong American Man: Complicating Discourses of 'Coming Out.'" *Hmong Studies Journal* 13, no. 1: 1–27.

Nguyen Viet Thanh. 2002. *Race and Resistance: Literature and Politics in Asian America*. Oxford: Oxford University Press.

Pha, Kong Pheng, Louisa Schein, and Pao Lee Vue. "Hmong Sexual Diversity: Beginning the Conversation." Unpublished manuscript.

Rubin, Gayle. 1975. "The Traffic in Women: Notes on the 'Political Economy' of Sex." In *Toward an Anthropology of Women,* edited by Rayna Reiter. New York: Monthly Review Press.

———. 1993. "Thinking Sex: Notes for a Radical Theory of the Politics of Sexuality." In *The Lesbian and Gay Studies Reader,* edited by Henry Abelove et al., 3–44. New York: Routledge.

Said, Edward. 1979. *Orientalism*. New York: Vintage.

Schein, Louisa. 1999. "Diaspora Politics, Homeland Erotics and the Materializing of Memory." *Positions: East Asia Cultures Critique* 7, no. 3: 697–729.

———. 2000. *Minority Rules: The Miao and the Feminine in China's Cultural Politics*. Durham, N.C.: Duke University Press.

———. 2004. "Homeland Beauty: Transnational Longing and Hmong American Video." *Journal of Asian Studies* 63, no. 2: 433–63.

———. *Rewind to Home: Hmong Media and Gendered Diaspora*. Ms in progress.

Schein, Louisa, and Va-Megn Thoj. 2008. "Violence, Hmong American Visibility and the Precariousness of Asian Race." *PMLA (Publications of the Modern Language Association)* 123, no. 5: 1752–56.

———. 2009. "*Gran Torino*'s Boys and Men with Guns." *Hmong Studies Journal* 10 (December): 1–52. http://hmongstudies.org/ScheinThojHSJ10.pdf.

Schein, Louisa, Va-Megn Thoj, Bee Vang, and Ly Chong Thong Jalao. 2012. "Beyond *Gran Torino*'s Guns: Hmong Cultural Warriors Performing Genders." *Positions: Asia Critique* 20, no. 3: 763–92.

Schein, Louisa, and Bee Vang. n.d. "Micro-Exclusions, Raunch Aesthetics and In-Jokes: A Rogue Hmong Raciosexual Parody." *Visual Anthropology*.

Sedgwick, Eve Kosofsky. 1990. "Axiomatic." In *The Epistemology of the Closet*. Berkeley, Calif.: University of California Press.

Shimizu, Celine Parrenas. 2012. *Straitjacket Sexualities: Unbinding Asian American Manhoods in the Movies*. Stanford, Calif.: Stanford University Press.

Tu, Thuy Linh Nguyen. 2003. "Good Politics, Great Porn: Untangling Race, Sex, and Technology in Asian American Cultural Productions." In *Asian America. Net: Ethnicity, Nationalism, and Cyberspace,* edited by Rachel C. Lee and Sau-Ling Cynthia Wong, 267–80. New York: Routledge.

Vang, Bee. 2013. "Hmong Butch: The Antinomies of Being Fourth World." *Feminist Wire*, March 12. http://thefeministwire.com/2013/03/hmong-butch-the -antinomies-of-being-fourth-world/.

Vue, Pao Lee. 2012. *Assimilation and the Gendered Color Line: Hmong Case Studies of Hip-Hop and Import Racing*. El Paso: LFB Scholarly Publishing.

Warner, Michael. 1999. *The Trouble with Normal: Sex, Politics and the Ethics of Queer Life*. New York: Free Press.

Williams, Linda. 1991. "Film Bodies: Gender, Genre and Excess." *Film Quarterly* 44, no. 4: 2–13.

CHAPTER 11

Dangerous Questions

Queering Gender in the Hmong Diaspora

Bruce Thao

THOUGH PUBLIC ACKNOWLEDGMENT and recognition of Hmong lesbian, gay, bisexual, transgender, and queer (LGBTQ) within the Hmong community is a recent phenomenon, our existence is not new. What *is* new is the conceptualization of Hmong LGBTQ in modern American society, where gays and lesbians are highly visible in the media, and attitudes toward same-sex relationships have drastically shifted in the past few decades in the direction of acceptance. This sits in contrast with much of the current scholarship on the Hmong. The roles of men and women in Hmong culture and society are often discussed as patriarchal and stagnant. Yet this volume clearly demonstrates that this is not the case. This chapter examines how the insertion and exploration of queer identities within the Hmong diaspora both disrupt and deconstruct existing conceptualizations of gender, sexuality, and patriarchy in Hmong culture.

In her exploration of queer South Asian diaspora, Jasbir Puar (1998) states, "The constructions of diaspora that hinge upon masculinist constructions of home and travel are, for the most part, inattentive to gender and silent on sexuality. When queer subjects become visible within diasporic contexts, not only does sexuality become a topic of concern but the masculinist paradigms of diaspora are disrupted as well" (407). Puar forces us to contemplate not only where queer communities of color are located within the diaspora but also where and how we are included, excluded, or displaced (406). Similarly, JeeYeun Lee (1998) asserts that diasporic histories based on kinship and lineage can perpetuate patriarchal and oppressive systems or traditions. Gayatri Gopinath (2005) also applies a queer diaspora framework to her exploration of the South Asian diaspora. In doing so, she is able to critically analyze historical and current diasporic narratives of the home, family, and nation. By inserting a queer Hmong narrative into an analysis of Hmong diaspora, we are forced not only to reflect on what type of diasporic history we have been reproducing over time but also to reconceptualize notions of "cultural authenticity" (Lee 1998, 195). Since the Hmong have been historically displaced, a key question this chapter asks is, What does it mean to be both queer and Hmong and thus displaced within the diaspora?

Dangerous Questions

Acceptance of Hmong LGBTQ raises dangerous questions. It poses potential risks to the continuation of Hmong culture, clan systems, and lineage—at least as they currently exist. When queer Hmong are inserted into an analysis of diaspora, we *queer* the diaspora and we *queer* gender; we *queer* the heteronormative gender binary of male–female because our existence itself complicates traditional gender roles and norms.[1] We *queer* patriarchy because the existence of Hmong LGBTQ forces us to ask dangerous questions: Can a same-sex Hmong couple take the same last name? Can a Hmong marriage ceremony be performed for same-sex Hmong couples? And, if such a negotiation were to take place, who would pay the dowry? Questions such as these have the potential to disturb traditional male-dominated narratives of the Hmong diaspora and revolutionize ancient and modern Hmong cultural norms and traditions as we know them.

Puar (1998) discusses "complex reterritorializations" in reference to what occurs when South Asian diasporas attempt to "expel queer brown bodies from nation as well as culture" (411). In a similar vein, Hmong reterritorializations may occur when queer Hmong individuals or relationships are perceived as threatening to the fabric of Hmong culture. It may be a fear that the roles of Hmong sons and daughters, the customs within marriage ceremonies, and other rituals may be altered if we incorporate Hmong LGBTQ individuals or same-sex couples into them. For example, traditional Hmong ceremonies—such as the bestowing of an elder name on a Hmong man once he has established himself with a wife and children (*tis npe laus*)—come into question. Can you bestow an elder name on a female-to-male transgender Hmong person? What about on a gay Hmong man with a male partner and adopted children?

Fear of altering history and tradition may be one factor preventing the Hmong community from accepting Hmong LGBTQ. Another factor concerns the way that Hmong LGBTQ or same-sex couples may thwart the longevity of the Hmong as a whole. JeeYeun Lee (1998) discusses the concept of reprosexuality (citing Warner) and "generational transmission" (194). Reprosexuality is the "interweaving of heterosexuality, biological reproduction, cultural reproduction and personal identity" (194). It ensures the sustainability of a people over time and is particularly important to diasporic communities that may not be bound by geography. Thus, some Hmong may feel (whether consciously or subconsciously) that queer Hmong threaten to rupture the cultural and biological lineage of the Hmong diaspora because they cannot reproduce. Particularly for a community that has experienced centuries of persecution, war, migration, and statelessness, the livelihood of our people and fear of extinction is not a far-fetched idea. This fear, nonetheless, rests on the assumption that Hmong culture is static and that the traditional systems of patriarchy and an agrarian lifestyle, which were vital to our survival in Asia, have not changed over space and time and remain relevant today. I would argue that this is not the case, particularly in the United States. Rather, there have been many shifts in Hmong culture and society over time and as we migrated across the West. If anything, the inclusion of Hmong LGBTQ individuals, couples, and families into Hmong rituals and customs will invigorate and strengthen families and traditions.

This chapter seeks to push the boundaries of the male–female gender binary and the heteronormative frame that has been used both to perpetuate patriarchy in Hmong families and customs, and to approach the majority of scholarship on the Hmong. It does so by using data and stories from the first national assessment of lesbian, gay, bisexual, transgender, and queer Southeast Asian Americans in the United States: the Queer Southeast Asian (QSEA) Census (2010). This chapter makes an important move to situate queer Hmong within the diaspora and to explore how they claim space and power within it. It does so in alignment with the other chapters in this volume, which together counter prevailing static narratives of Hmong culture and gender in both academic and public discourse.

The process of locating queer Hmong in the diaspora is not without its challenges, which are similar to the struggles of Hmong American women who have risen to positions of power and influence in the past decade, facing contempt and discomfort from segments of the Hmong community—including men. In the past ten years, there has been a shift in the community as Hmong women have claimed space as leaders—both within and beyond the community. Queer Hmong are now experiencing a similar shift in the diaspora, emerging from relegated spaces of denial and silence and claiming their place as active and vibrant members of the community. How they do this and the ways they shift between spaces varies, urging further exploration.

The stories in this chapter reveal that most Hmong LGBTQ embrace their families, value Hmong culture, and seek to be loved and accepted for who they are. They do not reject Hmong culture. On the contrary, they have found or are finding ways to be authentic to their gender, sexual, and cultural identities as queer Hmong individuals. They carry with them immense burdens as they navigate which spaces and closets they are or are not "out" in. Nonetheless, through the negotiation of these identities and multiple spaces, they find agency and power.

The Epistemological Record

The Hmong have been in the United States for nearly four decades. Within that period, there have been only four academic publications on Hmong LGBTQ individuals and one unpublished doctoral dissertation, all of which have been produced since 2008.[2] The dearth of literature on Hmong LGBTQ is not surprising considering that the field of LGBT studies is relatively new, dating back to about the 1970s; that queer theory only became popularized in the 1990s; and that scholarship on Asian–Pacific Islander (API) LGBTQ only emerged shortly after. Following the civil rights movement in the 1950s and 1960s and the subsequent formation of ethnic and gender studies, LGBT studies arose in the 1970s in an attempt to shed light on the experiences of gays, lesbians, and bisexuals (Lovaas, Elia, and Yep 2006). Queer theory came about a couple decades later as a response to LGBT studies, expanding on the constructions and definitions of gender and sexuality articulated in LGBT studies.

It was not until the mid-1990s that the first literature on API LGBTQ was published. Seminal anthologies—such as David Eng and Alice Hom's *Q & A* (1998) and Russell Leong's *Asian American Sexualities* (1996)—were among the first to present critical analyses and narratives of API LGBTQ identity. The authors discuss the intersectionality of race, ethnicity, gender, sexuality, nationality, power, and privilege. Several themes emerge regarding authenticity, identity politics, diaspora, homosexuality as a perceived Western (or "white") "disease," silence, and "coming out." This literature provides a foundation upon which we can engage the experiences of Hmong LGBTQ. Nonetheless, there is a clear absence of Southeast Asian perspectives in the API LGBTQ literature since the 1990s. The majority of contributors have been East Asian, Filipino(a), or South Asian. As both the pre- and postmigration experiences of Southeast Asians are markedly different from those of other Asian American groups, it should come as no surprise that the experiences of Hmong LGBTQ also differ in various ways from those of other API LGBTQ. Further, as a stateless ethnic minority, the experiences of Hmong LGBTQ differ from those of other Southeast Asian LGBTQ.

Despite the minute amount of literature on queer Hmong to date, there continues to be growing interest in academia to explore the lived experiences of Hmong LGBTQ. This rise is similar to the emergence of LGBT studies following gay and lesbian social movements. It is only in the past ten to fifteen years that Hmong and other Southeast Asian LGBTQ have begun to organize, forming social justice organizations such as Shades of Yellow (a Minnesota Hmong LGBTQ organization), Freedom Inc. (a Wisconsin Hmong gender justice organization), and the Providence Youth Student Movement (PrYSM, a Southeast Asian and queer organization based in Rhode Island). All of these organizations formed ten to fifteen years ago in response to a need for visibility, advocacy, and community for queer Southeast Asians. The recent research comes on the heels of these social movements.

The first publication was Walter Boulden's 2009 study, in which he interviewed ten gay Hmong men between the ages of eighteen and thirty. Boulden draws out the intersecting experiences of racism and discrimination that individuals felt due to their racial and sexual orientation. He highlights the struggles the men faced in attempting to appease their families and uphold traditional gender roles while feeling that, as gay men, they could never fulfill those roles. Thus, these individuals' sexual identities complicated the functions of family and culture as protective factors against racism.

The second and third publications on queer Hmong were both by Bic Ngo in 2012. Ngo's work uses case studies of gay Hmong men in their mid-twenties and one bisexual Hmong woman. The author explores how these individuals expand conceptualizations of Hmong culture, identity, and sexuality. Ngo makes it a point to challenge literature or frameworks that view Hmong culture as static. On the contrary, she argues that the experi-

ences of her interviewees attest to the fact that Hmong culture is constantly being (re)negotiated and is consistently evolving. The stories Ngo
highlights also complicate the traditional coming-out narrative of the
white mainstream LGBTQ community and emphasize the importance
of maintaining family relationships while coming to terms with one's
sexual identity.

J. B. Mayo (2013) and Pahoua Yang (2008) explore similar themes in
their research. Mayo uses the case study of a young gay Hmong man to
examine both the difficulties queer Hmong face and the resilience gained
through the process of negotiating which spaces to come out in and which
to keep themselves closeted in. Yang (2008) interviewed eleven Hmong
participants: five gay men and six lesbian women, ages twenty to thirty-one.
Yang focuses on coming-out experiences, drawing particular attention to
the decision-making processes leading up to coming out, the shifting
dynamics in family and social relationships post–coming out, and the
identity formation and meaning-making processes of gay and lesbian
Hmong after coming out.

The current research on Hmong LGBTQ demonstrates that the experiences of gay and lesbian Hmong are complex and nuanced and encompass
intersections of race, ethnicity, gender expectations, and familial obliga-.
tions. Nonetheless, it is evident that these works focus primarily on gay
Hmong men (Boulden 2009; Mayo 2013; Ngo 2012a, 2012b; Yang 2008).
While research focused on gay Hmong men indeed complicates the
gender binary, it does not represent the spectrum of Hmong LGBTQ
experiences and, once again, privileges Hmong male voices. The inclusion
of lesbian, bisexual, trans, and gender-queer voices would deepen an analysis of gender and patriarchy in the diaspora, much as queer theory has
enhanced the field of LGBT studies.

Gaps within the Literature

The Queer Southeast Asian (QSEA) Census and this chapter also differ
from the existing literature on queer Hmong in other ways. While some of
the literature touches on aspects of racism and poverty, the QSEA Census
forefronts intersections of poverty, racism, homophobia, and gender discrimination. Also, while prior studies included only those individuals
eighteen and over, the QSEA Census surveyed those ages fourteen to
thirty-eight. Further, the QSEA Census widens the scope of inquiry to

include individuals who identify as gay, lesbian, bisexual, pansexual, transgender, queer, and gender queer. The data reveal that while there are many similarities among these groups, there are also notable differences. Just as studies of Hmong men are enriched by the inclusion of Hmong women, the inclusion of transgender and gender-queer individuals adds depth and nuance to this study and furthers our understanding of how gender and sexuality impact LGBTQ lives.

On Methodology: The QSEA Census

Beyond the content and participants in this study, what also distinguishes this research from those previously conducted with Hmong gay, lesbian, and bisexual participants is that it was created from within the queer Southeast Asian American community. The QSEA Census is a project initiated by four community-based organizations that came together in 2009 to form the QSEA Network: the Providence Youth Student Movement (PrYSM; Providence, R.I.); Shades of Yellow (SOY; St. Paul, Minn.); Freedom Inc. (Madison, Wis.); and Khmer In Action (KIA; Seattle, Wash.).[3] The desire to create and conduct the first-ever national assessment of queer Southeast Asian Americans was spurred by the need for comprehensive data and narratives of the daily realities facing this community. Without adequate data or information, it is difficult to engage mainstream organizations, funders, or ethnic communities and make a case for the unique needs and challenges facing queer Southeast Asians. All content was created by these organizations with feedback from supporting Asian–Pacific Islander LGBTQ organizations, such as the National Queer Asian Pacific Islander Alliance (NQAPIA). Questions were developed based on the organizations' firsthand knowledge of the issues facing queer Southeast Asians and nuances that were not captured anywhere else in the literature.

A twenty-eight-item, online survey was designed, with closed-ended questions assessing multiple areas, including gender identity; sexual orientation; socioeconomic status; whether one was out of the closet and to whom; levels of social support; experiences with gang involvement; and experiences of racism, homophobia, and genderphobia/gender discrimination. Each topic area also included an open-ended section where participants could share personal stories or experiences in as much or as little detail as they desired.

Survey creation began in 2010, and outreach and promotion of the survey was conducted over the course of one year. No compensation or incentive was provided to participants to complete the survey. Outreach and promotion of survey participation were led by the QSEA Network and partner organizations across the country. Methods of solicitation included word of mouth; social media; and outreach at LGBTQ and API conferences, community events, and social spaces, such as bars and dance clubs. Participants were invited to complete the survey if they identified as being of Hmong, Lao, Cambodian, Vietnamese, or Thai ethnic descent; were currently residing in the United States; and identified as gay, lesbian, bisexual, transgender, pansexual, queer, or questioning. Overall, a total of 364 surveys were completed. This chapter focuses on the 142 Hmong participants in the sample.[4]

The 142 Hmong American participants (average age = 23; range = 14–38) represent seventeen states across the United States. The majority of participants were from Minnesota, Wisconsin, and California, where a majority of Hmong Americans reside. Respondents were given several options when asked to report their gender identity: 49 percent identified as male, 44 percent as female, 3 percent as transgender, and 4 percent as gender queer. While the number of individuals who identified as transgender or gender queer is relatively low, it should be emphasized that this is the first study to ever include transgender Hmong or provide the option for individuals to identify as gender queer. Regarding sexual orientation, 42 percent identified as gay, 22 percent as lesbian, 20 percent as bisexual, 2 percent as pansexual, 5 percent as queer, and 9 percent as questioning (see Table 11.1). As demonstrated in Table 11.1, a much higher percentage of females identified as bisexual and questioning in comparison to males. Females were also the only respondents to identify as pansexual.

Gender identity is defined as one's "internal sense of being male, female, or something else" (NCTE 2014). The category of transgender refers to individuals "whose gender identity, expression or behavior is different from those typically associated with their assigned sex at birth" (NCTE 2014). Transgender persons may or may not have used hormones or surgery to transition to the gender with which they more adequately identify. Those who identify as gender queer do not identify completely as either male or female and may consider themselves more androgynous. Important to note is that the term "gender queer" as a gender identity should

TABLE 11.1

Self-Identified Sexual Orientation by Gender Identity

| | | GENDER IDENTITY | | | | |
		MALE (n = 69)	FEMALE (n = 63)	TRANS (n = 4)	GENDER QUEER (n = 6)	TOTAL
Sexual Orientation	Lesbian	—	44%	25%	33%	22%
	Gay	84%	—	25%	17%	42%
	Bisexual	9%	33%	—	33%	20%
	Pansexual	—	5%	—	—	2%
	Queer	3%	5%	50%	—	5%
	Questioning	4%	13%	—	17%	9%

not be confused with the umbrella term "queer," which is "used to refer to lesbian, gay, bisexual and, often also transgender, people" (NCTE 2014).

Sexual orientation, on the other hand, is "a term describing a person's attraction to members of the same sex or different sex" (NCTE 2014). The terms "gay," "lesbian," and "bisexual" are commonly understood sexual orientations. Less known is the term "pansexual," which refers to individuals who are attracted to persons of any gender identity. This is not to be confused with bisexuals, who may be attracted to either men or women; pansexuals may be attracted to men, women, or those who identify with another gender identity (Queers United 2008).

Intersections of Oppression

For Hmong LGBTQ, our existence presses up against walls imposed by gender norms as well as cultural expectations. Throughout these experiences, there is a continual search for a space to exist within the diaspora. JeeYeun Lee (1998) discusses the complexities for Korean American LGBTQ when attempting to trace their history through the Korean diaspora (192). There is a search for authenticity, a validation of their lived experiences.

For many Hmong LGBTQ, there lies a gradient of gender and sexual identities beyond male and female or gay and straight that individuals may feel more accurately represent them. As a result, however, queer Hmong end up displaced not only within the Hmong community but within queer spaces as well. For the Hmong participants in this study, quantitative and qualitative data reveal that individuals experienced racism, homophobia, and gender discrimination in multiple realms (at home, at work, at school, and in society in general) and from multiple actors (family members, friends, religious peers, coworkers, and others from within the Hmong and LGBTQ communities).

Across groups, there were high rates of experiences of racism. Overall, 76 percent of the sample ($n = 108$) reported experiencing racism in both straight and queer communities. These rates were similar across gender identity groups, suggesting the salience of race as a source of discrimination in comparison to sexual orientation, which may be less visible. Regarding homophobia, about 56 percent of the sample ($n = 79$) indicated that they have experienced homophobia in mainstream and API spaces. This rate was higher for males (68 percent; $n = 47$) than for females (40 percent; $n = 25$). All those who identified as transgender ($n = 4$) and half of those who identified as gender queer ($n = 3$) reported experiencing homophobia. Regarding gender discrimination, 39 percent of participants ($n = 54$) reported having experienced hatred or violence because of their gender identity or gender expression. All those who identified as transgender ($n = 4$) and two-thirds of those who identified as gender queer ($n = 4$) reported experiencing gender discrimination.

The QSEA Census also took into account socioeconomic status (SES) and its impact on the intersections of gender, sexuality, culture, and family. SES is a crucial factor to consider given that Southeast Asian Americans continue to experience high poverty rates, even after being in the United States for decades. Hmong continue to exhibit some of the highest poverty rates, with one in four Hmong families living below the federal poverty line (U.S. Census Bureau 2009). The implications of financial hardship on family dynamics and social relationships in the midst of negotiating one's cultural, racial, and sexual identity cannot be ignored and must be taken into account. In this sample, over half of respondents (53 percent) indicated that they or their families have been on public assistance at one point in their lives.

Many respondents shared that financial difficulty was an additional factor on top of the existing challenges of coming out and managing family
relationships:

> I hurt our family culture a lot when I came out and told them but
> my family is forgiving, that's why I love them dearly. My mother
> out of all of us needs help the most. She is a single mother who still
> supports her 7 children who live under her roof. I wish I can help,
> but I now have bills that are overdue and in collections. (Gender-
> queer lesbian, 23 years old)[5]

This experience demonstrates the struggles facing queer, low-income ethnic
minorities. To come out amid poverty, family struggles, cultural expectations, and gender norms takes great courage. This individual almost
lost their family in an attempt to share this part of themselves.[6] They consider themselves lucky that their family *forgave* them for coming out. This
individual's belief that revealing their sexual orientation to their parents
would evoke pain counters prevailing messages from gay mainstream culture, which emphasizes the need to come out. In Western gay mainstream
society, the rhetoric regarding coming out often centers around liberation
and being honest with oneself and one's loved ones. Yet this individualistic
approach clashes with Hmong beliefs, in which familial roles and responsibilities and saving face are highly valued. By maintaining family harmony
and assisting their family economically, this individual is still able to negotiate between identity and family.

Displacement across the Spectrum

Lesbian, Bisexual, and Queer Hmong Women

These individuals negotiate their identities and shift how they represent
themselves depending on the context and setting. Martin Manalansan
(2003), in exploring the narratives of gay Filipino American men, challenges the notion of the archetypal gay lifestyle (92). As he delves into the
complex lived experiences of the men he interviews, he shares how their
"selves and identities are remade and recast in different situations" (91).
He discusses the concept of diasporic intimacy, which is the interaction of
the external world (government, public) with one's private life, and how

those in the diaspora respond and engage at these intersections. For queer immigrants, as displaced bodies within a displaced group, the creation of diasporic intimacy can be difficult, given that home and familial life may be spaces of conflict. Yet Manalansan argues that this is precisely why an analysis of the everyday experiences of queers in the diaspora is crucial for understanding how they "create and rearticulate" their narratives (91).

Hmong women often face strict gender expectations as well as the policing of their sexuality. The QSEA Census revealed that Hmong lesbian, bisexual, and queer (LBQ) women face two main stereotypes that are at opposite extremes from each other in regard to their sexuality. On one extreme, they are told that the reason they are attracted to women must be because men do not find them attractive. They are blamed for this "undesirability," and this is used to explain why they are now "choosing" to be with women. A bisexual nineteen-year-old female shared, "It was usually my family member who would indirectly insult me, stating that I was with a woman because I wasn't wanted by men." In placing the blame for her sexual orientation on her lack of desirability to men, her sexual orientation becomes her "fault."

On the other extreme, LBQ women are viewed as overtly promiscuous—indiscriminant about whom they sleep with. This polarity in stereotypes of asexual versus hypersexual removes the freedom for women to choose whom they love or are physically intimate with while also assuming that they lack the intelligence to make such decisions on their own:

> When I came out as bisexual, my close guy friends were no longer "comfortable" with me hanging out with their girlfriends/wives. They were afraid that if their wives/girlfriends hung out with me anymore they might "turn gay" too. Of the other guy friends who weren't offended, they asked if I was "up for a threesome," thinking that just because I now identified as bisexual, that I was into threesomes. When a coworker found out I was bi, he made remarks and physically imitated sexual acts of oral sex with a woman. (Bisexual Hmong female, 27 years old)

This story illustrates the multiple layers of gender, sexuality, and culture facing a bisexual Hmong woman. She is deemed a sexual deviant who may snatch up the girlfriends and wives of Hmong men. She is also assumed to be overtly promiscuous and is thus contorted into an exotic object of a man's fantasy world. Even in the workplace, she faces sexual harassment from coworkers after they discover that she is bisexual. In all of these situations, judgment and stereotypes are placed upon this woman. Her sexual identity is stripped from her and used to degrade, fetishize, and condemn her.

Bisexual women also received criticism from within the queer community. One respondent explains, "I'm constantly questioned about my sexuality, where I need to defend myself with the heterosexual and homosexual community. As a bisexual woman, I'm asked to defend my position as someone who is attracted to men and women." Discrimination is a common experience for those who identify as bisexual, regardless of race or ethnicity.

Further, a twenty-two-year-old lesbian shared an experience of gender discrimination from Hmong elders, or "OGs":

> Every Hmong OG who has not been really exposed to "gay" will always question me if I'm a boy or girl. Then they'll question me why I'm like this and everything but I tell them straight up that I'm simply gay and this is how the new generation is. I'll have a lot of elders talk down on me, even some family relatives, but I'm who I am. It doesn't make me feel uncomfortable. It's just sad how some people can't accept some young Hmong gays like us.

These experiences of LBQ women reveal that according to others in the community, they are not supposed to be sexual—much like Hmong women in general. To uphold traditional Hmong notions of a proper Hmong daughter, women are supposed to be pursued by men but not engaged in sexual activity until they marry a man. If they come out as anything but straight, they are automatically thrown into one of the two aforementioned extremes. LBQ women are displaced because their gender expression or sexual orientation complicates and challenges the male–female gender binary and traditional gender roles. The impact of such dislocation is exacerbated for queer Hmong, for whom displacement within queer communities is compounded by the Hmong's history of geographic displacement. Manalansan (2003) argues that queer diasporic subjects from the Third World face numerous levels of displacement; for them, the "creation and reconfiguration" of home is difficult (13). Further, he adds that this negotiation occurs at a juncture between belonging and citizenship for gay Filipino immigrants. What differs between the gay Filipino men he interviewed, however, and the queer Hmong in this chapter is that as refugees, Hmong migration has never been a choice; it has always been the product of war or persecution. Queer Hmong in the diaspora, then, are carrying multiple histories of persecution on their backs—as a historically persecuted ethnic minority and as LGBTQ.

Hmong Gender Queer and Transgender

For those who identify as gender queer or transgender, their unique experiences are often perplexing to family or community members. Those who identify as gender queer typically do not identify with one gender; rather, they view themselves as fluid and gender nonconforming. Their experiences demonstrate once again how they are displaced within family, society, and the Hmong community. A twenty-four-year-old gay male who "does drag" (dresses in women's clothing and makeup) shared:

> I am a gay man but still am questioning my gender about whether I should transition or stay the same. I find it very difficult that people want you to choose between the two sexes because society does not allow for a man to play two roles. It's very hard to justify who I am and what I am doing when I am constantly being put down professionally, personally, and above all else even finding love has become more problematic for me.

For those who identify as transgender, they do not identify with the gender that was assigned to them at birth. They may or may not have undergone gender reassignment surgery or taken hormones, but may live their lives as the gender they identify with. In the Hmong community, as in larger society, this can be difficult for family or community members to comprehend.

A twenty-four-year-old female-to-male (FTM) transgender lesbian shared, "When my grandmother was alive she didn't quite understand the concept as to why or how, but she loved me unconditionally." This individual was able to share their truth with their grandmother and respect where their grandmother was in the coming-out process, recognizing that it was a process for both of them. In Manalansan's (2003) interviews with gay Filipino men, he explores the role and meanings behind silence from family members after one has come out (28). While some may interpret silence as disapproval, Manalansan's interviewees described that it might also indicate "a kind of dignified acquiescence and, more importantly, of abiding love" (30).

Gay, Bisexual, and Queer Hmong Men

While the experiences that lesbian, bisexual, and queer Hmong women face and the responses they encounter when coming out largely center around the policing of their gender and sexuality, Hmong men's experiences are often focused around expectations placed upon Hmong sons and the privileging of masculinity. In the stories shared in the QSEA Census, gay, bisexual, and queer (GBQ) Hmong men often felt caught between two worlds. There is pressure to uphold the Hmong male masculine persona and to lead the family until one gets married. Then after marrying, Hmong sons are expected to care for their aging parents. Yet knowing that they would never live up to these expectations, many gay Hmong men expressed fear, guilt, and anxiety. They knew that by being gay and wanting same-sex relationships they would be breaking traditions and shunned for not upholding their duties as Hmong sons.

Some gay Hmong men expressed concerns about not being masculine enough. Those who identified their behavior as more feminine discussed feeling judged by members of the straight and gay communities. Even within gay circles, masculinity is privileged. At times this may cause more feminine gay men to think negatively about themselves. "People always tell me about how femme I am and sometimes it bothers me but I can't help who I am. It's disturbing because sometimes I wish that I could be less femme and more masculine," explains a twenty-two-year-old gay male.

The stories and examples shared by Hmong LGBTQ demonstrate the challenges of trying to navigate Hmong culture and society within the confines of the male–female gender binary. For lesbian, bisexual, and queer females, some were too butch for the "straight world" and some were not butch enough for the "queer world." Their sexuality was also policed in the Hmong community, deemed as either asexual or sex fiends. In both queer and straight communities, gay, bisexual, and queer Hmong males were often viewed as not masculine enough. In their families, they were expected to carry out their duties as Hmong sons (including marrying a woman) regardless of their sexual orientation. Transgender and gender-queer individuals found it difficult to fit in anywhere and struggled to find acceptance in the home, at school, in the workplace, or in society. The only reason their positions are considered dangerous, however, is because they could upend traditionally male-dominated, patriarchal narratives of the diaspora that have been preserved over time. Yet it is not the goal of Hmong LGBTQ to erase a rich cultural history and legacy. These individuals simply want to be true to themselves, honor their families, and find a place where they can be who they are. It is this desire for connectedness within families and the diaspora that has spurred many queer Hmong to learn to navigate life in and out of the closet.

Navigating Closets

In this sample, an extremely high proportion of individuals (90 percent; $n = 128$) reported that they had "come out," or revealed their sexual orientation to another person. This rate should not be surprising considering that individuals who have come out may be more likely to participate in a survey for queer Southeast Asians or to be involved in networks where they would be exposed to the promotion of this survey. The average age of coming out was eighteen years old (range = 8–30). This was the case for both males and females. Yet for gender-queer individuals, the average age of coming out was fifteen; and for transgender participants, the average age was thirteen.[7]

Puar (1998) argues that "the significance and celebration attached to coming out appears to be understood as a conclusion to the linear teleology of a modernist, rational subject emerging unrepressed and therefore as empowered as any white queer" (414). This is not the case for Hmong LGBTQ. Whether one has or has not come out or has come out and "gone back in," these are conscious decisions that they are making, and there is power and agency within either decision. JeeYeun Lee (1998) asserts that "people in Asia, the Third World, or racial minority communities are not *more* homophobic, they are *differently* [emphasis in original] homophobic, in ways conditioned not only by beliefs, values, and circumstances but also by histories of Western imperialism and U.S. racism" (196). Gopinath (2005) also argues against discourses that privilege coming out. She suggests that this Western mentality is hegemonic, further pitting Eastern and Western understandings of sexuality against one another.

The literature on gay and lesbian Hmong articulates similar complex coming-out processes that problematize the traditional coming out model of the white LGBTQ mainstream (Boulden 2009; Mayo 2013; Ngo 2012a, 2012b; Yang 2008). In the QSEA Census, as in previous research, a recurring theme in the coming-out stories was a sense of burden and guilt around coming out to one's family. Being LGBTQ was not simply a personal matter; for queer Hmong, their sexual identity has implications for the entire family and clan. Thus, one's sexual orientation comes with responsibility. While this complexity is not specific to queer Hmong, what is unique is that their coming-out processes are embedded within a history of oppression and a perpetual struggle to survive as an ethnic minority group. While this context provides multiple challenges for Hmong LGBTQ struggling to find a sense of self and social support, they do find ways to maneuver these systems.

For Hmong LGBTQ, there is no definitive "in" or "out" of the closet. While the majority of those in the study identified as out, that did not mean they were out in all spaces. In a sense, when a queer Hmong person reveals their sexual orientation to a parent, they are pulling the parent into the closet with them until both are ready to share with others. Participants made conscious decisions regarding which spaces to be out in and with whom they share their gender or sexual orientation. Within families, coming out could mean coming out to a sibling, an aunt, a mother, or a cousin. These were processes that, for some, extended over years.

Finding Power in the Closet

Hmong LGBTQ strategically weigh the decision of whom to come out to and when. They may be out in some spaces and may not discuss their sexual or gender identity in other spaces. As indicated by the age of participants (the youngest, age fourteen) and the age individuals reported they came out (as young as eight years old), the queer Hmong community is (re)claiming who they are and creating pockets of power within familial and community spaces where they can be known and embraced.

Diana Fisher (2003) posits that queer immigrants in America complicate the binary of the closet as a space of either visibility or invisibility, in which being out is reified and being closeted is viewed as weak. Rather, Fisher theorizes the closet as a fluid space in which queer immigrants consciously move. This movement is strategic, intentional, and used to negotiate multiple spheres of ethnic identity, sexual identity, and familial roles. She explains that "here, advantages gained through perpetual motion suggest that the opportunity to move is a very real currency that cannot be underestimated as a tactical form of power" (174).

When coming out is viewed in this sense, queer Hmong no longer become pawns in a game of identity politics, in which one must choose liberation of their sexual identity over family. Rather, they can strategically choose to be out to some people in their lives and not out to others. The ability to maneuver between these spaces gives them power by allowing them to negotiate their familial roles, relationships, and multiple identities on their own terms. When this occurs, Hmong LGBTQ are also staking their claim as members of the Hmong community. They will not run away; they will not be ignored.

Shades of Yellow (SOY) is an example of a Hmong LGBTQ organization that has exerted its power by being a visible presence; a voice; and a safe space for Hmong LGBTQ, their allies, and their families to come together. SOY has provided support, education, advocacy, and leadership for Hmong LGBTQ and their allies for more than ten years in the Twin Cities. Despite being based in Minnesota, it has also engaged the queer Hmong diaspora globally through the Internet, social media, and its annual SOY New Year. Puar (1998) discusses how queer diasporas use cultural productions to exert political prowess. This is embedded within a "politics of location and a politics of placelessness" (416). The SOY New Year is a queer spin on the traditional Hmong New Year celebrations that take place each year in Hmong communities around the world. Hundreds of Hmong LGBTQ from across the country gather in Minnesota each year to celebrate their queer Hmong identity and their place within the Hmong diaspora. Performers engage in Hmong cultural (re)productions by performing traditional and contemporary Hmong, Thai, and Lao songs and dances in drag. In the past, SOY has hosted Hmong drag pageants as well. These are all ways that SOY has created spaces where Hmong LGBTQ can reclaim their place in the diaspora. Manalansan (2003) asserts that for queer diasporic communities, performance is a method of "rewriting scripts or modes of behavior" (14). For queer Hmong, spaces such as SOY and events such as the Hmong New Year are an assertion of queer Hmong identity and power.

So how do we adjust or customize Hmong traditions to incorporate and embrace Hmong LGBTQ, not only as members of the Hmong community but as members of our families? As individual families and clans grapple with these questions, we must continue to lift up the stories and examples of how families have accepted their LGBTQ children and their partners or adapted Hmong customs and traditions to honor and respect their children. These stories may serve as examples for clan leaders and community members to learn from if there are other Hmong families or communities wondering how to accept and embrace their LGBTQ family members.

Through the work of organizations such as SOY, Freedom Inc., and PrYSM, remarkable strides are already taking place and the 2015 Supreme Court decision means that the reality of same-sex marriages and families can no longer be ignored. Several SOY constituents are in same-sex relationships, raise children together, and regularly participate in family events and traditional ceremonies. Some SOY members have participated in Hmong clan meetings in which the topic of same-sex Hmong marriage ceremonies and the ways to host them have been discussed. Community leaders and clan leaders must reach out to and partner with organizations such as SOY to shed light on these conversations and to share best practices and expertise.

Conclusion

Just as queer theory pushed the field of LGBT studies to go beyond existing frameworks and perspectives, this chapter has demonstrated that even within the emerging literature on Hmong LGBTQ, there is a need for critical scholarship that challenges social constructions of gender and sexuality. This comes at a time when the sociopolitical climate and general attitudes toward LGBTQ in America (and globally) are shifting. Nonetheless, tensions remain regarding LGBTQ acceptance. Such tensions were evident in the controversy over the 2014 Winter Olympics being hosted in anti-gay Russia, in the persecution of gays in Uganda, and in the internal conflict among Catholics and countless other religions regarding homosexuality. This exploration of the lives, struggles, and agency of Hmong LGBTQ is merely a microcosm of the world in which we live. What is significant, however, is the examination of gender and sexuality amid a backdrop of the Hmong as a stateless ethnic-minority diaspora. This context provides multiple layers within which issues of displacement, dislocation, and intersectionality can be unearthed.

By exploring the lived experiences of Hmong LGBTQ, this chapter reveals that the experiences of Hmong LGBTQ expand and challenge existing conceptualizations of the male–female gender binary, gender norms, and patriarchy; and that there are power and agency in the ways in which queer Hmong navigate narrowly defined gender and cultural norms as well as a racist and classist American society. Our experiences as queer Hmong cannot be fully understood or discussed without an interrogation of the intersections of racism, homophobia, genderphobia, classism, and patriarchy. It is what makes us who we are and what fuels our resilience. Hmong LGBTQ are not going anywhere. Rather, we are embracing our sexual, gender, and cultural identities and working arduously to maintain ties and relationships with our families. In doing so, we counter Puar's "complex reterritorializations" (1998, 411).

This research has also demonstrated that the experiences of Hmong LGBTQ are multifaceted and complex. An exploration of the challenges and negotiations of identity that queer Hmong encounter complicates typical conceptualizations of Hmong cultural norms and gender and fa-milial roles. This chapter upends academia's focus on Hmong male war-riors or Hmong female victims that has dominated the literature. Both of these narratives only perpetuate the privileging of a heteronormative lens and inherently perpetuate patriarchy. This chapter also reveals that despite experiencing rejection, confusion, or denial regarding one's sexual orien-tation or gender identity, Hmong LGBTQ continue to exhibit a strong sense of familial responsibility and a desire to maintain cultural and family ties. Hmong LGBTQ counter the Western binary of coming out versus staying in the closet, in which being out and visible is privileged. These individuals are committed to preserving relationships and educating their families, even if that means going back into the closet. Yet there are power and agency in those decisions.

Future research must move beyond a gaze fixed on gay Hmong men as the quintessential representation of all that is queer and Hmong. The voices and experiences of queer women, transgender, and gender-queer individ-uals must be represented in order for critical scholarship to be developed. In addition, research cannot ignore the intersections of identities and op-pressions that impact Hmong LGBTQ. While these interrogations can be applied to other queer Southeast Asians as well, the Hmong as a stateless ethnic-minority group provide a unique case with which to engage such inquiry. Research on Hmong communities must take into account queer

Hmong individuals and consciously explore how the inclusion of a queer lens can both enhance and enrich scholarship and analyses.

In the face of manifold experiences with racism, homophobia, gender discrimination, and classism, there is a spirit of resistance and resilience within Hmong LGBTQ that can only be defined as inherently Hmong. Their present experiences are tied to a history of oppression as a stateless ethnic minority that has resisted colonization for centuries. The refusal of queer Hmong to be rejected, mistreated, or marginalized should be celebrated as part of the DNA that has kept Hmong people and their culture alive. Beyond that, what this research also demonstrates is that by delving into the realities facing Hmong LGBTQ and inserting a queer Hmong identity into the Hmong diaspora narrative, new questions emerge at the intersections of identity, culture, gender, and sexuality. We are forced to consider what acceptance of Hmong LGBTQ looks like, what it would mean, and how it would alter (or enhance) Hmong cultural norms and traditions. These are the mere beginnings of conversations that must lead to substantive research and programming if we are to meet the pressing needs of Hmong LGBTQ and provide support to families and communities.

Notes

1. The term "queer" is commonly used as an umbrella term for those who identify as gay, lesbian, bisexual, or transgender. It is often considered a political term, as its usage in relation to one's sexual orientation is often to signify solidarity with other gay, lesbian, bisexual, and transgender persons as well as to reclaim the term as a positive descriptor, as opposed to the often negative connotation associated with it (NCTE 2014). When used in this chapter, the term "queer Hmong" is meant as an umbrella term for Hmong LGBTQ that both empowers and liberates the community.

2. See Mayo 2013; Ngo 2012a, 2012b; and Yang 2008.

3. Khmer In Action is no longer operating.

4. To learn how to obtain a full copy of the QSEA Census, visit www.shadesof yellow.org or contact SOY at community@shadesofyellow.org.

5. Because participants completed the survey online, all quotations of respondents shared in this chapter have been copied and pasted directly as they were written and submitted unless otherwise noted.

6. For individuals who identified as gender queer or transgender, "they" is used as the preferred gender pronoun within the text.

7. I would like to note that coming out is a privilege. There are many within the queer community for whom coming out is not a choice. Due to their gender expression or presentation, some may assume they are gay, lesbian, transgender, or other. To be able to "pass" as straight is a privilege that should be acknowledged.

Works Cited

Boulden, Walter T. 2009. "Gay Hmong: A Multifaceted Clash of Cultures. *Journal of Gay and Lesbian Social Services* 21:134–50.

Eng, David L., and Alice Y. Hom, eds. 1998. *Q & A: Queer in Asian America.* Philadelphia: Temple University Press.

Fisher, Diana. 2003. "Immigrant Closets: Tactical-Micro-Practices-in-the-Hyphen." *Journal of Homosexuality* 45:171–92.

Gopinath, Gayatri. 2005. *Impossible Desires: Queer Diasporas and South Asian Public Cultures.* Durham, N.C.: Duke University Press.

Hom, Alice Y. 1996. "Stories from the Homefront: Perspectives of Asian American Parents with Lesbian Daughters and Gay Sons." In *Asian American Sexualities: Dimensions of the Gay and Lesbian Experience,* edited by Russell Leong, 37–47. New York: Routledge.

Lee, JeeYeun. 1998. "Towards a Queer Korean American Diasporic History." In *Q & A: Queer in Asian America,* edited by David L. Eng and Alice Y. Hom, 185–206. Philadelphia: Temple University Press.

Leong, Russell, ed. 1996. *Asian American Sexualities: Dimensions of the Gay and Lesbian Experience.* New York: Routledge.

Lovaas, Karen E., John P. Elia, and Gust A. Yep. 2006. "Shifting Ground(s)." *Journal of Homosexuality* 52, no. 1–2: 1–18.

Manalansan, M. F. 2003. *Global Divas: Filipino Gay Men in the Diaspora.* Durham, N.C.: Duke University Press.

Mayo, J. B., Jr. 2013. "Hmong History and LGBTQ Lives: Immigrant Youth Perspectives on Being Queer and Hmong." *Journal of International Social Studies* 3, no. 1: 79–91.

National Center for Transgender Equity (NCTE). 2014. "Transgender Terminology." January 14. http://transequality.org/Resources/NCTE_TransTerminology .pdf.

Ngo, Bic. 2012a. "The Importance of Family for a Gay Hmong American Man: Complicating Discourses of 'Coming Out.'" *Hmong Studies Journal* 13, no. 1: 1–27.

———. 2012b. "There Are No GLBT Hmong People: Hmong American Young Adults Navigating Culture and Sexuality." In *Hmong and American: From Refugees to Citizens,* edited by Vincent K. Her and Mary Louise Buley-Meissner, 113–32. St. Paul: Minnesota Historical Society Press.

Puar, Jasbir K. 1998. "Transnational Sexualities: South Asian (Trans)nation(alism)s and Queer Diasporas." In *Q & A: Queer in Asian America*, edited by David L. Eng and Alice Y. Hom, 405–22. Philadelphia: Temple University Press.

Queers United. 2008. "Diversity Lesson 101: 'Pansexuality.'" *Queers United.* June 11. http://queersunited.blogspot.com.

U.S. Census Bureau. 2009. 2007–2009 American Community Survey, 3-Year Estimates.

Yang, Pahoua K. 2008. "A Phenomenological Study of the Coming Out Experiences of Gay and Lesbian Hmong." PhD diss., University of Minnesota.

CHAPTER 12

Finding Queer Hmong America

Gender, Sexuality, Culture, and Happiness among Hmong LGBTQ

Kong Pha

I WRITE THIS CHAPTER with three great hopes. My first hope is for researchers to begin taking the question of gender, sexuality, and sexual orientation in Hmong America as a serious intellectual subject. My second hope is for this chapter to shed a small amount of light on the lives of Hmong LGBTQ people living in America today. My third hope is for this chapter to galvanize Hmong LGBTQ to start documenting and writing about their own lives. We must begin to analyze discourses of sexuality in the Hmong community as they relate to the larger proliferation of sexual dialogues emerging around the world. Sexuality is not just becoming a topic of interest; the questions about sexuality itself have changed in much of queer studies literature. I have been captivated by the turn to affect in race and queer studies since the early 2000s as it relates to emotion, but more importantly, I am interested in seeing how those inarticulable and unseen forces affect our lives. These forces may indeed include emotion, but they also encompass feelings that we cannot seem to make out, those tensions between our hearts and our heads, and new and unconventional ways of doing and knowing academic scholarship. This new move toward unconventionality is indeed queer. It is with queerness itself that I will engage with past and current discourses of gender and sexuality in the Hmong American community. Most literature that has been written about the Hmong LGBTQ community (and there are not that many examples) has focused mostly on their hardships and struggles. I seek not only to explicate the happier moments in Hmong queer lives but also to read the negative feelings differently from "culture," as has always been done in the literature. Hmong queers cannot simply contemplate sadness every single day of their lives. They exert agency and devise strategies to negotiate their sexual identity, ethnic identity, and gender roles in order to live happy and content lives. This chapter will detail my entrance into this community and explore the trajectories of Hmong queer community and identity development, and how popular and historical discourses affect the everyday lives of Hmong LGBTQ people.

The philosopher Sara Ahmed (2010) states that "happiness shapes what coheres as a world" (2). How can we cohere to the Hmong LGBTQ world when all of our epistemological pursuits are only in relation to the suffering that stems from their status as "victims" of the Hmong culture? How can we seek to illuminate the Hmong LGBTQ experience when all that we ever know about their lives are their struggles without knowing how they identify their everyday experiences regarding gender, ethnicity, and sexuality? This chapter will further the discussion about Hmong women, gender, and power by first examining an understudied population in the Hmong community. Furthermore, by addressing sexuality, we can begin to see how central it is in shaping family dynamics, community, and happiness among Hmong women and men. We can then begin to understand and examine how sexuality can act as an identity of empowerment in the Hmong community.

Background

In 2002, park rangers in Fresno, California, found seventeen-year-old Pa Nhia Xiong and twenty-one-year-old Yee Yang dead. Xiong and Yang's story, entitled "Embracing the Forbidden," was part of a series on Hmong teen suicides in the *Fresno Bee* called Lost in America. The article—and the entire series—clearly articulated the "clash" between Hmong and American culture, stating, "The lesbian couple committed suicide together, knowing their love would never be accepted by their families or the Hmong community, which strictly forbids homosexual relationships" (Ellis 2002). Pa Nhia's brother is quoted in the article as saying, "The culture couldn't take it. In this country, men marry men and girls marry girls, but not in our culture." Pa Nhia's mother called her relationship with Yee "not normal" and "strange." Ultimately, Ellis ends the article with a quote from the mother: "This is good . . . because Pa Nhia talked about wanting to be a boy so that she could have more freedom" (Ellis 2002). In death, Pa Nhia would somehow be happier. The Lost in America series suggested that a clash of cultures has produced unhappiness and gender inequality harboring pregnancy and death, and has demonized homosexuality as taboo and "forbidden." What is considered "Hmong culture" is then detached from and becomes incoherent when gender and sexuality are articulated. Furthermore, culture becomes the site of contestation that obscures identities. This chapter seeks to demystify this discourse and to set a framework for understanding the Hmong identity away from a static notion of culture and toward a way in which various forms of difference can emerge.

In her seminal essay "Thinking Sex," Gayle Rubin (1984) states that "the time has come to think about sex" (267). Rubin is correct that in times of social stress, sexuality must be brought upon us to bear in order to conceive of the ongoing destruction that we continuously face. That is, the violence of war, racism, and poverty seems to be so overbearing that we often forget that sexuality is itself a site of contention. Sexuality has always been a crucial site of understanding Hmong society, yet conversations or academic inquiries about questions of sexuality have remained minimal. Homosexuality (or what I refer to in this chapter as queerness) is a recent development in discourse regarding Hmong sexuality; however, sexuality itself has long played a role in understanding Hmong subjects. Hmong racial formation has always depended on the hyperheterosexualization of Hmong society, which, consequently, has always been part of the American understanding of the Hmong people. What I call hyperheterosexuality includes bride kidnapping, bride price, marrying at a very young age, having up to as many as fifteen children, transnational marriages between older Hmong men and younger Hmong women, forced marriages, and polygeny (the belief that people evolved from several different pairs of ancestors). Not only are these practices hyperheterosexual, but they are also deemed as deviant and thus nonnormative. What constitutes as "Hmong identity" is then informed by the practices and beliefs about family, reproduction, and sex within Hmong society. This view of the hyperheterosexuality of Hmong society lends itself to an epistemology of panic. Sex is conflated with anxiety about Hmong sexual perversity, and moral judgments are cast upon Hmong society for its "intolerant" attitudes toward homosexuality.

In the prominent 1985 California court case *People v. Kong Moua*, Kong Moua was accused of raping and kidnapping Seng Xiong. The case ended in a plea bargain in which the judge acknowledged that Moua did not intend to rape or kidnap Xiong but was instead following the Hmong custom of "marriage by capture." Marriage by capture involves a man who abducts a woman without her consent—and, in most cases, despite her protests. For him, notions of sex in this case were mitigated by "culture." Such an understanding of Hmong marriage and sexuality raises legal, political, and epistemological questions about who exactly are the Hmong and what defines "sex" in Hmong society. This example of the use of Hmong culture and sexuality brings up some important questions. What line can we draw between "rape" and "culture" as not to conflate the two? And also, what does sexuality within a particular cultural or vernacular context say about morality in the larger conversation on sexuality?

In another example, on March 22, 2011, the Minneapolis–St. Paul radio station KDWB played a parody song that depicted perverse and "comical" aspects of Hmong sexuality. The song starts by saying there is no room for a couch in a Hmong house and that all family members sleep on the floor because of the "Hmong family of twenty-four." The second verse goes on to say that "Hmongs get pregnant early," with the "first baby at sixteen" and "seven kids by twenty-three" and "over the hill by thirty." Ultimately, the song concludes that the Hmong live like "sardines" because they live in a "two-room house packed with kids." This image of overproduction presents racialized knowledge that perpetuates Hmong sexual perversity and renders it as comedy. As Roderick Ferguson (2003) has shown through his explication of the racialization of nonheteronormative black subjects, the racialized and pathologized notion of Hmong sexuality continues to reveal itself through the refugee subject. Hmong sexuality itself is the problem that prevents the everyday practices of survival and well-being, such as not having a place for a couch in the house. Hyperheterosexuality, or having "too much" sexuality, disallows spaces for a comfortable life. Here, Hmong sexuality is construed as hyperheterosexual and overproductive, in contrast to heteronormative heterosexuality, and presents a crisis of Hmong refugee sexuality.

Another particular notion of hyperheterosexuality circulating within Hmong and mainstream discourse concerns the sexual exploitations of Hmong women by Hmong men who travel back to the homeland. Anthropologist Louisa Schein (2004) writes that, "at the transnational scale, gender binary has taken on a new valence as homeland becomes the quested-after feminine and sex becomes something that can be longed for from far away. Transnational erotics remixes sex and space, refashioning the most intimate of interiorities. Physical distance and proximity come to be articulated complexly in the contours of homeland desire" (458). Epistemologies of Hmong racial and subject formation manifest in this discourse of desires based on a narrative of sexual exploitation. Hmong American movies such as *Dr. Tom* reproduce this discourse of sexual inequality. In the video, a Hmong American man looking for a young woman goes back to Thailand and spots a woman named Nkauj Iab at the market. He ultimately breaks her apart from her lover by seducing her family with wealth and promises of going to America. In reality, Tom is nothing but a janitor back in America. Nkauj Iab's world is turned upside down after Tom goes back to America, leaving her waiting for him as the film concludes. Schein (2004) has done extensive readings of the film, in which she seeks to give the Hmong women in Thailand agency within these supposed exploitative relationships. Conversations that Schein has had with the director of *Dr. Tom* and Hmong audience members reveal that most of them do indeed agree that the relationship is exploitative and immoral (450). Nonnormativity, then, renders Hmong sexuality, and Hmong people, as deviant subjects within American society.

It is within this discourse that Hmong hyperheterosexuality masks same-sex desires and LGBTQ identities. A subsequent question in which to situate this critique is, Where do queerness and same-sex desire and identities fit into this framework of Hmong hyperheterosexuality in particular, and sexuality in general? That is, while Hmong sexuality is nonnormative within mainstream sexual politics, queerness is rendered as an illegible mode of sexuality within Hmong society, as evidenced by Xiong and Yang's knowledge that "their love would never be accepted by their families or the Hmong community, which strictly forbids homosexual relationships." In the same *Fresno Bee* article, Xiong's mother, Mai Yia Yang, was quoted as saying, "If she did not have that friend, maybe she would not be dead. . . . I have talked to her several times, saying, 'I know it's your friend, but it's not normal.' To the Hmong, we never have that way. It's kind of strange. Always husband and wife. What these two girls have is not acceptable" (Ellis 2002). This type of homogenizing of Hmong culture renders homosexuality as impossible, incomprehensible, and illegible, unless homosexuality is conflated with death. It also allows for a particular epistemological emergence concerning Hmong racial formation—namely, that within Hmong culture, only a particular sexuality can be made to be legible, which already exists as the hyperheterosexual, never the homosexual.

This chapter signified a way for Hmong communities to discuss sexuality. Furthermore, new forums, such as videos and blogs, emerged that tackled sexuality and sexual orientation. Unfortunately, after the incident in Fresno, the voices of Hmong queer women disappeared from the media. Instead, much of the popular discourse regarding sexuality shifted toward male sexuality. The establishment of Shades of Yellow (SOY), the first Hmong LGBTQ organization in the world, may be a catalyst for a larger conversation on sexuality in Hmong culture (Wanglue 2010). Phia Xiong and Xeng Lor founded SOY in 2003 as an informal gathering for others like themselves. The first SOY New Year occurred on January 21, 2006, enabling a larger discussion regarding homosexuality in the Hmong American community (Jurewitsch 2006). With a pageant under way that included queer people both in and out of drag, the SOY New Year was a watershed moment for the Hmong LGBTQ community. Many articles recount the establishment of SOY and its origins as a "social group," transitioning into a "non-profit" or "activist" organization (Glover 2010). Yet women played a minimal role in the early stages of SOY's development. Hmong queer women were introduced as "lost," but the popular discourse in this shift in affect to "activist" and "equality" has silenced the female voice, even when Hmong LGBTQ are fighting for equality. Fighting for equality represents both fighting for mainstream visibility and fighting for acceptance within the Hmong community. The notion of activism for equality, while essential, still paints Hmong LGBTQ as victims of their culture. An article by Laura Salinger (2010) in *Asian Wisconzine,* an online magazine on topics of interest to Asians living in Wisconsin, emphasizes "culture" as it pertains to gay Hmong individuals. She writes, "The Hmong culture, with a holistic and age-old religion, currently affords little recognition of gay or lesbian individuals. It is something that is barely, if at all, discussed" (Salinger 2010). At the end of the article, Salinger reminds us of Pa Nhia's and Yee's suicides and how "hard" it is to be gay. Thus, race, sexuality, and "culture" are highlighted as contributing to sadness and hardship.

While it is not my aim to situate Hmong queer women within the narrative of women's empowerment, I will continue to question the intersections of race, gender, and sexuality to understand how queerness and "women" come together within the trends of women's leadership in the Hmong community. The emergence of sexual discourse in Hmong America is not separate from women's emergence in the Hmong community. In

2006, Hmong American Partnership (HAP) hired its first Hmong American woman executive director. According to historian Chia Youyee Vang (2010), "The rapid increase of Hmong American women obtaining higher education has resulted in those serving as elected officials, executive directors of national organizations[,] managers[,] educators[,] and news reporters" (76). She also emphasizes the establishment of the Professional Hmong Women's group and Paj Ntaub Voice, a literary movement led by Hmong American woman Mai Neng Moua. Politicians like Mee Moua advanced the cause of Hmong American women's leadership by serving in the Minnesota state senate.

Changing gender relations is again entering the larger conversation about queerness and race in American culture. In fact, there seems to be a gender divide between gay men and lesbians that needs more conversation. This chapter highlights this tension and sheds light on gendered dynamics of queerness among Hmong LGBTQ individuals. In Queer Twin Cities, a roundtable discussion between Gilbert Achay, Brandon Campos, Elliot James, Andrea Jenkins, Nicole Kubista, Kelly Lewis, Kevin Moore, and Jason Ruiz highlights the significance of queer color and gender politics. Achay articulates the problems by addressing terminology and its racial implications, stating, "I also don't identify with the debate over GLBT versus LGBT. I think that was some debate that was trying to focus on diversity but it doesn't focus on ethnic diversity, cultural diversity, or religious diversity. They were just focusing on who had more power—gays or lesbians" (Twin Cities GLBT Oral History Project 2010). Instead, queer studies is beginning to shift from "naming" techniques of queer identity toward more critical conversations around affect, race, indigeneity—and hopefully culture and refugeeism. Therefore, while my point in this chapter remains crucial in highlighting gender dynamics, I want to complicate this male–female divide as well by illuminating how queerness allows for different exchanges among Hmong LGBTQ individuals. Yet gender must also remain a crucial part of Hmong studies discourse, particularly about visibility and equality. Completely dismissing gender erases a significant aspect of queer subjectivity.

I attended the first Txuj Ci Showcase on March 10, 2010, at the University of Minnesota, a talent show that seeks to give space for Hmong LGBTQ to display their talents, such as singing, dancing, and spoken word. The coming-out spoken-word performance "From St. Paul to San Francisco and Back to St. Paul" by Linda Her, a Hmong lesbian, caught my attention.

From the first line, "Dear culture of my roots," to the last line, "There's no place like home," the piece details Her's journey from St. Paul to escape the oppressive atmosphere of her family to San Francisco to explore her sexual identity. A round of applause erupted after her moving performance as Linda teared up on stage. An article on the event—"Hmong GLBT Group Expands Horizons with Talent Show"—appeared in the *Minnesota Daily* shortly after. This was indeed the first Hmong LGBTQ talent show, and it was perhaps the first time that many Hmong had been exposed to any Hmong LGBTQ individuals, as the article suggested (Lymn 2010). It was evident that the performers were predominantly Hmong queer women, yet the article marginalized the efforts of these women and their work in "expanding the horizons" of GLBT voices—that is, other than Linda Her, who identifies as a "queer lesbian." But Her, who was the most adored performer of the night, was silenced to a neutral voice, rather than a voice that would "expand horizons." The article does not address the fact that she cried and brought many people to tears, and that she had won the title of Mr. SOY during the SOY New Year Pageant. The Txuj Ci showcase was highly gendered, and without much critical analysis, reporting on Hmong LGBTQ events and cultural productions are reduced to neutral entertainment events that seem to lack any political underpinnings.

The shift from a sad queer Hmong woman to a powerful LGBT advocate who is trying to redefine culture is queer indeed. Yet such articulation denies the experiences of Hmong LGBTQ people in social movements, and perhaps even presupposes the notion that minority cultures have become insignificant in queer identities and subjectivities. This also begs the question, Have they then achieved full recognition in the mainstream LGBTQ community itself? In her study of Brazilian lesbians, Tomi Castle (2008) finds that they want more than just civil rights and legal recognition of their existence; they strive for full participation in Brazilian civic and public life. Castle's findings suggest a larger sociological network of activism at play. Implicit in this notion are similarities in Hmong queer women activism. Oskar Ly became the interim executive director of SOY after Kevin Xiong's resignation. The St. Paul–based *Asian American Press* hailed this as "a new chapter" and described Ly as a "unifying force" (*Asian American Press* 2010). This exclusion of political acts within queer ethnic minority communities and the assumption of cultural productions as apolitical and thus insignificant within the larger mainstream LGBTQ movement continue to render Hmong LGBTQ as voiceless, and women in these movements as passive. This cycle perpetuates the invisibility of gender and sexuality in regard to race, ethnicity, and culture, and the eventual life cycles of Hmong LGBTQ individuals.

Methodology and Reflexivity

How did Pa Nhia and Yee become so "lost" that death was the only answer to their "problem"? How was "shame" involved? What are the ramifications of their story on Hmong culture in a changing and globalized world? When did a Hmong queer identity emerge? To answer these questions, I propose a research project that considers their deaths within a larger conversation about gender, sexuality, and culture. What specific cultural forms are not oppressive to Hmong LGBTQ identity, self, and essence as human beings? My approach seeks to detach culture from oppression. I am employing psychologist Karl Rogers's theory of humanism to study the experiences and culture of the Hmong queer community. Humanist psychologists "take an optimistic view of human nature," and their approach "emphasizes the unique qualities of humans, especially their freedom and their potential for growth" (Weiten 2008). According to anthropologists Matthew Gordon and Carolina Izquierdo (2008), "Anthropologists specialize in understanding, through extended fieldwork, the complex cultural meanings that exist within a given society." Furthermore, anthropologists must engage in ethnographically sound research to unravel the "linguistic formulations of well-being" and "how these play out in people's daily lives, words, and worlds." Through ethnography, I can uniquely situate the "human" within the context of gender, queerness, and culture, and the affective ramifications of doing so.

While nearly no literature exists about Hmong LGBTQ, we can begin to analyze the emergence of Hmong queer women's and men's experiences in the larger frame of Hmong women's emergence. Ethnography can be used to effectively explore new areas of Asian America, and especially Hmong America (Manalansan 2003). Then there are, of course, queer studies scholars, such as Weston (1997), who venture into unconventional fieldwork, where resources and support are scarce. While it is critical to acknowledge that most of the literature in this study is from popular culture and fieldwork, it is also important to challenge different ways of knowing. As ethnographers, we are responsible for connecting and engaging in the strands of meanings attached in our informants' social, psychological, and material worlds. Our task is to read experiences and cultural productions (material, linguistic, affective, and so on) in relation to culture itself. It is here that we can begin to engage in the assemblages of invisible emotions and affects with the visible intersections of race, gender, and sexuality.

Issues of labeling and linguistics have struck me as problematic in the course of my research project (and in the course of my entire life). Thus, I only focused on individuals who are eighteen years of age or older and identified as "Hmong" or "Hmong American," and as "lesbian," "gay," "bisexual," "transgender," or "queer." The specific number of people have varied through the years, but through informal talks, interviews, and participation, I can interpret how their lives, language, feelings, and emotions are constantly reframing the Hmong culture. I will use "Hmong LGBTQ" interchangeably with "Hmong queers," because I take "queer" to encompass the entire spectrum of nonnormative sexuality. This chapter seeks to explicate the emerging meanings of gender and sexuality in Hmong America through my inquiry of Hmong LGBTQ experiences and history. This is not to say that I am speaking on behalf of all Hmong LGBTQ. The experiences of the individuals in this study do not reflect the experiences of all Hmong LGBTQ people. Instead, I am simply using their voices and experiences to map out the importance of sexuality and sexual orientation in the larger Hmong historiography and cultural discourse. I am interjecting my own reflexivity as a gay Hmong man as well as trying to rearticulate and represent what gender, sexuality, emotional well-being, and the good life in Hmong America really means. With this narrow definition and interdisciplinary methodology, I can better situate my research question: What does it mean to live a good queer Hmong life? Using the interdisciplinary literature review indicated earlier to guide me with the intellectual study of culture, emotion, ethnicity, gender, and queerness, I hope to bring a new form of activism toward social justice in Hmong American studies (Hale 2001).

Many disciplines have recently turned to autoethnography as a form of critical analysis. However, I am using this form of narration precisely because of the limited research in this area and, admittedly, the limited research I myself have been able to carry out. In employing this research methodology, I turn to Leon Anderson's (2006) method of analytic autoethnography. Anderson argues that the attributes of analytic autoethnography include "(1) complete member researcher (CMR) status, (2) analytic reflexivity, (3) narrative visibility of the researcher's self, (4) dialogue with informants beyond the self, and (5) commitment to theoretical analysis" (378). Analytic autoethnography can critically represent my own place in the social world I am analyzing while trying to understand all the movements and aesthetics that surround me. I am asking questions similar to those that Renato Rosaldo asks in his *Culture and Truth* (1989): What are the complexities of my social identity? What life experiences have shaped it? While ethnographic projects attempt to represent a culture as accurately as possible, it is impossible to ignore the subjectivities embedded in the identities and interpretations of the researcher. Autoethnography can incorporate subjectivities into the objective analysis of the particular social world under study. I endeavor for an analysis in which all Hmong LGBTQ, including myself, are working together to understand and cohere a world in which those inarticulable forces of gender, sexuality, race, culture, and emotions assemble.

Pa Nhia and Yee's story broke my heart as a young child and triggered my consciousness of the intersecting inequalities (racism, homophobia, heteronormativity, classism, ableism) of our everyday lives. I met many of my informants in a snowball effect resulting from my involvement in Hmong LGBTQ events. Most of these events consisted of very informal gatherings and discussions, allowing me to conduct interviews and informal conversations with participants at house parties, parks, stores, and clubs. I have also included my observations of the Txuj Ci Hmong LGBTQ talent show and the SOY New Year in 2011. I have been very open with my informants about my intentions of "studying them." My queer Hmong friends have taken great joy and excitement in my willingness to hang out with them and document their experiences. They joke that they are glad to have someone who "understands" them studying them. However, I still do not understand how their culture manifests in their activities and experience. It is an intellectual endeavor that I have yet to undertake. I still have much to understand about Hmong queer lives as they relate to specific issues of culture. Sara Ahmed (2010) points out that "happiness is not just how subjects speak of their own desires but also what they want to give and receive from others" (91). I am using Ahmed's argument of the sociality of emotion by extending my encounters to men and women. In *Global Divas*, Martin Manalansan (2003) writes that he is "interested in the ways the seemingly mundane activities in daily life construct a vital arena in which to investigate various under-explored issues, specifically the connection between everyday life, intimacy, and diasporic queer identity formation" (90). Julie Bettie's (2003) study of high school girls also involved "hanging out" with girls in "coffee shops, restaurants, . . . the shopping mall, . . . the school parking lot, near the bleachers behind the school, at birthday parties, and . . . on the floor of girls' bedrooms" (16). It is these sites of the everyday life that, I argue, are the most significant in understanding a culture. Engaging in dialogue with my informants within the framework of my own emotional revolution is autoethnography beyond the self.

Happiness and Parody

If happiness is so central to leading a good life, then why do we deny happiness to others? Why do we pretend that others have happiness? Why do we compromise others' happiness for our own, and vice versa? Daniel Nettle (2005) states that "happiness . . . is not something that can be so easily measured. . . . Assessing it involves making a judgment about what the good life consists of and the extent to which one's life fulfills it" (23). Hmong queers also strive for happiness in life. Yet their happiness constitutes a different set of ideals. Much of Western notions of "happiness" involve the idea of "coming out." Rust (2003) explains that coming out can be a psychologically straining process in which professional support may be necessary. None of my informants went through therapy or any psychological intervention. They "came out" on their own. There are notions of affirmation and acceptance that play a part in coming out to oneself. It was just a natural thing that they accepted as part of who they are without question. Gina puts it this way:

> G: In middle school, though, I met my first girlfriend. But, during
> that time I was dating my boyfriend too. I had boyfriends
> before girlfriends. And he cheated on me, and then I was seeing
> this girl. And it didn't work out 'cause she wasn't from here. That
> was it. . . . After that I stopped dating until my senior year in
> high school. Then I met my girlfriend, my partner, or whatever.
> Then, oh shit, Gina, you're a lesbian. You really like girls! Cause
> I don't think I ever felt that way about a girl, or about anyone, in
> such a long time. I met her and it just worked.
>
> KP: So you first realized you were attracted to girls, for sure,
> definite, in your senior year of high school?

G: Uh huh, that was a reality check. . . . It just happened automatically. It was normal. Nobody said anything.

Gina's coming-out experience to herself was unconscious. While it is true
that there are moments when one must consciously and overtly think
about one's (homo)sexuality, most of my informants often went about
their daily lives unconscious of when they "came out." This is a way of coping with the hardships of life, a form of maximizing happiness and mini-
mizing suffering. One informant, Dang Vang, says, "It's just natural for me.
If I think about it, it forces me to suffer." For Gina and Dang, valuing the
covert itself is a way to work with the culture of silence and the absence of
words. This is not to say that it is better to suppress those feelings of injury
that constitute much of queerness and that scholars of queer studies have
described many times over. Contrary to the mainstream notion of *having
to overcome this sadness* by "coming out" (with a prior presumption that
the queer is always sad *because* she constantly thinks about her sadness),
unconsciousness is intentional in that it allows the subject to manage and
reclaim those feelings of being unsettled in a way that is coherent to him or
her. Not thinking about those feelings is both queer and intentional in that
it provides a way to know the impact of one's suffering more intersubjec-
tively between various ethnic, gendered, and sexual selves without having
to necessarily "face" the normative temporal trajectory (of coming out) of
sadness itself.

In addition to queering one's emotion in trying to cohere culture,
queering family is another way that sexuality, gender, culture, and emotion
(parody and laughter) can be a way to cohere the Hmong social world.
During the Creating Change 2011 Conference in Minneapolis on February
3, 2011, my "mommy" and "daddy" officially adopted me. Mommy and
Daddy are a biologically female same-sex couple. It was here that I realized
the happiness they share through the use of parody. Mommy, Daddy, my
great aunt, and four siblings were all present in the car as we drove from
Hell's Kitchen—a bar in downtown Minneapolis—back to the Hilton
Hotel. Mommy and Daddy were arguing with each other when my great
aunt interjected with, "*Ua cas es, neb ob niag niam txiv ntawm neb yuav sib
ceg ua luaj li?*" [Why are you married couple arguing so much?] Daddy,
being the "man" that she is, harshly responded, "*Yog nej niam ntag!*" [It's
your mom's fault!] All the children involved themselves in this conversation as we all humorously tried to stop the argument:

KP: Oh . . . *neb tsis paub hais tias neb sib sib ceg mas peb cov me*
    nyuam no yeej mob mob siab thiab na! [Oh . . . you both do not
    know that your arguing does make us children very worried!]
  S: *Kuv ces, twb tsis xav nyob nrog neb ob niag laus ko li lawm os! Kuv*
    xum khiav xwb os. [I don't even want to live with you old couple
    anymore! I just want to run away.]

In Hmong American linguistics, the semantics surrounding parody creates
humor. My sibling's elongation of the word *"ces"* emphasizes her disgust
with Mommy and Daddy's argument. Yet because she is not their biological
daughter, the situation becomes one of comedy. She transforms the situation to embody and caricature heterosexual arguments; it is as if she really
were their daughter who wanted to "run away," but is not. She can subject
her "parents" to ridicule in this context. The impossibility of this situation
allows us to shed light on the norms of gender and sexuality in Hmong
culture in a comedic and funny manner.

Donna Goldstein (2003) suggests that humor in her informants' lives
constitutes political resistance to the harshness of everyday life; it is a rebellion of sorts (16–17). Perhaps not thinking about the historical injuries
of sexuality and replacing memory with parody and the construction of an
imagined kinship system are defense mechanisms against the painful
thoughts of invisibility and exclusion in Hmong culture as experienced by
Hmong LGBTQ. Such performances can be seen in the gay men's circles
that I had become a part of in the last several years. My "brothers" Tou and
Chris were especially instrumental in enacting and perpetuating parodical
acts. They, too, are the "sons" of Mommy and Daddy. Mommy and Daddy
had come to "supervise" us on a night at the Saloon, a gay club in downtown Minneapolis. Tou and I were dancing together when Mommy yelled
out to us, "Incest"! Everyone else laughed, and we continued. It is not that
she actually condemns incest, but she is caricaturing notions of shame in
Hmong culture. Shame, as Arlene Stein (2006) articulates, makes us hide
our vulnerability and deepest held beliefs and identities and compels us
to falsify characteristics that make us seem powerful and normal. We are
reminded that queerness and other modes of "abnormal" sexual behavior
are unacceptable and should be frowned upon, especially in the Hmong
culture. We are not engaging in actual incest, but yet we are imitating it
through our claims of brotherhood. Only in this queer space does our
mommy "allow" us to engage in this activity. Mommy here plays a role in

mediating what is queer, acceptable, and funny. Acting as the figure of our mother, one who either upholds or deviates from culture, she seeks to render our behavior as ambiguous, reinforcing the humor embedded in our performance (Chentsova-Dutton and Tsai 2007). The idea that our mother can blatantly condone our "incestuous" behavior represents humor and power. Yet the exchange also makes the notions of "family" and "culture" ambiguous. Our kinship constitutes a subtle reformation of the roles that mothers play in Hmong American society by giving the green light to, and making ambivalent, other modes of sexual behavior.

Family here is crucial to understanding queer subjectivity within the Hmong American context. Bic Ngo's (2012b) conversation with Fong, a gay Hmong American man, shows the importance of family in negotiating queerness. Fong had agreed to marry a woman so that his parents could "save face" within the Hmong community. Loss of face could mean that a Hmong family will suffer negative consequences, such as being the subject of gossip and rumors or facing ostracism from other family members or relatives. Yet Ngo writes that this does not mean that Fong chose his family over his gay identity. Rather, the complexity in which Fong negotiated his identity by marrying a woman while having a boyfriend allowed his family to come to terms with his sexuality while maintaining "face." Fong did not "come out" and reject his family or the Hmong kinship system, as we would perhaps have it in the dominant discourse. Family in the context in which I have described it, with the reconfiguration of a "mommy" and "daddy," signifies a renegotiation of family that fits with queerness. The parents, who are central to Hmong kinship systems, can become figures that can be queered in order for queerness to be understood. Re-seeing parents in a way that is queer by playing their roles is not a benign matter. The goal is to make the situation funny so that the parents can be deconstructed as always serious or always oppressive. It is a political act in trying to re-create a system that incorporates elements of Hmong kinship systems that can exist within a queer paradigm. Parodying how the parents can or should act by "allowing" incest or homosexuality to exist not only deconstructs the Hmong kinship system as heteropatriarchal and oppressive to queers but also liberates and gives new meaning to how such systems themselves are queer and subject to renegotiation.

I am not marginalizing the sadder moments of our queer lives. My questions regarding happiness are merely a way to get at how Hmong queers use agency to construct good lives. I am also not subverting or recuperating happiness as a way to diverge attention away from sadness, pain, or misery in our queer lives. As Heather Love (2007) argues, "Feelings of shame, secrecy, and self-hatred are still with us. Rather than disavowing such feelings as the sign of some personal failing, we need to understand them as indications of material and structural continuities" (21). Through my research, I have witnessed sadness, guilt, ambivalence, confusion, anger, regret, and estrangement among my informants. In *The Vulnerable Observer*, Ruth Behar (1996) says that "as an ethnographer for whom the professional ritual of displacement continually evoked the grief of diaspora, I distrusted my own authority. I saw it as being constantly in question, constantly on the point of breaking down" (21). I can see this breakdown of the researcher as authority in my research. While participating in a session in which three queer women, one heterosexual woman, and myself (the only male individual) were present, I began to spew out the story of my father leaving our family, my mother's attempted suicide and thoughts of abortion, my own suicidal thoughts, and my soul searching, all while crying hysterically. I had thought that being the first person to speak might elicit similar stories about sadness, family, and eventual happiness from the rest of the members. It was from this vulnerable position that I realized that crying was not a sign of sadness for me but a sign of how much happier I was now than before—and, by extension, how much happier the other participants must also be. At that moment I was not the observer or authority; instead, I was a participant who was being counseled along with everyone else. It was this moment of vulnerability that was most useful in my analysis of emotion and family in Hmong queer women's culture. Again, invoking Love, our past histories of injury are still with us, but to engage with them in connecting the links between our past and present lives makes for a more holistic understanding of how we have come to negotiate our feelings with that of family and culture.

On a trip to Des Moines, GL and I had a long conversation about her upbringing. She went into detail about running away from home at the age of twenty-one. She was living with her girlfriend at that time while working two jobs, one from 8 am to 4 pm and another from 4 pm to 11 pm. Eventually, GL came back home in what Bee Cha (2002) calls the "Theory of Necessary Return." Gina had also gone away from the Hmong community for four to five years due to her "hatred of Hmong people." Again, she also returned. Race is embedded in the way that Hmong queers see themselves. Asian American youths who go away eventually return to their ethnic enclaves because of racism. Such phenomena are apparent in the lives of the Nisei during the first half of the twentieth century (Kurashige 2003). While Cha is not arguing that the Theory of Necessary Return is necessarily all good, he states, "Although we cannot escape the gravitational pull of the Return theory, we must return a different and better Hmong person. The future of the Hmong should be what we are trying to create and not just what we are trying to preserve" (33). While I agree with him, I also argue that coming back to the ethnic community is a way of reading culture itself. To leave culture behind as a technique of embracing one's queer identity does not necessarily guarantee liberation. To realize culture in the instance of the return allows the subject to reformulate her existence in the context of why she went away in the first place. One's proximity to culture enables a sort of ontological reflection on one's state of being. Separating the body from (or bringing the body to) culture does not guarantee liberation. Instead, it is how one responds to this proximity to culture that allows one to decide how to live in the Hmong social world in a way that is best for one's mind, body, and soul. It is this framework of internalized oppression and "going away" that enables Asian American youth, and particularly Hmong queer individuals, to articulate their saliency and contentment—or coming-to-terms-with—their ethnicity and sexuality.

Conclusion

I have argued in this chapter that sexuality remains central to Hmong social life. There are emotional and affective registers to thinking about sexuality, gender, and identity. As we can see in Schein's (2004) research on Hmong American videos, the material manifestation of erotic longing in relation to video making is surreal and must be thought of more complexly in relation to sex, sexuality, and sexual desire. Schein also highlights the "diasporic subjectivity" of Hmong Americans. That is, Hmong American men who consume media can establish imaginaries of community and identities and materialize their "erotic subjectifications" into "actual returns [to the homeland] in pursuit of erotic encounters, or, sex" (Schein 2004, 458). Affect here is not simply a matter of sensing; rather, it puts social and political significance into the formation of Hmong queer subjectivities, identities, and communities. Continuing this trend, I am arguing that there are particular emotional and affective registers of thinking about Hmong queer lives. As Jasbir Puar (2007) suggests, perhaps affect is *not* the same as emotion but rather serves as "continuing efforts to elaborate different and alternative modalities of belonging, connectivity, and intimacy" (208). Emotions, affect, and feelings, may become blurred within abstract theories, but when we think about people's material realities, perhaps we can say that affect is the critical mechanism of trying to belong, to not overtly think of one's sexuality, in order to achieve that thing called "the good life."

It is at this point that I ask myself what makes me happy. Am I happy carrying out this ethnography? Gina, GL, Yeng, Dang, Mommy, Daddy, and all my other queer informants all seek happiness in life. Parody, comedy, and the closeness that we all share when articulating sexuality, ethnicity, and family become central to how we understand well-being and happiness in life. Sadness and homophobia are not intrinsic to any particular culture (Murray 1996, 3). Instead, the historical absence of such topics in Hmong culture gives flexibility to Hmong queer individuals' re-creation of what "Hmong," "family," "gender," and "happiness" mean. It is the flexibility of culture to become ambiguous and confusing that gives life to happiness. Notions of happiness are not enshrined in a particular locality or temporality as much as they are embedded in an ongoing re-creation of meanings in everyday life. Life itself is a performance embedded with social epithets. Queerness is only a category of life. Queer Hmong individuals re-create life through multiple strands of relationships: their partners, other LGBTQ, heterosexuals, their biological families, and their social families. David Eng and Alice Hom (1998) state, "We can no longer accept that notion that considering race and homosexuality together drains the lesbian/gay and queer movements of its political energies or social efficacies" (14). Being Hmong and being LGBTQ can coexist, and this coexistence is worth considerable intellectual examination.

Pa Nhia's and Yee's deaths have inserted into our consciousness the importance of sexuality in Hmong American culture. Early reports of their suicides cited "culture" as one of the main reasons why they could not live their lives as they chose. This interpretation of their deaths has perpetuated the myth that the Hmong culture is oppressive to women, and now queers. Instead, a more nuanced look at this case tells us that perhaps Pa Nhia's mother is happy because her daughter can be reborn into a boy, so she can "have more freedom." The mother's understanding of the queer life is not fixed but flexible in terms of perceiving what queerness means. I seek to use this case to examine what we know about the Hmong culture more broadly and explore how it is changing. As David Murray (2009) states, "Of course when a place is labeled homophobic, it is the people of that place who are being identified as such. What struck me was the way in which this term was being used as a sociocultural trait, or more accurately, as a sociopathological cultural trait, in which a group of people's sexual attitudes were being judged and the speaker's sociosexual culture and place were generally compared favorably to that of the 'Other' culture and place" (viii). Pa Nhia and Yee are subjects caught up in the complexities of power relations in a world in which sexuality becomes opaque and incomprehensible. Critical inquiries about sexuality in the Hmong community from positive perspectives will help us navigate the way that Hmong culture and identity are a mobile force that is shaping the emotional and affective lives of Hmong LGBTQ (Her 2012). This chapter is part of a conversation within a larger discourse of questions, such as: What is the Hmong identity today? How do Hmong people find meaning and agency in their lives in a land of heterogeneity, contradictions, and politics? How are Hmong women and men reclaiming their own emotions and histories of struggle? To what ends can we achieve happiness, and is there really such a thing? How do we negotiate the emotional process of rearticulating culture? What are our emotional attachments to culture? This chapter is only the beginning of my journey into queer Hmong America, as there are more avenues to be explored.

Works Cited

Abu-Lughod, Lila. 1988. "Fieldwork of a Dutiful Daughter." In *Arab Women in the Field: Studying Your Own Society,* edited by Soraya Altorki and Camillia Fawzi El-Solh, 139–61. Syracuse: Syracuse University Press.

Ahmed, Sara. 2010. *The Promise of Happiness.* Durham, N.C.: Duke University Press.

Anderson, Leon. 2006. "Analytic Autoethnography." *Journal of Contemporary Ethnography* 34, no. 4: 373–95.

Asian American Press. 2010. "Oskar Ly Takes Over as SOY Director." *Asian American Press,* December 8. http://aapress.com/community/oskar-ly-takes-over-as-soy-director/.

Behar, Ruth. 1996. *The Vulnerable Observer: Anthropology That Breaks Your Heart.* Boston: Beacon Press.

Bettie, Julie. 2003. *Women Without Class: Girls, Race, and Identity.* Berkeley: University of California Press.

Boulden, Walter. 2009. "Gay Hmong: A Multifaceted Clash of Cultures." *Journal of Gay and Lesbian Social Services* 21:134–250.

Calmes, Jackie, and Peter Baker. 2012. "Obama Says Same-Sex Marriage Should be Legal." *New York Times,* May 9. http://www.nytimes.com /2012/05/10/us /politics/obama-says-same-sex-marriage-should-be-legal.html?_r=0.

Castle, Tomi. 2008. "Sexual Citizenship: Articulating Citizenship, Identity, and the Pursuit of the Good Life in Urban Brazil." *Political and Legal Anthropology Review* 31:118–33.

Cha, Bee. 2002. "Being Hmong is Not Enough." In *Bamboo Among the Oaks,* edited by Mai Neng Moua, 22–33. St. Paul: Minnesota Historical Society Press.

Chentsova-Dutton, Yulia E., and Jeanne L. Tsai. 2007. "Gender Differences in Emotional Response among European Americans and Hmong Americans." *Cognition and Emotion* 21, no. 1: 162–81.

Chou, Rosalind S. 2012. *Asian American Sexual Politics: The Construction of Race, Gender, and Sexuality.* Lanham: Rowman and Littlefield.

Crenshaw, Kimberle Williams. 1995. "Mapping the Margins: Intersectionality, Identity Politics, and Violence Against Women of Color." In *Critical Race Theory,* edited by Kimberle Williams Crenshaw, Neil Gotanda, Gary Peller, and Thomas Kendall, 357–83. New York: New Press.

Ellis, Anne Dudley. 2002. "Embracing the Forbidden." *Fresno Bee,* August 11. www .capm.state.mn.us/pdf/HmongTeenSuicideReport.pdf.

Eng, David L., and Alice Y. Hom. 1998. Introduction to *Q&A: Queer in Asian America,* edited by David L. Eng and Alice Y. Hom, 1–21. Philadelphia: Temple University Press.

Ferguson, Roderick. 2003. *Aberrations in Black: Toward a Queer of Color Critique.* Minneapolis: University of Minnesota Press.

Glover, Katharine. 2010. "Twin-Cites-Based Shades of Yellow Promoting Visibility for Hmong Gay and Lesbian." *Minnesota Post,* April 8. http://www.minnpost. com/arts-culture/2010/04/twin-cities-based-shades-yellow-promoting -visibility-hmong-gay-and-lesbian-comm.

Goldstein, Donna. 2003. *Laughter Out of Place: Race, Class, Violence, and Sexuality in a Rio Shantytown.* Berkeley: University of California Press.

Gordon, Matthew, and Carolina Izquierdo. 2008. "Introduction." In *Pursuits of Happiness: Well-Being in Anthropological Perspective,* edited by Matthew Gordon and Carolina Izquierdo, 1–19. New York: Berghahn.

Gregory, Steven. 2003. "Men in Paradise: Sex Tourism and the Political Economy of Masculinity." In *Race, Nature, and the Politics of Difference,* edited by David S. Moore, Jake Kosek, and Anand Pandian, 323–55. Durham, N.C.: Duke University Press.

Gupta, Akhil, and James Ferguson. 1997. *Anthropological Locations: Boundaries and Grounds of a Field Science*. Berkeley: University of California Press.

Hale, Charles. 2001. "What Is Activist Research?" *Items and Issues: Social Science Research Council* 2, no. 1–2: 13–15.

Her, Vincent K. 2012. "Searching for Sources of Hmong Identity in Multicultural America." In *Hmong and American: From Refugees to Citizens*, edited by Vincent K. Her and Mary Louise Buley-Meissner, 31–46. St. Paul: Minnesota Historical Society Press.

Her-Lee, Lindy. 2006. "Hmong Gay: When Men Fall in Love with Men, and Women with Women." http://www.lchr.org/a/38/3g/archives/HmongGay LindyEnglish051906.html.

Hollan, Douglas W., and Jane C. Wellankamp. 1994. *Contentment and Suffering: Culture and Experience in Toraja*. New York: Columbia University Press.

Jurewitsch, Sao Sue. 2006. "A Hmong New Year Celebration Like No Other: Hmong GLBT Community, Families, and Friends Mark New Beginning." *Hmong Times*, February 1. http://hmongtimes.com main.asp?SectionID=31&SubSectionID=1 90&ArticleID=383.

Kurashige, Lon. 2003. "The Problem of Nisei Biculturalism." In *Major Problems in Asian American History*, edited by Lon Kurashige and Alice Yang Murray, 277–84. Boston: Houghton Mifflin Company.

Love, Heather. 2007. *Feeling Backward: Loss and the Politics of Queer History*. Cambridge, Mass.: Harvard University Press.

Lymn, Katharine. 2010. "Hmong GLBT Group Expands Horizons with Talent Show." *Minnesota Daily*, March 11. http://www.mndaily.com/2010/03/11/hmong -glbt-group-expands-horizons-talent-show.

Manalansan, Martin, IV. 2003. *Global Divas: Filipino Gay Men in the Diaspora*. Durham, N.C.: Duke University Press.

Masequesmay, Gina. 2003. "Emergence of Queer Vietnamese America." *Amerasia Journal* 29, no. 1: 1–18.

Matthews, Gordon, and Carolina Izquierdo. 2009. "Introduction: Anthropology, Happiness, and Well-Being." In *Pursuits of Happiness: Well-Being in Anthropological Perspective*, edited by Gordon Matthews and Carolina Izquierdo, 1–19. New York: Berghahn Books.

Murray, David A. B. 2009. "Introduction." In *Homophobias: Lust and Loathing across Time and Space*, edited by David A. B. Murray, 1–15. Durham, N.C.: Duke University Press.

Murray, Stephen O. 1996. "Male Homosexuality in Guatemala: Possible Insights and Certain Confusion from Sleeping with the Natives." In *Out in the Field: Reflections of Lesbian and Gay Anthropologists*, edited by Ellen Lewin and William L. Leap, 236–60. Urbana: University of Illinois Press.

Narayan, Kirin. 1993. "How Native Is a 'Native' Anthropologist?" *American Anthropologist* 95, no. 3: 671–86.

Nettle, Daniel. 2005. *Happiness: The Science Behind Your Smile*. New York: Oxford University Press.

Ngo, Bic. 2012a. "The Importance of Family for a Gay Hmong American Man: Complicating Discourses of 'Coming Out.'" *Hmong Studies Journal* 13, no. 1: 1–27.

———. 2012b. "There Are no GLBT Hmong People: Hmong American Young Adults Navigating Culture and Sexuality." In *Hmong and American: From Refugees to Citizens*, edited by Vincent K. Her and Mary Louise Buley-Meissner, 113–32. St. Paul: Minnesota Historical Society Press.

Ostrander, Susan. 1999. "Gender and Race in a Pro-Feminist, Progressive, Mixed-Gender, Mixed-Race Organization." *Gender and Society* 13, no. 5: 628–42.

Puar, Jasbir. 2007. *Terrorist Assemblages: Homonationalism in Queer Times*. Durham, N.C.: Duke University Press.

Rosaldo, Renato. 1989. *Culture and Truth*. Boston: Beacon Press.

Rubin, Gayle. 1984. "Thinking Sex: Notes for a Radical Theory of the Politics of Sexuality." In *Pleasure and Danger: Exploring Female Sexuality*, edited by Carol S. Vance, 267–319. Boston: Routledge.

Rust, Paula C. 2003. "Finding a Sexual Identity and Community: Therapeutic Implications and Cultural Assumptions in Scientific Models of Coming Out." In *Psychological Perspectives on Lesbian, Gay, and Bisexual Experiences*, 2nd ed., edited by Linda D. Garnets and Douglas C. Kimmel, 228–69. New York: Columbia University Press.

Salinger, Laura. 2010. "Gay—and Hmong." *Asian Wisconzine*, December. http://www.asianwisconzine.com /1210HmongAndGay.html.

Schein, Louisa. 2004. "Homeland Beauty: Transnational Longing and Hmong American Video." *Journal of Asian Studies* 63, no. 2: 433–63.

Silver, Nate. 2012. "Support for Gay Marriage Outweighs Opposition in Polls." *New York Times,* May 9. http://fivethirtyeight.blogs.nytimes.com /2012/05/09/support-for-gay-marriage-outweighs-opposition-in-polls/.

Stein, Arlene. 2006. *Shameless: Sexual Dissidence in American Culture*. New York: New York University Press.

Stolberg, Sheryl Gay. 2010. "Obama Signs Away 'Don't Ask, Don't Tell.'" *New York Times,* December 22. http://www.nytimes.com/2010/12/23/us/politics /23military.html.

Twin Cities GLBT Oral History Project. 2010. *Queer Twin Cities*. Minneapolis: University of Minnesota Press.

Vang, Chia Youyee. 2010. *Hmong America: Reconstructing Community in Diaspora*. Urbana: University of Illinois Press.

Vryan, Kevin D. 2006. "Expanding Analytic Autoethnography and Enhancing Its Potential." *Journal of Contemporary Ethnography* 35, no. 4: 405–9.

Wanglue, Richard. 2010. "SOY Is the First Hmong Organization for Lesbian, Gay, Bisexual, and Transgender." *Suab Hmong International Broadcasting News*, March 21.

Warren, Carol A. B. 2001. "Gender and Fieldwork Relations." In *Contemporary Field Research: Perspectives and Formulations*, 2nd. ed., edited by Robert M. Emerson, 203–23. Long Grove: Waveland Press.

Weiten, Wayne. 2008. *Psychology: Themes and Variations*. Belmont, Calif.: Wadsworth Cengage Learning.

Weston, Kath. 1997. "The Virtual Anthropologist." In *Anthropological Locations: Boundaries and Grounds of a Field Science*, edited by Akhil Gupta and James Ferguson, 163–84. Berkeley: University of California Press.

Xiong, Vang Tou. "The Challenges of Hmong Gay Men in Minnesota." MS thesis, Minnesota State University, Mankato.

Yang, Pahoua K. 2008. "A Phenomenological Study of the Coming Out Experiences of Gay and Lesbian Hmong." PhD diss., University of Minnesota.

Afterword

Cathy J. Schlund-Vials

My mother's garden is more than a plot of land with growing vegetation. Her garden is about the power of love, faith, endurance, and vision. There, in her garden, I am showered with love and the history of our people—Hmong. Her view on gardening is rooted to our people's history. From our journeys from land to land, fighting for survival, Hmong had to envision the future existence of our roots. In order to make that vision a reality, our foremothers had to nourish and care for their garden the same way my mother has tended hers. . . . Without our mothers and foremothers, the history and existence of my people would have been lost in the shuffle of life's tragedies. . . .

Their garden is a symbol of their independence, vision, beauty, strength, perseverance, and courage. It is there in this garden that I am rooted and encouraged to spread—to multiply by leaps and bounds like dandelions.

—Ka Vang, "Inheriting My Mother's Garden"

THE CAPITAL OF THE SO-NICKNAMED "Ocean State," Providence, Rhode Island, sits approximately fifty miles from Boston, Massachusetts, and Hartford, Connecticut, at the convergence of two rivers (the Moshassuck and the Woonasquatucket) and the head of Narragansett Bay. Founded in 1636 by Roger Williams—a religious exile from the Massachusetts Bay Colony—Providence Plantations reflected vis-à-vis divine nomenclature the English Protestant theologian's conviction that it was heavenly destiny that had brought him and his followers to the settlement.[1]

In subsequent years and successive decades, Williams's settlement—which was originally envisioned as a colonial haven for religious minorities—would not only emerge as the political center of the Rhode Island colony but also become a significant commercial site. Such mercantile prominence was facilitated by the confluence of multiple rivers, which enabled the city's nineteenth-century industrialization, along with its advantageous port position along the Atlantic seaboard.[2] During the American Revolutionary War, Providence transformed into an admittedly different type of sanctuary: the city, spared from the trials and tribulations of bellicose British occupation, became a de facto refuge for quartered colonial troops, who were granted nearby access to military hospitals and barracks.[3]

Presently, Providence is among the most diverse cities in New England. Aided by the passage of the 1965 Hart-Celler Act (also known as the Immigration and Nationality Act, which removed nation-based quotas in favor of hemispheric designations), the ongoing migration of African Americans from south to north, and the late twentieth-century influx of Southeast Asian refugees after "the American War in Vietnam" (1959–1975), Providence is home to a sizable Latino/a and African American population, which constitutes 38.1 percent and 16 percent of the population, respectively. Rhode Island's capital also persists as a hub for Portuguese-speaking communities from Portugal, Brazil, and Cape Verde. Last, but certainly not least, the city endures as a base for Asian immigrants and Asian Americans, who make up 6 percent of the population.[4] While the majority of these individuals are Cambodian refugees and their descendants, the greater Providence–New Bedford–Fall River tri-city area functions as a regional nucleus for the state's Hmong population, which currently totals 1,015.[5]

Providence's historical refugee foundations, along with its status as an identifiable Hmong resettlement site, prove an appropriate backdrop for this afterword's concluding consideration of *Claiming Place: On the Agency of Hmong Women* (edited by Chia Youyee Vang, Faith Nibbs, and Ma Vang), an anthology that productively remaps, fruitfully recalibrates, and constructively relocates the position of Hmong women—and Hmong sexualities—from the margins to the center of scholarly discourses about race, refugees, community, and nation. As a parallel frame and in a more immediate vein, the city's registers as a growing Hmong hub are compellingly accessed and directly acknowledged in this afterword's opening epigraph, taken from Ka Vang's short essay "Inheriting My Mother's Garden" (1997). A Hmong American poet, writer, and children's literature author, Vang's personal history—synopsized in the opening excerpt—is one inherently iterated, to varying degrees and divergent ends, in each of the provocative essays that comprise *Claiming Place*. To recapitulate, born in 1975 in Long Cheng [Long Tieng], a covert military installation operated by the Central Intelligence Agency (CIA) during the Laotian Civil War (also known as the "secret war," 1953–1975), Vang and her family soon found themselves in a politically untenable, critical position. As the second Indochina War came to a dramatic close with the April 17, 1975, Khmer Rouge takeover of Cambodia's capital, Phnom Penh; the April 30, 1975, fall of Saigon in Vietnam; the May 14, 1975, evacuation of General Vang Pao (which involved the concomitant withdrawal of U.S. military personnel); and the May 15, 1975, Vietnamese Army invasion of Laos (which facilitated the Communist Pathet Lao takeover of the country), Vang and her family members, along with tens of thousands of Hmong, endured profound instability and faced unimaginable human rights violations under a new regime that considered them—as anticommunist "freedom fighters" and abandoned allies of the United States—"enemies of the people."

Over the next decade, thousands of Hmong like Ka Vang and her mother would make the dangerous journey across the war-torn landscape and over the Mekong River into neighboring Thailand; many would eventually settle in the United States, assisted by the passage of two refugee acts: the 1975 Indochina Migration and Refugee Assistance Act, and the 1980 Refugee Act. While the majority of Hmong currently live in California, Minnesota, and Wisconsin, there are—as made clear by Providence's contemporary demographic imaginary—smaller communities along the Eastern seaboard; Hmong have also resettled in the southern United States and in the American West. Consistent with this afterword's initial East Coast focus and indicative of heterogeneous resettlement realities, it is on the one hand not incidental that Vang's contemplation of her mother's horticultural "inheritance" opens within an economically depressed area "on the south side of Providence," in a once emptied lot turned into a "bountiful garden." On the other hand, and to tactically reiterate, Providence's history as a multivalent, multigenerational site of asylum, inclusive of multiple displaced populations and diverse subjectivities, renders palpable the ways in which the Hmong experience is by no means peripheral but instead crucial to reading the United States not so much as a "nation of immigrants" but as a long-standing "country of refugees." These refugee passages presage Vang's haunting articulation of both the conditions that historically brought Hmong "into being" and the agentic feminist visions that promulgate and sustain Hmong community formation in the United States, particularly the knowledge of "mothers and foremothers," whose legacies involve "love, faith . . . [and] endurance."

Such Hmong refugee passages, linked to overarching histories of state-authorized violence and ongoing negotiations with the actualities of resettlement, evocatively intersect with what Yên Lê Espiritu characterizes as integral to "an engaged critical refugee studies project," which must "do more than critique" by "integrat[ing] sophisticated theoretical rigor with the daily concerns of real people as they navigate their social worlds."[6] Espiritu's categorization of "an engaged critical studies project," wherein everyday realities are necessarily considered within the context of flexible social imaginaries and more rigid racializations, accentuates the principle stakes of *Claiming Place,* a collection that indefatigably reckons with numerous sites of systemic oppression (via frames of race, class, gender, and sexuality) while attending to past and present strategies of resistance both within and outside Hmong communities in the United States, Laos, and Thailand. From Mai Na Lee's consideration of strategic marriage in "The Women of 'Dragon Capital' " to Prasit Leepreecha's evaluation of divorced Hmong women in Thailand, from Faith Nibbs's assessment of Hmong women's cyberagency to Julie Keown-Bomar and Ka Vang's coauthored contemplation of family assets and cultural wealth, and from Geraldine Craig's material analysis of Hmong textiles (specifically the *paj ntaub*) to Aline Lo's cinematic evaluation of "reel Hmong women" in Abel Vang's *Nyab Siab Zoo, Claiming Place* revises the dominant script of Hmong womanhood by eschewing trauma-driven passivity and stereotypical essentialism in favor of an all-too-infrequent yet welcome valuation of diasporic Hmong feminism and agency. Equally important, *Claiming Place*—as manifest in Louisa Schein's "Thinking Diasporic Sex," Bruce Thao's "Dangerous Questions," and Kong Pha's "Finding Queer Hmong America"—gainfully expands these feminist frames to encapsulate oft-elided queer subjectivities and sexualities. Correspondingly and accordingly, the diverse essays that make up this collection—written by scholars and practitioners in the humanities, social sciences, and cultural studies—collectively render urgent an identifiable yet necessarily multisided (and multisited) Hmong feminist critique. In so doing, the contributors to *Claiming Place* have substantively cultivated, à la Ka Vang's maternal garden, a particular place for contemplating and envisioning Hmong women's agency.

· To be sure, while *Claiming Place* is the first collection of its kind to take seriously the dynamic dimensions of women's agency in a way that moves us toward a Hmong feminist critique, it is also one that—to once again draw on this afterword's epigraphical consideration of *cultivated space*—judiciously charts the historical and scholarly contours of Hmong studies as a vibrant yet emerging field that has received limited but growing recognition within Asian American studies, Southeast Asian American studies, critical refugee studies, and gender/sexuality studies. To clarify, despite mid-twentieth-century roots in the civil rights movement, antiwar protests (specifically with regard to the second Indochina War), and Third World liberation, Southeast Asian American studies has only recently emerged as a recognizable subfield; while this new intellectual formation suggests an expanding of Asian American studies, Hmong studies still occupies a decidedly marginalized and problematically subsumed position vis-à-vis Filipino studies, Vietnamese American studies, and even Cambodian American studies. Whereas Hmong studies remains at this point *unforgivingly peripheral* within Asian American studies, the field's unflagging focus on refugeeness simultaneously connects it to prevailing directions in Asian American studies, expressly the turn to critical refugee studies. As the essays in *Claiming Place* make clear, when set within a syncretic milieu of wartime militarization and militarized humanitarianism, Hmong studies is necessarily linked to other sites in Southeast Asian American studies, which encompass what Ka Vang avers are communal "journeys from land to land" and refugee experiences that involve "fighting for survival." Finally, and urgently, the field assumes even greater importance when situated perpendicular to the expansive contours of twenty-first-century American imperialism. Certainly, as Espiritu's previously discussed call for "critical refugee studies" reminds us, the refugee as humanitarian recipient has troublingly been co-opted in discourses intended to justify U.S. militarization abroad, as evidenced in recent memory by the occupation of Iraq and Afghanistan as per the auspices of the ongoing "War on Terror." Moreover, the refugee as human rights subject remains convoluted in the face of juridical nonculpability, made apparent by the lack of prosecutions for crimes committed by authoritarian regimes. Such subjectivity is likewise unstable vis-à-vis bordered notions of personhood, which adhere to the limits of a clearly delineated nation-state.[7]

As editors, Chia Youyee Vang, Faith Nibbs, and Ma Vang—like the other contributors to *Claiming Place* and reminiscent of Ka Vang's epigraphical assertion—tend to these numerous polemical "inheri-tances," which ineludibly involve war, relocation, and resettlement and unescapably encompass paradoxes, contradictions, and ruptures. Such inheritances—or legacies—foreground *Claiming Place*'s fundamental intervention, which entails an unparalleled project of reclamation and re-vision. This two-sided engagement—etymologically evident in the Latin prefix "re-" which captures a sense of "again" and "back"—is at the titular level apparent in Chia Youyee Vang's "Rethinking Hmong Women's War-time Sacrifices," Ma Vang's "Rechronicling Histories," and Leena N. Her's "Rewriting Hmong Women in Western Texts," found in the collection's first section. Correspondingly, each essay takes as a rightful first premise the need to remediate, reimagine, and reinscribe the frames through which Hmong womanhood has traditionally and problematically been con-ceived through strictly military agendas, U.S. foreign policy, and refugee accounts that repeatedly—and wrongly—stress a nonagentic, disem-powered female subjectivity. Accordingly, as the introduction to *Claiming Place* underscores and as Her's evaluation of anthropological primordialism make clear, scholarly assessments of Hmong have recurrently and inaccu-rately promulgated a fixed, traditionalist reading of Hmong community formation that privileges masculinist, heteronormative subjectivities at the expense of Hmong women's agency, feminist articulation, and robust queer activism.

In drawing to a close, it is this focused consideration of Hmong femi-nist articulation and heretofore unrivaled attention to Hmong sexualities that supports a total reading of *Claiming Place* as a substantial counterhe-gemonic, critical refugee studies project, which in the end fulfills the fluid promise embedded in its title. Expressly, the use of the gerund form of "claim" (the nonfinite verb "claiming") from the outset suggests an activity that is by no means fixed but instead ongoing; such ongoingness operates as a provocative modifier for "place," which, according to the *Oxford Eng-lish Dictionary*, can refer to "a particular position or point in space" and "a portion of space available for or being used by someone else." Taken together, this collection's varied negotiation of diverse claims, its overt insistence on revisionary analysis, and its implicit contention that schol-arly attention be paid to undermined and unmined archives forcefully and compellingly lay bare the expansive spaces of Hmong studies and the undeniable dimensions of Hmong women's agency, encapsulated by Ka Vang's closing characterization of "independence, vision, beauty, strength, perseverance, and courage." And in so doing, *Claiming Place* engenders a future space to consider the open-ended possibilities and capacious contours of Hmong feminist critique.

Notes

1. Convinced the Church of England was corrupt, Williams (1603–1683) and his followers left Salem, Massachusetts, in 1636 and eventually made their way to present-day Providence, Rhode Island, where they encountered the Narragansett tribe. Williams purchased a land title from leaders of the tribe, which became the site of Providence Plantations. See Conley 1986.

2. This proximity to other sites figured keenly during the period of the transatlantic slave trade; indeed, Rhode Island was a major hub for the trade, notwithstanding the fact that it was the first colony to pass an abolition law in 1652. See Coughtry 1981.

3. See Conley 1986.

4. Ibid. The use of "the American War in Vietnam" is intended to signal a dominant reading of U.S. involvement in Southeast Asia; however, as Mariam Lam potently reminds us, such nomenclature elides the expansiveness of the conflict (outside Vietnam) and disremembers regional geopolitics (between Thailand, Burma, Laos, Cambodia, the Republic of South Vietnam, and North Vietnam).

5. This number emerges from the 2010 U.S. Census. See "2010 U.S. Census Hmong Populations." The states with the largest Hmong populations include California (91,224), Minnesota (66,181), Wisconsin (49,240), and North Carolina (10,864). As of the 2010 census, an estimated 260,076 Hmong lived in the United States.

6. See Espiritu 2015, 13.

7. Ibid. Such co-optation via dominant narratives about refugee subjectivity is provocatively discussed in Espiritu 2006.

Works Cited

Conley, Patrick T. 1986. *An Album of Rhode Island History, 1636–1986*. Norfolk, Va.: Donning.

Coughtry, Jay. 1981. *The Notorious Triangle: Rhode Island and the African Slave Trade*. Philadelphia, Penn.: Temple University Press.

Espiritu, Yên Lê. 2006. "The 'We-Win-Even-When-We-Lose' Syndrome: U.S. Press Coverage of the Twenty-Fifth Anniversary of the 'Fall of Saigon.'" *American Quarterly* 58, no. 2 (June).

———. 2015. *Body Counts: The Vietnam War and Militarized Refuge(es)*. Berkeley, Calif.: University of California Press.

"2010 U.S. Census Hmong Populations." Hmong National Development, Inc. http://www.hndinc.org/cmsAdmin/uploads/dlc/Research-Center-Data-Tables.pdf.

Acknowledgments

WE ACKNOWLEDGE THAT THE EDITORS contributed equally to this book, so the order of the byline does not represent the order of contribution. Each of us has conducted research on Hmong related topics for many years. We have wanted to see a volume like *Claiming Place.* In the fall of 2011, Chia served on a planning committee with Lynet Uttal and Nengher Vang to organize the Hmong American/Diaspora Institute, sponsored by the Asian American Studies Program at the University of Wisconsin–Madison. It was at that 2011 institute that Chia, Ma, and Faith had discussed how the advancement of Hmong studies had still not moved women beyond patriliny. These discussions eventually led the three of us to pursue this project. We issued a call for papers in late November 2011 and received many abstracts from a broad range of researchers from North America, Europe, and Asia. We further perused articles on topics we felt were important but not represented in the selected submissions. Many months later, we had what became the chapters of this book.

Ma and Chia would like to acknowledge how their participation in workshops they helped coordinate as part of the Critical Hmong Studies Collective gave them feedback on their work and to identify gaps in the literature. With support from the Institute for Advanced Studies, Louisa Schein and Chia co-organized the first workshop in summer 2007 at the University of Minnesota, and Ma and Chia coordinated a second meeting of the Critical Hmong Studies Collective sponsored by the Hmong Diaspora Studies Program at the University of Wisconsin–Milwaukee in spring 2009. Both of these events were important in helping to shape their ideas about Hmong studies, as more than half of the contributors to this volume came from participants in those workshops. Faith credits her involvement in this project to conversations with Chia at a Hmong studies workshop, which accentuated the dearth of agency given Hmong women in scholarship, and to her colleague and friend Dr. Caroline Brettell (coeditor, *International Migration: The Female Experience,* 1986), who always challenged her to look at the ways culture shapes the constraints, opportunities, and coping mechanisms experienced by migrant women.

We all are indebted to the many colleagues who expressed much excitement at different stages of the process. Our deepest gratitude must first be extended to Doug Armato, director of the University of Minnesota Press, for his interest in compiling a volume on Hmong women and gender before he knew its content, saving us from having to convince publishers of the importance of our project. As the volume progressed, we were fortunate to work with Pieter Martin, senior editor at University of Minnesota Press, whose patience and guidance helped to further shape the final product. In its early stages, Merry Wiesner-Hanks at UW-Milwaukee gave us feedback on our conceptual framework. As she is a distinguished historian of women and gender history, we benefited from her careful review of our call for papers. We are also grateful to the outside reviewers, whose comments were valuable in shaping the final manuscript into a much stronger and coherent volume. A debt of thanks is due to the many scholars who have waited for this volume with enthusiasm. Their continued encouragement provided valuable support as we faced the many challenges and discouragements that go along with working on such a project.

We would like to thank our dedicated contributors for staying on this journey with us. When we began the project, we could not have imagined the bumpy road ahead. Their willingness to reevaluate the many dimensions of Hmong lives across time and place helped to make this book the unique piece that it is. While the void in the Hmong women and gender literature cannot be filled by this one publication, their tireless work has paved the way for more critical publications in the field. We are indebted to this assemblage of influential and emerging Hmong studies scholars, whom we have been privileged to work with. Many thanks are due to our spouses, families, colleagues, and friends for their encouragement, patience, and companionship throughout this project.

Finally, we would like to thank the Hmong women and men, past and present, who shared their stories and experiences with our contributors, affirming our position that they have always been active agents in their own lives. May the pages of this book extend a new platform for them to claim place.

Chia Youyee Vang, Milwaukee, Wisconsin
Faith Nibbs, Dallas, Texas
Ma Vang, Merced, California

Contributors

GERALDINE CRAIG is associate professor of art at Kansas State University.

LEENA N. HER is instructor of work experience, Santa Rosa Junior College.

JULIE KEOWN-BOMAR is director of University of Wisconsin–Extension's Northwest Region. She is author of *Kinship Networks among Hmong-American Refugees*.

MAI NA M. LEE is associate professor of history at the University of Minnesota. She is author of *Dreams of the Hmong Kingdom: The Quest for Legitimation in French Indochina, 1850–1960*.

PRASIT LEEPREECHA is a lecturer of ethnic studies and development at Chiang Mai University. He is coeditor of *Challenging the Limits: Indigenous Peoples of the Mekong Region* and *Living in a Globalized World: Ethnic Minorities in the Greater Mekong Subregion*.

ALINE LO is assistant professor of English at Allegheny College.

FAITH NIBBS is the founding director of the Forced Migration Upward Mobility Project, which started as a project she directed while serving as research assistant professor of anthropology at Southern Methodist University in Dallas, Texas. She is author of *Belonging: The Social Dynamics of Fitting In as Experienced by Hmong Refugees in Germany and Texas* and coeditor of *Identity and the Second Generation: How Children of Immigrants Find Their Space*.

KONG PHA is a doctoral student in American studies at the University of Minnesota.

LOUISA SCHEIN is associate professor of anthropology and women's and gender studies at Rutgers University. She is author of *Minority Rules: The Miao and the Feminine in China's Cultural Politics* and coeditor of *Translocal China: Linkages, Identities, and the Reimaging of Space* and *Media, Erotics, and Transnational Asia.*

CATHY J. SCHLUND-VIALS is associate professor of English and Asian American studies at the University of Connecticut. She is author of *Modeling Citizenship: Naturalization in Jewish and Asian American Writing* and *War, Genocide, and Justice: Cambodian American Memory Work* (Minnesota, 2012).

BRUCE THAO is a Bush Foundation Fellow and consultant.

CHIA YOUYEE VANG is associate professor of history at the University of Wisconsin–Milwaukee. She is author of *Hmong America: Reconstructing Community in Diaspora* and *Hmong in Minnesota.*

KA VANG is instructor of Hmong language at the University of Wisconsin–Eau Claire.

MA VANG is assistant professor of humanities and arts at the University of California–Merced.

Index

Agency: of Hmong LGBTQ, 282–83, 295–99, 304, 310, 317; of women, 18–19, 24, 77, 117–22 passim, 125–27, 129–31, 134–36, 140, 156, 159, 202, 220–23, 230–31; of women, collective, 118, 121–23, 126, 128–30, 134, 136, 138–40, 156, 221, 230–31, 234, 239, 241–42; of women, through needlework, 195–96, 199, 202, 204, 207, 215; through writing, 23–24, 172. *See also* Social media: empowering role

Ally, Hmong as, 29, 40, 49, 51, 113

Animism, 153, 160–61, 195

API (Asian-Pacific Islander) LGBTQ, 283–84, 286

Art and design, 196–200, 202, 211

Artistic expression, limited by culture, 128, 177

Asian chic (fashion), 200–201, 211–12

Assimilation, 22, 221, 227; resistance of, 195, 202; to Western culture, 9, 14, 120, 128, 199, 207, 209–10, 241; to Western culture, difficulties with, 31, 47; to Western culture, effect on gender norms, 13, 130, 213

Australia, Hmong in, 9–12, 204, 206, 208

Beauty pageants, 199, 209–10

Binarization, 87, 118, 224, 261–62, 273; gender, 282, 294, 299, 306; used to describe Hmong, 14, 17, 49, 120. *See also* Stereotypes

Bisexual, 261, 272, 286–88, 312; Hmong men, 294; Hmong women, 290–92, 294

Blogs, 173–74, 180–81, 187, 308

Bouam Loung, Laos, 105–6

Bride capture, theft, or kidnapping, 93, 107, 120, 305–6

Bride price, 65–66, 133, 151, 154, 158, 204, 305

Buddhism, 152, 160

Burial, ritual, 204–5, 208

Casualties (war dead), 45–46, 69–70, 76–77, 253

Ceremony, divorce, 145

Ceremony, wedding, 132, 145–50, 153, 281

Chemical warfare, 29, 42

Chiang Mai, Thailand, 150, 154–56, 158, 160–61, 207

Children: adult reliance on for interpretation of language and culture, 47, 126–27, 136; gender equality, 159; Internet use and, 173; tradition of having many, 8, 305–6

Christianity, 68, 77, 153, 160, 243n10, 252, 258, 261

Church, Christian, 9, 153

CIA (Central Intelligence Agency, U.S.), 88, 96, 99, 101–3

Cinema: diasporic, 220–25, 234, 236–37, 239, 241–42; Hmong, 220, 225–26, 253, 255, 264, 269–70

Clan membership, change as result of marriage or divorce, 145, 147–48, 150. *See also* Natal lineage: return to after divorce

Clans: Hang, 93; Lo, 90–92, 94, 98, 111; Ly, 90–94, 102–4, 111; Lynhiavu, 104; Moua, 90, 93–94, 104–5, 109, 111; Thao, 94, 102; Vang, 109; Vue, 93; Xiong, 99; Yang, 90–94, 103

Class: differences, 144; due to divorce, 151; due to economic status, 209; due to education, 21, 57; due to employment, 76; due to gender, 156; due to language skills, 76

Clothing: modern, 208–9, 211, 213; traditional, 3, 7, 10, 76, 147, 196–98, 201–2, 204, 208–10, 213–14, 264. *See also* Needlework (paj ntaub)

Colonialism, 40, 48, 75, 205, 251; challenges to, 33; of discourse, 4; resistance of, 39, 195, 300; in U.S./ Hmong relationship, 31–32, 48

Colonial Route 6 (CR6), 105–6

Colonial Route 7 (CR7), 93, 102, 105–6

Communist: aggression, 30, 102; areas, 39; persecution, 29, 41–42; takeover, 39, 42

Community: women's leadership in, 125, 137–40, 156, 162, 282–83, 308–9; women's participation in, 121, 136, 140, 240

Convention on the Elimination of All Forms of Discrimination against Women, 162

Culture: as capital, 120, 123, 128, 136–37, 139–40; change, 118, 128, 131, 158, 161–62, 196, 207–9, 211, 221, 237, 242, 281–82, 285, 300, 321; expectations

of, 79, 122, 124, 129, 132, 136, 153, 177, 187, 228, 288, 290, 294; expectations of, for social engagement, 176–78, 180–82, 184–87, 189, 232, 237; LGBTQ and, 281, 300, 310–11, 321; negotiation of, 120, 152, 169, 181, 240

Dancing, 209, 210, 287, 297, 309

Dang, Fay, son of Blia Lao Lo, 93, 98

Daniels, Jerry "Hog," 102, 106

Dating: exogamous (dating outside one's ethnicity), 131, 135; online, 254; transnational, 131–32, 271. *See also* Marriage: exogamous; Marriage: transnational; Relationships: transnational

Depression, 32, 147, 180, 303, 308, 315, 318, 320

Diasporic cinema. *See* Cinema: diasporic

Displacement: cultural, 280–81, 291–92, 298; physical, 30, 32, 38–43, 47–48, 51, 60, 69, 76, 79, 149, 206, 220–21, 224, 241. *See also* Migration

Divorce, 99, 107–8, 132, 158–59; effects on women, 131–32, 134, 144, 148–55, 159, 161–63; infidelity as grounds for, 145, 154; increase in, 145, 149; prevention of, 148; spirituality and, 144, 149–50, 152, 158, 160–62

Dowry. *See* Bride price

Drag (men dressing up as women), 293, 297, 308

Dr. Tom (movie), 253–55, 263, 266, 269, 307

Economic mobility, 57, 60, 65, 79, 151, 159

Education, 22, 57, 61, 75, 157–59, 162; arts, 196, 211, 214–15; gender gap, 21, 63, 121, 128, 158; higher, 120–22, 124–29, 132, 137, 139–40, 150, 196,

202, 214, 309; lack of access, 22, 121, 132; parental expectations of, 52n6, 124–25, 128, 140; of women, 62–63, 65, 71, 74, 76, 79, 120–22, 124–27, 155, 157, 159, 162, 309; of women, frowned upon, 63, 65, 71–73

Employment: of married women, 74, 76, 132; of women, 8–9, 57–58, 65, 67, 69, 73–76, 79, 151, 153–54, 159, 241

English language: acquisition, 9, 14, 63, 67, 136, 203; acquisition, difficulty with, 47, 49, 134; benefits of fluency, 63–64, 136. See also Literacy

Eroticization: of criminality, 259; of homeland, 226, 236–37, 239; of the Orient, 249; of women, 223, 229, 255, 264–65, 272

Erotics, 250, 263–64, 267, 270, 274, 275n10, 319; transnational, 255, 272, 306–7, 319

Face, saving or losing, 154, 176–78, 181, 184, 187–88, 290, 317

Facebook, 169, 173–74, 179–82

Family, as support network, 118, 120–23, 126–27, 129, 134, 138–39. See also Agency: of women, collective

Fantasy, sexual. See Sexual: fantasy

Farming: desire to escape, 67, 79, 151, 271; effect of war on, 42, 206

Fashion, 200–202, 210–14

Fashion design: Asian American, 211; Hmong American, 212–14; shows, 199, 212–14

Female gaze, cinematic device, 230, 233, 242. See also Male gaze

Feminization of men, 259, 273

Filipinos, 57, 62, 78–79, 81n8, 177, 293

Film. See Cinema

Folksongs, traditional, 44, 77–78. See also Singing

Foucault, Michel, 5–6, 171, 275n10

Freedom Inc., Wisconsin Hmong gender justice organization, 284, 286, 298

French, language, 62, 93

Fresno, California, 100–101, 110, 210, 304, 308

Freud, Sigmund, 262

Gang members, stereotype, 19, 259. See also Stereotypes

Gay, 286–88, 293–94, 299, 308–9, 312

Gender: binary, 282, 294, 299, 306; discrimination, 285, 292, 300; education and, 21–22, 63, 128; equality, 157, 162, 241, 309; sexuality and, 280, 286, 291, 303, 305, 311, 313

Gender hierarchy, 7, 12–13, 15, 17–18, 132–33, 138–39, 145, 148–49, 156, 159, 177, 221; challenges to, 173, 180, 183, 188–89, 195, 225–26, 237, 281, 292; refusal of, 9, 15, 76, 79, 119, 131, 133. See also Patriarchal: practices; Patriarchal: structure, challenges to; Patriarchy

Gender norms/roles, 9, 12, 21, 24, 61, 63, 71, 73, 134, 197, 232, 236, 240, 316; acting outside of, 71, 132–34, 153–54, 185, 288; change in, 57–58, 60–61, 63, 71, 79, 130, 155–57, 159, 161–62, 221, 223, 226, 235, 239–42, 281; limitations resulting from, 129, 222, 226; online debates about, 170, 178–79, 189; queering of, 280–81, 299; struggles with, 179, 185–88, 241, 299

Gender politics, 170, 172, 199, 213, 309

Gender queer, 286–87, 289, 299; Hmong, 286–87, 289, 293, 295

Gran Torino (movie), 120, 243n2, 259, 265, 275n8

Her, Linda (lesbian spoken word artist), 309–10

Hero, Hmong as, 29, 38. *See also* Warrior: Hmong as

Heteronormativity, 24, 281–82, 299, 306–7, 313

History: constructed through memory, 50–51; erasure of, 35, 39, 41, 50–51, 61

Hmong, refugees, lack of written record, 57, 205. *See also* Secret war, the: lack of written record

Hmong American Partnership (HAP), 309

Hmong Association of Thailand, 155

Hmongtown Market, St. Paul, Minnesota, 207–8

Hmong Veterans' Naturalization Act of 2000, 29

Hmong women's online organizations, 179

Homeland nostalgia or longing, 199, 210, 222, 241, 264; as cinematic theme, 220–21, 224–26, 234–37, 239, 242, 253, 255

Homophobia, 261, 272, 285–86, 288, 295, 299–300, 313, 320–21

Homosexuality: unacceptable in Hmong culture, 257–58, 260–61, 304–5, 307, 316; as Western or white "disease," 283

Hospital, Sam Thong, 70, 74

Humanitarian aid, 42–44, 56, 62, 79

Humor, 315–17, 320

Hyperheterosexuality, 251, 305–7

Hypersexuality, 259, 291, 294

Identity: creating or crafting, 198–200, 202–4, 215, 240, 285, 290, 296; gender and, 286–87, 289; LGBTQ and, 280, 297, 300, 307, 309, 311,

313–14, 319–20; sexuality and, 285, 297, 304, 310; politics and, 261, 283, 297

Illiteracy, 63, 67, 77–78, 152. *See also* Literacy

Internet, use by Hmong, 169–71. *See also* Social media

Intersectionality (the intersection of forms or systems of oppression, domination, or discrimination), 87, 128, 197, 281, 283–85, 289, 291–93, 298–300, 308, 312–13

Johnson, Lyndon, President, 105

Kaitong, title, 92–93, 101. *See also* Phutong; Tasseng

KIA (Khmer In Action), 286

Kinsey, Alfred, 262

Kinship, system or structure, 7, 111, 119, 132, 149, 223, 230, 234, 238, 241–42, 280, 316–17

Knowledge: Western (academic) construction, 9, 28, 31, 48, 51, 120, 123, 282, 299; of Hmong women, 4–6, 11, 13–15, 17–19, 22, 24–25, 59–60, 121. *See also* Stereotypes

Lair, Bill, Colonel, 103–5

Lao language: learning, 21, 62, 75–76; literacy, 93

Latehomecomer, The, by Kao Kalia Yang (2008), 172, 204

Lesbian, 286–88, 290–94, 304, 312, 314

LGBTQ (Lesbian, Gay, Bisexual, Transgender, Queer): changing Hmong attitudes toward, 258; coming out, 260–61, 272–73, 283, 285–86, 290, 293–95, 297, 299, 314–15, 317; coming out, effect on family/clan, 296

LGBTQ Hmong, 280–85, 288, 292–93, 296–97, 299–300, 303–5, 308–14, 317–18, 320–21; lack of literature on, 283–85, 298, 303, 311; men, 294; negotiating the Closet (whether to come out or not), 285, 295–97, 299; non-acceptance of, 281, 316; as threat to Hmong culture, 281; women, 290–91, 294, 299, 308, 310, 318. *See also* API LGBTQ; Bisexual; Gay; Lesbian; Queer/Queerness; Transgender

Literacy, 73, 76, 81n19, 136, 205; French language, 62, 93; Hmong language, 76–77, 136; Lao language, 21, 62, 64, 75–76, 93; Meo language, 64. *See also* English language; Illiteracy

Lo, Blia Yao, son of Pa Tsi Lo, 91–93, 95, 111

Lo, Pai, third wife of Vang Pao, 95, 98

Lo, Pa Tsi, 91–92, 95

Long Cheng, Laos, 42–44, 69, 76, 102–3, 209

Luang Prabang, Laos, 22, 207

Ly, Foung, father of Touby Lyfoung, 96–97

Ly, Nhia Long, father of True Ly, 101–2

Ly, Nhia Vu, grandfather of True Ly, 91–92, 95, 101, 111

Ly, Tou Pao, brother of True Ly, 102–3

Ly, True, second wife of Vang Pao, 95, 101–3

Lyfoung, Touby, 92–94, 96–97, 99, 102–4, 111

Lyfoung, Touxa, son of Touby Lyfoung, 104

Mae Sa Mai, Thailand, 159–60

Male gaze, cinematic device, 228–31, 236–37. *See also* Female gaze

Marriage: arranged, 251–55, 265, 267–68, 272, 305; companionate or by choice, 254, 267, 272; changing attitudes/practices regarding, 129–34; exogamous, 80n6, 134, 138–39; infidelity, 130–32, 154; political alliance, 88–91, 93–94, 96, 98, 101, 104, 106, 111; provider of political capital, 89–90, 93, 96, 98, 101, 104, 111; provider of social capital, 48, 133, 222, 267; transnational, 131–34, 237, 305. *See also* Dating: exogamous; Dating: transnational; Relationships: transnational

Marriage Equality Act, U.S., 298

Masculinity, 280; Hmong, 258–60, 265–66, 273, 294

Media, Hmong, 253, 255, 264, 310

Mekong River, 31, 46, 50, 92

Memory, in construction of history, 50–51

Men, as objects of sexual desire, 271, 291

Meo, 64, 80n3

Miao, Hmong in China, 252, 264, 271, 273

Migration: forced, 29–31, 34–35, 38–41, 44–48, 74, 206, 221, 293; secondary, 48; to United States, 38, 48, 56, 206, 254–55. *See also* Displacement

Military Region II, 30, 103

Minneapolis-St. Paul, Minnesota, 106, 110, 207–10, 212, 214, 256, 286, 297, 306, 309–10, 315–16

Monogamy, 252–53, 272; as U.S. law, 258

Moua, Cher Pao, father of Chia Moua, 104–6

Moua, Chia, fourth wife of Vang Pao, 95, 104–7, 109; death, 110

Moua, Mai Neng, 23, 240, 309

Moua, Mee, Minnesota state senator, 10, 140n2, 309

Moua, Nhia Chou, father of Song Moua, 108–9

Moua, Song, sixth wife of Vang Pao, 95, 107–10; death, 110, 113n14

Muang Phuan, Laos, 92, 94. *See also* Xieng Khouang: Laos

Music, 44, 128, 139, 209–10, 264

Na Khang, Laos, 103, 105–6

Natal lineage, return to after divorce, 150–52, 162

Needlework (paj ntaub), 10, 16, 172, 178, 195–96, 206–7, 212–14; baby carriers, 202–4; as cultural expression/translation, 197–98, 202, 204, 210, 214–15; shift from geometric to pictorial representation, 198, 203, 206–8, 211; non-traditional forms, 198, 206–7; ritual uses of, 202–5; selling, 8, 16, 206–8; as story cloth, 204, 206–8; as text, 197, 202–7, 210, 215. *See also* Rituals: practice of; Rituals: religious

Network of Hmong Women in Thailand, 144, 155–56, 162

New Year celebrations, 138; beauty pageants, 209; bullfighting contest, 102; Fresno, CA, 101, 110; participation limited by gender status, 228, 236; poetry, song, and dance during, 177, 209; rituals, 150; traditional clothing, 198, 208–9, 214. *See also* SOY: New Year celebration

Nong Het, Laos, 41, 92, 102, 104

North Vietnamese army, 44, 105–6

Nurses, Hmong women, 56–57, 64–66, 69, 108

Nursing: profession, 21, 56, 60, 62–63, 68; training program, 57, 62–64, 66–67

Obligation, to family, 126, 129, 135, 254, 268, 284–85, 290, 294, 299

Oldest child, pressures on/ expectations of, 124–25

Oral history, 13, 25, 29, 34–35, 50

Oral tradition, 89, 204

Other, as indication of difference and/ or inferiority, 4–6, 16–17, 87, 198, 212, 249–51, 257, 260, 272–73, 321

Paj ntaub. *See* Needlework (paj ntaub)

Paj Ntaub Voice (literary movement), 309

Pansexual, 286–88

Parents, as positive influence, 123, 214

Parents, expectations of for their children, 124–28, 135–36, 139–40

Pathet Lao army, 44

Patriarchal: practices, Hmong women refusal of, 9, 15, 79, 238–39; practices, limiting factor for Hmong women, 9, 14–15, 64, 117–19, 129, 132–33, 155; structure, challenges to, 8, 140, 188–89. *See also* Gender hierarchy; Gender norms/roles

Patriarchy, 35, 117, 119, 121, 137, 140, 202, 220–21, 265, 282, 299; cultural, 15, 17–18, 20, 23, 79, 251. *See also* Gender hierarchy; Gender norms/roles

Patrilineal kinship, 7, 117, 132, 137, 144, 149, 160, 162, 221, 223, 229, 234, 238–41, 280

Patrilocal residence, women live with husband's family after marriage, 149, 153

Phou Pha Thi, Laos, 105–6

Phou San mountain range, Laos, 92, 104–5

Phum ritual. *See* Rituals: religious, phum

Phutong, title, 94. *See also* Kaitong; Tasseng

Place: as process of leaving, 41; as sense or way of knowing, 39, 43–44, 48, 51

Plain of Jars, Laos, 92–93, 99, 102, 104

Poetry, 23, 172, 177–78, 180, 229

Polygamy. *See* Polygyny

Polygeny, the belief that humans evolved from several independent pairs of ancestors, 305

Polygyny: the practice of men having more than one wife, 24, 72, 90, 104, 120, 131–33, 141n4, 149, 154–55, 234, 238, 251–52, 254, 257, 265, 272; choice of women after divorce, 141n4, 154–55; as excuse for rape or assault, 72; Western disapproval of, 253

Pornography, 269

Poverty, effects of, 125, 289–90, 305

Power: economic, of Hmong women, 57, 88, 120, 207; political, of Hmong women, 88, 120

Professional Hmong Women's Network (Galore), 309

Promiscuity, assumption of, 60, 73, 75, 149, 153, 291. *See also* Prostitution: assumption of

Propaganda, Hmong folksongs as, 77

Prostitution, 60, 73, 267, 271; assumption of, 71–75. *See also* Promiscuity: assumption of

PrYSM (Providence Youth Student Movement), Southeast Asian and queer organization based in Rhode Island, 284, 286, 298

QSEA (Queer Southeast Asian) Census, 282, 285–86

QSEA (Queer Southeast Asian) Network, composed of PrYSM, SOY, Freedom Inc., and KIA, 286–87

Queer Hmong. *See* LGBTQ Hmong

Queer/Queerness, 197, 229, 286–88, 300n1, 305, 307, 309–12, 316–17, 320

Racialization: of Asians, 201, 211–12; of Hmong, 31–32, 258–61, 273, 306, 330; of people of color, 261

Racism, 67, 121, 138–39, 251, 284–86, 288, 295, 299–300, 305, 313, 319

Radio: as propaganda tool, 44, 77; as morale booster, 44

Rape. *See* Sexual: assault

Refusal, ethnographic (a refusal to tell or to tell all), 31, 35–36, 46–48, 50–51, 148

Relationships: couples of disparate ages, 134, 255, 265, 272, 305; transnational, 131–32, 253, 255, 263, 265, 270, 272. *See also* Dating: transnational; Marriage: transnational

Reputation. *See* Face: saving or losing

Rights: human, 28, 157–58, 329, 331; women's, 155, 157–58, 161–62

Rituals: burial, 204–5, 208; LGBTQ and, 281–82; practice of, 23, 156–57, 160, 162, 195; to protect husband in war service, 45, 204; religious, ua neeb koos plig (to protect souls of family members), 150; religious, hu plig (soul calling), 150, 161; religious, lwm tsiab (driving out evil spirits), 150; religious, lwm sub (driving out evil spirits), 150; religious, nyob nruab hlis (shelter

Rituals (*continued*)
after giving birth), 150; religious, phum (reunification of divorced daughter with natal family and spirits), 160–62; wedding, 146–48; wedding, lwm qaib (blessing ritual), 146, 158; wedding, pe (bowing), 146, 163n6; wedding (food and drink offering) laig dab, 146; wedding, qaib faib sia (spiritual separation), 147, 150; wedding, umbrella, 148. *See also* Needlework (paj ntaub): ritual uses of; Spirits: household
RLA (Royal Lao Army), 96, 102

Sadness. *See* Depression
Same-sex Hmong: couples, 281; marriage, 298; relationships, attitudes shifting toward, 280
Sam Thong/Samthong, Laos, 57, 64, 68, 108
Secrets, family, 38, 48
Secret war, the, 22, 28–30, 32, 37, 50, 56, 61, 88–89, 98–99, 111, 220; lack of written record, 28–29, 39, 205. *See also* Hmong, refugees: lack of written record
Sedgwick, Eve, 262
Sewing: as income, by men, 207; as profession, by women, 76. *See also* Needlework (paj ntaub): selling
Sex before marriage, taboo, 292
Sexual: advances, unwanted, after divorce, 153–54; assault, 72, 305–6; "deviancy," 73, 250–51, 291, 305–7, 316; exploitation, 256, 306–7; fantasy, 263, 272, 274, 292; harassment, 292; impropriety, 251; orientation, 286–88, 303, 308, 312; orientation,

discrimination due to, 284, 292. *See also* Sexuality
Sexualities, 257–58, 272
Sexuality, 10–11, 59–60, 63, 71–73, 129–30, 149, 153–54, 213; Christianity and, 252, 258, 260, 298; discourse of, 250–51, 303–9; morality and, 250, 306; norms, change in, 252; studies, 249–50, 272; Western norms, 250, 272. *See also* Sexual
Shaman ritual, 3, 150, 206, 243n9
Singing, 177–78, 229, 297, 309. *See also* Folksongs: traditional
Social justice, 256, 284, 312
Social media: anonymity, 183–85; as community, 171, 185–89, 297; empowering role, 169–70, 172, 182–86, 188–90; enabling communication not possible face to face, 169, 178, 181–84, 187–88; democratizing effect, 169–70, 178, 183, 185; use by immigrants, 169–70, 172; as validation, 185–88; as voice, 171–72, 175, 180–81, 183–84, 187–89. *See also* Agency
Social mobility, 21, 57–58, 60, 65–66, 69, 75–76, 78–79, 126–27, 129, 151
SOY (Shades of Yellow), Minnesota Hmong LGBTQ organization, 284, 286, 297–98, 308, 310; New Year celebration, 308, 310, 313. *See also* New Year celebrations
Spirits: evil, 68, 150, 202–3, 205; household, 145–46, 148, 155, 160. *See also* Rituals
Spiritual exclusion, as result of divorce, 144, 149–50, 152, 155, 160
Spirituality, 144, 146–47, 150, 204, 206. *See also* Animism; Buddhism; Christianity

Starvation, threat of, 42–45, 74, 79
Statelessness, 171, 282, 284, 298–300
Status, matrilineal transfer of, 89–90, 94, 98, 101, 111
Stereotypes: of Hmong, 125, 200–201, 212, 306; of Hmong men, 258–60, 264–65; of Hmong men as gang members, 19, 259; of Hmong men as warriors, 38–39, 71, 259, 273, 299; of Hmong women, 4, 6–7, 10, 130, 265; of Hmong women as victims, 19, 72, 87, 117, 119, 131, 133, 254, 265–66, 299
Storytelling. *See* Oral history
Suicide, 93, 155, 256, 304, 308, 318, 320

Tailoring. *See* Sewing
Tasseng, title, 93. *See also* Kaitong; Phutong
Teachers, Hmong, 57, 75–76
Textiles, as fine art, 196–97, 199
Textiles, Hmong, 196–200, 203, 210, 215. *See also* Needlework (paj ntaub)
Thao, Sia, first major wife of Vang Pao, 95, 99–101
Thao, Xia. *See* Thao, Sia
Thoj, Va-Megn, filmmaker, 256
Tradition: continuation of, 215; fear of losing, 281; Hmong women as bearers of, 4, 7, 195, 233; incorporating LGBTQ Hmong into, 281, 297–98; levirate, to marry dead husband's brother, 76, 96, 99
Transgender, 281, 286–87, 289, 293, 295, 299, 312
Twitter, 173, 179
Txuj Ci Hmong LGBTQ talent show, 309–10, 313

UN (United Nations) General Assembly, 162

United States: Empire, 28, 31, 48; Imperialism, 33, 35, 66, 79, 88, 295; Naturalization, 29; as rescuer, 29, 48, 117
USAID (United States Agency for International Development), 42, 56–57, 62, 75, 78

Vang, Maikue, textile artist, 195, 199, 201–2, 207, 209, 215
Vang, Neng Chue, father of Vang Pao, 94–95, 97
Vang, Neng Chue, son of Vang Pao and Sia Thao, 101
Vang, Pao, 43, 65, 96–99, 102–10, 209; arrest, 100–101, 110, 113n13; death, 37, 100, 110; family marriage tree, 95, 97, 112nn7–8; rise to power, 87–89, 94, 101, 111; sisters, 37–38; wives, 88, 95–110 passim
Vang, Sue, 76, 109
Vang Pao Elementary School, Fresno, California, 110
Vientiane, Laos, 22, 62, 64, 67, 78, 109

Warfare, chemical, 29, 42
Warrior, Hmong as, 38–39, 71, 259, 273, 299. *See also* Stereotypes
Wat Tham Krabok, Thailand, 38, 39, 207, 256–57
Wedding ceremony. *See* Ceremony: wedding
Widowhood, 158, 221, 228–31, 239, 241, 253
Women: marginalization of, 7, 29, 61, 117, 125–26, 149, 155, 171, 185, 189, 221, 223, 225, 228, 239, 241–42, 310; as objects of sexual desire, 257, 264–65, 291–92. *See also* Men: as objects of sexual desire

Women, Hmong: as bearers of
    tradition, 4, 7, 195, 233; as civilian
    soldiers, 44–45; as peacekeepers,
    104
Writing, as act of agency, 23–24,
    172

Xieng Khouang, Laos, 62, 64, 75,
    93–94, 96, 98–99, 102. *See also*
    Muang Phuan: Laos

Xiong, Nonmala, fashion designer,
    195, 199, 201–2, 207, 209, 214–15
Xiong, Pa Nhia, 304, 311, 313, 320–21

Yang, Kao Kalia, author, 172, 204
Yang, Thao Tou, Communist
    nationalist hero, 91
Yang, Yee, 304, 311, 313, 320–21
Yellow rain, 29, 42
YouTube, 173–74, 179